THE INVENTION *of* RELIGION

The
INVENTION
of
RELIGION

FAITH AND COVENANT IN THE BOOK OF EXODUS

JAN ASSMANN

TRANSLATED BY ROBERT SAVAGE

PRINCETON UNIVERSITY PRESS
PRINCETON & OXFORD

Copyright © 2018 by Princeton University Press

Published by Princeton University Press
41 William Street, Princeton, New Jersey 08540

In the United Kingdom: Princeton University Press
6 Oxford Street, Woodstock, Oxfordshire OX20 1TR

press.princeton.edu

First paperback printing, 2020
Paperback ISBN 9780691203195
Cloth ISBN 9780691157085

Library of Congress Control Number: 2017963671

British Library Cataloging-in-Publication Data is available

This book has been composed in Adobe Text

Printed on acid-free paper. ∞

Printed in the United States of America

Incipit exire qui incipit amare.

—*St. Augustine*

CONTENTS

ILLUSTRATIONS

FOREWORD

A NUMBER OF YEARS AGO, Fred Appel gave me the idea for a book on Exodus. My first thanks go to him; without his initiative, this book would never have been written. I declined his initial invitation by pleading the many Old Testament scholars who, it seemed to me, would be far better suited to the task. By the time Fred renewed the invitation some years later, I had come to the realization that the Exodus theme had actually preoccupied me all my life.

What became clear to me was that the Book of Exodus is not just about the departure of the people of Israel from Egypt but also about the establishment of a completely new type of religion, or even "religion" as such. In the ancient world, this complex of election, covenant, and loyalty was something completely new; it by no means emerged from what came before it, despite incorporating many preexisting elements. From the internal viewpoint of the biblical texts, this innovation is experienced and presented as "revelation"; from the external perspective of historical analysis, it can be understood as "invention," albeit invention of a kind that has nothing to do with fiction. It is not the case that a lone genius called Moses was suddenly struck by inspiration. Rather, over many decades, perhaps even over many centuries, a collective experience attained a form of binding, ultimate truth that appears in Exodus as an act of otherworldly foundation. That is what we mean by the word "revelation," an idea that has no equivalent in the ancient languages. Yet no single word could do justice to this unprecedented new idea. It needed instead to be developed in a "Grand Narrative." Faith based on revelation, this complex of election and promise, covenant and loyalty—that is what we, the inheritors of this extraordinary invention, understand today by "religion." In the idea of incarnation, of (the word of) God entering the world in human form, and of a book sent into the world from heaven, Christianity and Islam adopted the motif of otherworldly foundation. Entering into this new religion required turning one's back on Egypt. That is the theme of the Book of Exodus, which does not—like the myth of old—end with the people's arrival in the Promised Land, but with the entry of God and his people into a joint foundation.

The world that the Israelites had to leave behind them in order to enter into the new kingdom of holiness was Egypt and not Assyria, Babylonia, the Kingdom of the Hittites, or some other ancient realm. Ancient Egypt therefore represents that world in exemplary, ideal-typical fashion. For this reason it is legitimate to view this new religion from an Egyptian (i.e., Egyptological) point of view. From this vantage point, there are two quite different ways of looking at the Hebrew Bible. One sees Israel embedded in the cultures of the ancient world and primarily detects continuities and parallels: between Egyptian hymns and biblical psalms, between Egyptian love songs and the Song of Solomon, between Egyptian and biblical sacrificial rites, taboos, and ideas of purity, between Egyptian and biblical representations of (sacral) kingship, and much else besides. The other foregrounds the discontinuities, antitheses, and ruptures in the relationship. It sees in Israel a new force that pits itself against the old world order as some-thing radically heterogeneous and, in so doing, lays the foundations of the world we know today. Whereas I used to read the Bible, during my first quarter century as an Egyptologist, entirely under the spell of the first approach, I have since become far more attuned to the other, dis-continuous, antagonistic, revolutionary aspect of ancient Israelite and above all early Jewish religion, and hence also to the symbolic meaning of the departure from Egypt.

This book aims at neither a retelling nor a commentary, although it naturally cannot avoid traveling some way down these two well-trodden paths to the biblical Exodus tradition. Above all, what I am aiming at here is a "resonant reading," a necessarily subjective interpre-tation of the biblical texts that reflects—to as great an extent as pos-sible—my own Egyptological and general cultural interests and his-torical experiences. More than twenty-five years ago, as a visiting Egyptologist, I was invited by the Stroumsa family to a Seder in Jeru-salem. My friends thought it would be meaningful, from a professional point of view, to commemorate the suffering endured by the children of Israel in their Egyptian house of bondage. That unforgettable evening of endless storytelling and song gave me heart as I embarked on this project.

I frequently walk past a sign that reads: "Use only under supervision and with expert guidance." The sign stands in front of a high ropes course at the local sports center. I was often reminded of such a high ropes course when coming to grips with the Old Testament. Fortunately, supervision and expert guidance were never wanting. Michaela Bauks, Ronald Hendel, Bernd Janowski, Othmar Keel, Daniel Kroch-malnik, Bernhard Lang, and Konrad Schmid all read the first draft of the manuscript and offered numerous corrections, changes, and references; where their suggestions have been taken on board, they have been individually acknowledged in the notes. I extend my thanks, too, to the Berlin theologian, Rolf Schieder, as well as Thierry Chervel, editor of the online magazine *Der Perlentaucher,* and his assistant, David Assmann. In his book *Are Religions Dangerous?* (2008), Rolf Schieder produced what is probably the most searching critique to which *Moses the Egyptian* has so far been subjected. He was kind enough to join me and a panel of invited speakers in an extremely productive debate that subsequently found a forum in *Der Perlentaucher.* In the course of the debate I learned a great deal that allowed me to refine and hone my arguments.[1] In this context, I am particularly grateful to the Viennese theologian Jan-Heiner Tück, who twice invited me to Vienna to discuss my ideas with a wider audience.

My heartfelt thanks likewise go to Ulrich Nolte, who edited the original German version with care and imagination and also selected the illustrations, along with Maximilian Eberhard and Matthias Golbeck. The manuscript was completed in Weimar during a four-month fellowship at the International Collegium for Research in Cultural Technology and Media Philosophy, a disciplinary focus that might at first glance appear far-removed from the topic of Exodus. However, the specific theme that brought together ten Fellows in Weimar in Winter 2013–14 could not have been more apposite: "Memorization: The Construction of Pasts." In remembering the departure from Egypt, we are indeed dealing with the construction of a past that a community appropriates for itself in order that they may, on that basis, embark on a new beginning and forge a new identity. My project benefited greatly from the discussions about memory, history, media, and constructivism conducted in Weimar. I thank both directors, Bernhard Siegert and Lorenz Engell, for inviting me to join the Collegium and their coworkers for their energetic support. Last but by no means least, I want to thank Robert Savage for the diligence and ingenuity of his rendering my sometimes convoluted German into readable English.

Biblical quotations are taken from the Authorized or King James Version, although these have occasionally been modified where the wording is unclear to modern readers or potentially misleading. The sacred name YHWH is rendered in the form of the tetragrammaton rather than as "the Lord." Line breaks generally follow shorter semantic-syntactic units, not the Masoretic versification, so as to convey something of the figured—albeit not strictly poetic—style of the narrative.

THE INVENTION *of* RELIGION

INTRODUCTION

The Exodus from Egypt remains our starting point.
—*Sigmund Freud*[1]

In the beginning was belief: belief in *one* God.
—*Heinrich August Winkler*[2]

The big bang of modernization occurred with the [...]
exodus from the world of polytheistic cultures.
—*Aleida Assmann*[3]

THE BOOK OF EXODUS contains what may well be considered the most grandiose and influential story ever told. Its theme is a watershed in the history of the human race, comparable only to such momentous milestones on the road to modernity as the invention of writing and the emergence of states: the shift from polytheism to monotheism. This was an evolutionary caesura of the first importance, at least for the Judeo-Christian-Islamic world. Even if it would take the Christianization and Islamization of the ancient world to reveal the full extent of its revolutionary impact, the story told in the Book of Exodus represents its founding myth. Exodus is thus not just the founding myth of Israel but that of monotheism as such, a key constituent of the modern world. The historian Gottfried Schramm, for one, sees in the departure from Egypt the first of "five crossroads in world history."[4]

To write the reception history of the Book of Exodus is therefore an impossible undertaking: its influence has been immeasurably vast, its impact all but ubiquitous. I propose instead to consider the source of that unique impact and lay bare the mythic core from which it draws its appeal. Myths lend themselves to countless retellings and revisions. They have the power to reveal new dimensions of life, to reorient human existence or even set it on a new footing, shedding light on situations and experiences that they invest with meaning. Myths are narrative elements that, configured and reconfigured in various ways, allow societies, groups, and individuals to create an identity for themselves—that is, to know who they are and where they belong—and to navigate complex predicaments and existential crises. With the help of the Osiris myth, for example, the Egyptians worked through the problem of death in their culture, while Sigmund Freud understood and treated his patients' neuroses in light of the Oedipus myth.

The Book of Exodus is devoted to the two most important questions on which human minds have dwelled since time immemorial: the question of the role played by the divine in our lives and the question of who "we" are. Both questions take on a specific form in the light of the Exodus myth and they are inextricably intertwined, since who "we" are is determined largely by what God has in mind for "us." The Egyptians appear never to have asked themselves such questions. They considered themselves not as "Egyptians" but simply as human beings, having emerged from God together with every other living thing (including deities) at the origin of the cosmos. God, for his part, has no special plan or destiny in mind for us; his sole purpose is to keep the universe on track, a task in which we humans can support him by performing religious rites. History did not appear to the Egyptians as a project structured around promises and their fulfillment, but rather as an ongoing process that had to be kept in harmony with primordial mythic patterns through cultural practice and so preserved from change. The Exodus myth, by contrast, relates how God freed the children of Israel from Egyptian bondage, singling them out from all the other peoples in order that they might jointly realize the project of a just society. A greater difference can hardly be imagined. Whereas the Egyptian myth tells a story about how the universe was created, the biblical myth of Exodus recounts how something wholly new came to be established within a world that had been created long ago. As presented in the myth, this groundbreaking new order arose in two ways: through revolution and revelation. In order to free the children of Israel, God first had to break the power of their oppressors; and in order to make them his chosen people and covenant partners in a new religion, he first had to reveal himself to them and proclaim his will.

A clear distinction needs to be made between the Exodus story and the Book of Exodus. The Exodus story goes far beyond what is dealt with in the Book of Exodus, for without the motif of the Promised Land that story cannot yield its full meaning. The escape from Egypt can be narrated only retrospectively, from the place foreseen at the time of departure as the ultimate destination. This is a story told by those who have arrived, not by those still wandering in the wilderness; by those who have been confirmed in their possession of the new, not by those who have only been emancipated from the old. The motifs of departure and Promised Land thus already belong together in the original myth before being subjected to literary development in the second to fifth books of Moses, as well as in the Book of Joshua. In the Torah, which prefaces this "Ur-Pentateuch" with the Book of Genesis and leaves out the Book of Joshua with the advent in the Promised Land, the Exodus story was confined to the biography of Moses, whose death marks its endpoint. The Exodus story centers on the three primal motifs of departure, covenant, and Promised Land. Those are the mythic kernels from which the account of Israel's departure from Egypt draws its transformative power across all its countless retellings. The Book of Exodus, by contrast, is restricted to the motifs of departure and covenant. It ends not with the Israelites' entry into the Promised Land but with God's entry into a form of symbiosis with his chosen people.

Accordingly, the Book of Exodus is split into three parts. The first part, chapters 1–15, tells the story of *liberation* from Egyptian captivity. The second, chapters 16–24, concerns the *binding* of the Israelites to the new covenant offered them by God. Interestingly, their oppression in Egypt and the religion that liberates them from it are both given the same Hebrew word here: *ʿăbōdâ* or "service." Human service signifies oppression, divine service denotes freedom. Revelation is the overall theme that shapes both parts, however. The third part, which follows in chapters 25–40, stands in for the Promised Land, understood as the goal that inspired the children of Israel to set out from Egypt.[5] This concluding part of the book is also the longest, although it has enjoyed nothing like the historical influence of the other two. It describes how the Temple (or Tabernacle), priesthood, and cult were set up. In other words, it concerns the institutionalization of the covenant in the form of a new religion. It is now widely accepted that this third part was added by the Priestly Source, which collated the Books of Genesis and

Exodus into a comprehensive historical narrative toward the end of the sixth century BCE.

The Exodus story is also referred to outside the Book of Exodus in surprisingly few biblical texts. Apart from passing allusions in some of the prophets, there are a handful of psalms indicating that tales of God's saving deeds had a fixed place in the liturgy of the postexilic cult of the Second Temple. Here, two points become quite clear: these tales are commemorative acts, intended to preserve past events from oblivion by handing them down to future generations; and, in addition to the three core mythic motifs of departure, covenant, and Promised Land mentioned above, we find here a fourth: the sins of the fathers, which the chosen people had to expiate by wandering in the wilderness for forty years after making the covenant at Sinai until their descendants finally reached the Promised Land. The histories of salvation and damnation go hand in hand, the former brought to mind amid the pangs of the latter. The great liturgy recited in the interconnected Psalms 105–7 begins by recapitulating the tale of the forefathers and Joseph, invoking God's promise "to give the land of Canaan" to Abraham and his seed (105:7–24), before recalling the exodus and the plagues of Egypt. Psalm 106 continues with the parting of the Red Sea and the various pitfalls into which the ill-tempered Israelites stumbled during their years in the wilderness, culminating in the gravest sin of all: the adoption of Canaanite customs in the Promised Land, upon which God drove them out and scattered them among the peoples. Psalm 107 is then the hymn of thanksgiving offered by those whom God brought back from "out of the lands, from the east, and from the west, from the north, and from the south" (107:3).

The Exodus story thus singles out the chosen people in three ways. It distinguishes them from Egypt as the epitome of the old system, which they are enjoined to abandon definitively and unconditionally; from their Canaanite neighbors in the Promised Land, who represent a false, blasphemous religion; and from the "fathers," who remind the Israelites of their own sinful past. It is this final motif, with its dual injunction to both repudiate the "sins of the fathers" and assume collective responsibility for them, that has come to seem uniquely significant in Germany today.

Although the Exodus myth had been told considerably earlier—as allusions in Hosea, Amos, and Micah, dating from the eighth century BCE, make abundantly clear—the era of its literary elaboration and cultic institutionalization only dawned in the sixth century BCE, the period of Babylonian captivity. In particular, its great moment came with the return from exile, when "Israel" had to be reinvented as an ethnic and religious identity and established on the basis of a political, social, and religious constitution. With the help of the Exodus story, those faced with this task succeeded in creating a memory that defined them as a group, anchoring them in the depths of time while also committing them to a common future. What they were doing was more than just history-writing; they were declaring their allegiance to an identity, fashioning a collectively binding self-definition in the medium of narrative and memory. In the two forms of storytelling and lawgiving, the narrative and the normative, the Book of Exodus codifies the *one* all-transforming, truly epochal revelation in which God emerged from his inscrutable concealment—for the Jews, once and for all; for Christians and Muslims, for the first time—to manifest his will to his people, so establishing a completely new relationship to the world, to time, and to the divine.

The revelation on Sinai provides the model for all later revelations, the foundation for a new form of religion that rests on the twin pillars of revelation and covenant and can therefore be termed a "religion of revelation," in sharp contrast to the "natural" religions that have flourished since time immemorial without reference to any such foundational event. Michael Walzer has read the Exodus tradition in its political dimension as the matrix of all revolutions;[6] analogously, I would like to interpret it in this book as the matrix of all revelations.

"Exodus" is not just the name given to a book in the Bible, however. It is also a symbol that can stand for any radical departure, any decampment for something entirely new and different. When Augustine, in his commentary to Psalm 64, remarks, *incipit exire qui incipit amare* ("the one who begins to love begins to leave"), he has in mind leaving behind the *civitas terrena*, the realm of worldly affairs and preoccupations, to enter the *civitas Dei*, the kingdom of God. This is not a physical movement from one place to another but rather an internal, spiritual exo-

dus: *exeuntium pedes sunt cordis affectus* ("the feet of those leaving are
the affections of the heart"). Accordingly, "Egypt" refers to the mun-
dane world where the pious dwell as strangers and suffer persecution
for their faith, as recalled in the aria of a Bach cantata, sung on the
second Sunday of Advent to words by Salomon Franck (BWV 70), that
looks forward to Christ's second coming: "When will the day come
when we leave the Egypt of this world?" When Kant famously declares
enlightenment to be "man's exit from his self-incurred immaturity," he
is likewise drawing on the symbolism of Exodus.[7]

When talking about a turning point in the history of the entire
human race, the idea of an "Axial Age" immediately springs to mind.
The philosopher Karl Jaspers used this idea to encapsulate reflections
that go back to the late-eighteenth-century Iranologist Anquetil-
Duperron, the discoverer of the Zend-Avesta.[8] Anquetil-Duperron,
recognizing that a number of movements like Zoroastrianism had
arisen at roughly the same time in different parts of the ancient world,
from China to Greece, spoke of a "great revolution of the human race."[9]
From the outset, the biblical shift to monotheism was also placed in
this context. Indeed this shift, extending from the appearance of the
early prophets in the eighth century (Isaiah, Hosea, Amos, Micah) to
the completion of the Torah some four to five centuries later, falls
neatly within the time frame of 500 BCE +/– 300 years identified by
Jaspers as the Axial Age. In brief, the Axial Age is marked by the discovery of transcendence. Around this time, a series of charismatic figures—Confucius, Laozi, Mencius, Buddha, Zoroaster, Isaiah and the
other prophets, Parmenides, Xenophanes, Anaximander, and others—
subjected traditional institutions and concepts to a radical critique on
the basis of newly discovered absolute truths, which they had arrived
at either through revelation or through methodical reflection.[10] The
shift described in the Exodus story would thus present only one of
many symptoms of a contemporary global development that saw humankind as a whole making a giant leap forward, as Jaspers asserts.

I take Jaspers's Axial Age theory to be one of the great scientific
myths of the twentieth century, comparable to Freud's theory of the
Oedipus complex. Like Freud's doctrine, it has the virtue of uncovering overarching patterns that had previously gone unnoticed; but it can
also—and this is the other side of the coin—go too far in its tendency

to lump together disparate phenomena under a catch-all category, overlooking important differences in the process.[11] The concept of the Axial Age refers to cultures and worldviews that distinguish between immanence (the this-worldly realm, home to the conditional and contingent) and transcendence (the other-worldly realm, home to the unconditional and absolute). On that basis, they tend to take a critical stance toward the world as it actually exists. Yet this is a question less of an "age" than of the presence of certain media conditions for recording intellectual breakthroughs and making them accessible to later generations. These include writing, of course, but also processes of canonization and commentary that endeavor to stabilize textual meaning. Once secured in this way, ideas can be disseminated in space as well as in time. It seems clear to me that, during the Persian period, Zoroastrianism and the pre-Socratic philosophers influenced the universalistic monotheism that was being developed in Jerusalem in the wake of the great prophets of exile, Deutero-Isaiah and Ezekiel. Yet the Exodus story, with its "monotheism of loyalty," must be regarded as a phenomenon sui generis. As such, it needs to be appreciated in its specificity and not prematurely filed under the all-encompassing rubric of a global "Axial Age." What is incontestable, at any rate, is that this story laid the foundations for a decisive shift that is entirely typical of the Axial Age. That shift is fully accomplished when the meaning of the divine covenant is expanded to cover the "kingdom of God" and the exodus from Egypt becomes the cipher for the soul's exodus from "this world," the *civitas terrena*, into the City of God.

PART ONE

GENERAL FOUNDATIONS

CHAPTER ONE

THEME AND STRUCTURE OF THE BOOK OF EXODUS

Incomprehensibilis voluit comprehendi—the ungraspable one wanted to be grasped.

—*Pope Leo the Great*[1]

The Christian faith contends that the inscrutable God emerged from his concealment to reveal himself in history, once and for all time.

—*Jan-Heiner Tück*[2]

THE FOLLOWING OVERVIEW of the Book of Exodus skips over many details that will be dealt with more thoroughly in later chapters. On the one hand, it aims to clarify how the biblical book is structured; on the other, it seeks to draw attention to certain "primal scenes" that have played a key role in how the book has been read and taken up.

Exodus (Chapters 1–15)

The first part of the book begins with an exposition before the drama of revelation gets underway in chapter 3. This exposition, in turn, is divided into two sections. The first section (chapter 1) recalls the suffering of the Israelites, while the second (chapter 2) tells of the birth and upbringing of Moses, their future liberator. The afflictions of the children of Israel in Egyptian captivity are depicted in the darkest possible colors, indelibly imprinting the image of ancient Egyptian culture in the memory of Islam and the West as the epitome of inhuman oppression. At the very moment when this oppression takes on genocidal dimensions with Pharaoh's decree that all male Israelite children be cast into the Nile, a son is born to a Hebrew couple. Placed in an ark and fetched from the waters by an Egyptian princess, he receives from her the name of Moses and is raised at court as her own child. Years later, having witnessed with his own eyes the cruelty inflicted on a Hebrew, Moses slays the overseer and flees abroad, to the land of Midian. In Midian, which we are to understand as lying in the north of the Arabian Peninsula, east of the Gulf of Aqaba, Moses marries the daughter of a priest and tends to his flocks.

In this short exposition, we can already see several points emerging that were to be of the utmost significance for the reception history of the Exodus story; I will return to them in the first section of chapter 4. They include the uncanny affinity of the Egyptian ordeal to the later fate of the Jews, particularly in the era of National Socialism, and the anticipation of anti-Semitic clichés like "foreign infiltration" and a "fifth column" (the idea that "they might support our enemies in time of war"). In the second part of the exposition, recounting the birth, rescue, and flight of Moses, it is above all the elided story of his childhood as a prince at the pharaonic court and as an initiate into the Egyptian mysteries that has fueled people's imagination since classical antiquity.

With this two-part exposition, the groundwork is laid for the great theme of the Book of Exodus: revelation. The idea that the gods disclose their will to mortals in portents, dreams, and oracles is nothing new and can be found in different forms in all religions. This form of continuous revelation is part of the existing world and demands that humans cultivate one quality above all others: attentiveness. In order to stay in contact with the gods, they need to develop finely tuned techniques of observation and interpretation. However, none of these divine revelations and declarations even remotely resembles the definitive, founding, and binding event that is the Exodus revelation. The revelation narrated in the Book of Exodus does not belong in the world as it actually exists; rather, it intervenes in that world, remaking it from the ground up. It does not continually recur in various forms as an accompaniment to the everlasting processes of the universe; it happens once and for all time. What it requires of mortals, more than anything else, is that it be remembered. On no account is this revelation to be forgotten. On the contrary, it must continually be brought to mind in its world-changing, radically innovative significance. The Book of Exodus does not just tell of this revelation, it also establishes an indestructible monument to its memory. We have here a story that is destined never to be forgotten, one that will captivate and transform the lives of all who read and hear its "good news"—indeed, the entire New Testament stands wholly under the spell of the Book of Exodus and represents a decisive phase in its reception history.

The grand revelation that dominates the Book of Exodus proceeds in six steps:

1. Ch. 3–6   Revelation of the name (prelude). YHWH manifests himself to Moses in his true name and announces his plans to him. This first step consists in an intimate form of revelation addressed only to Moses and has no other witnesses.

2. Ch. 7–15   Revelation of power. YHWH reveals his overwhelming power to Pharaoh and the Egyptians in ten plagues and the miracle of the Red Sea. This second step, in contrast to the first, takes place on a cosmic scale; it is addressed to Pharaoh and witnessed by both Egyptians and Israelites.

3. Ch. 19–24 Revelation of the covenant. YHWH reveals himself to his chosen people as the one who redeemed them from Egyptian bondage and gives them the laws as the basis and condition for the covenant he offers them. The people are the addressees and witnesses of this third, crucial step.

4. Ch. 25–31 Revelation of the Tabernacle as model and its description. Here Moses is again the sole addressee of the revelation, which takes place from within a cloud on Sinai, hence under conditions of the utmost seclusion.

5. Ch. 33–34 Revelation of the divine being. Finally, YHWH reveals himself once again to Moses alone, when Moses succeeds in pacifying him after the crisis of the Golden Calf. In the process, the prophet's appearance is so drastically transformed that, from then on, he can communicate with his people only with a veil over his face.

6. Ch. 35–40 Institutionalized divine presence. After the Tabernacle is built, YHWH descends in his "glory" (*kābôd*) in a cloud settling above and within the sanctuary in order that he now may dwell among his people. This culminating step in the revelation process should not itself be understood as an act of revelation, however, since it leaves behind a lasting presence.

God Reveals His Name

The first step of the revelation is in two parts. The first part (3–4:17) relates in four sections the actual revelation that Moses experienced at the burning bush. I will return to this narrative kernel, which was destined to exert a far-reaching influence in the reception history, in chapter 5. The second part (4:18–6) deals with Moses's attempts to communicate this revelation to his compatriots and also, above all, to Pharaoh.

1. Leading his flocks one day beyond their usual pasturelands to Horeb, the "mountain of God," Moses sees a bush that is burning without being consumed by the flames. Intrigued by the sign, he steps closer and is granted a revelation. God becomes audible as a voice from the burning bush, solemnly identifying himself as the God of his forefathers Abraham, Isaac, and Jacob. Moses demands a name and receives the famously enigmatic reply, "I am that I am" (*'ehyeh 'ăšer 'ehyeh*), an answer that plays on the name YHWH (3:1–14).

2. God makes known to Moses his plan to free the children of Israel from Egyptian bondage and lead them to the land flowing with milk and honey he had promised their forefathers. Acting as God's emissary, Moses is to convey the good news to the Hebrews while also petitioning Pharaoh to let them journey three days into the wilderness to sacrifice to their God. However, God knows that Pharaoh will refuse the request. This gives him an opportunity to use his miracle-working power to compel the release of his people (3:15–22).

3. Moses, doubting his own credibility, is equipped by God with three magic skills that will establish his credentials as divine emissary: the ability to transform staffs into snakes, water into blood, and healthy into leprous skin (4:1–9).

4. In the face of the continuing reluctance shown by Moses, who pleads his "slow tongue," God assures him of his support and sends him an assistant in the form of his brother, Aaron, who will speak on his behalf to the people and to Pharaoh, just as Moses will speak on God's behalf to Aaron (4:10–17).

The tale of Moses's departure for and arrival in Egypt is oddly punctuated with new directives and appearances from God. These make clear that, from now on, God is steering the course of events, without there being any need for each of his interventions to be once again heralded by an epiphany and ceremonious self-introduction. He has revealed himself and is now "there," just as he had announced with the formula "I will be what I will be" (*'ehyeh 'ăšer 'ehyeh*). Moses bids farewell to his father-in-law, Jethro, and God reminds him of what he has to say to Pharaoh. Here the fateful words appear: "Israel is my son, even my firstborn." If Pharaoh refuses to let him go, God will slay Pharaoh's firstborn son (4:18–23). On the way to Egypt, Moses meets with a puzzling incident: God tries to kill him and Zipporah saves him by quickly circumcising her son—the trace of an archaic legend that was probably inserted here by association with the death of the firstborn (4:24–26). God then makes another appearance and sends Aaron ahead to greet Moses. The rest is quickly and succinctly told. Moses confers with Aaron, who passes on God's message to the assembled elders; Moses performs "the signs in the sight of the people. And the people believed" (4:27–31).

At this point, the story could go straight on to Moses and Aaron's audience with Pharaoh and their display of magic tricks, but first the action is slowed down by an interpolation that takes up a further two chapters (5 and 6). The brothers appear at the court to pass on God's command: "Let my people go, that they may hold a feast unto me in the wilderness." Yet Pharaoh knows nothing of this God, requires no miracles attesting to his power, and dismisses them out of hand. Instead of negotiating with them further, he aggravates the Hebrews' labor conditions by canceling the supply of straw they use in making bricks. Now they will have to "scatter throughout the land of Egypt to gather stubble instead of straw" for their bricks. This unfortunate turn of events makes the people lose faith in Moses's God-given mission. Moses, too, grows despondent and turns again to God, who reassures him that he will vanquish Pharaoh "with a strong hand" (5:1–6:1).

On the one hand, this interpolation anticipates the actual moment when the brothers will demonstrate their magic before Pharaoh and thus usher in the cycle of "signs and wonders" by which God compels the release of Israel. On the other hand, it duplicates the story of the Israelites' afflictions by adding a new degree of punitive intensity to the slavery depicted at the outset. The interpolated episode could end here

(6:1), but God once again launches into a solemn self-presentation that reprises his revelation in the burning bush. "I am YHWH," he declares, "and I appeared unto Abraham, unto Isaac, and unto Jacob, by the name of El Shaddai, but by the name YHWH was I not known unto them." Then God once again recalls the covenant he made with the forefathers and his pledge to give them the land of Canaan. He explains that he has seen how the Israelites suffer "under the burdens of the Egyptians" and has decided to free them "with outstretched arm, and with great judgments," that they may be his people and he their God. The motifs of the covenant and God's promise emerge even more clearly here than in the scene at the burning bush. With that, the character of this revelation as "good news" entrusted to the bearer of that news, Moses, also becomes clearer. All the more disappointing is the reaction of the Israelites, who "hearkened not unto Moses for anguish of spirit, and for cruel bondage." Once again Moses turns to God, who once again dispatches him and Aaron to the people and to Pharaoh.

At the end of chapter 6 our text takes up the thread where it had been dropped in verse 12. There, Moses had once again broached the problem of his heavy tongue, a problem that God had long since solved by appointing Aaron to help him. Here it is repeated a third time (6:30) and God again calms the prophet down by explicitly appointing Aaron to be his spokesman before Pharaoh (7:1–2, cf. 4:16). Once again, God initiates Moses into his plan to harden Pharaoh's heart in order to force him to free the Hebrews by sending him as many "signs and wonders" as possible. The multiple repetitions and redundancies show that we are dealing here with a text worked on by many hands. I will discuss the textual history in chapter 3.

God Reveals His Power

The second step in the revelation, which becomes ever more grandiose and terrifying as it unfolds, begins when Moses and Aaron appear before Pharaoh to repeat their demand. This section of the story, which extends over some eight chapters, can only be understood when it is grasped as divine revelation. Traditionally it has been summarized under the heading of *magnalia Dei*, the mighty acts of God, a term that brings together the aspects of revelation and salvation. The same aspects also define the Christian concept of revelation that builds on the events in Exodus. On a narrative level, in terms of their function within the parameters of the narration, the plagues of Egypt make little sense: why does the story dwell on them at such length when only a single terrible plague—the pestilence, for example—should have been enough to punish Egypt and liberate Israel? The chief concern of the story at this point, however, is to demonstrate God's transcendent, awe-inspiring power as comprehensively as possible. As God himself says to Pharaoh: "If I had raised my hand to strike you and your people with disease, you would have been completely destroyed. But to show you my power I have let you live so that my name might be declared throughout all the earth" (9:15–16).

When Moses and Aaron present their credentials to Pharaoh with the miracle of the snake, Pharaoh summons his wise men and sorcerers to match the feat. They do so but are humiliated when Aaron's staff, in serpentine form, swallows their own. Pharaoh still refuses to budge, so God sends Moses to Pharaoh the following morning as he is walking by the water. The magic contest now expands to a cosmic scale, since Moses, by performing his next miracle at the Nile, transforms the entire river and all the drinking water in Egypt into blood. His second demonstration of his magical powers thus becomes the first of the ten "plagues" visited by God on Pharaoh and Egypt to compel the release of Israel, his "firstborn son."

The first nine plagues, grouped in threes with the aid of tags like "tomorrow" and "go forth," reveal a certain internal order. The first three plagues perpetuate the sorcery competition contested by Aaron with his staff. "Nile" and "frogs" belong together, and just as the waters of the Nile teem with frogs, so the dust (dried Nile mud) brings forth clouds of gnats. The second group of three has a common denominator in the theme of sickness. The vermin unleashed in the fourth plague are obviously more dangerous than the merely bothersome gnats; together with the pestilence and boils of the fifth and sixth plagues, they threaten the bodies of both livestock and human beings. The final group of three is distinguished by the cosmic-meteorological character of the plagues. This is evidently true of the hail and darkness caused by the seventh and ninth plagues, respectively, and it is indirectly true of the locust swarm of the eighth, which is brought to Egypt by the east wind and carried away again by the west wind. These three plagues are also linked by the fact that Pharaoh finds them particularly unbearable and at first relents, only to harden his heart again once each plague has passed. That was previously the case only after the second and fourth plagues (frogs and vermin, respectively).

The tenth plague, the slaughter of the firstborn, is heralded at considerable length (chapter 11) and presented in a completely different format: unlike the other nine, it is not reported in narrative form but is instead embedded in God's prescriptions for the Passover feast (Pesach) and the Festival of Unleavened Bread (matzah), instituted to commemorate the exodus from Egypt. The former falls on the night of departure, the latter in the following week, when the Israelites, in their haste to put Egypt behind them, lacked the time to leaven their dough and so ate unleavened bread instead (12:15–20; cf. 23:24; Lev 23:5–6). Here the connection between revelation and memory emerges with particular clarity: "And this day shall be unto you for a memorial [*zikkārôn*]; and ye shall keep it a feast to YHWH throughout your generations; ye shall keep it a feast by an ordinance forever" (12:14).

The night of departure—the night when the Israelites stay in their homes, awaiting the signal to set out, and feast on the sacrificial lamb with whose blood they have daubed their doorways to ensure that YHWH passes them over as he stalks Egypt slaying all the firstborn—forms the primal scene of the Passover feast, which is still reenacted to this day in Judaism on the night of Seder and also underlies the Christian Easter festival as a subtext. The actual plague, the killing of the firstborn, is dispensed with in two verses following twenty-eight dedicated to establishing the Pesach and Matzah festivals; two further verses record the reaction of Pharaoh, who finally gives permission for the Israelites to leave with all their goods. These include the gold- and silverware they receive as gifts from the Egyptians prior to their departure (11:2–3, 12:35–36): an important motif already announced to Abraham (Gen 15:14) and Moses (Ex 3:21–22). This gold will later be used to cast the Golden Calf, as well as playing a role in building the Tabernacle.

The remainder of chapter 13 is taken up with the exodus of the Israelites, whom God leads through the desert in the east, appearing as a pillar of cloud by day and a pillar of fire by night. In the fourteenth chapter, the greatest of all the signs and wonders takes place, the climax of the second act in the drama of revelation: the crossing of the *yam sûf* or "Sea of Reeds," which in postbiblical times commonly meant the Red Sea. Once again God takes matters in hand, revealing to Moses his plan to lure Pharaoh into pursuing the Israelites with his entire army only for it to be destroyed with a final blow. When the Egyptians come within sight of the people encamped by the sea and panic spreads among the Israelites, God commands Moses to stretch his staff over the sea and part it, allowing the people to cross the dry land to safety on the other side. The waves then return to engulf the Egyptians following in hot pursuit, so that "there remained not so much as one of them" (14:28).

Moses and the rescued Israelites now offer up a song of thanksgiving in nineteen verses: "I will sing unto the Lord, for he hath triumphed gloriously: the horse and his rider he hath thrown into the sea." Miriam, Moses's sister, and all the women join in a round dance to the beat of their tambourines (20–21). Miriam's victory song ranks among the oldest pieces of Hebrew poetry on account of its ancient form and diction. If we are not to take it for deliberately archaic, then it is certainly much older than the story in which it is embedded. Indeed, it may be considered the earliest testimony to the Exodus myth, possibly dating back at least to the tenth or ninth century and hence before Hosea and Amos, who refer to the myth in the second half of the eighth century.

Plagues, Pesach, and the miracle of the Red Sea form the second act in the drama of revelation, in which God manifests himself to the world—if not in his physical form, then at least in the consequences of his all-surpassing power and greatness. Visibility is what matters: "And Israel saw the great work which YHWH did upon the Egyptians" (14:31). For the Egyptians, God's saving deeds have the character of "heavy punishments" (*šĕpāṭîm gĕdōlîm*), for the Israelites, that of "signs and wonders" (*'ōtōt ûmōpĕtîm*). In their cumulative force, they build up to an extraordinarily powerful and lastingly influential image— a mental hieroglyph, as it were, recalling the pictogram of Pharaoh smiting his enemies[3]—that is conjured up with the constantly recurring formula: "with a mighty hand, and with outstretched arm" (*bĕyād ḥăzāqâ ûbizrōʻa nĕṭûyâ*: Deut 4:34, 5:14, 7:19, 11:2, 26:8; Ps 136:12; Ez 20:33). These saving deeds, a narrative high point that has had a particularly wide-ranging impact in the book's reception history, will be discussed in chapter 6.

Sinai—Calling, Covenant, and Law (Chapters 15–24)

The Way to Sinai

Moses's song of thanksgiving draws a line under the first part of the Book of Exodus, which tells of his people's actual departure from Egypt. The second and third parts deal with their entry into a new order, which is not to be confused, however, with the "promised land," the ultimate fulfillment of the promise made to Abraham, Jacob, and Moses. This new order is rather, in the first place, the covenant founded on God-given laws and, second, a closeness to God institutionalized in cultic practice: nothing less than a symbiosis with God, who will henceforth dwell "among his people." These parts can be more concisely summarized than the first. Chapter 15 verses 22–27 as well as chapters 16–18 recount five events that befell the Israelites on their way from the "Sea of Reeds" to Sinai. The first three have to do with the problem of securing necessary provisions in the desert. In Marah the parched Israelites are unable to find water that is fit to drink: "And the people murmured against Moses, saying, What shall we drink?" (15:24). Moses cries out to God, who shows him a piece of wood that he can throw into brackish water to make it sweet. In addition, we are told that God here gave them laws to live by (*ḥōq ûmišpāt*), although this actually happens later, in the context of the "Sinai pericope" (Ex 19–Num 10, more narrowly Ex 19–24). In this context, God also pledges to be a healer to his people (*'ănî rōpĕ'ekā*) and to protect them from the diseases he has brought upon the Egyptians, provided they obey his commandments (*miṣwôt*) and laws (*ḥuqqîm*). We can see here the trace of an alternative, presumably older version of the Exodus myth that knows nothing of the "Sinai pericope."

Food is in short supply in the desert as well. The people long for the "fleshpots of Egypt" and once more "murmur" against Moses and Aaron. God then causes bread to appear in the form of the enigmatic manna from heaven, giving precise instructions about how and when it is to be gathered and consumed. On the sixth day, he provides double rations, since nothing is to be harvested on the Sabbath (which, strictly speaking, is first established with the revelation of the Decalogue on Sinai). For dinner, God satisfies the Israelites' yearning to eat meat with quails, which "covered the camp."

The third crisis takes place in Rephidim, where no water is to be found. For the third time, the people "murmur" and appear to be on the verge of stoning their leader. God commands Moses to strike a rock with his staff, causing fresh water to gush forth. In the Book of Numbers, which increases the number of Israelite mutinies to ten, this episode recurs in a different version and is judged in an altogether different light.

The fourth crisis breaks out when Israel is attacked by Amalek in Rephidim (17:8–16). This crisis, too, is surmounted with the same miraculous means that had accompanied and made possible the exodus ever since the snake miracle at Pharaoh's court. While the Israelites under Joshua fight against Amalek, Moses stands with Aaron and Hur on the hill and raises his arms toward the sky. As soon as he lowers them, Amalek gains the upper hand. At last, Aaron and Hur bring a stone for Moses to sit on and support his arms on both sides. Amalek is ultimately defeated in this way. God commands Moses to commemorate the victory in a book so that all memory of Amalek may be extinguished. Moses instead immortalizes the incident by building an altar, calling it "The Lord is my banner" and proclaiming: "YHWH will be at war with Amalek from generation to generation." As a consequence, Amalek is remembered to this day as Israel's quintessential archenemy and a figure of everlasting obloquy.

The fifth episode is peaceful in nature and reprises the theme of jurisdiction. Jethro, Moses's father-in-law, pays a visit and, learning from Moses of the miracles God has performed to save his people, acknowledges that YHWH "is greater than all gods" (18:1–12). The following day, he sees how Moses wears himself out from dawn until dusk judging disputes and instructing his people in God's "statutes" (*ḥuqqîm*) and "instructions" (*tôrōt*). Such a workload is unsustainable, so Jethro advises him to appoint honest, capable men "to be rulers of thousands, and rulers of hundreds, rulers of fifties, and rulers of ten"; these men

will judge the less important cases, leaving Moses to bring the harder
cases before God while also educating the people about God's statutes
and laws. So it comes to pass, and Jethro returns home (18:13–27).
Here, too, the laws that will only be announced in the following "Sinai
pericope," the third act in the revelation, are already presupposed. All
this suggests that the Sinai pericope represents a later addition to the
story, intended to make Israel's laws and constitution a part—the
crowning part, no less—in the drama of revelation that began at the
burning bush and continued in the "signs and wonders" in Egypt. Although God was the source of law and justice in the older version as
well, these figured as elements in the dialogues between God and
Moses accompanying the departure from Egypt, rather than forming
a grandiose act of revelation in their own right. That had to wait until
the compositional stage which united the Exodus and Sinai narratives
into a single continuous, steadily intensifying drama of revelation: in
all likelihood, the Priestly Source.

God Reveals the Covenant

The term "Sinai pericope" refers to the section of the story from the
people's sojourn at Sinai to the proclamation of the law. The pericope
extends from Exodus 19 to Numbers 10, with Exodus 25–40—which
belong together as what I consider the third part of the book—repre-
senting a Priestly addition to the Book of *Exodus (the asterisk here
indicates that we are dealing with a reconstructed urtext). Chapters
19–24 form the third, climactic act in the drama of revelation. They
frame the proclamation of the law in the four chapters 20–23, fore-
grounding a different linguistic register that might be called "pre-
scriptive" (rather than "descriptive") or "normative" (rather than "narrative"). Here, the forward momentum of descriptive storytelling
is blocked by a massif of commandments, prohibitions, admonish-
ments, threats, and promises. These are radically different speech acts.
Far from referring to a reality whose existence is assumed to lie before
and beyond such acts, they create, by the very fact of their being uttered and transcribed, a reality that is summoned into being when
certain frame conditions are in place: in this case, the making of the
covenant.

Of course, such "performative" speech acts can be found at the level of human speech as well. Through performative utterance, we all have the ability to create situations that assume binding reality for me and for those around me: for example, by saying "I do" at the altar, confessing or pronouncing a verdict in a court of law, absolving the penitent from sin in the confessional, or swearing an oath before witnesses. Yet a very different, vastly more comprehensive and compelling reality is created when a god expresses himself in this form—and not just any god, but *the* God, YHWH, the one and only, even if he no longer issues these commandments and prohibitions as the creator who brought the entire universe into being by fiat but as the liberator making a covenant with those he has freed from Egyptian bondage.[4] The liberation from Egypt is the frame condition under which God's normative speech acquires performative force. What that means for how the Book of Exodus was read hardly needs emphasizing: the covenant is what first invests the book with binding validity. While that holds true of the Bible as a whole, the Hebrew Bible no less than the Christian, it is especially so for the Book of Exodus, since unlike most other books of holy scripture, Exodus does not simply presuppose these frame conditions but tells how they came about, explicitly proclaiming and codifying their authority.

This alliance between book and covenant constitutes what has ever since gone by the name of "revealed religion." A canon of sacred texts forms the foundation of these religions, which in turn provide the framework for the canonicity of the sacred texts.[5] The history of a sacred text is thus fundamentally different from that of a profane work like the Homeric epics or the dramas of Shakespeare. Such works also "live on," so to speak, in the framework of a society that endows them with classic status, but they do not explicitly establish that framework; rather, it is determined by the laws of art, according to which the Book of Exodus would have to be found severely wanting. However impressive and influential this book may appear in the light of its religious significance, it is anything but a seamless literary masterpiece. It resembles instead a very strange kind of painting: a collage repeatedly retouched by later brushes.

Performative texts can be found in other religions too, presumably in all of them. Under exactly prescribed and scrupulously observed frame conditions, blessings or curses are pronounced, rainclouds summoned, demons exorcised, the sick healed, and so on. It is only in revealed religions, however, that God's performative utterances lay the foundation for an entire community and a way of life. The Book of Exodus is the first example of such a comprehensive foundation. It presupposes the Book of Genesis with the creation of the universe, since it relates how something new and unique, the covenant between God and his chosen people, emerged within the already created world; and it forms, in turn, the precondition for all the stories that will subsequently be told within the framework of the reality established here.

But back to the story. After the two collections of laws are proclaimed, the Decalogue and the "Covenant Code," the covenant is solemnly sealed (chapter 24). God orders a group of delegates consisting of Moses, Aaron, Nadab, Abihu, and seventy of the elders to come up to him on the mountain, since a legally binding covenant requires a certain representative public to witness it, although only Moses is to "come near the Lord," that is, within earshot. Before this, Moses secures the people's consent to the "judgments" handed down on the mountaintop. He then sacrifices to the Lord, sprinkling half the blood on the people and declaring: "Behold the blood of the covenant, which YHWH hath made with you concerning all these words." Jesus will invoke and supersede this formula when introducing the last supper: "This is the blood of the new covenant."

Thus authorized, Moses and the delegates selected by YHWH climbed the mountain "and saw the God of Israel." No description is offered of this vision except for the surface under YHWH's feet, "like a pavement of sapphire as clear as the sky itself." With this revelation, God signals his assent to the covenant: "Also they saw God, and did eat and drink." With that, the ceremony of the covenant is over. But Moses must return once more to the mountaintop to be given the stone tablets. Covering the mountain is a cloud in which the glory (*kābôd*) of the Lord appears to the Israelites like a devouring fire. Moses must wait six days; on the seventh, he is called up from its midst. Moses ventures into the fiery cloud and stays there for forty days and forty nights. Thus ends the first part of the Sinai pericope.

Divine Presence (Chapters 25–40)

God Reveals the Tabernacle

The third and longest part of the Book of Exodus gets underway some-what abruptly at this point. "Let them make me a sanctuary," YHWH says to Moses, "that I may dwell among them" (25:8). At its dramatic high point, the story becomes bogged down in a seemingly endless catalog of items for the construction and interior design of a tabernacle. This catalog is run through twice: first as the fourth act in the drama of revelation, in the form of YHWH's instructions to Moses (25–31), ending with him receiving the two "tables of stone, written with the finger of God" (31:18); then as the report of their implementation, ending with the entrance into the Tabernacle of the cloud and YHWH's *kābôd* (35–40). The finale in the drama of revelation is taken up with the creation of a permanent, securely institutionalized framework for the form in which YHWH can be "there" for his people. This thirteen chapter-long catalog is interrupted in the middle by three chapters of highly dramatic narrative in which the entire enterprise is once again radically called into question.

The first six chapters (25–31) deal with the production of the four most sacred objects—the ark of the covenant, the *kappōret* (Tyndale's "mercy seat"), the altar of burnt offering, and the golden lampstand—as well as the elements for constructing and furnishing a tabernacle, the clothing and ornaments worn by the priests, and the basic characteristics of the cult.[6] God even nominates an artist to direct the project: Bezalel, Uri's son and the grandson of Hur (who, alongside Aaron, had held up Moses's arms in the battle against Amalek). These instructions have the character of a revelation in which God presents the Tabernacle that is to be constructed both in the form of a visible model (*tabnît*) and through a description of its individual components.

Revelation of the Divine Being: Breach and Reconciliation

Meanwhile, forty days have passed since the people saw Moses disappearing into the fiery cloud, and they have given up all hope of ever seeing him alive again. They beg Aaron to "make us Elohim which shall go before us; for as for this Moses, the man that brought us out of the land of Egypt, we know not what is become of him." By construing the word "Elohim," gods, in the plural, they show that they have forsaken the one true God. What is puzzling is that Aaron, who ought to know better, willingly complies with their demand, ordering golden jewelry to be collected and made into a molten calf. The Israelites now proclaim: "These be thy gods, O Israel, which brought thee up out of the land of Egypt." Aaron builds an altar for the calf and ordains that a great feast be celebrated the following day. The Israelites sacrifice animals to their new totem and descend into a state of orgiastic revelry; indeed, it is difficult to see how they could behave any more sinfully. When Moses, descending from Sinai with the stone tablets, sees the people dancing around the Golden Calf, he shatters the tablets in his rage and orders the execution of three thousand men. By worshipping the Golden Calf, the Israelites have already disobeyed the first two commandments: to have no other gods and no graven or molten images. With that they have willfully broken the terms of the covenant. YHWH resolves to annihilate them but Moses manages to talk him out of it. I will discuss this episode in more detail in chapter 10.

Chapter 33 begins with a new speech by YHWH. Guided by an angel, Moses is to lead his people into the Promised Land. YHWH himself will not escort them there, "because you are a stubborn people, and I might destroy you along the way" (33:3). In God's eyes, the living community wished for on both sides has become a thing of impossibility, since the people obviously lack the sanctity required to uphold their end of the bargain. Moses acts on God's decision to dwell no more among his people by removing the Tabernacle from the camp—although it has not actually been erected yet—and pitching it some distance away. The cloudy pillar descends there, the people worship it from afar, and YHWH speaks to Moses "face to face, as a man speaks to his friend" (33:11).

This sentence forms the introduction to the following exchanges between Moses and YHWH, which reveal Moses in his full, previously unseen greatness and bring him almost face to face with God. After Moses has succeeded in pacifying God, he dares petition him to make himself visible in his presence as a sign of reconciliation. Although YHWH grants him this extraordinary favor, he takes precautions to ensure that Moses does not come to any harm. He places him in the crack of a rock and, as he passes by, offers only his "back parts" to the prophet's sight. Additionally, in a final act of revelation, he famously describes his essence—in a high point of biblical theology—as "gracious and merciful God."

Moses again pleads with God to "go among us" (34:9) and God renews the covenant in solemn terms. The scene ends with a Dodecalogue, a series of twelve commandments that only partially coincides with the Decalogue. The grandiose scene of Moses's divine vision forms the conclusion and fifth act in the process of revelation. In its intimate character as a revelation intended for Moses alone, it corresponds to the scene at the burning bush. As a result of his direct exposure to the divine being, Moses's appearance is permanently transformed: "the skin of Moses's face shone" (or, in an alternative rendering, his face was "horned"). He must now cover his face with a *masweh* ("cover," "veil"? the word occurs only here), since no mere mortal can endure so powerful a manifestation of the sacred.

The Tabernacle Is Built

In the next five chapters (35–39), God falls silent; instead it is Moses who speaks, directing the building of the Tabernacle at God's behest. The first step is to stipulate the working hours: work can be done only six days a week, since the seventh is set aside for the Sabbath rest: "Whoever does work therein shall be put to death. Ye shall kindle no fire throughout your habitations on the Sabbath day" (35:2–3). God's instructions for building the Tabernacle had ended with this warning to observe the Sabbath; the orders given by Moses begin with it. Next, Moses details the offerings or sacrifices that people are expected to make in order for the Tabernacle to be built. Everyone, "man and woman," is called on to volunteer their services to the best of their ability. The individual components and precious materials are once again enumerated on this occasion: the *miškān* (God's dwelling place within the Tabernacle) as well as the articles contained therein—the ark of the covenant, the table, the lamps, and the incense altar—the altar of burnt offering at the entrance together with the surrounding hangings, as well as the priestly garments. Thus all contributed "whose heart made them willing to bring for all manner of work, which YHWH had commanded to be made by the hand of Moses" (35:29). Lastly the craftsmen are called to work under Bezalel and Aholiab.

The Revelation Concludes: God's Permanent Presence

Chapter 40—and hence the Book of Exodus—concludes with God's entrance into his new dwelling place: "the cloud abode thereon, and the glory of YHWH [*kĕbôd* YHWH] filled the Tabernacle." The longed-for closeness to God has now been placed on a permanent footing.[7] God has moved in. The visible presence of the cloud and the invisible presence of his glory (*kābôd*) together form a miraculous sign similar to the signs and wonders in which God had displayed his power and majesty for all in Egypt to see, albeit no longer in the form of a theophany spectacularly distinguished from the ordinary course of events but rather as an everyday state of affairs. When the cloud covers the Tabernacle, Moses cannot enter it; when it lifts, this is a sign for the Israelites to break camp. Then it draws before them, appearing by day as a cloud and by night as a pillar of fire.

With that, the stage is set for all the regulations, edicts, commandments, and laws subsequently issued by God. These are recorded in the directly ensuing third and fourth books of Moses. Nonetheless, the story that makes up the theme of the Book of Exodus has come to an end with the construction of the Tabernacle and God's entry into his "dwelling place." That story had begun with the account of the trials of the children of Israel in Egyptian bondage, a situation of the utmost remoteness from God—until God heard their cries and set about rescuing them; and it ends by depicting a lived closeness to God in the form of a literal, visible community that bears several of the characteristic features of fairytale.

Without wanting to give undue emphasis to the scholastic chapter divisions,[8] which are external to the text, a certain symmetry can nonetheless be detected in the story. Interpolations though they may be, the chapters still give a good idea of the narrative's proportions, the space allotted to its respective themes. Sixteen chapters are devoted to the final closeness to God, first when the building instructions are given, then—following the interlude of the crisis, which places everything in doubt once more, and its triumphant overcoming in the glorification of Moses—when those instructions are carried out. The account of the exodus proper takes up fourteen and three-quarters chapters, from the oppression in Egypt to the crossing of the Red Sea and Moses's song of thanksgiving. The theme of "community with God" thus takes up more space than that of "exodus"! In between—that is, between chapter 15a, the song of thanksgiving, and chapter 25, when the building instructions are given—lie nine and one-quarter chapters, the first three devoted to the path to Sinai, the following six to the handing down of the law and the covenant at Sinai. The book's proportions thus distribute the three central themes of "exodus," "covenant," and "Temple" in a ratio of approximately 3:2:3.

From this we can see how much space is taken up by the theme of the Tabernacle in the Book of Exodus, and hence also its importance in the story, which stands in such stark contrast to the significance accorded it in the subsequent reception history. Were it not for the story of the Golden Calf, which forms the middle section (B) in the composition, this part would probably have attracted the least attention, especially since the reprise (A'), which recounts how the commands given in A were carried out, merely runs through the same catalog of items in a slightly different order. As it stands, however, this part reflects the whole salvational history in miniature, since the crisis recounted in the middle section assumes the dimensions of a second fall from grace. Under the quite different conditions of covenant and election, it radically calls into question the entire salvational project of restoring the harmony between God and his creation destroyed with the first fall. The theme of divine presence only becomes clear in its relative weighting and in its proportions when seen against the broader background of the Priestly Source.

I shall have more to say about the textual history in chapter 3, where I will also expand on what is meant by "Priestly Source" (P). In brief, I take it to mean a composition that brings together the Books of Genesis and Exodus into a single, all-encompassing work of history, one that extends all the way from creation to the revelation on Sinai. The third part of the Book of Exodus should therefore be understood as the conclusion, not just of this book, but of the entire "Priestly Source" history. It is generally agreed that this part—fixated as it is on Temple

and cult—first arose in the course of the Priestly redaction and represents the goal and climax of the entire story, beginning with the creation of the universe and ending with the creation of religion in the
form of God coming down to dwell among his people. The paralleliza-
tion of creation and Temple has clear Egyptian and Babylonian antecedents.[9] Unlike in those antecedents, however, the Temple does not
arise in the process of creation; rather, it is founded through revelation
in the course of history, at the end of millennia full of vicissitudes.

If we reexamine the book's structure from this vantage point, we
must therefore include the Book of Genesis and take the entire "Priestly
Source" conception and composition into account. The Book of Genesis is split into primordial (1–11) and patriarchal (12–50) history. Primordial history, in turn, is divided by the caesura of the flood, the first
part stretching from Adam to Noah (2–9), the second from Noah to the
Tower of Babel (9–11). The story of the Patriarchal Age, meanwhile, is
clearly articulated into Abraham (12–25), Isaac (26–27), and Jacob
(28–35) cycles, each named after its respective protagonist, as well as
the highly literary tale of Joseph (37–50). By comparison, the Book of
Exodus is not so clearly structured, since the protagonist, Moses, dominates the book from start to finish. Whereas the narrative of Genesis
is chronologically organized through the succession of generations
(*tôlĕdōt*), the narrative of Exodus is spatially structured through
changes in location; these correlate to large sections within which
fairly clear thematic focal points can be distinguished:

1. Egypt (here ch. 4)
   The sufferings of the Israelites in Egyptian bondage (1)
   The birth of the savior, Moses's upbringing and flight (2)
2. Midian (here ch. 5)
   Moses's call from God at the burning bush (3–4:17)
   Moses's partnership with Aaron and return to Egypt (4:18–31)
3. Egypt (here ch. 6)
   Moses and Aaron's talks with Pharaoh and the first nine plagues (5–10)
   The Passover night, tenth plague (11–13:16), and passage through the
   Red Sea (14–15:21)
4. Desert (here ch. 9)
   The people's "murmurings" and the quail and manna miracles (15:22–16)

The miracle of the water at Massah-Meribah, victory over Amalek, arrival (17–19)
5. Covenant at Sinai (here ch. 7–8)
   Decalogue, laws, covenant (20–24)
6. The Tabernacle (here ch. 10)
   Instructions for the Tabernacle (25–31)
   Crisis and renewal of the covenant (32–34)
   Construction and furnishing of the Tabernacle (35–40)

Unlike the Book of Genesis, the Book of Exodus is held together by a single narrative thread, leading from a catastrophic point of departure to a triumphant conclusion: from an oppressed minority to God's chosen people, from the utmost distance from God to the most intimate symbiosis with God. In the eyes of the Priestly authors of this history, a goal has been attained for which even Genesis, with its tales of creation, primordial history, and patriarchal history, provides only the prelude. The Priestly Source formulates the founding legend of the new religion launched into the world on Sinai.

CHAPTER TWO

THE HISTORICAL BACKGROUND

Event and Remembrance

> There are no pure facts of memory. [...] Whatever cannot be
> made the subject of a descriptive statement [...] becomes
> susceptible to narrative transformation.
>
> —*Hans Blumenberg*[1]

AT SOME STAGE OR OTHER, every reader of the Book of Exodus is
confronted with the vexing question of the historical truth of the events
behind the tale. How easy things would stand if the Book of Exodus
were simply a work of history and the events recorded there had actually taken place at some identifiable point in the past! Since we are
dealing here with truly extraordinary events—genocidal persecution,
natural catastrophes, a sea that parts to allow the Israelites free passage
before closing over their pursuers, awe-inspiring revelations in the
Sinai desert—it is hardly surprising that such events inspired stories
intended to provide a lasting memorial to what happened, even as they
constantly recast it in a different light. We would thus be dealing with
a series of unprecedented events, on the one hand, and their elaboration and reception in narrative form, on the other. By studying how
these events were retold while also drawing on as many independent
testimonies, sources, and historical traces as possible, we could hope
to arrive at as objective an account as possible of what actually happened (for example, a reconstruction of the historical Moses).

Such hopes for enlightenment with regard to the historical background of the events reported in the Bible were once placed in Egyptology. Did the Egyptian sources have nothing to say about the Israelites' stay in the country? Were they silent on the subject of their

departure?[2] Was not Moses an Egyptian by name? Perhaps he had supported Akhenaten, the monotheist heretic-pharaoh, and been forced to quit the country after the forces of restoration had triumphed?[3] Or did the historical Moses lie behind a different usurper driven into exile at a later date, one with a similar name such as Amenmesse[4] or the Syrian Beja, who adopted a courtly name modeled on Ramesses, Ramose?[5] In addition, archaeologists of ancient Palestine went hunting for traces of the conquest that followed upon the Exodus—signs of widespread destruction, major changes in material culture and the like—but no evidence directly supporting the biblical account turned up.[6] It was hoped that the excavation of Jericho would provide missing information about the "occupation," but it revealed that the city had fallen into decline long before the events recounted in the Bible could have taken place and was resettled only much later.

Such questions about historical reality end in a blind alley. The biblical stories contradict each other, while extrabiblical sources are in short supply. The "historical Moses" has vanished into thin air and a verifiable exodus cannot be reconstructed from the stories.

In this book, I want therefore to search for the meaning of the Exodus-and-Moses tradition, not in whatever residues of real history it might preserve, but in what it had to say to its audiences down the ages—and what it still says to us today—when it invokes the legendary past. What actually happened on the flight from Egypt? Who was the real Moses? These are questions that cannot meaningfully be asked of the Exodus-and-Moses tradition. Instead, I propose to ask: Why is the story told and from whose perspective? Which standards of judgment are applied in its telling? Nobody would ever dream of reading the Books of Jonah or Esther with a view to acquiring information about the historical reality of the characters and events reported there; similarly, if we bracket out the historical event of the exodus and the historical Moses from our investigation, we can regard the tradition as a purely symbolic narrative: *etsi Moses non daretur*. No longer seeking the meaning of the tradition in whatever historical facts it may contain, we are free to interrogate it for what it can tell us—and what it told all who heard and studied the story down the ages—about ourselves, our heritage, our future, and our relationship with God and the world. After all, that is what constitutes the vitality of a tradition—and the

Book of Exodus must surely be considered one of the most vital books in all the Bible.

Three levels need to be distinguished here: history ("what really happened"), myth (the stories handed down about it), and literature (how these traditions have been elaborated in writing). In this case, as mentioned, we must make do without the historical dimension. That is not to deny that the stories in the Bible may contain a kernel of truth. On the contrary, it is highly likely that some event, experienced as a miraculous act of salvation, served as the crystallization point for a story—or a cycle of stories—that subsequently brought together a multitude of diverse historical experiences and memories. But that also means that the one great, decisive, utterly transformative and foundational event recorded in the Book of Exodus never took place, or at least not in this form.

Rather than asking, "What really happened?" the mnemohistorical approach asks how it was remembered; it examines why, by whom, for whose sake, and in which forms this past became meaningful. The line of questioning can also be reversed, such that, rather than starting out from the tradition and inquiring into the historical events that might underpin it, we proceed instead from the events documented by the sources and archaeological finds and investigate the traditions that may have attached themselves to those events. That, too, is part of mnemo-history. Applying this approach to the historical times and places to which the Exodus tradition refers, and in which it developed, yields a whole range of possibilities for linking that tradition with various historical contexts. Of particular interest is the incontrovertible evidence pointing to contacts between the Egyptians and their West Semitic neighbors (whether Canaanite, Palestinian, Syrian, or Hebrew)—contacts that must surely have left their mark, not just on the archaeological record,[7] but also on the oral and literary tradition, that is, the cultural memory of the peoples and tribes concerned.

Memories

The Hyksos

In this regard, the "Hyksos" should be mentioned in first place. *Hyksos* is the term used by the Greeks to render the Egyptian *ḥeqaʾ ḥasût*, "ruler(s) of the foreign lands." The term refers not just to the rulers but to the entire colony of migrants who pushed into Egypt from the northeast toward the end of the eighteenth century BCE and settled in the Delta, probably under pressure from a wave of far-roaming Indo-European horse people, the Hurrians, who founded the kingdom of Mitanni on the Upper Euphrates and established city-states in northern Syrio-Palestinian and Lebanese territory. Once settled in Egypt, the Hyksos established their capital in Avaris, a city in the northeastern Delta directly adjacent to the later Ramesside capital, Pi-Ramesses. In the seventeenth and sixteenth centuries, the lords of Avaris were able to expand their kingdom and subjugate the Middle and Upper Egyptian nomes. As overlords of Egypt, they adopted the Egyptian royal titulary and ruled the land for around 110 years.[8]

We are thus dealing here with a substantial group of Semitic migrants who settled in what the Bible calls the Land of Goshen and stayed in Egypt for a good two centuries, before they were eventually driven out in a long-running war of liberation waged against them by the Upper Egyptian nomarchs of Thebes. Nothing could be more understandable than to identify this group with the Israelites. There are significant discrepancies, to be sure: far from being enslaved by the Egyptians, the Hyksos ruled over them; they were not freed from Egypt as a result of protracted negotiations and power plays but were, on the contrary, expelled from the country by force. But these very inversions reinforce the impression of a link. A wide range of sources provides information about these Hyksos. First, archaeological finds attest to an unambiguously un-Egyptian, Palestinian culture that then partially assimilated to its new surroundings. Second, there are Egyptian inscriptions relating to the Theban wars of liberation. Finally, there are texts from a later date making clear that the Hyksos experience had an important place in the cultural memory of Egypt.

Another link between the Hyksos and the Israelites can be established via the god Seth, who had a principal cultic site in Avaris, the Hyksos capital. The Hyksos had brought their god Ba'al or Hadad with them from Palestine. Arrived in Egypt, he was equated with Seth, who murdered his own brother, Osiris, and personified all the qualities loathed by the Egyptians: brute force, dishonesty, sexual misconduct, chaos, and so on. Through this *interpretatio semitica*, this veritable anti-god—identified by the Greeks with the demonic Typhon—gained im-

mensely in importance, coming to assume in the eastern Delta the features of the great thunder god worshipped in the Middle East and
among the Hittites. The Ramesside dynasty, which originated in the
Delta, was closely associated with Seth; no fewer than three pharaohs
(Seti I, Seti II, and Setnakhte) bore names incorporating the god's. The
Ramessides restored the cult of Seth-Ba'al, which had been abandoned
in Avaris following the expulsion of the Hyksos, and commemorated
the event in a stele (fig. 1).[9] It represents the first—and for a long time
remained the only—instance of a historical anniversary recorded in the
annals of history. Can it be pure coincidence that this unique memorial
sets the age of the Seth-Ba'al cult in Avaris at four hundred years, exactly the same period of time that, according to Genesis 15:13, the Israelites dwelled in Egypt (430 years, according to Exodus)? Is it purely
by chance that the date cited for the establishment of the cult in Avaris,
1650, coincides with the rise to power of the Hyksos?[10]

It would appear, then, that the "four hundred years" the Israelites
spent languishing in Egypt represent a "resonance phenomenon" of
the cultural memory associated with the Egyptianized Ba'al. There is
even evidence for the equation of Seth-Ba'al with YHWH. It is anything but improbable that, under Ramesses II, the four-hundredth-
anniversary celebrations of the Seth-Ba'al cult of Avaris extended all
the way into Canaan, which was ruled by Egypt at the time. This would
have allowed the association of Egypt and a four-centuries-long sojourn to take root and endure in the cultural memory of this region.

A further motif—one that could have played a role not just in the
collective memory of Egypt—is associated with the cult of Seth-Ba'al
of Avaris. In a historical narrative of the Ramesside period, the Hyksos
king Apophis is remembered as a monotheist:

> King Apophis chose for his Lord the god Seth. He did not worship any
> other deity in the whole land except Seth.[11]

This backward glance at the Seth cult of the Hyksos may also resonate
with the experience of the Amarna period, when the pharaoh
Akhenaten chose the sun "to be the Lord" and "worshiped no god in
all the land except Aten."

Yet even in traditional Egyptian mythology, the god Seth is already
associated with loneliness, at least in the negative sense that he dis-

FIGURE 1. The 400-year stele: Ramesses II's memorial commemorating the establishment of the Seth cult in Avaris, the Hyksos capital. c. 1250 BCE.

plays asocial behavior. In a ritual "for warding off evil," Seth is characterized as

> he who rejoices in division and hates society (*snsn*), who relies (only) on his (own) heart among the gods.[12]

Seth is an unwed bisexual rapist[13] whose company no god could abide in a normal cultic constellation, as *paredros* or consort. In his Canaanite reinterpretation as a storm and weather god, however, he acquires the positive traits of one who battles against the chaotic powers of the sea (Jam) and the summer drought (Mot, "death"). As such, under the Ramessides he offers his support to the sun god and appears

at the bow of the solar bark fighting the water snake, Apep. He is also
depicted in this pose on numerous Palestinian stamp seals. Furthermore, among the Ramesside rulers he takes on the features of a war
god, an ʾiš milḥamah, much like YHWH in Exodus 15:3. In this capacity
he receives a temple in the capital and is named patron of one of the
four divisions of the Egyptian army. Michael Brinkschröder concisely
summarizes the results of the iconographic research carried out by
Othmar Keel and others: "At first, Seth was amalgamated with the
Syrio-Palestinian god Baʿal into a novel kind of 'divine molecule'
(Keel), a war-like storm god. This image of the deity, in turn, had a
decisive influence on how the Yahweh of the first Iron Age (1200–1000
BCE) was viewed."[14] A late connection between Seth and YHWH is
made in Greco-Egyptian texts that link the god Iao—the rendering into
Greek of the Hebrew divine name[15]—with Seth and the donkey, since
the name resembles the obviously onomatopoeic Egyptian word for
"donkey."[16] "They dedicate, in a shrine, a statue of an ass and sacrifice
a ram in his honor, apparently in derision of Ammon."[17] Plutarch relates that Seth, the murderer of Osiris, was driven out of Egypt and
spent seven days fleeing into Palestine. There he fathered two sons,
whom he named Jerusalem and Judah.[18]

The most important medium to have preserved the memory of the
Hyksos in the Egyptian cultural memory and beyond, into Greco-
Roman times, is the king list, which gives the names of the Hyksos
kings as the fifteenth and sixteenth dynasty. The priest Manetho, who
drew on these sources toward the start of the third century BCE to
write a Greek-language history of Egypt that was probably commissioned by Ptolemy II ("King Talmai" of the Jewish tradition, who is
also said to have sponsored the Septuagint, the translation of the Bible
into Greek[19]), fleshed out the skeleton of this list with stories. While his
work is no longer extant, the very passages on the Hyksos that interest
us most were transcribed by Flavius Josephus, who identified the Hyksos with the Israelites and their expulsion with the exodus from Egypt.

In his pamphlet Contra Apionem, "Against Apion," Josephus compiled a dossier of pagan testimonies on the subject of the Jews. He had
two ends in mind. On the one hand, he set out to prove the venerable
age of the Jewish people; on the other, he wanted to refute the lies that
Egyptian authors, particularly Apion, had circulated about the Jews.

These two goals correspond to two lengthy excerpts from Manetho's *Aegyptiaca*. The first (*C. Ap.* 1.73–105)[20] serves the chronological argument and refers to the expulsion of the Hyksos. According to Josephus, Manetho writes of them that they are people of obscure origin (*anthrōpoi to genos asēmoi*) who invaded and occupied Egypt without encountering serious resistance; Manetho interprets their name as "shepherd kings" (from *Šas.w* = "nomads"). They pillaged Egypt with the utmost cruelty, burning down cities, destroying temples, slaughtering some and enslaving others. Manetho then lists six Hyksos kings with their reigns. The Hyksos ruled Egypt for 511 years until the Theban kings rose up against the foreign overlords. The Hyksos dug in at Avaris. Following a fruitless siege, King "Thutmose" promised them free passage to a land of their choice. The Hyksos, still some 240,000 strong, then moved with all their goods to Syria, but their fear of the Assyrians led them to settle instead in the country known to Manetho's contemporaries as Judea, where they founded the city of Jerusalem. To be sure, Manetho speaks neither of Jews nor of Hebrews, and he makes no mention of Moses. For Josephus, however, his naming of Judea and Jerusalem is enough to corroborate the link to the biblical Exodus, assuming that Josephus is to be trusted and these two names really did appear in Manetho's original account. The fact that the Jews figure here as rulers, whereas according to tradition they suffered as captives in Egyptian servitude, sits uneasily with Josephus's version of events. But a solution to this contradiction lay at hand. In a different copy, says Josephus, probably meaning another section of Manetho's work, an etymology of the word "Hyksos" entirely different from the generally accepted one is to be found. In this passage, the component *hyk* is traced back to the Egyptian *ḥ'q*, "captive," rather than to *ḥq'*, "ruler." The word as a whole thus means "captured shepherds," not "shepherd kings."[21]

Flavius Josephus was certainly not the first Jew to hear Egyptian recollections of the Hyksos and be reminded of the exodus. Such tales were still very much alive in late-period Egypt, where they would have been encountered by the many Jews who sought refuge there following the destruction of the Temple. The strikingly negative tone of these tales, which depicted the Hyksos period as a time of great suffering, must have posed a problem for the Jews who identified with the Hyksos. We will come back to this in the context of the "plagues of Egypt." At any rate, we cannot dismiss the possibility that

- Canaanite memories of a two-hundred-year spell in Egypt and a final violent expulsion were retained at least among certain tribes in different forms of oral tradition;
- Egyptian memories of the Hyksos as tyrants and blasphemers could have provoked a Jewish countermemory or counternarrative in which, on the contrary, the Israelites appear as victims of oppression and the Egyptians as tyrannical slave-drivers.

Amarna

Time and again, most prominently by Sigmund Freud, a connection has been proposed between Moses and Akhenaten, the pharaoh who in the mid-fourteenth century BCE abolished the traditional religion in Egypt and replaced it with a new cult of the one sun and light god Aten. Moses, it is claimed, borrowed the idea of monotheism from Akhenaten. Others, such as the Egyptian author Ahmed Osman, have gone so far as to claim that Akhenaten and Moses are the same person. This theory would suggest that memories of the Amarna period could also have flowed into the Moses-Exodus myth.

Although completely without foundation, the theory appears to find support in another excerpt from Manetho. While Josephus cites it in connection with the exodus of the Israelites, it actually relates to the Amarna experience. A Heliopolitan priest by the name of Osarsiph appointed himself leader of a large group of lepers (*miaroi*) and took the name of "Moyses" (see chapter 6). What emerges from this story is that Moses and Akhenaten (evidently hidden behind the name of Osarsiph) were already associated with each other in antiquity, long before Freud, even if in all likelihood they had nothing to do with each other in historical reality.

It is in Psalm 104, rather than the Book of Exodus, that we find a memory trace that unambiguously points back to the Amarna period. Verses 20–30 cannot be understood as anything other than a loose and abridged translation of the "Great Hymn":[22]

Psalm 104	Great Hymn
20 Thou makest darkness, and it is night: wherein all the beasts of the forest do creep forth.	27 When you set in the western lightland, 28 Earth is in darkness, 29 as if in death.
21 The young lions roar after their prey, and seek their meat from God. 22 The sun ariseth, they gather themselves together, and lay them down in their dens. 23 Man goeth forth unto his work and to his labour until the evening.	33 [...] Every lion comes from its den, the serpents bite. [...] 38 At dawn you have risen in the lightland to shine as the sun of the day. 42 Awake they stand on their feet, you have made them get up. 45 [...] The entire land sets out to work.
24 YHWH, how manifold are thy works! in wisdom hast thou made them all: the earth is full of thy riches. 25 So is this great and wide sea, wherein are things creeping innumerable, both small and great beasts.	76 How many are your deeds, 77 though hidden from sight.
26 There go the ships: there is that leviathan, whom thou hast made to play therein.	53 [...] Ships fare downstream 54 and back upstream.
27 These wait all upon thee; that thou mayest give them their meat in due season.	56 [...] The fish in the river 57 dart before you;
28 That thou givest them they gather: thou openest thine hand, they are filled with good. 29 Thou hidest thy face, they are troubled: thou takest away thy[23] breath, they die, and return to their dust. 30 Thou sendest forth thy spirit, they are created: and thou renewest the face of the earth.	58 Your rays penetrate the depths of the ocean. 126 [...] When you rise, they live. When you set, they die. You are lifetime itself, one lives through you.

Not only are most of the motifs of Psalm 104 also to be found in the Great Hymn; with the sole exception of verse 24 (= Aten hymn verses 76–77), they even appear in the same order. To be sure, a number of the motifs appropriated from the hymn appear in a different theological light in the context of the psalm. This is true, above all, of the night motif, which is negatively connoted in the hymn as the absence of God (i.e., the sun) yet positively connoted in the psalm, where God no longer represents the sun but stands for a transcendent and omnipresent power: even nocturnal predators come under his care. The psalm must likewise reinterpret the motif of life's intermittent renewal: in the hymn, the alternation of life and death occurs as waking and sleeping, set to the rhythm of sunrise and sunset, whereas in the psalm it is determined by the breath exhaled and inhaled by God.

Because of these reinterpretations, most Old Testament scholars deny that the psalm derives from the Aten hymn;[24] yet there is not a single later Egyptian text that so closely resembles the Aten hymn as the Hebrew psalm. For my part, I do not harbor the slightest doubt about its dependence. Yet how is it to be explained, given the immense distance in time separating the two texts? Akhenaten's hymn was written around 1350 BCE, Psalm 104 presumably at least eight centuries later. One possible explanation looks something like this: in the Amarna period, Palestine largely stood under Egyptian dominion. The Egyptian vassals would have been kept informed about the religious revolution underway in Egypt, if only so as to avoid embarrassing blunders in their correspondence with Pharaoh's court. Abridgments of the hymn in Babylonian translation could thus have been sent to Palestine and from there found their way into Canaanite poetry, in which the first nineteen verses of Psalm 104 quite clearly originate. Naturally, the theological differences between the two texts are obvious. Where the Amarna hymn praises the sun and its works, the psalm celebrates the transcendent creator. Such differences do not mean, however, that the texts have nothing to do with each other, only that the Egyptian (now Canaanite) text had to be subjected to revision in order to find a place in the psalter.

Since in Egypt even Akhenaten and his next of kin were subjected to a radical *damnatio memoriae*, to the extent that all material remains of the religious coup were destroyed, no official tradition could commemorate what had been a deeply divisive and, for most Egyptians, traumatic experience. This is not to say, however, that this historical episode vanished without trace in the collective memory.

The Amarna trauma did not just retroactively alter the memory of the Hyksos, who now appeared as "Seth monotheists" and blasphemers; it also had a formative influence on how foreigners—especially Asians—were imagined and perceived for generations to come. Accordingly, legends arose in which reminiscences of the Amarna time were fused with memories of the Hyksos as well as later experiences of Assyrian conquest, Persian and Greek suzerainty, and finally also the encounter with the Jews. In this way Akhenaten and Moses, the monotheistic coup and the exodus from Egypt, came to be retroactively interlinked. They were paired in collective memory despite having had nothing to do with each other in real history. We need to relinquish the idea of any direct causal link between the Amarna religion and the genesis of biblical monotheism. Not just the gulf in time but equally the divergence in content between the two movements is simply too great. Akhenaten's repudiation of traditional cosmotheism flowed from a new cosmology that derived all existence and growth from the life-giving effects of the sun. The belief in a single god proclaimed by the prophets of Israel has nothing to do with cosmology; it demands exclusive fidelity to YHWH. The modern concept of "monotheism" conceals the unbridgeable differences between the monistic theory of Akhenaten and the religious idea of the prophetic YHWH faith.[25]

Ḫabiru/ʿapiru

In Egyptian, Babylonian, and Canaanite sources of the fourteenth to twelfth century, we encounter a group called ʿapiru or Ḫabiru, a label that corresponds precisely to the Hebrew self-characterization as *ibrim*.[26] To be sure, ʿapiru or Ḫabiru is not an ethnic category but the pejorative term for a way of life and social position, somewhat akin to the English exonym "gypsy," taken in the general sense of "vagabond" or "traveler" (now largely superseded by "Romani" or "Roma" for just this reason). Many theologians and historians have therefore rejected the identification of ʿapiru with the Hebrews. Furthermore, the Babylonian concept of Ḫabiru cannot possibly relate to the Hebrews, since this term refers to people whose presence is attested far earlier, and in quite different locations, than could be expected of the Hebrews.

Nonetheless, it is entirely possible that a group of Canaanites who rejected the Egyptian occupying force and its vassals may have cultivated an "alternative lifestyle" as seminomadic breeders of small livestock; that they self-consciously positioned themselves outside the city-states and in opposition to them; and that they consequently appropriated this term of abuse for themselves. The term *'apiru* ("wanderers," "vagrants," "bandits," "outlaws") is semantically as well as phonetically particularly apt for a group that based its shared identity not just on biological kinship but also (and especially) on a common—alternative and oppositional—social praxis. These *Ḫabiru* or *'apiru* appear in the sources—especially in the correspondence, discovered in an archive in Amarna, conducted between the Egyptian court, its Palestinian vassals, and the neighboring kingdoms of Mitanni, Hatti, and Babylonia—as a movement that is not just nomadic but also rebellious, directed above all against the city-kings who derived their power from Egypt and hence against Egypt itself. Even if we refrain from simply identifying the *Ḫabiru* or *'apiru* with the Hebrews, the question still arises whether anti-Egyptian memories of this group could somehow have found their way into the later Exodus-Moses mythology.[27]

It should not be forgotten that, during the four hundred years between 1500 and 1100, the Egyptians exercised effective sovereignty over Canaan. At the time, it was the practice of colonial masters not only to subjugate the natives but also to deport them to their own country, where they could be exploited as a captive labor force. Around 1100, when Egypt lost control of its Canaanite vassals, these foreign workers would have returned to their homeland, perhaps nursing a lifelong grudge against their former overlords. Moreover, it was not necessary to have lived in Egypt to suffer from Egyptian oppression. In a series of landmark essays, Ronald Hendel has advanced the thesis that memories of late Bronze Age (fifteenth to twelfth century) Egyptian colonial rule in Canaan survived in the Exodus story.[28] The Exodus myth could have drawn its key motifs from an anticolonial, "nativist" resistance movement against the colonizing power,[29] gaining all the more in forcefulness and emotional impact from the mid-eighth century onward, as colonial oppression resumed under the Assyrians and continued unabated under the Babylonians, Persians, Seleucids, and Romans.

Waves of Migration, Sea Peoples

Toward the end of the second millennium, the Mediterranean world was gripped by the greatest wave of migration it had witnessed hitherto. It swept away both the Mycenaean culture and the Hittite Empire; Egypt, too, was forced to defend itself at great cost against the unwanted influx of people; and it marked more generally the end of the Bronze Age and the onset of the Iron Age. The Philistines were caught up in this wave, proceeding via Crete to Palestine and giving the country in which they settled the name it bears today. Other regions of the Mediterranean likewise still bear the names of these migrants, as they are attested in Egyptian sources. Just as Palestine goes back to the Peleset, so Sicily derives from the Sikelesh, Sardinia from the Shardana, the Tyrrhenians and Etruscans from the Tursci, the Achaeans from the Ekwes, and the Lycians from the Lukka. The prophet Amos preserved a memory of these migrations while also linking them with the Exodus:

> Are ye not as children of the Ethiopians unto me, O children of Israel? saith YHWH. Have not I brought up Israel out of the land of Egypt? and the Philistines from Caphtor (Crete), and the Syrians from Kir? (Amos 9:7)

There is uncertainty about the location of Kir, but Caphtor indisputably refers to Crete, and the migration of the Philistines via Crete to Canaan as one of the "sea peoples" has been archaeologically proven beyond doubt. The Philistines brought with them a new material culture and drove out the inhabitants of the coastal region, who fled into the mountainous hinterland. There, small settlements arose in the twelfth and eleventh centuries. Today, we see in these displaced settlers the origins of Israel, but they did not come from abroad; rather, they only moved around within Canaan.[30] From this period or perhaps slightly earlier—around 1200—dates the oldest and only explicit reference to a group called "Israel," on the famous Israel stele of the king Merneptah.[31] It is entirely possible that at some stage a Canaanite tribe of this name migrated to Egypt and later moved back, possibly led by a man called Moses.

The example of the Philistines shows how immigration comes to be reflected in the archaeology. Similar phenomena would have to be expected of the "Hebrew migration," if it ever took place. In their material culture and their anthropological characteristics, however, the Hebrews cannot be distinguished from the other inhabitants of the country.[32] We are dealing here with a phenomenon of cultural semantics, not historical memory.

What is important, at any rate, is the insistence with which the Bible dwells on Israel's "allochthony," its foreign origin. The Abraham myth has Abraham, Israel's ancestral father, migrating from Mesopotamia to Canaan, while the Exodus-Moses myth has Israel, grown to a great nation in Egyptian captivity, taking flight from Egypt. Even YHWH is depicted in several key passages as a foreign god who came up from the south:[33]

> YHWH came from Sinai, and rose up from Seir unto them; he shined forth from Mount Paran, and he came with ten thousands of saints: from his right hand went a fiery law for them. (Deut 33:2)

> YHWH, when thou wentest out of Seir, when thou marchedst out of the field of Edom, the earth trembled, and the heavens dropped, the clouds also dropped water. The mountains melted from before YHWH, even that Sinai from before YHWH, the lord of Israel. (Judges 5:4–5)

> God came from Teman, and the Holy One from Mount Paran. Selah. His glory covered the heavens, and the earth was full of his praise. And his splendor was like the sunrise; rays flashed from his hand, where his power was hidden. (Hab 3:3–4)

The "Shasu (shepherd-nomads) of Jehu (JHW)," mentioned in fourteenth- and thirteenth-century Egyptian texts alongside the "Shasu of Seir" and "Shasu of Edom," also come into consideration as bearers of memories that may have found entry into the Exodus tradition. The motif of foreign origin has an obvious symbolic significance: it makes clear that Israel has nothing to do with the Canaanites settled in the country and that YHWH has just as little to do with the native gods.[34] On the other hand, the possibility cannot be ruled out that memories of this turbulent time of migrations heralding the end of the Bronze Age may have been retained.

Theocracy

At the time of the Davidian and Solomonic monarchy, when Israel and Egypt stood in close contact, Upper Egypt witnessed the emergence of a theocracy in the truest sense of the word. This was not a "representative theocracy," a state headed by a ruler acting as son and stand-in of the sun god, in line with the normal construction of pharaonic sacral kingship. Rather, it was a direct theocracy, with the god Amun himself ruling the state by oracular decree. Equally unusually for Egypt, the secular regent serving the god-king as high priest combined priestly, military, and administrative authority in his own person. In the eighth century, the system was changed so that a princess of the dynasty ruling from Tanis (and later from Sais) now headed the theocracy as "divine consort." Espoused to the god Amun, these divine consorts were pledged to strict celibacy and chose their successor through adoption, in consultation with the secular ruler. They wrote their names inside a cartouche and were recognized as rulers of the Thebaid; in reality, however, their official duties were seen to by their majordomos, who laid out burial sites of unparalleled majesty and extensiveness in Thebes.

In many respects, this substate construction accords with the post-state notion of theocracy found in the Bible. At any rate, we cannot rule out the possibility that this Egyptian institution of the eleventh to sixth centuries may have exerted a certain influence on the biblical—that is, Deuteronomist—idea of the state, an idea whose elaboration in the Persian period likewise coincides with an epoch of substatehood.[35]

Experiences

Miraculous Redemption from Mortal Danger

Just as not all the details of the Exodus narrative—the ten plagues, the parting of the sea, the revelation at Sinai, the trek through the desert and subsequent settlement—can be accorded the status of unvarnished historical truth, so too would it be wrong to deny it any element of truthfulness and take it for a purely fictional composition, albeit one enriched by memories from various sources. There could very well have been some extraordinary event, experienced by those who lived through it as YHWH intervening to save them from mortal danger, over which memory could then cast its mythicizing spell. Such an event is celebrated in the song of thanksgiving offered up by Miriam following the crossing of the Sea of Reeds and the drowning of her pursuers:

> I will sing a song unto YHWH,
> 　　for he hath triumphed gloriously;
> and the horse and rider[36]
> 　　hath he thrown into the sea. (Ex 16:21)

It is almost unanimously agreed that this short song, accompanied by Miriam on the tambourine, represents one of the oldest surviving examples of Hebrew poetry, possibly dating as far back as the second millennium BCE. The song unmistakably has its basis in an escape experienced as nothing short of miraculous. Expanded over time into Moses's great song of thanksgiving (Ex 15:1–18), we can imagine it having its fixed liturgical place in an annual feast day commemorating the flight from Egypt. These two couplets contain *in nuce* the entire story of the Red Sea crossing, and with it the germ of the Exodus narrative that may have developed from it. Nothing is more plausible than to speculate that a Bedouin tribe in Egyptian captivity, calling itself the "children of Israel" or "nomads of Jehu," was pursued by Egyptian troops while attempting to cross the border and could only be saved from annihilation by a chain of events that verged on the miraculous.

Miriam's song and Moses's song of thanksgiving both recall the Egyptian genre of "proclamations of divine power" (*sedjed ba'u*), which plays a significant role in texts of "personal piety."[37] Anyone who has been saved through the intervention of a god erects a stele recording his experience. Thus we read on a Berlin stele from the thirteenth century BCE:

> I shall praise Amun,
> I shall compose hymns in his name;
> I shall praise him
> To the height of the sky and the breadth of the earth,
> I tell of his might to those who travel up- and those who travel downstream:

Beware of him!
Declare him to son and daughter,
To the great and small!
Herald him to generations,
Not yet born!
Herald him to the fish in the river
And the birds in the sky!
Declare him to those that know him and to those that know him not!
Beware of him!

You are Amun, Lord of the "silent,"
Who comes at the voice of the poor!
When I called to you in my distress
You came to rescue me.
To him who was wretched you gave breath,
You rescued me from bondage.
You are Amun-Ra, Lord of Thebes,

Who rescues him who is in the underworld;
For you are he [who is merciful,]
When one calls to him,
You are he who comes from afar![38]

Not just the songs of Miriam and Moses but the Exodus story as a whole may be regarded as just such a "proclamation of divine power" writ large.

The "Secession of the Northern Tribes": The First Occasion for Remembering the Exodus?

So far I have attempted to identify the event that might have triggered or catalyzed the Exodus story, as well as to list the various memories that may have entered into that story as it was worked up over time. I want to conclude this chapter by reaffirming the mnemotheoretical principle that the past is never remembered as such and for its own sake, but always in relation to present-day needs and conditions. "The call to which memory responds," Henri Bergson wrote, "emanates from the present."[39] In the biblical account of the history of Israel, there are two such "presents" from which the call for memory could have initially emanated and found a response in the myth of the departure from Egypt, two situations in which it was necessary to (re)establish "Israel" as an ethnic, political, and religious unit: one in the tenth century BCE, the other in the sixth.

If the Book of Kings is to be believed, the first great moment for remembering the departure from Egypt could have arrived in 931 BCE, when, following the death of Solomon, the northern tribes rose up in revolt against his successor, Rehoboam, and severed ties with Jerusalem. The breakaway tribes felt compelled to legitimate this step by establishing a new political identity for themselves.[40] The date can be deduced from the campaign led by Sheshonk I (the biblical Shishak) against Israel, said to have taken place in the fifth year of Rehoboam's reign and fairly securely dated in Egyptian chronology to 926 BCE.[41] The separatists, we read, elected Jeroboam I as their king. He set up two golden calves to be worshipped, one in Bethel and the other in Dan, consecrating them to YHWH as the redeemer from Egyptian bondage: "Behold thy gods, O Israel, which brought thee up out of the land of Egypt" (1 Kings 12:28). Assuming this report to be historical, we have here an act commemorating the exodus from Egypt, whichever form the Exodus myth may have taken in this early period of the Northern Kingdom. In other respects, too, there is much to suggest that the newly established Northern Kingdom made the departure from Egypt its foundational myth or "state ideology."[42] This also explains why allusions to the Moses-Exodus myth first appear in the prophets Hosea and Amos, who were active in the Northern Kingdom, rather than in those of the Southern Kingdom, Isaiah and Micah (Micah 6:4 and 7:15 are believed to be later additions).

Archaeologists like Israel Finkelstein and Wolfgang Zwickel have disputed, however, that there ever was a United Monarchy under David and Solomon.[43] They maintain that Israel and Judah never broke up but existed independently of each other from the beginning. The exciting story of Jeroboam is evidently a literary novella that nonetheless, by virtue of its two references to King Shishak/Sheshonk I, has some foundation in historical fact; in this respect, it differs sharply from the Joseph novella.[44] The first time the pharaoh appears, it is to grant asylum to Jeroboam (1 Kings 11:40); on the second occasion, it is to lead a military campaign against Rehoboam (14:25–26). What cannot be disputed, in any event, is the vitality of the memory of Jeroboam I and the secession of the northern tribes in the historical memory of later centuries.

The reason given for the secession is that Rehoboam wanted to make the statute labor introduced by Solomon even more onerous: "My father made your yoke heavy, and I will add to your yoke: my father chastised you with whips, but I will chastise you with scorpions" (1 Kings 12:14). In the Book of Kings, the corvée introduced by Solomon to construct the Temple and other building projects is described in the same terms used in the Book of Exodus to describe the Israelites' forced labor for the pharaoh. The parallels are indeed striking, particularly since in both cases the working conditions are shown to grow ever more burdensome. In the harsh light cast by the Book of Exodus, Solomon, this proverbially wise and God-fearing king who built the Temple and whose rule is unmistakably blessed by God, appears as a second pharaoh, a tyrant who oppresses his people with hard labor.[45] Jeroboam, on the other hand, at first appears almost as a second Moses sent to free his people from bondage. From the mouth of the prophet Ahijah, God calls him to rule over the new kingdom of Israel. Just as Moses grew up at Pharaoh's court but then had to flee abroad, so Jeroboam enjoyed Solomon's favor before being forced into exile. And just as God sent Moses from Midian back to Egypt after Pharaoh's death, so Jeroboam returns to Israel after Solomon's.

In both stories, however, those who have fled oppression lapse into the sin of idolatry and bow down before golden calves. Aaron casts a molten calf at the people's bidding, while Jeroboam sets up two golden calves in Dan and Bethel; in both cases, these are consecrated with the cultic proclamation cited above: "Behold thy gods, O Israel, which brought thee up out of the land of Egypt." In the Book of Kings, we had interpreted this formula as a recollection of the exodus from Egypt. In the story of the Golden Calf as found in Exodus 32, however, we have before us a reminiscence of the "sin of Jeroboam."[46] Between these two commemorative acts—Jeroboam's memory of the exodus from Egypt and the author of Exodus 32's memory of the sin of Jeroboam—lies the fundamental shift from the Canaanite cult of the monarchy to the exclusive YHWH faith of the exilic and postexilic period in early Judaism.

This shift caused Jeroboam's institution of the cult to appear as idol worship and theological backsliding of the most reprehensible kind. Apart from the golden calves in Dan and Bethel, he is said to have built shrines on high places and appointed priests even though they were not Levites—all this in flagrant violation of the terms set down in the covenant (which, to be sure, could not yet have existed in the tenth century). With that, Jeroboam created in the Northern Kingdom the very situation that, according the account given in the Book of Kings (2 Kings 22 ff.), Josiah was to abolish three centuries later with the utmost severity and cruelty. This idolatry, the worship of foreign gods at local cultic sites, is what Hosea denounces as "harlotry" and adultery, a line of attack subsequently taken up by Jeremiah and Ezekiel in the Southern Kingdom.

Israel Refounded: The Principal Occasion for Remembering the Exodus

Compared with the secession of the northern tribes, we stand on much firmer ground in the sixth and fifth centuries BCE, the era of Babylonian exile, the return of the *bĕnê haggôlâ* to Jerusalem and especially the rebuilding of the Temple, cult, and "Judaism." This reinvention of Israel offers the classic case of a "present" from which the past is invoked and given literary form. Chronological certainty is provided by the prophets Haggai and Zechariah, who were called on by YHWH to rebuild the Temple and who place their visions and revelations within the narrow time frame of Darius I's first years in power, between 520 and 518 BCE.[47] We can thus identify the point in time at which—speaking with Bergson—"the call to which memory responds" was sent out as a matter of some urgency. This is not to suggest that the past, in the form in which it was remembered and used to make a fresh start with "Israel" by those returning from exile, represents a reconstruction in all particulars. Some details stick out in the narrative, resisting their complete integration to the twin functions of storytelling and identity-founding commemoration. Rudolf Smend, for example, has shown this in relation to "Moses as a historical figure."[48] Two things stand in the way of any narratological or ideological interpretation of the Moses story: his Egyptian name and his repeatedly mentioned foreign marriage, which is variously connected with a Midianite, a Cushite, and a Kenite woman. Between 520 and 450, nothing could have been further removed from the order of the day.

The correspondences between the events of the narrative and Israelite experiences at the time of narration make clear the extent to which contemporary experiences as well as age-old memories flowed into the Exodus story and the Book of Exodus:

Events of the Exodus Narrative	Events at the Time of Narration
Egyptian oppression Emancipation from Egyptian slavery Departure of the children of Israel	Assyrian and Babylonian oppression 587: fall of Jerusalem, destruction of the Temple, deportation of the elite
Revelation of the law at Sinai and covenant Building of the Tabernacle	50–70 years of "Babylonian captivity," compiling of legal and cultic traditions
Wandering through the desert The people's complaints (the "sins of the fathers") and punishment of the guilty generation (40 years in the wilderness)	c. 520: return of the Jews under Persian rule, emphatic repudiation of the "sins of the fathers" Resistance of those who stayed behind to the religious and other demands of the returnees Resistance, too, of those who had successfully integrated in Babylon to the demand that they return to a devastated Jerusalem
Occupation of Canaan	520–450: rebuilding of the Temple, renewal of the covenant, and reestablishment of Israel as "Judaism"

The events listed in the two columns stand in a relationship of either correspondence (oppression, departure and return, "sins of the fathers," occupation and rebuilding, the covenant made and then renewed, building of the Tabernacle and rebuilding of the Temple) or inversion (emancipation and deportation) to each other. Of course, I am not proposing that we read the Exodus story as a kind of roman à clef, a narrative that simply projects contemporary relations and figures onto a fictional past. My aim is to understand the situations and experiences from which the "call to memory" emanated, and to find out how strongly the literary formation of memory was shaped by contemporary experience. Above all, however, there is one motif that connects the remembered past with the present: the "sins of the fathers."[49] In the story, this serves to justify the punishment of forty years spent wandering in the desert that bars the forefathers entry into the Promised Land; in the present, it allows the fall of Jerusalem and the loss of the Promised Land to be interpreted as a punishment for the disloyalty shown by the people, and especially the court, in worshipping foreign gods alongside YHWH. The great historical recapitulations in Ezekiel 20, Psalm 106, Nehemiah 9, and elsewhere all draw a bow from the Golden Calf to the fall of Jerusalem.

Through the "sins of the fathers" motif, the Exodus story takes on a tragic cast, with the result that the motif of promise is associated not with fulfillment but with failure. Evidently, the praiseworthy memory of God's saving grace is inseparably linked with the shameful recollection of one's own unworthiness. This motif of sinfulness and guilt is especially prominent in the extensive and comprehensive retelling of the Exodus story found in Nehemiah, a protagonist of Israel's postexilic reinvention. This tragic dimension, which stands in such stark contrast to the story's triumphalist account of the downfall of the Egyptians and expulsion of the Canaanites, was added to the tradition through the experiences of rupture, defeat, and deportation. Under these circumstances, bringing the Exodus story, with its promises, salvational deeds, and divine guarantees of support, into the present represents a typical act of "contrapresentist" memory: an intervention designed to repair the breach and salvage the covenant.

CHAPTER THREE

TEXTUAL HISTORY AND
THE HISTORY OF MEANING

Redaction as "Cultivation of Meaning":
Textual Layering in the Bible

The Hebrew Bible presents us with a peculiar dilemma. A number of more or less conspicuous signs in this collection of texts point to centuries of accretion: redundancies, inconsistencies, internal contradictions, clear interpolations and omissions, glosses, addenda, and so forth. While this multiplicity of layers and voices is most strikingly apparent in the first books of Moses, it continues in the other books of the Pentateuch, as well as in the "former" and "latter" prophets. At the same time, however—and this is what makes the situation so unique—it looks as if this anthology had somehow absorbed or suppressed all its contemporaries. Outside the Bible, almost nothing has been preserved that could allow comparison with these writings, providing us with information about the literary genres to which they belong or shedding light on their cultural, social, and historical backgrounds. The Bible is practically the sole surviving example of Hebrew literature from the tenth to the fourth century BCE.

That is not the case in other cultures. There are other epics besides the Homeric and Mesopotamian ones, for example. Older versions and different epics can still be read alongside the twelve-tablet version of the Epic of Gilgamesh. In addition to the Egyptian Book of the Dead, there are plenty of Pyramid and Coffin Texts gathered in older collections of such literature, as well as other funerary inscriptions from outside these collections. Yet, apart from the literature codified in the Hebrew Bible, almost nothing has survived from before the Hellenistic period, when a "Deuterocanonical" body of writing in Hebrew, Aramaic, and Greek started to develop in the shadow of the emerging canon. It may safely be assumed that the texts collected in the Bible represent around one-twentieth of what was written in Israel during the corresponding period. By comparison, the texts that have come down to us from ancient Egypt also represent, at best, only about five percent of what was written in Egypt between 3000 BCE and 300 CE. Whereas here the selection of texts was dictated by chance, however, in Israel a consciously restrictive process of canonization was at work. That makes an enormous difference.

In response to this unique state of affairs, Old Testament exegesis developed an equally unique apparatus of "diachronic" analysis. In the process, two dominant ways of reading the Bible were elaborated: one, more theological in nature, investigates the structure and spiritual message (or "kerygma") of the text as it has come down to us in its final form; the other, more philological approach attempts to reconstruct its genesis with the means of diachronic text analysis. As an extreme example of diachronic interpretation, one need only compare Christoph Berner's *Die Exoduserzählung* (The Exodus Story) with Dominik Markl's *Der Dekalog als Verfassung des Gottesvolkes* (The Decalogue as the Constitution of God's People), an example of synchronic exegesis.

When it comes to the impact made by a book, only the final form in which the book became widely known is of interest to us, not the preliminary stages in its composition. The works by Goethe that laid claim to posterity, for example, were not his *Urfaust* and *Wilhelm Meister's Theatrical Calling* but the masterpieces in which those unpublished early works came to fruition: *Faust I* and *II* and *Wilhelm Meister's Apprenticeship* and *Journeyman Years*, respectively. In the case of the Book of Exodus, as of the four other books in the Torah, an additional factor comes into play. Only their final versions have attained the status of supreme and binding authority, where every word is taken to bear the direct imprint of the divine will. Moreover, it is not just the Book of Exodus that is responsible for the extraordinary influence and lasting appeal of the Exodus myth. Even more crucial are the motifs or narrative kernels the book contains, which also figure in a number of psalms and books of prophecy: motifs of departure, election, covenant, law, and divine presence. Since my aim here is to study the Exodus story from the viewpoint of the cultural sciences, these ideas and their historical context are of primary interest to me. What is essential for this angle of questioning, methodologically indebted to the history of ideas and to mnemohistory, is not just a synchronous perspective but also, within limits, a diachronic one.

For our purposes, it is enough for now to make out four stages of development:

1. the orally transmitted myth;
2. the first version of the Book of *Exodus as an originally freestanding literary composition alongside other pre-Priestly writings such as the *Deuteronomist, the *patriarchal narratives, and the *tale of Joseph;
3. the ur-*Priestly Source (which has not come down to us in this form), bringing together *Exodus and a first version of the Book of *Genesis (creation story, patriarchal narratives, and story of Joseph) into a single overarching historical composition;
4. the post-Priestly path through various compositional stages to the canon of biblical books (the Tanakh), where the Book of Exodus figures as the second book of the Torah and the Torah figures as the first and most sacred part of the "three-tiered" canon of Torah, prophets, and "hagiographies."

The decisive and, for its time, quite unparalleled feat lies in the unification of the patriarchal narratives and the Exodus story into an all-encompassing outline of history, beginning with the creation of the universe and ending with that of the mobile temple.[1] This feat was once ascribed to the source texts J (Yahwist), E (Elohist), and JE (Jehovist) and placed in the tenth to eighth centuries BCE. Today, that reconstruction finds very little support. In this book, I follow a tendency that sees in it the work of the Priestly Source (P). In this view, P is not a source text that was only fragmentarily preserved in the final text and had to wait until a later redaction to be combined with the non-Priestly components of the Books of Genesis and Exodus into a comprehensive work. Instead, it represents a compositional and redactional stage that itself undertakes that unification. I also do not posit any preexilic precedents for such a sweeping historical enterprise.[2] Rather, I contend that the refoundation of Temple, city, and "Israel" as a religious, ethnic, and political (albeit substate) identity was what first provided the impetus for a comprehensive project anchoring the history of the people in a cosmogony. All readers of the Hebrew Bible who are interested in more than the text's diachronic strata must decide upon a version that, in their eyes, represents a meaningful whole. For many, that was once the "Yahwist" or the "Jehovist" (combining J and E); for others, it is the canonical final form in which the biblical text has come down to us. For me, in this book, it is the Priestly Source. As the foundational document of the Second Temple, this composition creates a narrative extending all the way from the creation of the universe to the construction of the ur-Temple; accordingly, I contend that P comes to an end in Exodus 40.[3] The advantage of this approach is that it allows us to link the first comprehensive codification of the Exodus tradition with a concrete historical situation: the postexilic and posttraumatic epoch of a new beginning.

Two forms of textual labor appear to bear particular responsibility for the diachronic expansion of the biblical texts. The first form is compositional: by cutting and pasting snippets of material into a textual montage, it aims to create a meaningful whole from the diverse sources at hand. The second is exegetical: through the means of commentary, explication, and interpolation, it aims to amplify, reinterpret, and clarify the text's meaning as far as possible. In biblical studies, this process of continuous elaboration is referred to as *Fortschreibung*. I see both methods at work in the creation of the Priestly text. Whereas the compositional aspect comes to the fore in the Book of Genesis, threading the patriarchal narratives into novella cycles, linking them with the highly literary story of Joseph and prefacing them with the myths of primordial history, in the Book of Exodus it is the exegetical aspect— the work of *Fortschreibung*, of commentary and cumulative revision— that predominates.

Behind the architectonic labor of compilation and composition, on the one hand, and the exegetical labor of emendation and commentary, on the other, stand two quite different, albeit by no means mutually exclusive goals. As noted previously, the compositional approach envisages an all-encompassing work of history, beginning with the creation of the universe and leading right up to the present day (of the Temple). What is unique about the Priestly history is its theological focus on revelation, such that God emerges all the more resolutely from his absolute transcendence the more Israel steps into the role of his chosen people, the partner and arena of his dwelling in the world. To this stands opposed the older Deuteronomist work of history, already begun in exile, which starts with the exodus from Egypt and ends with the fall of Jerusalem. The Deuteronomist tradition is characterized by the moral, covenant-theological perspective that sees the course of history dictated by the people's wavering fidelity to the covenant. Both histories represent something completely new in the ancient world. By beginning with the creation of the universe, an idea dubbed "historiogenesis" by Eric Voegelin,[4] the Priestly text follows the example of Sumero-Babylonian and Egyptian king lists; yet these lists eschew any interpretive or evaluative perspective and cannot qualify as works of history owing to their lack of narrative elaboration. The work of composition is expressed, beyond the mere collation of different source texts, in procedures intended to establish and maintain coherence; such procedures include linking passages, cross-references, foreshadowing, harmonizing interpolations, and more. On the other hand, the work of commentary does not purport to deliver a *grand récit* or master narrative but instead serves to cultivate meaning.

A distinction must be made between "cultivating the text" (*Textpflege*) and "cultivating meaning" (*Sinnpflege*).[5] Cultivating the text involves preserving the letter of the text and also—so far as possible—its prosody. That is particularly vital for magical and ritual texts, where a single slip of the tongue can ruin everything.[6] In the case of the Indian Vedas, the written tradition was not credited with such accuracy, so a perfected mnemotechnics took their place. In Egypt, by contrast, no such faith was placed in memory, and writing soon established itself as the preferred medium for preserving sacral texts. This was the prerogative of the "lector priests," who appear in the Bible as *ḥartummîm* and play a special role in the Exodus story, as we will see later (chapter 6). In the case of the Egyptian Book of the Dead, philological procedures for cultivating the text were elaborated, including the production of a standardized text—complete with variants—from the range of available manuscripts.

Highly sophisticated methods were also developed at the Library of Ashurbanipal in Nineveh. All kinds of information were entered at the bottom of a tablet: the series to which the tablet belonged; the first lines of the tablet on which the text continued; the tablet number (if the text spread over several tablets); an indication that it was the final tablet in the series (where applicable); the original of which the tablet was a copy; a collation statement; the number of lines; the name of the copyist, date, and ownership mark (*ex libris*). These concluding remarks were often extended into a longer text, a "colophon," threatening with a curse any future scribe who dared make even the slightest alteration to the text. What can be inferred from these copies (and their copyists) is a typically Oriental, almost religious attitude to the written word that culminates in the Judaism of a later age. The "canon formula" forbidding the scribe from deleting, augmenting, or altering anything in the text handed down to him also appears in two passages of Deuteronomy (4:1, 13:1), although the warning did nothing to spare such texts from continuous editorial interference in the process of their transmission. This process was clearly about "cultivating meaning" rather than "cultivating the text"—at least until the growing sacralization of these texts lent them the character of magical-ritual immutability, with a corresponding shift in emphasis to wording and prosody.

The obligation to cultivate meaning is associated with texts that play a central role in the socialization and education of future generations. These are the "cultural texts" in which a society glimpses the fitting receptacle of the norms, values, and orientations deemed worthy of being handed down to the young, the embodiment of a cultural identity to be reproduced from one generation to another. In Egypt and Mesopotamia, with their highly complex systems of writing, studying cultural texts meant learning to read and write. The texts were learned by heart and then written down from memory at the teacher's behest. By laboriously mastering the art of writing in this way, students became familiar with the central texts and genres, poetics, and narratives of their culture as well as its key moral values and economic and administrative techniques. The same could also be said of Israel.[7] Here, the writing system with its twenty-two letters was infinitely simpler, yet the missing vowel signs meant that texts could be read only by those knowledgeable enough to supply them. Moreover, the less knowledge of written signs was called for, the more important became the text itself. Just as everything depends on wording and prosody in texts with aesthetic and magical (in the broadest sense of the term) properties, so everything depends on understanding the meaning in cultural texts.

These texts demand to be "taken to heart," not just memorized but consciously lived out and enacted from day to day. This requires that they be continuously brought up-to-date through the insertion of glosses, additions, and emendations that aim to bridge the widening gap between the old text and the ever-changing conditions for understanding it.[8] The more important the cultural text from a normative and educational point of view, the more intense the efforts devoted to cultivating its meaning.

This goes some way to explaining the textual form in which the Pentateuch—and thus also the Book of Exodus—has come down to us: on the basis of its unparalleled significance in establishing a Jewish identity, its meaning was cultivated with corresponding intensity in the form of ongoing interpolations and glosses.

Nothing gives a more impressive sense of how meaning was cultivated through *Fortschreibung* than the diachronic analysis to which Christoph Berner has subjected Exodus 1–18. The twenty successive redactional stages he has distinguished generally tend to explicate the text by introducing additional details, to amplify and intensify its drama, and to establish coherence, especially between the Books of *Genesis and *Exodus brought together in the Priestly Source. But they can also bring about a shift in perspective that leaves its mark on the content. In the pre-Priestly *Exodus story, for example, YHWH performs three spectacular miracles to demonstrate his power before launching his final, decisive strike, the slaughter of the firstborn; in their Priestly reinterpretation, these are now embedded in a magic contest between YHWH, Moses, and Aaron on one side, and Pharaoh with his sorcerer-priests (*ḥartummîm*) on the other. In all these additions, the aim is to bring out the meaning—or one particular meaning—as clearly as possible. I find this model far more convincing than the so-called documentary or Wellhausen hypothesis. Whereas the latter brings to bear a quasi-architectonic interest in the production of ever more comprehensive textual syntheses, the former is guided by the hermeneutic interest in a continuous actualization and explication of meaning—a process that continued, even upon completion of the canon, in the burgeoning commentary literature. To be sure, these twin dynamics—the compositional and the hermeneutic—are by no means mutually exclusive.

As David Carr has emphasized, cultural texts live and breathe in memory and performance, not in the archives. The most important frameworks for the performance of such texts are provided, on the one hand, by the family—the famous chain "from father to son"[9] so often evoked in the Bible—and the "school," understood not as a building for public instruction but rather as variable master-student relations. On the other, they are secured by the great festivals in which foundational traditions are brought to life in various forms. These include song, dance, and recitation, as well as public readings like the one depicted in Nehemiah 8. Here, we also encounter a special way to cultivate meaning:

> And Ezra the priest brought the law before the congregation both of men and women, and all that could hear with understanding, upon the first day of the seventh month.

> And he read therein before the street that was before the water gate from the morning until midday, before the men and the women, and those that could understand, and the ears of all the people were attentive unto the book of the law.

> [...] And Ezra opened the book in the sight of all the people, for he was above all the people. And when he opened it, all the people stood up. [...] And Jeshua [...] and the Levites, caused the people to understand the law: and the people stood in their place.

> So they read in the book in the law of God distinctly, and gave the sense, and caused them to understand the reading. (8:2–8)

"For the first time in history," Yosef H. Yerushalmi remarks of this report, "a sacred text ceases to belong exclusively to priests and becomes the common property of the people. Here we witness, at one and the same time, the birth of scripture and the birth of exegesis."[10] In the words of Othmar Keel, what is described here is "the first divine liturgy, a form that took over from the ancient Oriental (and Classical) sacrificial cult and later became the dominant form of worship in synagogues, churches and mosques."[11] With this form of divine service, however, temple and school also move closer together: public worship becomes a form of instruction and education. Josephus had already identified what was unique about Jewish worship in its preparing "the entire body of the people [...] for religion."[12] The pedagogical methods involved in religious schooling must be understood in a similar way. The teacher recites the text to be memorized—or the student recites it by heart—and offers a section-by-section commentary. At a certain stage of the transmission process, the text then acquires such a patina of authority and holiness that the commentary can no longer be written into it but must be set alongside it as a separate text. In Judaism, this commentary long remained the preserve of the oral tradition as the "Oral Torah" (*tôrâ šebě'al-peh*) until, under the conditions of the diaspora, it was set down in writing as the Mishnah and Talmud.

Aleida Assmann has suggested that a distinction be made between "hodegetics" and "hermeneutics."[13] Hodegetics (from the Greek *hodēgeîn*, "to show the way") is the typical method for explicating the text in the student-teacher situation, where the master sheds light on the obscured meaning by providing oral commentary. Hermeneutics presupposes a system of interpretive rules—for example, the doctrine of the fourfold sense of the scriptures—that first arises under conditions of canonization. So far as canonization is concerned, a distinction between text form and text corpus needs to be made. Canonization of the text *form* pertains to magical and aesthetic texts; it has no place when it comes to cultural texts, which demand that they be "taken to heart." Canonization of the text *corpus* is something altogether different. It involves the selection of a number of authoritative, highly esteemed texts from the complete body of the (oral and written) tradition. For the Bible, the first steps in this direction are thought to have been taken in the Hellenistic era, around the time that the Greek "classics" were being canonized by philologists in Alexandria. The anthologization of the five books of Moses as the "Torah" (law, instruction), which was to become the foundation of the three-tiered TaNaKh made up of Torah, Prophets (*něbî'îm*), and Hagiographa or Writings (*kětûbîm*), goes back further. It forms the fourth stage in the genesis of the Book of Exodus.

Near unanimity prevails only when it comes to dating the third stage, the Priestly redaction; it coincides with the development of early Judaism in the Second Temple period. A crucial epochal turning point thus lies between the first two and the last two stages in this summary textual history: the passage from ancient Israelite to early Jewish religion.[14] That marks off the third stage from the rest, which is why I will also treat it as the most important, so far as the book's history is concerned.

We first encounter the myth (stage 1) in the early prophets of the Northern Kingdom, Hosea and Amos, who preached around 730–719 BCE, during and after the catastrophic conquest of the Northern Kingdom by the Assyrians in 722.[15] It could be far older than that. Given that it represents the foundational myth of a secession movement, it could have originated in the northern tribes that broke away from the Solomonic kingdom toward the end of the tenth century BCE (as suggested above).[16] It is not inconceivable, however, that it dates back even further, to the settlers who retreated into mountainous terrain before the advancing Philistines, or to the *Ḥabiru*, who turned their backs on the city-kingdoms that collaborated with Egypt.

At this stage, the myth primarily contained the material narrated in chapters 1–15 of the Book of Exodus: slavery and emancipation, accompanied by signs and wonders. However, the motifs of the chosen people, their covenant with God, and their entry into the Promised Land must already have been present here in embryonic form, since only in the triad of beginning (emancipation), middle (covenant), and end (colonization) is the myth at all imaginable in its presumed original version, even if the elaboration of the covenant idea through the handing down of the law, the institution of the cult, and everything else related in chapters 16–40 had to wait until a much later stage. This base myth also informs the psalms and other passages in the Bible—surprisingly few in number—that refer to the Moses-Exodus myth. The Book of Nehemiah, written around 450 BCE, brings together the themes of "exodus" and "lawgiving" for the first time outside the Torah.[17]

While the myth's genesis lies in the nearer or more distant past, located sometime in the centuries when Israel was first emerging as an ethnoreligious identity, its actualization in the early prophets of the Northern Kingdom, Amos and Hosea, falls in the period when that identity was facing its gravest threat, as the expansionist Neo-Assyrian Empire conquered the Northern Kingdom and deported its inhabitants en masse. For Hosea, the ideas of election and covenant are of central importance. In expressing them, he draws on bridal and filial metaphors. On the one hand, he accuses the Israelites of "prostituting" themselves with other gods, placing the blame for the catastrophe squarely on their sins and faults; on the other, he bases his hope that the covenant will be renewed and the people saved on the precedent provided by the exodus: "I called my son out of Egypt" (Hos 11:1);[18] "I am the Lord thy God from the land of Egypt" (12:9, 13:4); "And by a prophet [Moses] YHWH brought Israel out of Egypt, and by a prophet was he preserved" (12:13). The filial metaphor (although not the bridal one) also makes an appearance in the Book of Exodus:

> And thou shalt say unto Pharaoh, Thus saith YHWH, Israel is my son, even my firstborn: And I say unto thee, Let my son go, that he may serve me: and if thou refuse to let him go, behold, I will slay thy son, even thy firstborn. (4:22–23)

A century and a half later, the image of betrothal and marriage was further developed by the prophets Jeremiah and Ezekiel, who experienced firsthand the catastrophe that visited the Southern Kingdom when Judah was conquered by the Babylonians in 597 and 587. Like Hosea, they invoke the myth of emancipation, election, and loving commitment when faced with an existential threat, they interpret the disaster as the just punishment meted on Israel by an enraged lover, and they draw hope from the continued validity of God's election, covenant, and promise.

Amos has a very different agenda from Hosea. He is less concerned with the emotional resonance of the covenant than with its normative dimension. His theme is law and justice. Like Hosea, he too accuses Israel of infidelity, but what he denounces is not harlotry with other gods but injustice and oppression. Amos—or rather YHWH—invokes the revealed act of emancipation in order to justify his claim to obedience: "Also I brought you up from the land of Egypt, and led you forty years through the wilderness, to possess the land of the Amorite" (2:10); "Hear this word that YHWH hath spoken against you, O children of Israel, against the whole family which I brought up from the land of Egypt!" (3:1); "I have sent among you the pestilence after the manner of Egypt" (4:10). Also belonging in this series is the extraordinary passage, already cited above, denying that the Israelites have been uniquely chosen by God: "Are ye not as children of the Ethiopians unto

me, O children of Israel? saith YHWH. Have not I brought up Israel out
of the land of Egypt? and the Philistines from Caphtor, and the Syrians
from Kir?" (9:7). Whereas Amos holds injustice and oppression responsible for the sin of breaching the covenant, for Hosea it is the worship of other gods. While both tendencies demand absolute, unstint-
ing, and exclusive loyalty to the one YHWH, who freed the Israelites
from Egypt and entered into an alliance with them, one tendency sees
such loyalty in cult-theological terms, the other in terms of social
ethics.

Isaiah, the great prophet of the Southern Kingdom and the contemporary of Amos, Hosea, and Micah, makes no mention at all of the
Moses-Exodus myth. It may therefore be assumed that the Exodus
tradition was at home in the Northern Kingdom, where it was presumably handed down in Levitical circles. The Levites played a role
in ancient Israel comparable, in some respects, to that of the Brahmins in India. Prohibited from owning land, they made a living by
raising small livestock and roaming the land as itinerant sacrificing
priests. At a time when the cult was not yet centralized in Jerusalem,
they carried out rituals wherever their services were needed. As the
principal custodians of religious tradition, they were entrusted with
the ritual and liturgical rules as well as the myths and historical narratives of their people. They differed from the Brahmins in their inferior
social status, which in Israel as in other ancient societies was chiefly
determined by land ownership, as well as in their role as warriors:
they bore arms and acted as a kind of roving police force.[19] Among the
biblical Levites, we occasionally come across Egyptian names like
Moses, Phinehas (*Pa'-neḥsi*, "the Nubian"), and Putiel (*Pa-di-El*, "gift
of El" = Theodore), the maternal grandfather of Phinehas.[20] They may
indicate that memories of a spell in Egypt and subsequent emigration
were particularly well preserved in this tribe.

I place stage 2—the emergence of an independent literary composition—in the period between the fall of the Northern Kingdom and the
return from Babylonian captivity, hence between 720 and 520, the two
centuries in which the pre-Priestly Sources arose.[21] The fall of Jerusalem, the demise of the Southern Kingdom, and the deportation of the
elite in 587–586 divide this stage into 2a, the preexilic period, and 2b,
the period of exile. One can well imagine that the two catastrophes—

the fall of the Northern Kingdom in 722 and that of the Southern Kingdom in 587–586—made it seem especially urgent that the disrupted
traditions be preserved in written form. A parallel case can be found in
Egypt, where the fall of the Old Kingdom toward the end of the third
millennium BCE occasioned a literary flowering.[22] The representative
work of this epoch, the Deuteronomist, already brought together the
Exodus myth and the revelation of the law. It is widely assumed that
this was a book in its own right before being incorporated into the
Torah. *Deuteronomy—the asterisk indicates that we are dealing here
with a reconstructed urtext—displays linguistic and spiritual affinities
with the prophet Jeremiah and must date from the period of the late
monarchy (2a) or early exile (2b). It is also believed by many that this
original version was identical with the book that, according to 2 Kings
22, was unearthed in the Temple during restoration works in 622 BCE
and identified as a book of Moses. This Ur-Deuteronomy was held to
be the work of a circle opposed to the conciliatory, ideologically flex-
ible politics of the court. The Kingdom of Judah had fallen under Assyrian suzerainty, creating a climate receptive to Aramaic-Assyrian
religious practices and ideas.[23] According to this theory, with the fall of
the Assyrian Empire and the child Josiah's ascension to the throne of
Judah, the opposition felt that its time had now come. Against the per-
missive ways of the court, it upheld a piece of writing that made the
continued existence of the people conditional on their unwavering fidelity to their covenant with YHWH and insisted on the strict observance of the law. This text was then framed with the legend of its discovery told in 2 Kings 22, which presented it as the Torah of Moses.
Several researchers have since cast doubt on this early dating of *Deuteronomy.[24] But even if *Deuteronomy first emerged in the early exilic
period, the legend's relation to this book can count as assured. The
practice of "pseudepigraphy" (the false ascription of authorship)
should not just be viewed as pious fraud. The book codified normative
traditions associated with the name of Moses and was certainly written
in his spirit, even if it has no stronger claim to have been written by the
man himself than the other books.

The Book of *Exodus dates from roughly the same period. Like
*Deuteronomy, it probably also combined the departure from Egypt
with the giving of the law. *Exodus and *Deuteronomy bring the cov-

enant idea, represented by Hosea and Ezekiel with the aid of bridal and nuptial metaphors as a *hieros gamos*, a sacred union between God and Israel, into the form of a political alliance on the Assyrian model. This is now no longer a metaphor for their relationship but the relationship itself. The question of which book is older and alludes to the other, *Deuteronomy or *Exodus, is a controversial one and does not need to be settled here. The redactors of the Pentateuch, reading Deuteronomy as a paraenetic (hortatory and explanatory) recapitulation of what happened in Exodus, placed it afterward as the fifth book of Moses. The original version of the Book of *Exodus is the image that, retouched and modified multiple times, lies before us in canonic form as the second book of Moses. The most important of these retouches belong in stage 3.

Stage 3 falls in the Persian period, between 520 and 450 BCE, when cult and Temple were restored following the return from exile. This was the time when the founding text of early Judaism, the *Priestly Source, was written. It combined two originally independent, alternative founding myths of Israel, the tales of the patriarchs (Abraham, Isaac, and Jacob) and the Moses-Exodus myth, together with the creation and flood myths, into a comprehensive historical composition modeled on the Babylonian and Egyptian king lists, which likewise take the origin of the universe as their starting point.[25] Owing to its strong Babylonian overtones, the Book of *Genesis must have been written in and after exile under the influence of Babylonian myths and Persian theological ideas. It represents God from a universalistic perspective as the creator of heaven and earth, interacting with the human race as a whole as well as those individuals—Adam and his descendants, Noah and his descendants, Abraham and his descendants—deemed worthy of his company. The Book of *Exodus, by contrast, adopts a decidedly particularist perspective that has God rescuing his chosen people from Egyptian bondage.

Egypt comes off very well in the Book of Genesis. Genesis 13:10 compares the area around Sodom and Gomorrah before their destruction with the Garden of Eden and the land of Egypt. Genesis 12 tells how a famine in the land drives Abraham to Egypt, where he is treated generously. Joseph, sold by his brothers into Egyptian slavery, rises there to become the second most powerful man in the state; and when his family later follows him to Egypt, likewise driven by hunger, the hospitality and largesse with which they are received leaves nothing wanting. Egypt appears here as a paradisiacal land, a refuge to all who go hungry and suffer persecution.[26]

The Joseph novella, whose striking narrative qualities suggest that it must have led an independent literary existence before the authors of the Priestly Source included it as a bridge between Genesis and Exodus, tells how Jacob's family emigrated to Egypt where Joseph, one of their own, had attained the highest honors. The Book of Exodus links up at this point: proliferating at an almost miraculous rate, after 430 years the clan in Egypt has become so populous that it now outnumbers its hosts, who, fearful of losing their supremacy, resort to near-genocidal forms of oppression. God delivered them from this intolerable situation by sending his servant, Moses.

In the Book of Exodus, the pro-Egyptian image found in Genesis is turned on its head. Egypt now appears as the epitome of despotic rule, murderous oppression, and ungodly hubris, a land that the Israelites must resolutely put behind them if they are to enter into the new world of freedom, justice, and human dignity held out to them by God in his covenant. Whereas the Book of Genesis is keyed to integration, understanding, and harmonious relations, the Book of Exodus takes a stance of exclusion, hostility, and violence, showing affinities to Deuteronomy in its antagonistic, confrontational identity politics. Several Old Testament scholars have concluded from this that Israel had two different origin myths.[27] One begins, like so many other ancient myths of origin, with creation, and although this myth also has the primordial father Abraham emigrating from Mesopotamia to Canaan, it emphasizes the good relations he and his kinfolk establish with the natives of his new country and the things they have in common. It is true that Genesis 15:19, like many passages in the Book of Exodus, lists the tribes settled in the Promised Land—"the Kenites, and the Kenizzites, and the Kadmonites, and the Hittites, and the Perizzites, and the Rephaims, and the Amorites, and the Canaanites, and the Girgashites, and the Jebusites"—but there is no suggestion that they are to be mistreated, let alone driven out and annihilated. Nor is Abraham's emigration in any way motivated by persecution and emancipation. The other origin myth starts with the exodus from Egypt and emphasizes three things:

first, the sharp, irreconcilable contrast between the emigrants and their Egyptian hosts; second, the equally irreconcilable contrast between the emigrants and the native inhabitants of the lands they occupied; and third, the absolute—albeit not necessarily inimical—difference between God's chosen people and all other nations. It is precisely the Exodus myth that, by establishing Egypt and Israel as polar opposites, gives symbolic expression to a religiously defined singularity and otherness. And it is the Book of Exodus that, to this day, has perpetuated the negative image of Egypt as the house of slavery and oppression.

Both the Priestly Source and Deuteronomy were further expanded in the sixth and fifth centuries BCE. The Priestly Source took on the Book of Leviticus and probably also substantial parts of Numbers, while Deuteronomy was swelled by the "Deuteronomistic history" (Joshua, Judges, 1 and 2 Samuel as well as 1 and 2 Kings). The two traditions were then combined into an "Enneateuch," a nine-book work that was finally split into "Torah" and "Former Prophets." Although the Book of Exodus's prominent position within the Torah was not without consequence for its subsequent history, we can disregard here the further stages in the process of canonization. The Bible's vitality, its continuing presence in the cultural memory of the human race beyond the circles of rabbinic scholarship and Christian theology, does not depend on the ultimate canonic form of its books, which most laypeople would be hard put to summarize in the correct sequence, but in the enormous appeal of individual stories: the fall, the expulsion from Paradise, Cain and Abel, the flood, the Tower of Babylon, the destruction of Sodom and Gomorrah, the sacrifice of Isaac, Jacob stealing Esau's blessing and wrestling with the angel, Joseph in Egypt, Moses and the burning bush, the plagues of Egypt, the law given at Sinai, and the dance around the Golden Calf. These stories are familiar to us from countless paintings by the likes of Michelangelo, Rembrandt, Poussin, Chagall, and many more artists, both known and unknown. Such narrative variety and iconic vividness characterize the first two books in the Bible to a far greater extent than the remaining books in the Hebrew Bible, which come across as less coherent and mythic. Specifically, the Book of Exodus owes it phenomenal vitality to the religious ideas that it presents in the form of narrative ("Haggadah") and normative prescription ("Halacha"): revolution and liberation, covenant and election, revelation and faith, moral and juridical laws, sin and atonement.

Just as I will abstain from any further reconstruction of the canonization process, so I will also forgo any attempt to distinguish the different source texts used by the Priestly authors when composing the *Priestly Source. At one time there was general consensus that two principal source texts could be identified, the "Yahwist" and the "Elohist," both showing up fairly clearly in the Book of Genesis as dual lines of tradition. In the last thirty years, such consensus has collapsed, at least in Europe. Needless to say, this does not mean that the Book of Exodus is a creation ex nihilo, for it was preceded by the Exodus myth and no doubt draws on other preexisting texts, the most obvious and prominent being the "Covenant Code" (Ex 20–23).

The Priestly overpainting of an older Exodus canvas manifests itself in the text in the form of redundancies and internal contradictions. These make clear that we are not dealing with a homogeneous narrative here, but one worked on by a number of authors and redactors over a considerable period of time. Two scenes make this particularly apparent: the scene at the burning bush where YHWH reveals his name, declares his intentions, and sends out Moses to do his will (chapters 3–4) and the renewed account of Moses's mission (6:1–7:9). So far as the logic of the narrative is concerned, the second scene is not just unnecessary; it is downright absurd.[28] Here, Moses receives the same instructions for a second time. The author (or school) whose presence is palpable in this section evidently intended to build a bridge between Genesis and Exodus. This scene of revelation recalls the scene, depicted in Genesis 17, where God presents himself as El Shaddai and announces to Abram (who will now be called Abraham) his plan to make a covenant with him, to make him "exceeding fruitful" and give him the land of Canaan. Instead of working these explicit references into the burning bush scene, the Priestly redaction adds an almost identical appendix, clearly intended to link the originally independent novella cycles about the patriarchs and the Exodus story into a single comprehensive history that begins with the creation of the world and ends with the building of the Tabernacle and the institution of the YHWH cult at Sinai. In this it takes after the Babylonian and Egyptian

king lists, which likewise combine cosmogony and chronology. Where
the king lists secure a chronological framework through reign dates,
the biblical history leans on genealogy, and it is precisely in this sense
that here, after the first step in the process of revelation has been completed, the Book of Exodus draws a line by inserting the genealogy of
the Levites, the tribe of Moses and Aaron.

Indeed, the Book of Exodus starts off with a genealogical synopsis.
Chapter 1:1–5 lists the names of Jacob's twelve sons, who migrated with
their father to Egypt when Joseph ruled there as grand vizier and was
able to provide for them in times of famine. In reference to this beginning, the Hebrew title of the book is *šĕmôt*, "names." The genealogy of
the tribe of Levi, from which the brothers Moses and Aaron trace their
ancestry, follows at the end of chapter 6.

The Book of Genesis is structured entirely along genealogical lines.
It begins with the "genealogy" (*tôlĕdōt*, "generations") of heaven and
earth, followed by ten generations (seven, according to an alternative
reckoning) from Adam to Noah. After the flood there are ten generations up to Abraham, and the tales of the patriarchs (including the Joseph novella) encompass four more.

By combining *Genesis and *Exodus, the Priestly Source softened
the opposition between the inclusive, universalistic, and irenic tendency of the tales of the forefathers and the exclusive, particularistic,
and aggressive spirit of the Exodus story by integrating it into a higher
unity. For all that, an unmistakable tension still persists between the
Priestly Source, on the one hand, and the Deuteronomist (D) as well
as the associated "Deuteronomistic history" (DH), the second founding document of early Judaism, on the other. That history begins not
with creation but with the departure from Egypt, and it takes the story
past the covenant all the way up to the fall of Jerusalem and the end of
the monarchy in 587 BCE. The Priestly Source and the Deuteronomist
differ markedly in their theological tendencies. The Priestly Source is
concerned primarily with creation theology and cult theology. It combines a universalism of creaturality—there is only one God, the creator
of heaven and earth, and he is the god of all nations and all people—
with a particularism of holiness: he chose the people of Israel so that
he might dwell in their midst, provided that Israel meets his exacting
standards of sanctity by obeying his laws. The Deuteronomist and the

Deuteronomic school, by contrast, are interested predominantly in liberation and covenant theology. There are many gods but, for Israel, only one savior and liberator, who redeemed it from Egyptian bondage that it might serve him and follow his law, which offers release from servitude, from oppression and humiliation. Whereas the Priestly Source pursues the ideal of a "sacred people," the Deuteronomist follows that of a just society.

The ethnologist Mary Douglas has done more than anyone else to elucidate the differences between the Priestly Source and the Deuteronomist. Identifying four fundamental "thought styles"—isolationist, individualist, enclavist, and hierarchist—she associates the Priestly Source with a hierarchist mindset and the Deuteronomist (together with the historical works influenced by the Deuteronomic school) with an enclavist thought style.[29] Enclavists advocate a policy of strict self-separation from the outside world, while at the same time emphasizing equality and fraternity within their own community. Hierarchists tend to think more inclusively; because they discriminate among their ranks, they are more open to compromise in their dealings with the world at large. Thus the Book of Genesis clearly owes its universalistic perspective to the "hierarchist" spirit of the Jerusalem priesthood (P), while the particularist and separatist tendencies of Exodus betray the "enclavist" spirit of the Deuteronomist and the Deuteronomic school (D / DH).

Just as the idea of an institutionalized divine presence, YHWH's "dwelling" among his people, is of central importance for the Priestly Source, so too is the idea of the divine covenant—conceived in directly political terms—central for the Deuteronomist, together with the inseparably interlinked ideas of the chosen people, the laws, and the Promised Land. Here, too, divine presence is invoked, yet this is no longer a question of cult and priesthood (as in the Priestly Source) but of law, justice, and fidelity to the covenant. The difference between the two traditions can be traced back to the respective constituencies or demographic groupings whose views they represent. The constituency behind the Priestly Source is undoubtedly the Jerusalem priesthood, while the ideas reflected in the Deuteronomist and the Deuteronomistic History flourished in lay theological circles, among the educated scribes (*sôpĕrîm*) and city elites. This opposition was perpetuated in intertestamental and postbiblical times in the conflict between the Sadducees, the sacerdotal elite, and the Pharisees, the "learned" laity. From a Christian viewpoint, one could go a step further and recognize this opposition between priestly theology and lay theology in the tension between Catholicism and Protestantism, as well as within Protestantism between Lutheran orthodoxy and Pietism (in the German context) or between High Church Anglicanism and Puritanism, Methodism, and other dissenting movements (in an English context).[30] This opposition is inscribed in the Bible and contributes to the vitality of the biblical books, which are used not just as devotional literature but also as a source of arguments for interconfessional debate.

Chronologically speaking, the beginnings of the Priestly Source coincide with the years of renewal around 520–518 BCE when the prophets Haggai and Zechariah experienced their visions, early on in the reign of the great Persian king Darius I. That is the moment from which, to cite Bergson once again, "the call to which memory responds" emanated. In those years of a fresh start following the trauma of exile, the priestly historians drew up a past that provided a firm foundation for a new Israel, in the form of early Judaism, to rise up alongside the Second Temple.

From Myth to Canon and Back

The semantic core of the Exodus tradition, and the source of its immense influence, can be found in the myth of Moses and the departure from Egypt with its liberation-theological message. What is a myth? A myth is a story that is not just told time and again but told each time anew. It renews itself from one historical moment to the next, with each moment gleaning from it previously unsuspected nuances of meaning. In the terminology of semiotics, a myth is a "genotext" manifested in a potentially endless series of "phenotexts."[31] A myth unfurls in the dimension of time, which is to say that it belongs in the order of memory. In the order of memory there is no distinction between original and copy, hence there can also be no notion that the distance from the original increases each time a copy is made. There is no original memory, or, as Hans Blumenberg puts it, "there are no pure facts of memory."[32] As such, myth stands opposed to the logic of reproduction, which habitually works with such distinctions as original and copy, theme and variation, text and commentary, and so on. Here, there is the "original" or "reference text," in relation to which everything else appears more or less far removed.

Memory regulates the process of remembering and forgetting. Just as a memory wrested from oblivion actualizes and transforms the content of that memory, so too the mythic genotext is changed by being brought to language in a specific social and historical situation. Memory remembers what it finds important and lets everything else fade into the background, or even disappear altogether. What appears important is dictated by the formation and consolidation of a personal or collective identity, an "I" or a "we." We are what we remember: memory is framed, cultivated, and circumscribed by the identity sustained by these memories and kept alive in them. We give the name "myths" to stories that sustain a "we" and are framed, cultivated, and circumscribed by this "we." Myths are collective figures of memory, narrative *lieux de mémoire*, loci of a culture of remembrance. Whether they draw on real or fictitious events is beside the point; all that matters is that they claim a place in the order of memory, maintained there by a self-image that, in continually telling them anew, continually reassures itself of its roots and its goals, its truths and its dreams. This "we" is the totality of all those for whom a given memory—the memory of Moses, for example—still means something. It cannot be reduced to an ethnic, national, political, or religious identity. Myths found a cultural identity that runs athwart all such identities and has open, constantly shifting boundaries. A cultural identity is unstable, multilayered, contradictory, and heterogeneous. That is made abundantly clear, for example, in Arnold Schoenberg's opera *Moses und Aron*, which features elements from three distinct memory traditions: Jewish, Protestant, and philosophical. These traditions are nonetheless held together by the common cultural identity and the shared memory bank (or myth bank) that we call "the West." Moses is one of the preeminent "loci" in Western memory culture, one of its brightest beacons, even though his historical existence is sunk in the deepest obscurity and the light he sheds is drawn from memory alone.[33]

Yet can we speak without further ado of a "Moses myth"? That would appear to run counter to the authority of the Bible, which certainly invites us to tell the story time and again, but not to tell it differently with each telling. Far from it: once the process of redaction had come to an end, this story was codified and canonized as *historical* truth, set down in unalterably authoritative form as the second through fifth books of the Torah. Yet one cannot speak of canonization in the strict sense here: in the Jewish context, the concept applies only to legal principles and maxims for life (*hǎlākôt*), while in the Christian context it pertains only to officially recognized truths (dogmas), not storytelling (*'ǎggādôt*). Here, on the contrary, it is imperative to keep telling the tales, and to keep telling them anew, so that they may be kept alive in the collective memory.[34] Even though the border between story and doctrine in Christianity is not always so clearly delineated as that in Judaism between Halacha and Haggadah, any Christian, even a Christian theologian, is free to retell the story of Jesus differently to how it is told in the Bible.[35]

When contrasting the terms "myth" and "canon" here, we must avoid associating one with infinite variability and diversity and the other with monolithic rigidity and uniformity. As far as the canon of the Hebrew Bible is concerned, two points are of decisive importance. First, the Hebrew Bible is not a book like the Quran, the Adi Granth, or the Book of Mormon; it is a core library consisting of twenty-four books (by Jewish reckoning) or thirty-nine books (by Christian reckoning).[36] A core library sifts out a selection of particularly authoritative writings from the mass of literature that has been passed down to posterity. Clement of Alexandria reports that the Egyptian priests had a core library stocked with forty-two "indispensable" or "absolutely necessary" (*pany anankaiai*) books. The structure of the library resulted from the hierarchical order of the priesthood and the specialization of the different priestly ranks. The Hebrew Bible represents another such core library, and the key selection criterion was not uniformity but authoritativeness. Thus the Bible frequently, indeed almost systematically, juxtaposes voice and countervoice, Version A and Version B, since both are hallowed by tradition and the redactors were loath to sacrifice either. With respect to this polyphony within the Bible, Bernd Janowski speaks of the "contrastive unity of scripture."[37]

The other point to be made concerns the previously mentioned element of narrative freedom, which plays a greater role in Judaism than in Christianity. For example, although Thomas Mann's multivolume, idiosyncratic retelling of the Joseph story met with near-unanimous enthusiasm among Jewish readers, many Catholic readers voiced their severe disapproval.[38] The freedom characterizing the Haggadah corresponds to the sovereign disposition over mythic materials designated by Hans Blumenberg as "work on myth." Diversity prevails not just within the canon but outside it, too: alongside the Written Torah there is the Oral Torah where the unending exposition of the Written Torah takes the form of declaration and counterdeclaration, claim and counterclaim. The two Torahs are equal in stature, both having been given to Moses on Sinai according to rabbinic teaching.[39] When Blumenberg therefore describes myth as a story that is always told anew and unfolds its meaning in the fullness of its variants, this holds no less true of the biblical stories, at least as the Jews understand them. Thomas Mann had exactly the same freedom to set forth his own Joseph Haggadah in four volumes, and so take his place in the endless procession of those who have reinterpreted and retold the story, that was enjoyed by James Joyce when he decided to base his *Ulysses* on the Homeric Odyssey. The sole difference is that Joyce's masterpiece has secured for itself a place in the canon of world literature, whereas Thomas Mann's tetralogy—and for that matter every retelling of biblical material, no matter how skillfully done—could never hope to enter the biblical canon, which has been permanently closed off since antiquity. Whatever is still possible here has the status of commentary, yet commentary—and this is the crucial point—does not stand beneath the text but runs alongside it, attaining the dignity of inspired exposition in the Oral Torah tradition.

That is why "myth" and "canon" are not antonyms. The canonization of a story cannot put the brakes on the dynamism inherent to myth. The Moses myth has not just continually provoked new answers to the question "What does Moses mean to us?" in the genre of commentary; the story itself has also been retold in countless different ways. That holds true for ancient approaches to the Moses figure, from Philo's Moses biography, *De vita Mosis*, to the chapters devoted to the prophet in Flavius Josephus's *Antiquitates*, and it holds especially true for more recent treatments of the material, above all by Carl Leonhard Reinhold, Friedrich Schiller, Heinrich Heine, Arnold Schoenberg, Sig-

mund Freud, and Thomas Mann, as well as Martin Buber's classical
Moses and the breathtakingly audacious interpretation of the story
proposed by Ernst Sellin, which set Freud on the path to his "historical
novel" on Moses. Here, the biblical text is not merely interpreted but
thought further.[40] And when American presidents like George Wash-
ington, Thomas Jefferson, and Abraham Lincoln are hailed as a "second Moses," or Nelson Mandela is eulogized after his death as a "black
Moses," what is invoked here is the Moses myth rather than the biblical
Book of Exodus.[41] The Moses story is understood not as a one-off historical event but as a memory figure that reveals its truth in the very
act of remembrance and in the moment of remembering: as a myth, in
the fullest sense of the term. Miraculously, centuries of enlightenment,
historical-critical analysis, and demythologization have done nothing
to dull the Bible's luster in cultural memory. "Work on myth" arises
from the need to recast biblical material in a new form, to remember
the story in a new way, and to retell it in the context of a current historical moment that makes it appear in a completely new light. When, by
whom, and to what end the story is retold can be clearly understood
with reference to this historical context. For example, in the case of
Arnold Schoenberg, Sigmund Freud, and Thomas Mann, all three
were émigrés; all three turned to the Bible under the shock of Nazi
barbarism and anti-Semitic persecution; and all three sought to bring
the symbolic figure of memory known as "Moses" to the attention of
their time as a source of judgment and solace.

Moses stands for monotheism: this simple proposition would
quickly find assent among Jews, Christians, and Muslims. His name is
indelibly linked with the normative proclamation of the One God, normative in the sense that it stipulates strict exclusiveness and the clear-
cut distinction between the One True God and the many "other," foreign, forbidden, false, imaginary gods. This distinction, set out in
numerous (613!) injunctions and especially prohibitions, calls for a
decision to be made. Remembering Moses means remembering this
distinction, in whatever form it presents itself to the trials and tribulations of a given historical situation: between loyalty and betrayal, freedom and servitude, justice and injustice, purity and impurity, order
and chaos, civilization and barbarism, sensuality and spirituality, or
truth and untruth.

The "Mosaic Distinctions" and the Monotheism of Loyalty

I introduced the concept of the "Mosaic distinction" in my book *Moses the Egyptian* (1997), further elucidating it in *The Price of Monotheism* (2009). I take it to mean the distinction between true and false, a distinction that—and this was my main contention—first entered into the sphere of religion with biblical monotheism. First the Bible, and then the religions built upon it, distinguish between true God and false gods, true religion and false religions. While I would still defend this thesis today, I must admit that the distinction between true and false plays no role in the Exodus tradition. It should therefore not be called "Mosaic," given that the Exodus tradition is, after all, where we find Moses in the Bible. None of the three theological dimensions that play a role in the story of the departure from Egypt—the liberation-theological, covenant-theological, and cult-theological—is invested in the distinction between true and false. Instead, the dominant distinction that enters into the religious sphere under the auspices of Moses is that between loyalty and betrayal.[42]

When we take a closer look at the Exodus story, however, we ascertain that three distinctions play a fundamental role here. All three can therefore, with some justice, be termed "Mosaic." None has anything to do with truth and falsehood. At issue are the distinctions between (1) Egypt and Israel, (2) Israel and the nations, and (3) friend and foe, or loyalty and betrayal. Each forms the basis of one of the three sections into which the Book of Exodus is partitioned. The key distinction made in the first section is that between Israel and Egypt; in the second, it is that between Israel and the nations as well as friend and foe; in the third, the distinction between loyalty and betrayal is clarified through the example of the Golden Calf.

The distinction on which the first part is based is clearly that between captivity and freedom. More precisely, since "freedom" does not belong in the biblical vocabulary, it is that between human and divine servitude. Human servitude enslaves, divine servitude sets free. On several occasions it is stated that YHWH frees his people that they may serve him (Ex 7:16, 26; 8:20; 9:1, 13; 10:3, 7, 26; see 3:12; 23:25). At the same time, the confrontation of Egypt and Israel also involves the distinction between old and new. Egypt stands for the old that the Israelites must put behind them, freeing themselves from its yoke, in order to step into the new. In this sense, the departure from Egypt has about it something of a collective conversion experience. In the history of the Exodus story, the liberation- and redemption-theological impulse forms the decisive center of meaning.

With the covenant on Sinai, two new distinctions come into play, which likewise bear no relation to truth and falsehood. The first differentiates between outside and inside, belonging to the covenant and not belonging to it, exosphere and endosphere. God makes this covenant not with the world and the entire human race but with the children of Israel, whom he has chosen to be his people and led out of Egypt. Through the covenant and divine election, the world splits into Israel and the nations. It is important to emphasize that this distinction has nothing whatsoever to do with intolerance and violence. God cares for all peoples but he has something special in mind for Israel. That is why everything depends on Israel segregating itself from the circle of nations and insisting on its otherness. That is what the law is for. By following it, Israel sanctifies itself as God's people and marks itself out from all other nations. All people belong to God but Israel is his jewel. In antiquity, this principle of isolation from the nations was misconstrued as "misanthropy" and brought the Jews a great deal of suffering, hatred, and condemnation.[43] From an insider's perspective, this isolation looks quite different: by living in strict accordance with the God-given law, they seek to set an example for other nations. While the Priestly Source emphasizes the aspect of holiness, the Deuteronomist foregrounds the aspect of wisdom, education, and justice, which other nations should strive to emulate:

> Behold, I have taught you statutes and judgments, even as YHWH my God commanded me, that ye should do in the land whither ye go to possess it. Keep therefore and do them; for this is your wisdom and your understanding in the sight of the nations, which shall hear all these statutes, and say, Surely this great nation is a wise and understanding people.
>
> For what nation is there so great, who hath the gods so nigh unto them, as YHWH our God is in all things that we call upon him for?
>
> And what nation is there so great, that hath statutes and judgments so righteous as all this law, which I set before you this day? (Deut 4:5–8)

Seen from within, this second "Mosaic distinction" between Israel and the nations is completely nonviolent and nonpolemical. It is an act of self-exclusion that leaves others free to live by their own laws and worship their own gods. Seen from outside, however, it provoked numerous Judeophobic reactions and fanned the flames of ancient anti-Semitism.[44]

Through the covenant, Israel becomes a people that "shall dwell alone, and shall not be reckoned among the nations" (Num 23:9). Those are the words of Balaam, the Moabite diviner. Haman expresses similar views in the Book of Esther: "There is a certain people dispersed among the people in all the provinces of thy kingdom who keep themselves separate; and their laws are different from those of all other people" (3:8). As Bernhard Lang has pointed out, the Bible "always places the most telling statements in the mouth of a non-Israelite. The fictive stranger's perspective is used as a vehicle for self-description."[45] In the apocryphal Book of Jubilees, Abraham says to Jacob: "Separate yourselves from the nations! Eat not with them! Act not according to their works! Become not their associate! For their works are unclean, and all their ways are a pollution and an abomination and uncleanness."[46]

The interpretation of the law given in the letter of Aristeas belongs in this context, too:

> The legislator [Moses], armed by God with profound wisdom, surrounded us with impenetrable palisades and iron walls to prevent our mixing in any way with any of the other nations, remaining pure in body and soul, preserved from false beliefs, revering the one almighty God above the whole creation [...]. So that we should not besmirch ourselves with anything and not be spoiled by contact with the bad, he surrounded us on all sides with purity instructions, commandments on eating and drinking, touching, hearing and seeing.[47]

God himself decrees in Leviticus:

> I am YHWH, your God, which have separated you from other people. [...] And ye shall be holy unto me: for I, YHWH, am holy, and have severed you from other people, that ye should be mine. (20:24, 26)

As it is presented in the First Book of the Maccabees, the Maccabean Revolt broke out over this very question of the Jews' willful apartness

from other people. It was directed against an assimilationist reform
party that wanted to release itself from its obligations to the law and
collaborate with the Seleucid occupying forces: "Let us go and make a
covenant with the heathen that are round about us: for since we departed from them we have had much sorrow" (1:11). The Wars of the
Maccabees and the various Zealot movements mark the point at which
the principle of isolation (or sanctification) becomes bound up with
the distinction between friend and enemy. They would not be disen-
tangled until, in the interest of peaceful coexistence with the host nations of the diaspora, rabbinical wisdom developed a principle that
toned down the conflict between this call for strict separation, this
absolutism of difference, and the need to integrate into the host culture: *tôrâ 'im derek 'ereṣ*, "the Torah *with* the way (i.e., customs and
laws) of the (host) land" (Pirkei Avot 2:2).[48] In the nineteenth century,
Rabbi Samson Raphael Hirsch was to make this principle the basis of
his neo-Orthodox reform program.

Self-sanctifying segregation also explains the heavy emphasis placed
on the motif of allochthony (migration from abroad) in both the Exodus story and the patriarchal tradition. This motif causes Israel's genesis
as God's own people, in the sense of a political and religious identity, to
appear in the light of a *creatio ex nihilo*: the children of Israel were nothing, powerless, defenseless, unsheltered by the law and utterly without
dignity, until God chose them to be his people and led them into Canaan. Furthermore, the motif of foreign provenance makes clear that
the migrating Israelites have nothing in common with the nations already settled in the Promised Land. The holy people must at all costs
avoid making contact with them; indeed, sooner they be wiped from
the face of the earth than that Israel be seduced into worshipping at
their shrines and altars. Just as Israel must keep its distance from other
nations, so too must it keep their gods at bay. The ban on assimilation
thus has its counterpart in the ban on foreign gods. Therein—and not
in any factual origin in Egypt (Moses) or Mesopotamia (Abraham)—
lies the symbolic significance of Israel's allochthony.[49]

The third "Mosaic distinction" is struck within the covenant, in the
endosphere: that between friend and enemy. As the justification for the
ban on foreign gods and graven (or molten) images, it occupies a central and prominent position:

Thou shalt not bow down thyself unto them, nor serve them: for I, YHWH thy God, am a jealous God, visiting the iniquity of the fathers upon the children unto the third and fourth generation of them that hate me, and showing mercy unto thousands [of generations] that love me and keep my commandments. (Deut 5:9–10 = Ex 20:5–6; cf. Ex 34:7)

The distinction made here is that between God's friends and his enemies. Note that God is the object, not the subject of hatred and love. God is not the one who distinguishes between friend and foe; rather, it is humans—specifically, those who have been singled out to receive the law and made a solemn pledge to live by it—who make that decision by choosing to uphold or abandon their vows. Having entered into the covenant, they cannot now renege on their commitment without incurring God's wrath.[50] This is the most problematic of the three "Mosaic distinctions." It goes hand in hand with the "language of violence" that has scandalized enlightened opinion to this day, calling forth the usual clichés of an Old Testament vengeful God, a "God who punishes and kills."[51]

Within the semantic formation established by the covenant, there arises a new conception of violence alongside a new conception of sin. Violence refers here to the "zeal" (qin'â, from which 'ēl qannā', "the jealous, wrathful God"[52]) with which YHWH and his covenant partners enforce the terms of the covenant, as, for example, when Moses orders the mass execution of three thousand idol worshippers in the tale of the Golden Calf. Idolatry, the production and worship of divine images in contravention of the first commandment, becomes the most serious sin in the covenant-theological catalog. "Sin" and "violence" thus belong together. Indeed, they first emerge in this sense with the covenant and its law distinguishing friend from foe. But this distinction has nothing to do with truth and falsehood. It instead pits fidelity to the covenant against the backsliding tendencies of the unfaithful.

I therefore propose calling the form of monotheism illustrated in the story of the departure from Egypt, and associated with the name of Moses, a "monotheism of loyalty." It stands in contrast to a "monotheism of truth"—represented in the Bible not by Moses but by the exilic and postexilic prophets, especially Deutero-Isaiah, Daniel, and others—which evidently arose in the Persian period under the influence of Achaemenid Zoroastrianism. This monotheism concerns not the God who freed his people from Egyptian bondage but the creator of heaven and earth, beside whom there are no other gods they could revert to worshipping. Whereas the genuinely "Mosaic" monotheism of loyalty presupposes the existence of other gods—what sense could there be in staying true to God without rival gods to tempt his fickle people?—for the "monotheism of truth," these other gods do not exist and are consequently dismissed as "idols," manmade fetishes and fictions. Scholars of religion tend to reserve the term "monotheism" for this latter form, the former going by the name of "monolatry." The terminology is regrettable. It suggests that the covenant theology of the Book of Exodus is something typical and widespread, whereas it is in fact a unique and revolutionary phenomenon found only in the Bible. Furthermore, the distinction between monolatry and monotheism conceals the indissoluble bond forged between the monotheism of loyalty and the monotheism of truth in the later writings of the Old and New Testament as well as in the Quran. Nothing would be more wrongheaded than to assume that biblical monotheism has evolved from particularistic monolatry to universalistic monotheism. Rather, the uniquely biblical conception of a divine covenant and monotheism of loyalty proved so compelling that the exile period idea of the One, all-creating God was unable to displace it. On the contrary, the ideas of covenant, loyalty, emancipation, and providence are what constitute the essence of biblical religion and define its emotional content; they have shaped rabbinical Judaism and Christianity, especially Protestant Christianity, to this day. The particularist monotheism of loyalty and the universalist monotheism of truth coexist in the complex, polyphonic canon of biblical writing, with the monotheism of loyalty providing the *cantus firmus*.

The true-false dichotomy pertains solely to the monotheism of truth. Insight and knowledge are fundamental here, not fidelity and jealousy. Only here, in reference to this God, does the philosophical concept of truth have a place. This monotheism can also be found in a figure like Xenophanes of Colophon, a contemporary of the late and postexilic prophets. Likewise, ancient Egyptian religion and many other religious traditions acknowledge only one creator and originator of the universe, from whom all else flowed (including the other gods).

Here, the gap between such "cosmogonic" monotheism and "pure" monotheism appears narrow indeed.

In the semantic paradigm of Exodus, by contrast, the monotheism of loyalty takes center stage. God demands nothing less of his people than love and unconditional, absolute fidelity, which they demonstrate by abiding by his commandments and prohibitions. It is only possible to be loyal or disloyal where there are alternatives. We cannot betray our creator, since it is impossible for us to escape the confines of our own creaturality. But the Israelites can be disloyal to their liberator and covenant partner by returning to Egyptian captivity, defecting to other gods, or breaking his laws. The laws are neither true nor false; rather, they are binding and obligatory. That is why God is never addressed in the course of the Exodus myth as the creator of heaven and earth, only as the one who "brought thee out of the land of Egypt, from the house of bondage" (Ex 20:20; 29:46; Deut 5:6; Lev 19:36; 22:33; 25:38; 26:13; Num 15:4; Ps 81:11; see also Lev 11:45).[53] This is the god who distinguishes between friend and foe, showering his blessings on one and unleashing his fury on the other. Wrath and awe are a part of this covenant no less than love and grace, even if love proves the vastly more powerful emotion. The specificity of biblical monotheism lies in the idea of the covenant and loyalty. With that, a completely new form of religion, a new template for believing and belonging, had been invented. This new religion, founded on the concept of loyalty, finds authoritative expression in the Exodus myth. Deuteronomy, the first version of which probably dates from around 620 BCE, modeled the idea of the covenant on the loyalty oath that Esarhaddon made his vassals swear to the designated successor to the Assyrian throne, Ashurbanipal. The succession treaty tied the principle of political fealty to the relationship between god and his covenanted subjects.[54] In the Bible, however, the Assyrian model undergoes three decisive changes. First, the bond described in the Exodus myth is indissolubly linked with the concept of liberation: the laws only make sense when seen against the backdrop of Egyptian enslavement. Second, rather than being imposed on the people from on high, in the manner of the vassal treaty, the divine covenant is entered into freely and freely renewed each time it is broken; the biblical account places great emphasis on this. Third, the aspect of divine favor, benevolence, forbearance, and mercy plays an altogether different role than in the political model. That said, the friend-foe distinction quite obviously derives from this source and with it, too, the problem of violence.[55]

The Book of Genesis mentions neither friend and enemy nor God's wrath and jealousy, although outbursts of punitive force occur frequently enough, from the expulsion from Paradise through the flood and confusion of tongues to the destruction of Sodom and Gomorrah. But God's wrath never flares up at these violent interventions.[56] Wrath and jealousy first belong in the semantics of the covenant made on Sinai, as the Golden Calf story immediately makes clear. Lactantius already pointed this out in his text *De ira Dei*, connecting God's wrath with his "imperium," his role as lord of the covenant, not with his essence.[57] To this imperium belongs the dichotomy between friend and enemy. Even the "formula of grace" with which God reveals himself in his all-forgiving goodness after the episode with the Golden Calf (Ex 34:6–7) reinforces this distinction, emphasizing that no sin can be allowed to remain without consequences under the terms of the covenant. No religion without fear, as Lactantius puts it: *religio esse non potest ubi metus nullus est.*[58] Fear befits a god who not only, like many other gods of the time (Ra in Egypt, Shamash in Babylon, Zeus in Greece, Mithras in Persia, Varuna in India, Baʿal bĕrît in Shechem, and so on), watches over his people to ensure that contracts and laws are upheld, but also—and this is the revolutionary novelty of this religion—decrees those contracts and laws himself. This is the liberator from Egyptian captivity celebrated in the Book of Exodus, as opposed to the creator of heaven and earth introduced in Genesis. From a biblical viewpoint, of course, they are one and the same god, but creation and liberation reveal different conceptions of how God is experienced and how he shines his face upon the world.

The third of the Mosaic distinctions, that between friend and enemy, further involves what has been called "biblical anti-Canaanism."[59] This problematic phenomenon ought by no means to be brought into connection with the second distinction between Israel and the nations. The decisive difference between the second and third Mosaic distinction is that, whereas the second has nothing to do with violence, the third declares it a sacred duty. In this sense, violence is inherent to the monotheism of loyalty, however vigorously theological apologetics may deny it.[60] The other nations from which Israel separates itself out through the second distinction are not its enemies, with one exception: the seven nations settled in the Promised Land. These are drawn into the semantics of holy warfare, such that the friend-enemy distinction (which holds only within the covenant) is projected outward onto the people of the covenant's relations with their neighbors. Holy war[61]—the biblical term means "to execute the ban (ḥērem)"—and anti-Canaanism thus belong to the semantics of the third Mosaic distinction, which declares violence to be a sacred obligation.

A holy war is a war of extermination. Looting is strictly forbidden; instead, all the spoils of war are to be offered up as a sacrifice to the god in whose name the war is waged and whose support is vital to the success of the undertaking. In Deuteronomy 20 it is stated that a regular war (involving right of plunder) may be launched against far-off nations and cities, but that a holy war must be waged against the nations and cities of the Canaanites. There is nothing specifically biblical about the semantics of holy war.[62] Much the same terminology can be found in the inscription on the stele of King Mesha of Moab from the mid-ninth century BCE.[63] The "occasional monolatry" encountered here—an exclusive relationship to a single god improvised only for the special case of a holy war—certainly played an important role in the formation of the biblical monotheism of loyalty.

The equation of the Canaanites with the backsliders, the "despisers" of the covenant and the law within the Israelites' own ranks, suggests that these foreign "nations" stood in for their own past transgressions, which lived on in the many regions and social classes that remained stubbornly unconverted to monotheism. Othmar Keel, in particular, has drawn attention to this symbolic significance of biblical anti-Canaanism. "No very profound knowledge of the Bible is required," he writes, "to see that the abominations ascribed to these people, the altars and massebahs slated for destruction, were once a part of Israelite religion and not perpetrated by some devilish nations."[64] He goes on to note: "The 'anti-Canaanism' of Hosea and the Dtn-Dtr movement, like the anti-Judaism of the New Testament, denounces an aspect of its own past by seeking to identify and repudiate it as something alien."[65] This sentence makes three points clear: (1) We are dealing here with a phenomenon of conversion—the concept "Canaanites" refers to the

Israelites' own past and the unconverted among their own people; (2) this anti-Canaanism does not characterize the entire Hebrew Bible, only a particular tendency that first emerges with the prophet Hosea[66] and goes on to define the Deuteronom(ist)ic tradition; (3) this tendency is perpetuated not only in the anti-Judaism of the New Testament but also in the attitude toward indigenous populations shown by other colonialist movements identifying with the exodus, such as Puritan migrants to the USA, the Boers in South Africa, and the right-wing settler parties in Israel, all of whom have drawn on the relevant passages in the Old Testament to justify their violent actions.[67] Naturally, the texts must be understood against their historical background and should not be held responsible for how they have been—and still are—misused in different times and circumstances. But we should also bear in mind the hermeneutic principle that the (mis)uses to which a text is put are not entirely extrinsic to whatever semantic potential they may contain.[68] The friend-enemy distinction, and the violence it entails, are presumably indispensable for establishing the rule of law and can be explained accordingly, but the extension of God's law to outsiders, along with the outbursts of religious violence it legitimates in the name of holy warfare, have occasioned far too much devastation and bloodshed throughout history to be passed off as "God's word." It may be appropriate, as Othmar Keel has suggested, to recognize in such passages the "statutes that were not good" (ḥuqqîm lō' ṭôbîm) spoken of by God to Ezekiel (Ez 20:25).[69]

The monotheism of loyalty is also the spiritual site from which the Egyptian exodus is remembered. Loyalty and memory, like truth and insight, go hand in hand. Loyalty requires that YHWH's munificence in freeing his people from Egypt not be forgotten and that an awareness of the covenanted identity founded on Sinai be kept alive or rekindled. The covenant must constantly be affirmed, confirmed, and renewed. The Exodus story revolves, as we have seen and will see again, around the act of memorialization; not only does it set out what is to be preserved in memory, it also lays the foundations of the cultural mnemotechnics intended to anchor this memory for all time in the cultic, festive, quotidian, domestic, and public domains. Cultivating this memory entails, on the one hand, composing grateful panegyrics proclaiming God's saving grace and, on the other, acknowledging the people's sinfulness, as demonstrated in exemplary fashion in the great liturgical trilogy of Psalms 105, 106, and 107. Psalm 105 tells of God's miraculous deeds (*niplā'ôt*), from the tales of the patriarchs, the Joseph story, the suffering of the children of Israel in Egyptian captivity, and the plagues (here numbering only seven) to the Exodus. Psalm 106 extends this proclamation by confessing the sins of the fathers. They too are seven in number, echoing the seven Egyptian plagues, just as, in Exodus and Numbers, ten plagues correspond to ten instances of disobedience, transgression, rebellion, and unbelief (in God's counting: see Num 14:27). In the context of the Exodus story, the seven sins are followed by continued sinfulness in the Promised Land itself: assimilation to the sacrificial customs of the Canaanites. God's vengeful wrath, manifested in the fall of Jerusalem, the loss of land and Temple as well as Israel's dispersal among the nations, constitutes the real demonstration of the power that is proclaimed here. Even as he punishes them, God still abides with his people, the covenant still holds, and there is still hope for forgiveness:

> Nevertheless he regarded their affliction, when he heard their cry: And he remembered for them his covenant, and repented according to the multitude of his mercies. He made them also to be pitied of all those that carried them captives. Save us, YHWH our God, and gather us from among the heathen, to give thanks unto thy holy name, and to triumph in thy praise! (Ps 106:44–47)

The Exodus story is an act of remembrance, and remembering the departure from Egypt means keeping faith with the covenant. That memory sustains the hope for renewal and a fresh start. The present moment from which—to cite Bergson once again—a particularly audible call for the Exodus memory emanates can be dated with some precision. On the twenty-first day of the seventh month (i.e., October 17), 520 BCE, the prophet Haggai experienced a vision in which God proclaimed: "According to the word that I covenanted with you when ye came out of Egypt, so my spirit remaineth among you; fear ye not" (Hag 2:5). Seen from this late-sixth-century commemorative standpoint, when the various traditions were being brought together into an absolutely binding foundation for the newly reconstituted nation, state, and Temple, it must be asked why this new Israel was distancing itself with such extraordinary vehemence on two fronts: against Egypt and against the Canaanites. With the Persian conquest of Egypt, that country had lost all political relevance for Israel or Judea (until Judea again temporarily fell under Ptolemaic rule in the third century), while the Phoenicians and Persians had come to replace the "seven nations" that had to be driven out of the Promised Land. These two fronts are therefore to be understood symbolically: Egypt stands for oppression of all kinds, Canaan for idolatry. Those are the two spheres of sinfulness that are in flagrant breach of the covenant and draw down God's wrath. At the same time, they are the two spheres of justice and covenant fidelity to which the two tables of the law traditionally refer. Whereas the first table with the divine commandments is directed against proscribed forms of worship (Canaan), the second with its social laws targets all forms of social injustice (Egypt).

PART TWO

THE EXODUS

When will the day come when we leave the Egypt of this world?

—Salomon Franck[1]

Wherever you live, it is probably Egypt.

—Michael Walzer[2]

It is not only that one has risen up against us to destroy us; rather, in every generation they rise against us to annihilate us. But the Holy One—blessed be he—saves us from their hand.

—Pesach Haggadah

CHAPTER FOUR

THE TRIBULATIONS OF THE ISRAELITES AND THE BIRTH OF THE SAVIOR

Griefs are more valuable than triumphs, for they incur
obligations and call for a common effort.
—*Ernest Renan*[1]

Bondage in Egypt

The Book of Exodus starts off by depicting the torments endured by
the children of Israel after a new pharaoh came to power and drastically revised the terms of their guest status. The Israelites had migrated
as shepherds and prospered as free, more or less settled graziers in the
pastoral province of Goshen, in the eastern Delta. Now, under a new
pharaoh, they were commandeered to build the "store cities" of Pithom
and Ramses.

> And Joseph died, and all his brethren, and all that generation.
> And the children of Israel were fruitful, and increased abundantly, and mul-
> tiplied, and waxed exceeding mighty; and the land was filled with them.[2]

> Now there arose up a new king over Egypt, which knew not Joseph. And
> he said unto his people, Behold, the people of the children of Israel are too
> strong and numerous for us:[3]
> Come on, let us deal wisely with them;[4] lest they multiply, and it come to
> pass, that, when there falleth out any war, they join also unto our enemies,
> and fight against us, and [then] get them up out of the land.[5]

> Therefore they did set over them taskmasters [*śārê missîm*] to afflict them
> with their burdens [*sĕbālôt*]. And they built for Pharaoh store cities, Pithom
> and Ramses.

But the more they afflicted them, the more they multiplied and grew. And
they were grieved because of the children of Israel.
And the Egyptians made the children of Israel to serve with rigor [*pārek*⁶]:
And they made their lives bitter with hard bondage, in mortar, and in brick,
and in all manner of service in the field: all their service, wherein they made
them serve, was with rigor. (1:6–14)

The enslavement of the children of Israel and their ordeals in Egypt is
a theme that has enormous resonance in the Jewish, Christian, and
Islamic traditions. Without this burden of suffering, there could have
been no exodus; without this exodus, there could have been no new
dispensation in which relations between God and the universe, God
and humankind, the individual and society were fundamentally transformed in ways that bear on the past and future as well as the present.
This motif therefore warrants further consideration.

Let us begin by taking a closer look at this section of the text.
"Store cities" are stations stocked with provisions for supplying the
army and with garrisons for securing the key campaigning routes.
Neither "Ramses" (meaning the royal capital of the Ramessides, *Pi-
Ramesses*) nor Pithom (*pr-Jtmw* in Egyptian, "house of Atum") had
this function, but in the thirteenth century BCE, Nineteenth Dynasty
Egypt undoubtedly went through a building boom that must have
required an immense labor force. This is the only passage in the Book
of Exodus that refers directly to the time and place of the narrative.
Ramesses II, who ordered the city of Pi-Ramesses to be built, is thus
widely identified as the pharaoh of Exodus. While I do not rule out
the possibility that the passage may indeed refer to historical events
that took place under Ramesses II (1279–1225), I propose to read it—
along with the Book of Exodus as a whole—from a different angle:
with an eye to how it resonated with different audiences over the
millennia, just as the book itself resonates with the memories that
entered into it.

To start with these resonances, conscripted labor was as common in
the states of the ancient world as compulsory military service in their
modern counterparts. The state maintained a monopoly over construction and skilled manual labor, including the acquisition of materials

FIGURE 2. *The Hardship and Subservience of the Israelites in Egypt.* Woodcut by Julius Schnorr von Carolsfeld, mid-nineteenth century.

through expeditions and quarrying. Throughout the ancient Near East, conscripted labor was a customary form of taxation and could be paid in kind or in the form of labor service as an alternative to monetary payment. In Egypt, conscripted labor played a particularly important role owing to the annual flooding of the Nile, which put a halt to work in the fields for three to four months at a stretch, freeing up farm hands for other activities. Furthermore, huge cargoes that would otherwise have had to be arduously hauled overland could now be transported by ship. Workers were recruited from the rural populace, with craftsmen trained to become skilled laborers. We learn of this general obligation from the decrees that exempted particular groups, especially priests, from work duties. There can be no doubt that a high degree of social violence prevailed within the Egyptian organization of conscripted labor, duties, and taxes.

This "normal" degree of social violence pertaining to the work world in ancient Egypt should be distinguished from the heightened forms of constraint and coercion that, according to the Book of Exodus, were applied specifically to the Israelites. These go far beyond the demands of ordinary conscripted labor and are instead more typical of forced labor conditions. Forced labor was regularly imposed on prisoners of war and subjugated populations. Above all, it was the commonest means of punitive detention (there being no prisons, only a system of pretrial confinement). Those punished in this way were mostly consigned to backbreaking work in the quarries. Nothing would have seemed more natural in Egypt than to subject foreigners—especially prisoners of war, but perhaps also those deported from the occupied Palestinian territories—to these harsher strictures. The transition from conscripted labor, an accepted and far from dishonorable form of work in Egypt, to forced labor, which was considered highly demeaning owing to its punitive character and no doubt took place under conditions of strict supervision, presumably represents a first intensification of the repressive measures taken by the Egyptian state against the Israelites. The Hebrew concept of *bêt ʿabdôt*, "house of bondage," refers to this institution of forced labor.

The Hebrew word *mas*, applied as much to the corvée Solomon demanded of his own people as to the forced labor exacted from defeated cities and enslaved captives, makes no distinction between conscripted and forced labor. Deuteronomic martial law sets down a procedure for setting subjected cities or states to work (Deut 20:11), but this applies only to distant conquests. Canaanite cities were to be subjected to the "ban," meaning that all living things were to be put to the sword (Deut 20:17–18). Repeated references to Israelites requiring Canaanites in newly conquered territories (Jos 16:10; 17:13; etc.) and thereafter (Judges 1:27–35; 1 Kings 9:16) to work for them instead of expelling or destroying them are thus to be understood as directed against a practice expressly forbidden by Deuteronomic law. Under King Solomon, who spent twenty years building the Temple and royal palace in Jerusalem while also undertaking further construction projects in Hazor, Megiddo, and Gezer, the issue of forced labor became acute:

And King Solomon raised a levy out of all Israel; and the levy was thirty thousand men. And he sent them to Lebanon, ten thousand [men] a month by courses: a month they were in Lebanon, and two months at home: and Adoniram was [supervisor] over the levy. And Solomon had threescore and ten thousand that bare burdens, and fourscore thousand hewers in the mountains; Besides the chief of Solomon's officers which were [deployed] over the work, three thousand and three hundred, which ruled over the people that wrought in the work. (1 Kings 5:13–16)

In this report, there is not the slightest suggestion that the corvée introduced by Solomon was tainted by indignity, degradation, enslavement, suffering, or the deprivation of rights. We should not forget, however, that its continuation under Solomon's successor, Rehoboam, led the northern tribes to secede from the Jerusalem dynasty. When Rehoboam went to Shechem to be crowned king by "all Israel," representatives of the northern tribes approached him, saying: "Thy father made our yoke grievous: now therefore make thou the grievous service of thy father, and his heavy yoke which he put upon us, lighter, and we will serve thee" (1 Kings 12:4). The ill-advised king threatened them instead with an even worse fate: "My father chastised you with whips, but I will chastise you with scorpions" (12:14). At that, the northern tribes broke with him and left the assembly. When the chief supervisor Adoniram, of all people, was sent to negotiate with the breakaway tribes, "all Israel stoned him with stones, that he died" (12:18). This episode—whether historical or purely literary in origin—clearly shows the connotations associated in Israel with *mas*. A later Deuteronomistic redactor of the Book of Kings felt it necessary to emphasize that only Canaanites, not Israelites, were conscripted by the king (even if there ought to have been none left to conscript), so that Solomon's gleaming image might not be tarnished by pharaonic associations:

And all the people that were left of the Amorites, Hittites, Perizzites, Hivites, and Jebusites [...] that were left after them in the land, whom the children of Israel also were not able utterly to destroy, upon those did Solomon levy a tribute of bondservice [for his construction works] unto this day. But of the children of Israel did Solomon make no bondmen; but they were

men of war, and his servants, and his princes, and his captains, and rulers
of his chariots, and his horsemen. These were the chief of the officers that
were [deployed] over Solomon's work, five hundred and fifty, which bare
rule over the people that wrought in the work. (1 Kings 9:20–23)

All these reports feature exactly the same vocabulary used elsewhere to describe Egyptian servitude. They make clear that a Hebrew
had no need to move to Egypt to undergo the bitter experience of conscripted labor: it was familiar enough on home soil during the period
of the United Monarchy. In memory, though, it was Egypt that remained indissolubly linked with the idea of conscripted labor, transformed into slave labor by pharaonic injustice. Notwithstanding the
favorable impression of Egypt conveyed in the directly preceding tale
of Joseph, this association with enslavement continues to blacken the
country's image to the present day.

Chapter 5 relates how, following Moses's first audience with Pharaoh, the corvée system was tightened in such a way that it now definitively crossed over into degradation, forced labor, and persecution.
This was Pharaoh's reaction to Moses's petition that the Israelites be
given three days' leave to sacrifice to their god in the wilderness:

> And Pharaoh commanded the same day the taskmasters [*nōgĕśîm*, from
> *nāgaś*, "to strike"] of the people, and their officers [*šōṭĕrîm*], saying, Ye shall
> no more give the people straw to make brick, as heretofore: let them go and
> gather straw for themselves. And the tale of bricks, which they did make
> heretofore, ye shall lay upon them; ye shall not diminish ought thereof: for
> they be idle; therefore they cry, saying, Let us go and sacrifice to our God.
> Let there more work be laid upon the men, that they may labor therein; and
> let them not regard vain words. (5:6–9)

This excerpt is especially rich in genuinely Egyptian details. To this
day, bricks in Egypt are made from Nilotic mud, mixed with straw chaff
and dried in the sun. That explains why brick production is a form of
farm labor; the straw required as temper is abundant here so it does not
normally need to be supplied by the state. Mud bricks were used for all
forms of profane domestic architecture, including royal palaces. Only
sacral architecture (temples and graves) was built in stone. The Hebrews worked under "list-bearers," foremen from their own ranks who

kept a list of all the workers under their supervision (as is still customary in Egypt today; many such lists from ancient Egypt have survived),
as well as Egyptian overseers or superintendents. Above these stood
the "taskmasters" mentioned in Exodus 1:11. The Hebrew "overseers"
(*šōṭĕrê bĕnê yiśrā'ēl*) were responsible for their work output and were
thrashed if they failed to meet their quotas. Pictures in Old Kingdom
tombs suggest that "domain administrators" were similarly punished if
they fell behind in their duties.

Even in ancient Egyptian eyes, Pharaoh and his Egyptian taskmasters had committed a sin that could have grave consequences when they
were summoned before the Egyptian court of the dead. There, the deceased had to recite a long list of sins and swear not to have committed
any of them. Near the top of this list, alongside serious sins like injustice,
blasphemy, murder, and manslaughter, appears the following:

> I did not begin a day by exacting more than my due, my name did not reach
> the "helmsman of the bark" [= the sun god].

Evidently the idea that unfairly exploited laborers could lodge a complaint with the sun god was as prevalent in Egypt as it is in the Exodus
story. The story gets underway when the oppression of the Israelites
becomes so intolerable that they cry out to God in their suffering and
he responds. In the commandments handed down to God's people on
Sinai, we also repeatedly encounter the warning never to drive anyone
so far that they cry out to God (Deut 15:9; 24:15).

For the Israelites, Egyptian forced labor—and herein lies the particular resonance of the motif—became in all its ignominy a central element in their self-understanding and in their understanding of the divine. God is the liberator who led them out of Egypt, the house of
bondage. They themselves are continually reminded of this fact and
enjoined never to forget that they "were slaves in Egypt." They have
remained slaves, but from slaves (*'ăbādîm*) of the Egyptians they have
become the servants (*'ăbādîm*—the same word, but in relation to God
the translation "slaves" would be out of place[7]) of YHWH: "For unto
me the children of Israel are servants; they are my servants whom I
brought forth out of the land of Egypt: I am YHWH your God" (Lev
25:55). Servitude to God frees from human enslavement. "I am YHWH

FIGURE 3. "And they oppressed us and imposed on us hard labor." Woodcut from a modern Haggadah. Munich, 1948.

your God, [. . .] and I have broken the bands of your yoke, and made you go upright" (Lev 26:13).

It is worth sifting through the relevant passages in Deuteronomy and Exodus for the occasions when the memory of Egyptian slavery is invoked.[8] That happens, in particular, when Israelites themselves keep slaves from among their countrymen and -women:

> And if thy brother, an Hebrew man, or an Hebrew woman, be sold unto thee, and serve thee six years; then in the seventh year thou shalt let him go

free from thee. And when thou sendest him out free from thee, thou shalt not let him go away empty. [. . .] And thou shalt remember that thou wast a bondman in the land of Egypt, and YHWH thy God redeemed thee: therefore I command thee this thing today. (Deut 15:12–15)

The most prominent such admonition is the justification for the Sabbath law given in Deuteronomy:

Keep the sabbath day to sanctify it, as YHWH thy God hath commanded thee. Six days thou shalt labor [*taʻăbōd*, "serve"], and do all thy work [*mĕlaʼktekā*]:
But the seventh day is the sabbath of YHWH thy God: in it thou shalt not do any work, thou, nor thy son, nor thy daughter, nor thy manservant, nor thy maidservant, nor thine ox, nor thine ass, nor any of thy cattle, nor thy stranger that is within thy gates; that thy manservant and thy maidservant may rest as well as thou.
And remember that thou wast a servant in the land of Egypt, and that YHWH thy God brought thee out thence through a mighty hand and by a stretched out arm: therefore YHWH thy God commanded thee to keep the sabbath day. (5:12–15)

In the Book of Exodus, the rationale given for the same commandment is that, having created the world and everything in it, God rested on the seventh day. That is the specifically Priestly justification going back to the Priestly account of creation. Whereas the Priestly Source argues from a creation-theological perspective, Deuteronomy adopts a liberation-theological viewpoint, and it is from this latter perspective that the memory of Egyptian bondage is kept alive so that the true value of freedom can never be forgotten. The Feast of Weeks (Shavuot) is similarly celebrated in order to commemorate the ordeal of slavery in Egypt:

Seven weeks shalt thou number unto thee [. . .]. And thou shalt keep the feast of weeks unto YHWH thy God, [. . .] and thou shalt rejoice before YHWH thy God, thou and thy son, and thy daughter, and thy manservant, and thy maidservant, and the Levite that is within thy gates, [. . .]. And thou shalt remember that thou wast a bondman in Egypt: and thou shalt observe and do these statutes. (Deut 16:9–12)

More generally, this memory is used to justify the injunction not to infringe on the rights of strangers, orphans, and widows:

> Thou shalt not pervert the judgment of the stranger, nor of the fatherless; nor take a widow's raiment to pledge:
> But thou shalt remember that thou wast a bondman in Egypt, and YHWH thy God redeemed thee thence: therefore I command thee to do this thing. (Deut 24:17–18)[9]

The ban on gleaning harvested fields, olive groves, and vineyards is justified in the same terms:

> When thou gatherest the grapes of thy vineyard, thou shalt not glean it afterward: it shall be for the stranger, for the fatherless, and for the widow. And thou shalt remember that thou wast a bondman in the land of Egypt: therefore I command thee to do this thing. (Deut 24:21–22)

In the Book of Exodus, this justification appears in both passages of the Covenant Code that forbid the mistreatment of strangers:

> Thou shalt neither vex a stranger, nor oppress him: for ye were strangers in the land of Egypt. (22:21)

The psychological justification provided in the second passage is particularly impressive:

> Also thou shalt not oppress a stranger: for ye know the heart [*nepeš*] of a stranger, seeing ye were strangers in the land of Egypt. (23:9)

Since they themselves were strangers in Egypt, the Israelites can and must empathize with the strangers in their own land; since they were poor and without rights in Egypt, they should look after the rights and welfare of the poor in their own country; since they were slaves in Egypt and were forced to perform hard labor, they should allow themselves as well as their own slaves one day of absolute rest every six days and likewise on feast days. Only by remaining mindful of their trials and tribulations in Egyptian slavery can the Israelites hope to grasp the laws to which they covenanted themselves as a medium of freedom. In this sense, Egypt serves from a liberation-theological perspective as a counterimage to the divine covenant forged on Sinai.

The depiction of the sufferings of the children of Israel in Egyptian bondage thus performs two functions: a (liberation-)theological function as background and justification for the covenant laws and a narratological function as the starting point of a story that leads to its own overcoming and reversal. The extremely negative light cast on pharaonic Egypt as the epitome of inhuman despotism cannot be explained as a report—however tendentious—into the state of affairs in ancient Egypt at the time. Rather, it has a narrative function in the structure of the Exodus tale. What is depicted here is a turning point in salvific history, from the utmost desolation in Egyptian bondage to the covenant with a god whose laws promise salvation through divine presence and the Promised Land. This narrative structure explains why Egypt is depicted with such unrelieved negativity. The Egyptian world is painted in such dark colors not because the regime was really so horrendous but because it forms the starting point of a story that draws its tension from the contrast between oppression and freedom. In cultural memory, however, this depiction of Hebrew suffering has indelibly stained the image of ancient Egypt. Even today, it is still widely believed that the pharaohs must have enslaved their own people, as well as foreigners like the Israelites, in order to build the colossal monuments of Egyptian architecture, above all the Great Pyramids of Giza. Confronted by these mighty works, many tourists still imagine the lashings, threats, curses, and cries of pain that accompanied their construction by incessantly toiling slave armies. To this day, the word "pharaoh" is a term of abuse in the Arab world, and when the deposed Egyptian president Mubarak was characterized on the banners of revolutionaries as "Firaûn," the Pharaoh of Exodus would have been uppermost in their minds.

So far as the depiction of Egyptian oppression is concerned, the aspect that resonated most strongly with readers over the millennia was the anti-Semitic clichés that the text ascribes to the anonymous Pharaoh. According to the Exodus story, anti-Semitism or Judeophobia therefore appears to be older than the people of Israel itself, which did not even exist before the covenant! There is, first, the fear that the Hebrews, who already outnumber the native population, will increase still further, and second, the "fifth column" argument that they could ally with the enemy in the event of war and rise up against the Egyptians. Both fears arose in the context of modern nationalism and relate to the fear of minorities whose loyalty toward the state and its culture could be called into question. Such anxieties played a key role in the twentieth century; for example, they stood behind the Armenian genocide in Turkey (1915, in the shadow of the First World War), even if the term "fifth column" is first attested in the Spanish Civil War. Egypt thus becomes the archetype of all the persecutions heaped on the Jews in the course of their sorrowful history.

The emphasis placed on foreignness (allochthony or "migrant background") is common to both narratives of origin, the legends of the patriarchs and the Exodus story. Yet Abraham suffered no abuse in his Mesopotamian world; in turning his back on it, he was following God's call. The Exodus story emphasizes not just the Israelites' Egyptian origin but their suffering there, as aliens beset by forced labor and murderous persecution. One of the starkest formulations of this motif of foreign origin and suffering abroad can be found in the short version of the myth, known as the "short historical credo," recited by an Israelite when offering the first fruits of the land, presumably at Sukkot:

> My father was a wandering Aramean, and he went down into Egypt, and sojourned there with a few, and became there a nation, great, mighty, and populous:
> And the Egyptians evil entreated us, and afflicted us, and laid upon us hard bondage:
> And when we cried unto YHWH, God of our fathers, YHWH heard our voice, and looked on our affliction, and our labor, and our oppression:
> And YHWH brought us forth out of Egypt with a mighty hand, and with an outstretched arm, and with great terribleness, and with signs, and with wonders:
> And he hath brought us into this place, and hath given us this land, even a land that floweth with milk and honey. (Deut 26:5–11)[10]

The symbolic significance of Israel's former status as an alien nation lies in three points: first, it marks the Promised Land as the Israelites' true homeland; second, it characterizes them as "allochthonous"[11] in relation to that homeland in order to distinguish them as sharply as possible from the other tribes settled in Canaan; and third, it defines them as an "empathic civilization," a society that remembers its birth pangs and hence feels for those who are less fortunate. The memory of the sojourn in Egypt is meant to empower the Israelites to commiserate with the strangers, the poor, and the underprivileged in their midst. It is brought out in three contexts:

1. You should not oppress the stranger since you yourself were a stranger in Egypt.
2. You should not exploit slaves since you yourself were a slave in Egypt.
3. You will only understand the meaning of the laws you are beholden to obey if you do not forget that you were a slave in Egypt and were set free by YHWH.

Egyptian servitude thus forms a central element in Israel's image of itself and its God.[12] The Israelites are freed slaves who have not forgotten their wretched past. God is the savior who, in calling them from Pharaoh's service to be his servants, requires that they themselves practice an empathic, "redeeming"[13] justice (Lev 25:54–55).

The past—however traumatic or humiliating it may have been—is crucially important to the Israelites, for it makes them sensitive to the needs of the Other. "If you had never been foreigners and slaves in Egypt," the message seems to be, "you could never have founded a new form of society in which nobody is oppressed or degraded anymore." Learn, *mathein*, through suffering, *pathein*, as the famous Greek adage puts it.[14] The mythical motif of Egyptian captivity encapsulated the Israelites' all too real suffering under Assyrian and Babylonian rule; it also established a pattern for understanding, experiencing, and enduring later trials under Seleucid and Roman oppression as well as in the diaspora. To borrow a term used by Aleida Assmann and others, such a pattern may be characterized as "premediation"[15] or "prefiguration": "All cultures develop systems of prefiguration that help them work through events and give meaning to experiences."[16] The "Egyptian exile," Nehama Leibowitz writes, "prefigured every exile to which Israel was subjected, and just as the Egyptian bondage provided the motivation and impulse for many moral imperatives, so did the redemption from Egypt serve as a spur for religious duty."[17] That is the other side of the memory of suffering in Egypt: it contributed to the moral refinement of the Israelites.

Today, in the shadow of the appalling suffering that slavery and colonialism, two world wars, Shoah and Gulag have meted out on the human race, the biblical correlation of memory and justice has acquired an entirely new resonance and relevance. Only as a society that remembers its own history will the human race become an "empathic civilization," in Jeremy Rifkin's sense of the term,[18] and only as an empathic civilization will it be able to uphold human rights throughout the world and face the daunting challenges of globalization.

The Birth of the Child

With the account of forced labor, the account of the torments endured by the Israelites under conditions of Egyptian captivity has not yet come to an end. As chapter 1 continues, they now take on quasi-genocidal forms:

> And the king of Egypt spake to the Hebrew midwives, of which the name of the one was Shiphrah, and the name of the other Puah:
> And he said, When ye do the office of a midwife to the Hebrew women, and see them upon the stools [*'al-hā'obnoyīm*[19]]; if it be a son, then ye shall kill him: but if it be a daughter, then she shall live.
> But the midwives feared God, and did not as the king of Egypt commanded them, but saved the men children alive.
> And the king of Egypt called for the midwives, and said unto them, Why have ye done this thing, and have saved the men children alive?
> And the midwives said unto Pharaoh, Because the Hebrew women are not as the Egyptian women; for they are sturdy,[20] and are [already] delivered ere the midwives come in unto them.[21]
> And Pharaoh charged all his people, saying, Every son that is born ye shall cast into the river, and every daughter ye shall save alive. (1:15–22)

With this turn of events, the previously realistic depiction of Egyptian forced labor enters the realm of fairytale. It seems strange that two midwives would suffice for so evidently large a population; no less puzzling is the fact that they are called by name, a courtesy denied even the Pharaoh. The names are Hebrew, and the midwives are explicitly identified as Hebrews in the Masoretic text (*měyallědōt hā'ibrîyōt*). On the other hand, the midwives speak of the Hebrew women as if they belonged to a different race than the Egyptian women, whose birthing procedures they appear to regard as normal. The Septuagint offers the genitive form—"of the Hebrews"—rather than the adjective "Hebrew," so leaving open whether we are dealing here with Hebrew midwives or with Egyptian ones (as the logic of the narrative would suggest).[22]

To this day, the midwives Shiphrah and Puah live on in cultural memory as paragons of God-fearing virtue (*yir'at 'ĕlōhîm*) and heroines of civil disobedience.[23] The fear of God they represent, however, does not serve the interests of a "phobocracy,"[24] a rule of fear imposed by the powerful to instill obedience and deference in their subjects, as argued since ancient times by the enlightened critique of religion. On the contrary, it positively encourages resistance to unjust laws and commands. But does not the reference to the "fear of God" speak against the interpretation of the midwives as Egyptians? Not in the least. Both the other passages where the Torah speaks of the "fear of God" (*yir'at 'ĕlōhîm*) refer to foreigners: in one case to the Egyptians, whom Abraham had not credited with such fear when he took the precaution of passing off Sarah to them as his sister (Gen 20:11), and in the other to the Amalekites, who "feared not God" when they harried the Israelites on their long march:

> Remember what Amalek did unto thee by the way, when ye were come
> forth out of Egypt;
> How he met thee by the way, and smote the hindmost of thee, even all that
> were feeble behind thee, when thou wast faint and weary, and he feared not
> God. (Deut 25:17–18)

Fear of God is a civilizing principle common to all civilized people, not just the Israelites. The text does not mention "fear of the Lord" (*yir'at* YHWH) here but fear of God in general (*yir'at 'ĕlōhîm*), the God in question being not YHWH but Elohim, the divine as such. When the king's plan founders on the midwives' resistance, he no longer bothers to conceal his true intentions, moving from covert to overt genocide[25] by commanding his people to cast all male children—meaning the children of the Hebrews—into the Nile.

This section stands in an altogether different context of justification to the first. The first section deals with the iniquities and degradations suffered by the Hebrews while in Egyptian captivity; it forms the pendant to the liberty they enjoy as servants of the God who freed them and called them to be his people at Sinai. Moreover, their mistreatment is not allowed to go unpunished. It is avenged in the first nine of the ten plagues that God visited on the Egyptians. The second section stands in a very different narrative context, already belonging to the tale of the birth and rescue of the infant Moses told in chapter 2. The link between infanticide and rescue would later unfold its own afterlife as the anti-type or prefiguration of the massacre of the innocents in Bethlehem recounted in Matthew 2.

This last outrage, the slaughter of all male Hebrew children, stands in exactly the same relation to the previously depicted torments of forced labor as does the tenth plague, the slaughter of the firstborn among the Egyptians, to the account of the previous nine. Here, too, the narrative is formally and stylistically transformed. The first nine plagues follow the same basic format, rain down on the Egyptians one after the other, and almost all appear as natural phenomena that are not entirely unknown in Egypt. The tenth plague, the slaughter of the firstborn, differs markedly from the rest and is a specifically biblical theme rather than an Egyptian one. I will have more to say about this in chapter 6.

In the narrative context of the Book of Exodus, the depiction of the infanticide thus preludes the following account of the birth of Moses, who miraculously avoids being killed at Pharaoh's command:

> And there went a man of the house of Levi, and took to wife a daughter of Levi.
> And the woman conceived, and bare a son: and when she saw him that he was a goodly child,[26] she hid him three months.
> And when she could not longer hide him, she took for him an ark[27] of bul-rushes,[28] and daubed it with slime and with pitch, and put the child therein; and she laid it in the reeds[29] by the river's brink.[30]

> And his sister stood afar off, to wit what would be done to him.
> And the daughter of Pharaoh came down to wash herself at the river; and her maidens walked along by the river's side; and when she saw the ark among the reeds, she sent her maid to fetch it.
> And when she had opened it, she saw the child: and behold, the babe wept. And she had compassion on him, and said, This is one of the Hebrews' children.

FIGURE 4. The infant Moses is abandoned, forming the capital letter "S" in a fourteenth-century book illustration.

Then said his sister to Pharaoh's daughter, Shall I go and call to thee a nurse of the Hebrew women, that she may nurse the child for thee?
And Pharaoh's daughter said to her, Go. And the maid went and called the child's mother.

And Pharaoh's daughter said unto her, Take this child away, and nurse it for me, and I will give thee thy wages. And the woman took the child, and nursed it.
And the child grew,[31] and she brought him unto Pharaoh's daughter, and he became her son. And she called his name Moses: and she said, Because I drew him out of the water. (2:1–10)

In narrating the hero's birth, the biblical author draws on material that was familiar throughout the ancient Oriental world in the eighth and seventh centuries BCE: the legendary birth of King Sargon of Akkad, who in the twenty-third century BCE had united the Mesopotamian city-states into a mighty empire:

> Sargon, the strong king, the king of Akkad, am I. My mother was a high priestess, my father I do not know. [. . .] My mother, a high priestess, conceived me and bore me in secret. She placed me in a reed casket and caulked my hatch with pitch, then she abandoned me to the river, from which I could not escape. The river carried me, it brought me to Akki, the water drawer. Akki, the water drawer, lifted me out as he dipped his ewer. Akki, the water drawer, brought me up as his adopted child. Akki, the water drawer, appointed me as his gardener. When I was a gardener the goddess Ishtar loved me: for fifty-five years I ruled the kingdom.[32]

The parallels are obvious: secret birth, abandonment in a reed casket, adoption by the finder's family, divine calling. As Sigmund Freud and, above all, his student Otto Rank have pointed out, we are dealing here with an enormously widespread mythic schema that the Moses legend redeploys but also turns on its head at a decisive point. Typically, the adoptive family is of far humbler status than the highborn, often royal foundling. Only in the case of Moses, discovered by a princess and raised at Pharaoh's court, are things the other way around. With this story of his birth and upbringing, Moses is introduced as a hero and a new Sargon, a divinely appointed ruler. The reader can expect that Moses, too, will eventually take the throne. It is therefore all the more significant that he never does so. The reason why Moses is abandoned by his parents is also different. Moses is abandoned to save him from imminent execution by Egyptian thugs.[33] Sargon is abandoned to spare his mother, a high priestess evidently consecrated to a life of virginity, from scandal.[34] Both are plucked from the waters and end up performing great deeds: Sargon goes on to found the first Mesopotamian empire, while Moses becomes the savior of his people. If we ask about the "resonances" of the biblical story, it is clear that they again point in two directions: at once backward to the Assyrian birth legend (which the story echoes)

FIGURE 5. *Moses Abandoned.* On the left, the crestfallen Amram exits the scene with the three-year-old Aaron; to the right, the wreathed Nile god lies with the personification of Egypt, seen here wearing a Turkish fez. Nicolas Poussin, 1654.

and forward to the massacre of the innocents in Bethlehem (which it prefigures).

The principal difference between the birth legend of Moses and the tale of the slaughtered infants in Bethlehem lies in the motif of prophecy. Entirely missing in the case of Moses, it provides the spur to Herodian persecution in the case of the Christ child. The link between a prophesied future king and the murderous plans of the reigning monarch can also be found in an Egyptian story that has come down to us in a seventeenth- or sixteenth-century papyrus but may well be much older, since it refers to events from around the mid-third millennium.[35] King Khufu, the builder of the great pyramids, is given a prophecy by a wizard that he will be succeeded by three kings, the eldest of whom knows a certain secret concerning Khufu. This message is not to the king's liking. He demands to know precisely when and where these kings will be born and learns that the sun god himself has impregnated the wife of his priest with all three. Khufu is told the time and place, and we may assume that his intentions toward these children are far from benign. The triplets duly come into the world under miraculous circumstances and with divine support. A maidservant, quarreling with their mother, runs off to inform the pharaoh about the birth of the three kings, only to fall into the water on her way and be snapped up by a crocodile. Although the papyrus breaks off at this point, the outline of the story is clear enough. What is foretold here is evidently the birth of the three kings (not just one: these are the first three kings of the fifth dynasty) who will put an end to the tyrannical regime of the pyramid builders and usher in a new era of godly rule, signaled by the temples they will erect to the sun god. Khufu attempts to eliminate the children, and the missing ending to the papyrus must have told how that attempt is thwarted.

Khufu, Ramesses II, and Herod have one thing in common: they are remembered as three of the greatest builders of the ancient world. This allowed legends to spring up around their monumental, highly visible legacy, including the belief that such colossal buildings could not have been possible without a slave labor force and a cripplingly heavy tax burden. Such legends made their rule appear as a time of great suffering for their people (or, in the case of Ramesses II, a guest people). A similar legend told of Khufu is found in Herodotus, and for Ramesses we can find a distant echo in the Book of Exodus. Here the royal name has become the name of a city mentioned on three occasions in the Pentateuch: in Exodus 1 as the site and object of the Israelites' forced labor, and in Exodus 12:37 and Numbers 33:3 and 5 as the starting point of their travels.

The missing motif in Exodus of prophecy was subsequently added by Flavius Josephus in his retelling of the Exodus story:[36]

> One of those sacred scribes, who are very sagacious in foretelling future events truly, told the king that about this time there would be a child born to the Israelites, who, if he were reared, would bring the Egyptian dominion low, and would raise the Israelites; that he would excel all men in virtue, and obtain a glory that would be remembered through all ages. Which thing was so feared by the king, that according to this man's opinion, he commanded that they should cast every male child, which was born to the Israelites, into the river, and destroy it. (*Antiquitates* 2.9)

Josephus goes on to recount in some detail the tale of the child's abandonment and discovery by the Egyptian princess, providing a very interesting etymology of Moyses, the name she gave him: "mo" from the Egyptian *mw*, "water," and "yses" from the Egyptian *Ḥesy* (*hasie* in Coptic), "drowned in water (and thereby blessed)." This is understood by Josephus to mean "pulled out from water." Absurdly, the biblical text offers a Hebrew etymology for a name given by an Egyptian princess: Mōšeh, from *māšah*, "to pull," but this yields "the one who pulls" rather than "the one pulled (out from water)." Today we know that the name is Egyptian and simply means "born," from *mesi*, "to give birth." It generally appears with a divine name: Ramose "born from Ra," Thutmose "born from Thoth," Amenmose "born from Amun," and so on. It thus corresponds to the Greek name ending *-genes*, which for the three Egyptian names I have just mentioned would result in Heliogenes, Hermogenes, and Diogenes. An Egyptian divine name is naturally out of the question for the Hebrew Moses, so he is simply called "child," and in Egypt this abbreviated version without the divine complement is also attested.[37]

The discovery that the name Moses is Egyptian inspired Sigmund Freud, in particular, to far-reaching speculations that breathed new life into the Moses legend. If the name is Egyptian, he reasoned, then its bearer must have been Egyptian as well, and the birth story found in Exodus must have been fabricated to cover up this Egyptian heritage. It seems irrefutable that something has indeed been covered up or at least forgotten here. Why does the biblical narrator fail to mention that the Egyptian princess gave the baby a common Egyptian name, instead purveying a Hebrew etymology that simply does not stand up to linguistic scrutiny? The strategy suggests that this awkward detail may contain a historical clue. At any rate, the narrator did not invent the name "Moses" but found it already given and interpreted it as he saw fit. In doing so, he foregrounded the act of salvation from water, so foreshadowing the collective salvation from water in which the Exodus story culminates in chapter 14. The one pulled out from water here becomes the one who does the pulling, as expressed in the active participle *môšeh*: *yamšēnî mimmayīm rabbîm*, "he drew me out of great waters," the Psalmist sings in Psalm 18:16. That holds true of both the infant Moses and Israel at the Sea of Reeds.

Moses's Childhood and Upbringing

Understandably, the princess who finds the howling infant proves unable to breastfeed him, and his biological mother is called in to act as wet nurse. Saved from pharaonic persecution, then suckled by his own mother (who is even paid for her troubles), and finally adopted into the royal family—this is a happy ending of almost ludicrous improbability. The informed reader can only marvel at the mysterious ways in which God works. But God has not yet been mentioned at this stage (leaving aside the "God-fearing" midwives) and will appear only later, and then not on Egyptian terrain.

For the ancient Egyptians, childhood comes to an end at the age of ten; now the boy is ready for higher education and instruction. Strikingly, however, this theme is passed over in silence in the Book of Exodus. Here, the tale of how Moses was given his name runs straight into his return to his brothers' company as a grown man.

If we turn once again to consider the story's resonance, we see before us a case study for how an omission or lacuna can have a far more pervasive influence than many positive statements. This very gap in the narrative allows speculation to take flight, prompting readers over the millennia to provide their own, highly elaborate constructions. The process had already gotten underway in ancient times, albeit attested by fairly sparse remarks. Prior to his stoning, the deacon Stephen gave a stirring speech recapitulating the history of mankind's damnation and salvation, filling in the gap between Moses's childhood and maturity with the following information:

> And Moses was learned [*epaideúthē*] in all the wisdom [*sophia*] of the Egyptians, and was mighty in words and in deeds. (Acts 7:22)

Philo of Alexandria is already much more precise in his biography of Moses. From an early age, he reports, Moses disdained all toys and playthings, attending only to what could improve his mind. He received a comprehensive education and soon surpassed all his teachers in understanding and knowledge. He was taught arithmetic, geometry, the lore of meter, rhythm, and harmony—the whole domain of music—as well as the other arts by the Egyptian philosophers, who instructed him in "the philosophy which is contained in symbols" (*dia symbolōn*

philosophia), "which they exhibit in those sacred characters of hiero-
glyphics, as they are called, and also in that philosophy which respects
animals, which they invest with the honors due to God." Behind this
account stands a belief widely held among the Greeks of this late period and no doubt promoted by the Egyptians themselves. The Egyptians, it was maintained, had two forms of writing: a cursive script,
which was used for normal purposes of communication and record-
keeping, and a symbolic script reserved for the esoteric philosophy of
the mysteries, which was revealed only to the initiated few. Thus Diodorus, who in this point as in all others concerning Egyptian culture
and history excerpted Hecataeus of Abdera (late fourth century BCE),
remarks: "The Egyptians use two different scripts: one, called 'demotic,' is learned by all; the other one is called 'sacred.' This one is
understood among the Egyptians exclusively by the priests, who learn
it from their fathers in the mysteries."[38] That is the hieroglyphic script,
understood as a form of symbolic writing which Moses, according to
Philo, learned in the course of his courtly education as a gateway to the
philosophy stored up in those enigmatic characters.

In the seventeenth century, the English Hebraist John Spencer am-
bitiously ventured to derive all the Mosaic ritual laws from Egyptian
mysteries, that is, secret rites and symbols.[39] God, he argued, wanted
to give his chosen people as perfect a religion as possible. For that reason alone, he made them tarry for centuries in Egypt before sending
them a leader steeped in the arcane lore of the mysteries. Only after
being "nourished with the hieroglyphic literature of Egypt" (*hiero-
glyphicis Aegypti literis innutrium*) was Moses in a position to be chosen
as God's first prophet: "God wished that Moses should write the mystic
images of the more sublime things. Nothing could have been better
suited to this purpose than the hieroglyphic literature in which Moses
was educated."[40] Spencer was less concerned with the content of Egyptian theology than with the structure of religion as a semiotic system.
Spencer discerned that structure in the principle of hieroglyphs as an
esoteric code; they offered outsiders an attractive exterior while at the
same time reserving a higher wisdom for the initiated. There is thus a
structural resemblance between Egyptian rites and Hebrew ritual
laws: in both cases we are dealing with "hieroglyphs," symbolic forms
encoding a deeper meaning.

A century later, building on Spencer's argument for the origin of
Mosaic monotheism in the Egyptian mysteries, other scholars set out
to uncover not just the ritual but also the theology of the mysteries,
which they compared with Moses's proclamation of the One God.
Their primary concern, however, would be God's revelation at the
burning bush.

CHAPTER FIVE

GOD REVEALS HIS NAME

Moses at the Burning Bush

feu
Dieu d'Abraham, dieu d'Isaac, dieu de Jacob
—*Blaise Pascal*

Moses Is Called

And it came to pass in process of time, that the king of Egypt died: and the children of Israel sighed by reason of the bondage, and they cried, and their cry came up unto God by reason of the bondage.

And God heard their groaning, and God remembered his covenant with Abraham, with Isaac, and with Jacob.
And God looked upon the children of Israel, and God knew them.

Now Moses kept the flock of Jethro his father in law, the priest of Midian: and he led the flock to the backside of the desert, and came to the mountain of God, even to Horeb.

And the angel of YHWH appeared unto him in a flame of fire out of the midst of a bush: and he looked, and, behold, the bush burned with fire, and the bush was not consumed.
And Moses said [to himself], I will now turn aside, and see this great sight, why the bush is not burnt.

And when YHWH saw that he turned aside to see, God called unto him out of the midst of the bush, and said, Moses, Moses. And he said, Here am I.
And he said, Draw not nigh hither: put off thy shoes from off thy feet, for the place whereon thou standest is holy ground.

Moreover he said, I am the God of thy father, the God of Abraham, the God of Isaac, and the God of Jacob. And Moses hid his face; for he was afraid to look upon God. (Ex 2:23–3:6)

When the pharaoh dies in Egypt, God realizes that the time has finally come to attend to the needs of his suffering people. It is telling
that God takes the initiative himself rather than responding to their
prayers for help. The people seem to have forgotten all about him.
Rather than crying out to God, they simply cry out, and God does not
"answer" their prayers, he "hears" their cries and "sees" their suffering.
"God" had not been mentioned to this point in the narrative (with the
sole exception of the "God-fearing" midwives, Shiphrah and Puah,
who were rewarded with "houses" by God—surely a later interpolation). Now he is mentioned five times in five consecutive sentences.[1]
God "hears" (*šāmaʿ*) and "remembers" (*zākar*), he "looks upon" (*rāʾâ*)
his people and "recognizes" (*yādaʿ*)[2] their plight. On two occasions,
verbs of sensory perception are followed by verbs of inner realization:
to hear and remember, to see and recognize. The artfully established
contrast between the silence on the subject of God maintained in the
first two chapters and the accumulation of the divine name in verses
23–25 emphasizes God's dramatic intervention in human affairs, which
inaugurates a new chapter in salvational history. As YHWH, he will
from now on remain a constant presence in the action.

This text may be considered "one of the densest nodal points in the
entire Old Testament and one of the most influential texts in world
literature."[3] In a scene of pastoral tranquility, diametrically opposed to
all the hardship and terror that Moses had fled from in Egypt, God intervenes in history to put a stop to that hardship and terror. God could
not have staged this long-awaited intervention any more tenderly or
sparingly. Not in thunder and lightning, in earthquakes, howling
winds, and firestorms does God come down to appear before Moses,
but in a bizarre natural phenomenon seemingly designed to catch the
prophet's attention and draw him from afar: a dry, thorny shrub of the
kind that has sometimes been known to spontaneously combust where
steppeland gives way to desert yet here burns steadily without being
reduced to ash. The flame is "the angel of YHWH," the sign that announces his presence, but the voice that intones from the bush is God's
own: "Moshe! Moshe!"—and Moses answers "*hinnēnî*—here am I."

This divine call echoes an earlier passage where the same voice had
called out to another: "Abraham!" and he had answered: "*hinnēnî*—
here am I!" In both cases, God imposes a supreme, almost intolerably

FIGURE 6. Moses at the burning bush, blithely nibbled at by a billy goat. French book illustration (Noyon), c. 1210.

excessive burden on his servant. Abraham is commanded to take his son Isaac to a mountain and sacrifice him there as a burnt offering. Moses is ordered to proclaim this God to his people, demand their release from Pharaoh, and guide them through the desert to God's holy mountain. Abraham, who has far greater cause than Moses to disobey God's command or seek to plead his way out of it, tacitly assents and sets off with his son. Unlike Moses, he knows whom he is dealing with. For his part, Moses enters into lengthy negotiations with God. The voice continues:

> Put off thy shoes from off thy feet [a rhyme in Hebrew[4]], for the place whereon thou standest is holy ground.

God calls out to Moses on only two further occasions in the course of the narrative, both times at critical junctures: when he ascends Sinai to conclude the covenant and receive the tablets of the law (Ex 19:3) and at the start of Leviticus, when, after renewing the covenant and erecting the Tabernacle (*miškān*), he is for the first time commanded to receive new laws from within the *miškān*. The scene at the burning bush, however, is the only one where God calls Moses by name.

Only after removing his sandals does Moses learn whom he is dealing with: *'ānōkî 'ĕlōhê 'ābîkā*, "I am the God of thy father," the voice says, "the God of Abraham, the God of Isaac, and the God of Jacob." Only now does Moses take fright: "And Moses hid his face; for he was afraid to look upon God." The scene strongly recalls the description of Elijah's encounter with God at Sinai/Horeb:

> And he said, Go forth, and stand upon the mount before YHWH. And, behold, YHWH passed by, and a great and strong wind rent the mountains, and brake in pieces the rocks before YHWH, but YHWH was not in the wind. And after the wind an earthquake; but YHWH was not in the earthquake. And after the earthquake a fire, but YHWH was not in the fire. And after the fire a still small voice. And it was so, when Elijah heard it, that he wrapped his face in his mantle, and went out, and stood in the entering in of the cave. (1 Kings 19:11–13a)

Here, the contrast with a violent theophany (such as that depicted when God delivers the laws in Ex 19:16–25) is made explicit. Unlike Moses, Elijah immediately understands what is happening to him and hides his face. Abraham, who was often favored by such divine visitations, is never said to have been afraid or to have covered his face. Jacob, though, is gripped by fear upon awakening from his dream of a ladder reaching all the way to heaven:

> And Jacob awaked out of his sleep, and he said, Surely YHWH is in this place, and I knew it not. And he was afraid,[5] and said, How awesome is this place! This is none other but the house of God, and this is the gate of heaven. (Gen 28:16–17)

By introducing himself to Moses as the God of his fathers, YHWH alludes to the pact he had concluded with Abraham (Gen 15 and 17), which had remained in abeyance during the more than four centuries the Israelites had tarried in Egypt. On the one hand, something utterly new is heralded here, the story of God and his chosen people. On the other, this represents only the latest episode in an ongoing saga that had begun with creation, continued with Noah after the flood, and then, with Abraham, been placed in the light of divine election and promise. God had appeared before the fathers themselves as El Shaddai (Gen 17:1; 35:11). In Jacob's dream of a ladder to heaven, however, he introduces himself to Jacob much as he does later to Moses, as "the God of Abraham thy father, and the God of Isaac" (Gen 28:13).

This scene finds an echo in Blaise Pascal's famous "Mémorial," the parchment on which, in 1654, the thirty-one-year-old mathematician and philosopher recorded a life-changing religious experience. Wanting to hold fast to this experience under all circumstances, to preserve it from the vicissitudes of memory and fortune, Pascal sewed the parchment into his coat so it would always lie close to his heart. It was discovered there after his death by his manservant. It begins with the words:

> Fire.
> God of Abraham, God of Isaac, God of Jacob, not of philosophers and scholars. Certainty, certainty, emotion: joy, peace. God of Jesus Christ.[6]

This is Pascal's "burning bush" experience. The vision lasted "from around half past ten in the evening to about half past twelve." With tears of joy, he confesses his return to the faith of the fathers: "Jesus Christ! I have separated myself from him; I have fled from him, denied him, crucified him. Let me never be separated from him." He praises "renunciation, total and sweet. Total submission to Jesus Christ and to my [spiritual] director." The distinction made here by Pascal is revolutionary. Ever since classical antiquity, Christian (as well as Jewish and Islamic) theologians have sought to reconcile reason and faith by identifying the idea of the divine upheld by faith with the philosophers' god, the "unmoved mover" of the Aristotelian tradition or the *prôtos noûs*, the "primal intellect" of the Platonic tradition. Pascal holds the two conceptions of the divine to be irreconcilable; to embrace one means to renounce the other. By following the god "of the philosophers and scholars," he now sees that he had "fled from" the God of the Fathers, betrayed and forgotten him. What his nocturnal experience signifies to him is a reconversion, and this is also how the burning bush scene is to be understood.

Moses, raised at Pharaoh's court, together with his compatriots, resident in Egypt for hundreds of years and finally enslaved to form a captive labor force, had likewise broken off contact with the God of their fathers. The narrative hints at this by leaving God unmentioned until this scene. By now introducing himself to Moses as "the God of Abraham, the God of Isaac, and the God of Jacob," he invites the people—through Moses's intercession—to return or reconvert to the forgotten faith of their forefathers. This formulation not only emphasizes God's power and greatness but also stresses his continuing bond with Jacob's clan, a bond that has persisted through centuries of silence and suffering.

It is not Moses who has come back but God; he "turns around to grace," as the Egyptian phrase puts it. He fell silent over hundreds of years, disdaining to show himself to his ever-growing people during their Egyptian exile, in order to reveal himself all the more impressively now as their savior. Throughout their history, the Jewish people have repeatedly experienced periods of suffering when it seemed that God had turned his face from them and forgotten all about them:

> Awake, why sleepest thou, O Lord? Arise, cast us not off for ever.
> Wherefore hidest thou thy face, and forgettest our affliction and our oppression?
> For our soul [*nepeš*] is bowed down to the dust: our belly cleaveth unto the earth.
> Arise for our help, and redeem us for thy mercies' sake. (Ps 44:23–26)

In a situation of direst need such as that described by the Psalmist in relation to later events, the Exodus myth was recalled by the prophets before and after the downfall of the Northern Kingdom in 722 BCE, and the phases of its literary elaboration in the seventh and sixth centuries coincide with the subjection of the Southern Kingdom under Assyrian vassalage, the breakdown of that kingdom, too, and the deportation of its elites to Babylon, as well as the posttraumatic and postcolonial reworking of this past following the return to Israel. In such circumstances, the second book of Moses is a source of great solace, and the memory of the departure from Egypt is one that gives hope for salvation and a new beginning after even the worst disaster. Thus, the prophet Haggai remembers the departure from Egypt in 520 BCE in a bid to pressure the responsible parties into rebuilding the Temple:

Yet now be strong, O Zerubbabel, saith YHWH; and be strong, O Joshua, son of Josedech, the high priest; and be strong, all ye people of the land, saith YHWH, and work: for I am with you, saith YHWH of hosts.

According to the word that I covenanted with you when ye came out of Egypt, so my spirit remaineth among you: fear ye not. (2:4–5)

God Renews His Promise

And YHWH said, I have surely seen the affliction of my people which are in Egypt, and have heard their cry by reason of their taskmasters; for I know their sorrows;

And I am come down to deliver them out of the hand of the Egyptians, and to bring them up out of that land unto a good land and a large, unto a land flowing with milk and honey; unto the place of the Canaanites, and the Hittites, and the Amorites, and the Perizzites, and the Hivites, and the Jebusites.

Now therefore, behold, the cry of the children of Israel is come unto me: and I have also seen the oppression wherewith the Egyptians oppress them.

Come now therefore, and I will send thee unto Pharaoh, that thou mayest bring forth my people the children of Israel out of Egypt. (Ex 3:7–10)

YHWH renews his vow to Abraham that he will make him the father of a great people and give them the land of Canaan. On no fewer than six occasions, God promises Abraham that his seed will be without end and that he will enter into possession of a land occupied by others. In Genesis 12:2 and 13:15, he shows him that land and pledges to make him into a "great nation" that will be a blessing to all, and to make his "seed as the dust of the earth." In 15:5, it is foretold that his descendants will be as numerous as the stars in the sky; in 15:18, God draws the borders of the Promised Land "from the river of Egypt unto the great river, the river Euphrates"; in verses 19–20, he lists all the nations who dwell there: Kenites, Kenizzites, Kadmonites, Hittites, Perizzites, Rephaims, Amorites, Canaanites, Girgashites, and Jebusites. In 16:10, it is said that Abraham's descendants will "multiply" to such an extent that they can no longer be counted, and in 17:6, God promises to make Abraham "exceeding fruitful" ("fruitful" and "multiply" are already keywords in Gen 1:22 and 9:7). In 17:8, the land is promised to him in "everlasting possession." In 22:17, having tested his loyalty with the narrowly averted sacrifice of Isaac, God once again confirms that he will "bless" Abraham: "and in multiplying I will multiply thy seed as the stars of the heaven, and as the sand which is upon the sea shore," and his seed will be a blessing to all nations. This pledge of land, fruitfulness, and blessing is subsequently repeated to Isaac (26:3–4) and Jacob (28:13–14, in the dream of the ladder to heaven, and 35:9–15; see also 48:4).

That is the great promise God now renews before Moses. The promise of proliferation has already been fulfilled: Jacob's family had moved into Egypt with just seventy people (Gen 46:27), but by the time the Israelites set out on their exodus they are able to muster some 600,000 able-bodied men—perhaps three million souls in total. From now on, only the gift of land is still outstanding.[7] In Exodus 6:2–8, YHWH mentions the covenant and the pledge of land, renewing both for the Israelites. The nations living there are catalogued in the six passages containing this pledge (Ex 3:8; 3:17; 13:5; 23:26; 33:2; 34:24) and God vows that they will be "cast out" in the three passages following the covenant. The characterization of Canaan as a land "flowing with milk and honey" does not appear in the Book of Genesis, however. This turn of phrase is typically Deuteronomic and crops up in the parts of the Bible reflecting Deuteronomic influence. But it would also be out of place in the Book of Genesis, which is set in Canaan, after all. Abraham has no need to be told what kind of a country he is living in, or to have its praises sung to him. The other books of the Pentateuch take place outside of this country: in Egypt, in the desert and in Moab, where Canaan must constantly be brought to mind as the ultimate goal of a nation still hankering after the "fleshpots of Egypt." In connection with the rebellion led by Korah, Dathan and Abiram even praise Egypt as a "land flowing with milk and honey" (Num 16:13). What milk and honey have in common is that they cannot be acquired by toiling in the field, a cursed occupation ever since Genesis 3:17–19. They are associated with the fairytale idyll of a life of ease and plenty.

In the ancient Egyptian *Tale of Sinuhe*, which dates from the early second millennium BCE, the emigrant praises a region in Canaan called Yaa as a fabulously bountiful, paradisiacal land:

It was a good land, named Yaa. Figs were in it and grapes. It had more wine than water. Plentiful was its honey, abundant were its olives. Every kind of fruit was on its trees. Barley was there and emmer. There was no limit to any kind of cattle.[8]

"Figs and grapes" are in Egyptian literature what "milk and honey" are in Hebrew literature, at least in the Deuteronomic tradition. "I found figs and grapes there," begins the description of the paradisiacal "isle of Ka" where the shipwrecked sailor washes up in an Egyptian tale from the same period as *Sinuhe*.[9] Honey is also explicitly mentioned in the *Sinuhe* story, with the milk being replaced by the many kinds of cattle to be found there. To be sure, for an Egyptian the land of Yaa would not be a paradise without a plentiful supply of "barley and emmer."

This text, a masterpiece of ancient Egyptian literature, emerged over a thousand years before there was any written tradition in Israel. According to the biblical chronology, Sinuhe would have been an older contemporary of Abraham. But we must always bear in mind that this chronology is a product of the Priestly Source, which sought to arrange the various myths, sagas, novellas, and tales then circulating in Israel into a coherent narrative and chronological sequence. These undated texts were pressed into a more or less artificial time frame. In Egypt itself, the *Sinuhe* novel became a classic that had a fixed place in the curriculum for training scribes. Even Udjahorresnet, a contemporary of the priestly authors in the early Persian period, was still quoting from the text. As late as the time of the Priestly Source, the image of Canaan as a land of plenty was thus still current in educated Egyptian circles.

Tales of an earthly paradise can be found in other cultures, such as the land of Dilmun imagined by the Babylonians or the "island of Ka" in the aforementioned Egyptian *Tale of the Shipwrecked Sailor*. Yet these are not narratives of a promise made and then kept. At best, we could think of Elysium, the isle of the blessed in the Orphic mysteries and its presumed model, the Egyptian "Field of Reeds." The Egyptian dead set out on a journey to the afterlife that first leads them into the hall of judgment. If they emerge from the court "justified," as "transfig-

ured spirits," they pass into a region of ripe cornfields and fertile pasturelands, placid lakes and streams teeming with fish. There, they must
undergo interrogation to prove that they are indeed transfigured spirits, not mortals. This blissful place is also described as a shore. It is said
that anyone who catches a glimpse of it will become immortal, and
anyone who settles there will become a god. Most importantly, a tree
stands there offering eternal provisions and refreshment for anyone
who finds shelter in its shade.[10] Strikingly similar motifs can be found
in the gold tablets taken into the grave by those initiated into the Orphic or Bacchic mysteries.[11]

All this has nothing to do with the biblical Promised Land, however.
Canaan lies in the here and now, not in the hereafter; it is a specific lo-
cale, a place that can be visited and settled in, a country much like any
other. Above all, in the Egyptian and Greek myths, the individual can
enter into Elysium only postmortem and under particular conditions;
in the Bible, an entire nation emigrates there en masse and during its
lifetime. The sole common denominator is the motif of promise.

Promise is the crucial keyword. It implies a reorientation of mythical time from the past—"in illo tempore"—to the future. A myth of origin turns into a myth of salvation. Other cultures tell stories about divine history and human history. Sacral history is history that God has
or makes in partnership with human beings, and that is an exclusively
biblical idea, one that first comes into the world with the Hebrew
Bible.[12] Sacral history, *historia sacra*, is a project that God has entered
into with the human race, a completely novel idea that begins right
here. Everything leading up to this point was but prelude and promise.
Only once the children of Israel have swelled into a proper nation has
the time come for God to embark with them upon the project of *historia sacra*.

Excursus I: The Burning Bush in
Schoenberg's Opera *Moses und Aron*

No other artist has interpreted and refashioned the burning bush scene
more magnificently than Arnold Schoenberg in his opera *Moses und
Aron* (1932).[13] The opera was planned for three acts, although Schoenberg completed only the first two.

FIGURE 7. *The Burning Bush.* Gouache by Marc Chagall, 1966.

Before the curtain has even gone up, six solo voices sing four chords
suggesting God's presence, becoming audible yet still unarticulated in
words. Moses responds with the cry:

Unique, eternal, omnipresent,
imperceptible and unimaginable God!

Of the five divine predicates named by Moses, the last—"unimaginable"—is drawn out: this word is more important than the rest, and
it is also the one with which Schoenberg distances himself at the outset
from the Mosaic God of the Torah. "Unique" is the central divine predicate in the Torah (the Pentateuch), foregrounded both in the first commandment and in the prayer "Hear, O Israel": "YHWH, our God,
YHWH is one." God is praised as "eternal" in Psalm 90, for example, a
psalm traditionally ascribed to Moses: "Before the mountains were
brought forth, or ever thou hadst formed the earth and the world, even
from everlasting to everlasting, thou art God." God's omnipresence is
the theme of Psalm 139: "If I ascend up into heaven, thou art there: if I
make my bed in hell, behold, thou are there." God's invisibility is emphasized in Deuteronomy 4:15: "you saw no form [kol-těmûnâ] of any
kind on the day that YHWH spake unto you in Horeb out of the midst
of the fire." While these four divine predicates are thus attested in the
Bible, the fifth—unimaginability—goes beyond the biblical God. In
this regard, Schoenberg's Moses reveals himself to be a philosopher,
not a prophet and leader. While the idea that God cannot be imagined
may be conceivable, it is not one that can easily be "proclaimed."

This makes it all the more surprising that, in Schoenberg's restaging,
God calls out from the burning bush to Moses. For does not a God who
speaks contradict the idea of a God who cannot be imagined? How can
I hear a voice without imagining a body to which that voice belongs?
Schoenberg solves the problem in a way that frustrates any attempt to
imagine such a physical support. God's voice is realized by six voices:
soprano, treble, alto, tenor, baritone, bass, all multiply cast, in addition
to the six solo voices from before. "Now proclaim!" the voice says to
Moses. Moses thanks God for reviving the "thought" of his fathers in
him and implores him: "Do not compel me to proclaim it!" "My tongue
is slow," Moses objects, citing Exodus 4:10, and continues: "I can think
but not speak." Those last words are to be found nowhere in the Bible.

Schoenberg's Moses is a philosopher, untroubled by speech defects, who would concur with Wittgenstein that whereof one cannot speak, thereof one must be silent. He would rather graze his flocks in peace and not have to talk about God. His place is in the desert, his passion is thought, his medium silence.

God goes about solving the problem by splitting the task between the two brothers. He places the smooth-talking Aron[14] by the side of the deep-thinking Moses. Language becomes problematic as a medium of communication, not of expression. That is also what Wittgenstein had in mind. "Whereof one cannot speak" refers to dialogue with others, the universe of possible discourses. Moses could very well have articulated his thoughts in words, but no one would have understood them. Aron's remit is communication, not articulation. His task is to clothe Moses's abstract ideas in comprehensible words, that is, in figurative language.

The division of labor between Moses and Aaron in the Book of Exodus is telling: one is able to speak with God, the other with the people. Evidently, it is not possible to do both at once. God makes use of Moses; Moses makes use of Aaron as a mouthpiece. In the dialogue between God and Moses, God's plans assume spoken form (articulation); in the dialogue between Aaron and the people, they are disseminated and accepted (communication). Moses's "heavy tongue" symbolizes the difficulty faced by the prophet in making himself understood by the people. The prophet is a messenger tasked by God with delivering an incommunicable message. Schoenberg translates the contrast between Moses's pensive silence and Aaron's overflowing, richly metaphorical eloquence into the contrast between speaking and singing. For Moses, the score calls for a speaker with a "deep, very big voice." The pitch differences indicated in the notation are only meant to characterize his declamation. Aron, on the other hand, is a lyric tenor with an expressive bel canto.

The exchange between Moses and Aron in the opera's second scene reveals the sheer audacity of this conception. What the fervently pious Aron captures in words here and holds against Moses is precisely what was taught and proclaimed by the biblical Moses. Aron speaks enthusiastically of "grace," "love," and "faith," Moses of "knowledge," "cognition," and "thought." Grace is called *gratia* in Latin and the music accompanying Aron's entrance is marked "grazioso." Aron embodies grace and graciousness, whereas Moses stands for intellect and the law. According to a Christian view that goes back to Augustine, "law" and "grace" designate the opposition between Judaism and Christianity. From Moses on, Israel lives *sub lege*, "under the law"; from Christ on, *sub gratia*, "under grace." Are Judaism and Christianity opposed in this way in Schoenberg's Moses and Aron? No, for Aron goes on to speak of God's justice in the words of the Jewish, Old Testament Moses: "Thou punishest the sins of the father on his children and children's children! Thou rewardest those who are faithful to thy commandments! Thou hearst the cries of the poor and acceptest the offerings of the good!" Moses decisively rejects such reasoning. "Are we able to bring something about that forces thee to an outcome?" No: "Inexorable law of thought compels to fulfillment."

Whereas Schoenberg's Aron is the biblical Moses, Schoenberg's Moses is a character completely alien to the Bible, one that has its roots in Greek thought, in the religious critique of Xenophanes, the negative theology of the Areopagite, the searching rationality of Maimonides, the heretical theology of the Early Modern period and in Modernist iconoclasm. It is Aron who speaks of love of God, of God's justice, punishment and reward, grace and mercy, of the Promised Land flowing with milk and honey; it is Aron who performs the miracles ascribed to Moses or God in the Bible: the staff transformed into a snake, the hand afflicted by leprosy and then restored, the transformation of water into blood, the water struck from the rock, even the pillar of cloud by day and the pillar of fire by night to guide the people on their way—in Schoenberg's opera, these are all Aron's doing. In the eyes of Schoenberg's Moses, they are false images one and all, flashy showpieces that fall short of the "idea" of true monotheism and thus betray it.

There can be no doubt that none other than the biblical Moses stands behind Schoenberg's Aron, at least in the opera's first act. What is more, the biblical God stands behind Aron as well. When Moses capitulates before the resistance of his people, it is the voice of God— the six solo voices, that is—that calls "Aron!" and draws attention to his miracles with "Behold!" Though Aron's words and deeds may prove fundamentally inadequate to his brother's sublime idea of God, it is indisputably the biblical God that speaks and acts through Aron. The border that Schoenberg draws between Moses and Aron places the biblical God on Aron's side. With that, the entire Torah is denounced as a false, idolatrous image, and the biblical God falls victim to his own ban on graven images.

In Schoenberg's opera, Moses and Aron are radically, irreconcilably opposed. The opposition is that between truth and falsehood, true religion and idol worship—the same opposition that, according to the Enlightenment view, comes into the world with the revelation on Sinai. With that, a border is drawn and people are called on to take a stand on one side or the other. Schoenberg draws this border in a completely new sense by opposing not Israel and Egypt but Moses and Aron. In doing so, he imports the distinction into the midst of biblical monotheism itself, which is founded on the alliance between Moses and Aaron. There, the brothers work together harmoniously—with the single exception of the scene with the Golden Calf.

I Am That I Am

And Moses said unto God, Behold, when I come unto the children of Israel, and shall say unto them, The God of your fathers hath sent me unto you; and they shall say to me, What is his name? what shall I say unto them?

And God said unto Moses, I AM THAT I AM [*'ehyeh 'ăšer 'ehyeh*]: and he said, Thus shalt thou say unto the children of Israel, I AM hath sent me unto you.

<And God said moreover unto Moses, Thus shalt thou say unto the children of Israel, YHWH, the God of your fathers, the God of Abraham, the God of Isaac, and the God of Jacob, hath sent me unto you.>[15] This is my name for ever, and this is my memorial unto all generations. (Ex 3:13–15)

The name God reveals to Moses plays on the multiple allusions of the word YHWH. The form *'ehyeh*, from *hāyâ* ("to be"), means "I am" or "I will be there." However, the name YHWH contains a "w" that refers back to the verb *hāwâ*, "to blow." Perhaps the name recalls a primordial wind or weather god, like Hada and Baʿal. In any event, *'ehyeh* is not a divine name but the first-person singular imperfect of the verb *hāyâ*, "to be." This "to be" denotes a supportive being-there or being-with.[16] That the name *'ehyeh* is meant to be read in this way emerges clearly enough from the context, since from this point on God is constantly making his presence felt in both word and deed as he watches over the fluctuating fortunes of his people.[17]

On the other hand, the formula "I am that I am" (or "I will be what I will be") is tautological: as an example of the rhetorical figure known as *idem per idem*, it explains nothing. Other examples from the Book of Exodus include "I will be gracious to whom I will be gracious, and will show mercy on whom I will show mercy" (33:19) and "bake that which ye will bake, and boil that ye will boil" (16:23). From this perspective, a name is being withheld here rather than shared. By declaring "I am that I am," God leaves the question of his name unresolved. "I AM hath sent me unto you" sounds a little like the positively worded counterpart to the "no-one" with which Odysseus introduces himself to Polyphemus, leading the blinded cyclops to lament, "No-one has wounded me"—a cry that ensures no-one comes to his aid.

In *De docta ignorantia*, Nicolaus of Cusa takes the name *'ehyeh* to mean "I have no name and have no need of one, since I am all-encompassing." To bolster this claim, he refers —surprisingly enough— to Hermes Trismegistus, the Egyptian sage held to have written the *Corpus Hermeticum*, a Greek-language anthology of Platonizing treatises erroneously believed to date back to the very earliest times:

> It is obvious that no name can be appropriate to the Greatest one, because nothing can be distinguished from him. All names are imposed by distinguishing one thing from the other. Where all is one, there cannot be a proper name. Therefore, Hermes Trismegistus is right in saying, "because God is the totality of all things [*universitas rerum*], he has no proper name, otherwise he should be called by every name or everything should bear his name." For he comprises in his simplicity the totality of all things.[18]

According to Hermes Trismegistus, divine names can be found only in polytheism, where they serve to distinguish one god from another. Where there is only one God and where that God is identical with all that exists, and thus utterly indistinct from the universe, there is no need for names. Hermes Trismegistus, says Nicolaus, taught that God has no name because there is nothing that could set apart the divine being from anything else that exists. While the *Corpus Hermeticum* be-

came known in the West only later, Nicolaus had read the corresponding passage from Lactantius, the late-third- and early-fourth-century
Christian author, who likewise drew parallels between primal Egyptian wisdom and God's self-identification before Moses:

> He [Trismegistus] wrote books and those in great number, relating to the
> knowledge of divine things, in which he asserts the majesty of the supreme
> and only God, and makes mention of him by the same names which we
> use—God and Father. And that no one might inquire His name, he said that
> He was without name, and that on account of His very unity He does not
> require the peculiarity of a name. These are his own words: "God is one,
> but He who is one only does not need a name; for He who is self-existent is
> without a name." God, therefore, has no name, because He is alone; nor is
> there any need of a proper name, except in cases where a multitude of
> persons requires a distinguishing mark, so that you may designate each
> person by his own mark and appellation. But God, because He is always
> one, has no peculiar name.[19]

The passage quoted here by Lactantius comes from §20 of the treatise
Asclepius or *teleios logos*, originally written in Greek and handed down
in Latin translation. In a more modern translation, it reads: "The Creator has no name, or rather he has all names, since he is at once One
and All, so that one must either designate all things by his name, or give
him the name of all things."[20] This amounts to proclaiming that God is
one-and-all.

Nevertheless, *ho ōn anonymos* does not mean "the nameless one"
but rather "the one who exists and has no name." The stress falls on
existence, not anonymity. God is the quintessence of all that is, having
no need for a name because there is nothing distinct from him. That is
how Exodus 3:14 was already understood in the Septaguint: *egō eimi ho
ōn*, "I am the one who is." The Greek translation of the Hebrew Bible
thus establishes a connection to the philosophers' god, placing the
scene at the burning bush in the light of Platonic philosophy and
thereby turning it into a primal scene of divine revelation and philosophical knowledge. In his "Mémorial," Pascal cited verse 6, where
God presents himself as the God of the Fathers, and he played off this
God against the god of the philosophers. Those who read the Bible
though a Platonic lens, by contrast, could draw on verse 14 to equate

YHWH with eternal being. This is the God referred to by John in Revelation 1:4: "Grace be unto you, and peace, from him which is, and which was, and which is to come."

From here, there is but a step to the famous inscription on the "veiled image at Sais": "I am all that is, was, and shall be. No mortal has ever lifted my veil." Plutarch mentions this inscription in the ninth chapter of his treatise *On Isis and Osiris*. At Sais, he writes, "the seated statue of Athena, whom they consider to be Isis, also bore the following inscription: 'I am all that has been and is and shall be; and no mortal has ever lifted my mantle [*peplos*].' "[21] However immense the difference may appear to us today between Isis, who says "I am all that has been . . . ," and YHWH, who proclaims, "I am that I am," in the late-eighteenth-century intellectual climate of pantheism they seemed practically indistinguishable, just as Lactantius and Nicolaus of Cusa saw no difference at all between YHWH and the *deus anonymus* of the *Corpus Hermeticum*. "*Hen kai Pan*," "One and All!," Lessing is reported to have exclaimed, so nailing his colors to the mast of Spinozism and creating a sensation in German intellectual circles. Some greeted the revelation with enthusiasm; others reacted with outrage. Among the former was Friedrich Schiller. In his essay "The Legation of Moses" (1790), he traced Moses's idea of God back to the Isis of the Egyptian mysteries. He was following in the footsteps of his friend and colleague in Jena, Carl Leonhard Reinhold, who in his Masonic text *The Hebrew Mysteries, or, The Oldest Religious Freemasonry* (1787), had posited their equivalence:

> Brethren! Who among us does not know the ancient Egyptian inscriptions: the one on the pyramid at Sais: "I am all that is, was, and shall be, and no mortal has ever lifted my veil," and that other on the statue of Isis: "I am all that is?" Who among us does not understand the meaning of these words, as well as in those days of the Egyptian initiate, and who does not know that they express the essential Being, the meaning of the name Jehovah?[22]

For Reinhold, as for Lactantius and Nicolaus of Cusa before him, the statement "I am that I am"—taken to mean "I am the essential Being"—does not so much offer a name as withhold one. It proclaims an essentially nameless God, a *deus anonymus*, in whom he glimpses the deity of the Egyptian mysteries. If Moses grew up as a prince at Pharaoh's court, then he naturally would have been initiated into the mysteries of Isis. In Reinhold's account, Isis is the nameless god of the *Corpus Hermeticum*, the one-and-all. In her inscription at Sais, she reveals herself not with the words "I am Isis" but with "I am all," and her all-encompassing oneness explains both her anonymity and her hiddenness. Nothing less is implied by the "veil" that "no mortal has ever lifted."

Reinhold's text was written for his lodge brothers and would have remained unread—indeed, to this day it is very much a bibliographical rarity—had he not shared it with his friend Schiller, who immediately set about working it into "The Legation of Moses." This essay publicized Reinhold's theses far beyond the boundaries of Freemasonry.[23] Schiller offered no new arguments, instead preferring to draw out whatever struck him as particularly important in Reinhold's presentation of the case. Two ideas stood out, in particular: on the one hand, the idea of nature as the sublime deity of the mysteries: abstract, spiritual, anonymous, invisible, and lying almost beyond the reach of human reason—in Kant's words, the most sublime thought ever expressed:

> One has perhaps never said anything more sublime or expressed a thought in more sublime fashion than in the inscription of the temple of Isis (Mother Nature): "I am all that is, that was, and that will be, and no mortal has lifted my veil."[24]

On the other hand, Schiller was impressed by the idea of the "Mosaic compromise": Moses had had to distort and reduce the sublime idea of the divine celebrated in the Egyptian mysteries in order for it to become the engine of Israelite ethnogenesis, the basis for a political constitution and the object of a public religion. On this view, Moses was able to salvage the idea of God's oneness, but at considerable cost. In place of the supreme, nameless deity of the mysteries, Moses substituted the national god YHWH; the mystical vision of Nature was replaced by blind faith, compelled by miracles; and rational insight made way for an equally blind, violently enforced obedience. Reinhold had already said all this, but Schiller expressed the same ideas far more pithily and pointedly.

The idea of a nameless, all-encompassing divinity that Schiller—following in Reinhold's footsteps—found in the phrase "I am that I am"

represents, in his view, the epitome of the "sublime." In the eighteenth
century, an experience was described as sublime if it surpassed ordinary human understanding to elicit fear, trembling, and speechless-
ness. The sublime is unutterable, unnameable, unfathomable; it transcends whatever words and concepts we seek to pin it down with. The
idea of placing the deity of the Egyptian mysteries and the biblical
YHWH in the light of the "sublime" was Schiller's singular contribution to this debate. It was, it must be acknowledged, a stroke of genius.
It enabled him to find the most precise possible common denominator
for the anonymity of the hermetic God and the aniconic grandeur of
his biblical counterpart. "Nothing is more sublime than the simple
grandeur with which the sages spoke of the creator. In order to distinguish him in a truly defining form, they refrained from giving him a
name at all"[25]—so reads Schiller's paraphrase of the teaching of Hermes
Trismegistus, which in his eyes (and in Reinhold's, too) has the same
meaning as the revelation of the name in Exodus 3:14. The sheer audacity of this interpretation is breathtaking. The God of the Hebrew
Bible—or, more precisely: covenant theology—would accordingly be
a fiction, aimed at tailoring an ineffably sublime, philosophical, and
abstract idea of the divine to the limited understanding of mere
mortals.

The scene at the burning bush where the name YHWH is revealed to
Moses has had an influence as wide-ranging and far-reaching as any in
the Book of Exodus. The fact that this was the divine name associated
with the philosophers' god—God as (absolute) Being, beyond and
above all individual beings—runs strictly counter to the spirit of the
story, however, and poses a puzzling paradox. For with the name
YHWH, God reveals himself unambiguously in his loving concern to
free, reward, and punish his people, quite unlike the transcendent de-
tachment from worldly affairs, impersonality, and hiddenness that
typify the philosophers' god. The play on *hāyâ*, "to be," emphasizes
God's being-there for his people as the chosen object of his solicitude.

Isis is eternal presence, and in this respect the opposite of a god
who is not simply there but will manifest his presence whenever and
wherever he so chooses. When the Septuagint renders the Hebrew
'ehyeh 'ăšer 'ehyeh as *egō eimi ho ōn*, "I am the one who is," it negates
the future-oriented volition that speaks through this divine self-

introduction. In so doing, it directly translates the God of the Fathers into the philosophers' god. Yet the God of the biblical monotheism of loyalty heralded in the Book of Exodus stands under the sign of becoming, not being, at least as he reveals himself in the history-making interventions into human affairs that form the proper subject of the Bible. This God is not simply one among the world-preserving gods who has risen above his peers by proving himself greater and mightier than the rest; he is a wholly different, utterly new god, a god who transforms the circular time characteristic of a belief system geared toward maintaining the universe on its customary course into the forward-facing time of futurity.

What takes place here is a radical reshaping of cultural memory, a total reorientation in the dimension of time. This reorientation affects not just the future, now envisaged as the horizon for the fulfillment of God's promises of salvation, but also the past, which can only now be narrated in all its breadth. The ancient Near Eastern kingdoms, Egypt and Mesopotamia, kept king lists with reign dates that made it possible to plumb the past to fabulous depths. For them, however, this past could never have been told as a story. The past can be narrated only once it has acquired significance for the self-understanding or identity of the group that is doing the narrating. History, wrote Johan Huizinga, is the intellectual form in which a country takes account of its past. There is nothing self-evident about this. The king list is not a document for taking account of the past but an instrument of chronology, a calendar. For a society to take an interest in accounting for its past, it has to grasp the past as "its own," making it an integral part of how it sees itself. It must, as Claude Lévi-Strauss maintained, internalize the past for it to become the engine of its future development. Only the time saturated with God's living presence, the *historia sacra*, is a time that can be narrated as extensively as it is in the Bible.

CHAPTER SIX

SIGNS AND WONDERS

God Reveals His Power

I have broken the bands of your yoke, and made you go upright.

—*Leviticus 26:13*

Let my people go.

—*Spiritual*

Remember what YHWH thy God did unto Pharaoh, and unto
all Egypt; the great temptations which thine eyes saw, and the
wonders, and the mighty hand, and the stretched out arm,
whereby YHWH thy God brought thee out: so shall YHWH
thy God do unto all the people of whom thou art afraid.

—*Deuteronomy 7:18–19*

The Plagues of Egypt

God reveals his power in three stages: in the plagues visited on Pharaoh and his people, in the institution of the Passover feast to commemorate God's saving grace, and in the miracle of the Sea of Reeds,
which shows the meaning of this intervention to be the "redemption"
of God's chosen people. With that, the Exodus story created an idea of
revelation that was later to be adopted by Christianity. God steps out
of his backstage obscurity and onto the floodlit stage of history, not
that he might unveil the full extent of his power, but in order to save his
people. In this chapter, the three stages in the second act of the Exodus
revelation will be examined more closely and linked to how they have
been preserved in Jewish and Christian cultural memory. The plagues
of Egypt still stir the imagination, and the search for the possible causes
and traces of these ecological disasters shows no sign of abating. The

ritual commemorating the night of departure, the Seder, remains one of the most important festivals in the Jewish calendar. As for the sea miracle, God's decisive act of salvation, I will be casting a glance at George Frideric Handel's great oratorio, *Israel in Egypt*, which celebrates the Exodus from a perspective that is at once Protestant and probably also quite personal.

In the account given in the Priestly Source, the plagues are the result of a magic duel fought in Pharaoh's presence between the two brothers and the Egyptian "wise men and sorcerers." God had planned it this way:

> When Pharaoh shall speak unto you, saying, Shew a miracle for you: then thou shalt say unto Aaron, Take thy rod, and cast it before Pharaoh, and it shall become a serpent [*tannîn*]. (Ex 7:9)

So it comes to pass. Pharaoh reacts by summoning his "wise men and sorcerers," the "Egyptian *ḥartummîm*," who are masters in the magic arts.[1] Who are these *ḥartummîm*? The term has been identified as a rendering into Hebrew of the Egyptian honorific *ḥrj-tp* (*p-hritob* in Demotic; *ḥar-tibi* in Akkadian); *ḥrj-tp* actually means "chief" and is the abbreviated form of the title "chief lector priest" (just as "chef" is short for *chef de cuisine*).[2] These *ḥartummîm* reappear as interpreters of dreams and omens in two other very prominent passages in the Bible, the tale of Joseph and the Book of Daniel. In both cases, they are shown up as abject failures by their Hebrew rivals. Joseph divines that Pharaoh's dream foretells seven years of plenty followed by seven years of famine, while Daniel successfully interprets King Nebuchadnezzar's dream about the four successive kingdoms. He is also able to read the writing that appears on the wall during Belshazzar's famous feast.

Thanks to their proficiency in the magic arts, the *ḥartummîm* are able to match the brothers' feat and transform their staffs into snakes. Yet Aaron's staff swallows up the rest, costing them this opening round in the duel. Pharaoh, whose heart has been hardened by God, remains obdurate. God therefore commands Moses and Aaron to perform their next trick on the following day, when Pharaoh goes out to the river: the transformation of water into blood. Moses is to repeat his demand that Pharaoh free his people and then, if he refuses, announce the plague:

FIGURE 8. Musa (Moses) turns Aaron's rod into a dragon. Persian miniature, Herat, 1415–1416.

> YHWH, God of the Hebrews, hath sent me unto thee, saying, Let my people go, that they may serve me in the wilderness: and, behold, hitherto thou wouldest not hear. Thus saith YHWH: In this thou shalt know that I am YHWH: behold, I will smite with the rod that is in mine hand upon the waters which are in the river, and they shall be turned to blood. And the fish that is in the river shall die, and the river shall stink; and the Egyptians shall lothe to drink of the water of the river. (Ex 7:16–18)

On this environmentally catastrophic scale, the brothers' display of magic becomes the first plague. Yet here, too, the Egyptian *ḥartummîm* can give as good as they get: "And the magicians of Egypt did [the same] with their enchantments." Still, they are powerless to transform the blood back into water and so ward off the plague. Even though this unbearable situation drags on for seven days, "Pharaoh's heart was hardened, neither did he hearken unto them; as YHWH had said"

FIGURE 9. Moses and Aaron (right) compete with the Egyptian sorcerers (wreathed, in white togas). While Pharaoh (seated) gestures toward his sorcerers, Moses and Aaron point upward to God's power. On the left, a wreathed servant bears a standard. Perched on top is an ibis, the sacred animal of Thoth, god of magic. Nicolas Poussin, 1654.

(7:22). God therefore resorts to a new, darkly comic plague that shares with the first the motif of disgust:

> And YHWH spake unto Moses, Go unto Pharaoh, and say unto him, Thus saith YHWH, Let my people go, that they may serve me. And if thou refuse to let them go, behold, I will smite all thy borders with frogs: And the river shall bring forth frogs abundantly, which shall go up and come into thine house, and into thy bed-chamber, and upon thy bed, and into the house of thus servants, and upon thus people, and into thine ovens, and into thy kneadingtroughs: And the frogs shall come up both on thee, and upon thy people, and upon all thy servants. (8:1–4)

So it comes to pass. Yet even here, astonishingly, the *ḥartummîm* can still hold their own: "And the magicians did so with their enchantments, and brought up frogs upon the land of Egypt." For the first time, though, Pharaoh appears to relent, saying: "Intreat YHWH, that he may take away the frogs from me, and from my people; and I will let the people go, that they may do sacrifice unto YHWH" (8:8). As soon as God calls off the plague at Moses's intercession, however, Pharaoh again hardens his heart and reneges on the deal. A third round is therefore required. Aaron is told to "smite the dust of the land" with his staff, "that it may become lice throughout all the land of Egypt." And that is what happens: "all the dust of the land became lice throughout all the land of Egypt" (8:16–17).

The *ḥartummîm* seek to emulate this magic trick, too. This time, though, they are forced to concede defeat: "Then the magicians said unto Pharaoh, This is the finger of God" (8:19). The *ḥartummîm*—and this testifies to their wisdom—are the first to notice that a higher power is at work here.[3] What began as a contest of thaumaturgical prowess thus turns into an event that looks like divine punishment to the Egyptians while being interpreted by the Israelites as "signs and wonders" or "God's saving deeds."

There is scholarly agreement that the earliest pre-Priestly version of the plagues sequence, following the miracle attesting to the brothers' credentials (staffs into snakes) and before the decisive strike (death of the firstborn), was restricted to three plagues: water into blood, frogs, and lice. These three plagues correlate to the three elements of water, earth, and air; they thus form a meaningful whole. The Priestly Source expands the plagues into a series of five by adding wild animals and festering boils while setting them in the Egyptian framework of a magic competition.[4] The contest has a climactic structure:

0	Staffs into snakes	*ḥartummîm* hold their own
1	Water into blood	*ḥartummîm* hold their own
2	Frogs	*ḥartummîm* hold their own
3	Dust into lice	*ḥartummîm* are defeated and recognize the "finger of God"
4	Festering boils	*ḥartummîm* are themselves infected and can no longer even compete

The magic duel is a well-documented motif in Egyptian literature. The best-known example is the story of the contest between an Egyptian and a Nubian sorcerer in the second Setne tale.[5] "Setne Khamwas" is the hero of a cycle of stories, several of which have been preserved on two Demotic papyri dating from Ptolemaic and Roman times (Setne I and Setne II, respectively).[6] Behind him stands Khaemweset, son of Ramesses II and high priest of Memphis, who became renowned for taking in hand the restoration of numerous historic monuments. In Setne II, the Nubian magician turns up at the Egyptian court with a papyrus roll and challenges anyone to read the document he is carrying without breaking the seal. Setne Khamwas brings along his young son Siosiris, who accepts the challenge and successfully recites the contents of the sealed document. It tells of a magic contest that took place fifteen hundred years earlier. Three Nubian sorcerers appear before the Nubian king, each claiming that he is capable of visiting a plague on Egypt. The first can shroud Egypt in darkness for three days. The second can spirit Pharaoh to Nubia overnight, have him publicly flogged with five hundred stripes, and then whisk him back to Egypt within six hours. The third can visit three years of famine on Egypt. When the second is awarded the royal contract, he fashions a litter and four litter-bearers out of wax, animates them, and gives them their orders. Everything runs according to plan: they bring Pharaoh to Nubia in the dead of night, give him five hundred lashes under the king's eyes, and return him to his bedchamber, all in six hours. The maltreated pharaoh summons his magicians to plot his revenge, and one of them succeeds in putting the Nubian king through the same ordeal. This magician outmatches his opponent and the Nubian is forced to surrender. So much for the document. Siosiris then unmasks the Nubian as the revenant of the sorcerer from fifteen hundred years ago, at the same time revealing himself to be the reborn Egyptian magician. He conjures up a fire that consumes his Nubian competitor. The similarity of the afflictions intended for Egypt by the other sorcerers—three days of darkness, three years of famine—with the biblical plagues is startling, as is the similarity of the animated wax figures with the animated staffs.

Sorcery with wax figures is also cited in the trial documents relating to the harem conspiracy against Ramesses III and in many magical texts. The best-known example is the tale of the supreme lector priest Ubaoner in the magician stories found in the Westcar Papyrus, which I mentioned in an earlier chapter. When Ubaoner finds out that his wife has been receiving a lover in his absence, he creates a wax crocodile and casts a spell on it so that it will attack and devour her paramour as he takes his regular bath in the garden lake. He orders his caretaker to cast the figurine into the water at the right moment, where it immediately becomes a real, living crocodile and drags its victim into the depths. As soon as Ubaoner touches it, it turns back into a wax figurine.[7] The Priestly narrative of the magical duel evidently draws on legends associated at the time with the image of Egypt in the world.

In the post-Priestly redaction, the plagues already included in the Priestly narrative are augmented by plagues six to nine (diseased livestock, thunderstorm of hail and fire, locusts, darkness), extending the series to ten. The plagues are reported at varying lengths and in different degrees of detail. The first, second, fourth, and ninth plagues are of medium length with 12, 15, 13, and 9 verses. The third, fifth, and sixth plagues are dispatched with briskly in 4, 7, and 5 verses, while plagues seven and eight are allotted more space with 23 and 20 verses, respectively. The tenth plague, taking up three whole chapters, is disproportionately lengthy. They are summed up in the table below.[8]

	Ex	Prior warning	Time	Instruction	Agent	Ps 78	Ps 105	Jub 48:5
1 Blood (dām)	7:20	Yes	Morning	Take thy rod	Aaron	V. 44 (1)	V. 29 (2)	(1)
2 Frogs (sĕpardĕ'îm)	8:1	Yes	-	Go unto Pharaoh	Aaron	45b (3)	30 (3)	(2)
3 Lice (kinnîm)	8:13	No	-		Aaron	45a (2)	31 (4)	(3)
4 Wild animals ('ārōb)	8:16	Yes	Morning	Stretch out thy rod	God	-	-	(4)
5 Diseased livestock (deber)	9:1	Yes	-	Go unto Pharaoh	God	-	-	(6)
6 Boils (šĕḥîn)	9:10	No	-		Moses	50 (6)	-	(5)

FIGURE 10. The ten Egyptian plagues from a Haggadah. Venice, 1609.

continued

	Ex	Prior warning	Time	Instruction	Agent	Ps 78	Ps 105	Jub 48:5
7 Hail (bārād)	9:22	Yes	Morning	Stretch forth thine hand	Moses	47–48 (5)	32 (5)	(7)
8 Locusts ('arbeh)	10:12	Yes	-	Go unto Pharaoh	Moses	46 (4)	34 (6)	(8)
9 Darkness (ḥōšek)	10:21	No			Moses	-	28 (1)	(9)
10 Firstborn (hikkâ kol-bĕkôr)	12:29	Yes	-	-	God	51 (7)	36 (7)	(10)

The three right-hand columns of the table set out the parallels in two psalms and the Book of Jubilees, where the Egyptian plagues are likewise enumerated. In the final stage of redaction, two plagues were duplicated in order to arrive at the number ten: 3 became 3 + 4, 6 became 5 + 6. Psalms 78 and 105, probably from the postexilic period, almost certainly reflect the original version in listing only seven plagues. The second-century BCE Book of Jubilees, by contrast, already contains the canonic ten and lists them in the same order as they appear in the final version, with the exception of 5 and 6, which have been swapped. The number of plagues is explicitly emphasized in this text:

> Ten great and terrible judgments came on the land of Egypt that thou mightest execute vengeance on it for Israel. And YHWH did everything for Israel's sake, and according to his covenant, which he had ordained with Abraham that he would take vengeance on them as they had brought them by force into bondage. (Jub 48:7–8)

In the compilation of rabbinical sayings known as Pirkei Avot, there is a section devoted to things belonging in groups of ten that also mentions the Egyptian plagues:

> Ten miracles were performed for our forefathers in Egypt and another ten at the sea. Ten afflictions were wrought by God upon the Egyptians in Egypt, and another ten at the sea. (5:4)

Here the plagues are differentiated in their significance: for the Israelites they were "miracles" whereas the Egyptians experienced them as "afflictions." The distinction made in the Book of Jubilees between "signs and wonders" (48:2) and "terrible judgments" (48:7) is to be understood in much the same way. So, too, God announces his impending liberation of the Israelites in Exodus 6:6 "with a stretched out arm, and with great judgments" (*šĕpāṭîm gĕdōlîm*).[9]

The number ten plays an important role in the Exodus myth, featuring on three very prominent occasions: the ten plagues, the ten commandments, and the ten rebellions against Moses (and Aaron), three of which are reported in Exodus and seven in Numbers (see chapter 9). In each case, the number ten has a mnemotechnical function, serving to consolidate the memory established by the Book of Exodus.

The miracle at the Sea of Reeds, which the Israelites cross without even getting their feet wet before the pursuing Egyptian forces are inundated by the returning waves, numbers among the "signs and wonders," if not among the plagues in the narrower sense. This miracle has exerted a particularly tenacious hold on the scientific imagination, and there has been no shortage of theories proposing a natural explanation for the parting of the sea. First of all, it is far from clear what the "Sea of Reeds" (*yam sûf*) actually refers to: is it an inland body of water bordering on the Mediterranean—here Lake Serbonis seems the most likely candidate—or the Red Sea? The account given in chapter 14 offers two versions of what happened, one better suited to the Red Sea, the other to Lake Serbonis. According to the first version, the sea is "divided" and the waters tower on either side of the passing Israelites like a wall ("and the waters were a wall unto them on their right hand, and on their left" [Ex 14:22] —one of the legendary special effects in Cecil B. DeMille's film, *The Ten Commandments*). This scene brings to mind the Red Sea, which is deep enough and is also affected by strong tides, making it at least conceivable that the Israelites could ford across at low tide and the Egyptians be caught out as the tide turned. According to the second version, a strong wind blows from the east throughout the night to dry out the sea, which then floods back over the Egyptians:

Dixir Dñs ad Moysen Cleva virgam tuam t extende manum tuam
super mare ε divide illud ut gradiantur filii)srahel in medio
mari per siccum

FIGURE 11. Moses parts the Red Sea with his staff. The text above the image quotes Exodus
14:16 in the Vulgate: "Stretch out your staff and raise your hand over the sea and divide it,
that the children of Israel may pass through on dry land." From the *Hortus deliciarum* of
Herrad of Landsberg, c. 1180.

> And Moses stretched out his hand over the sea; and YHWH caused the sea
> to go back by a strong east wind all that night, and made the sea dry land.
> (Ex 14:21)

This far more realistic variant could have been set at Lake Serbonis,
a flat and treacherous body of water near the Mediterranean coast that
in ancient times is said to have swallowed up entire armies.[10] Textual
criticism ascribes the more realistic version to a pre-Priestly source,
whereas the more miraculous version involving the parting of the sea
belongs to the Priestly Source.[11]

We find a parallel for the juxtaposition of a soberly realistic and a
miraculously poetic version of the same event in the Egyptian transmission of the Battle of Kadesh in 1274 BCE. Three versions were
handed down: (1) a "poem"; (2) a "bulletin"; and (3) wall reliefs with
lengthy explanatory captions.

FIGURE 12. *Moses Crossing the Red Sea*. Fresco by Raphael in the Vatican Loggia, 1515–1518.

Ramesses II and his army had been caught in an ambush. According to the "Poem of Pentaur," a poetic account of the battle, the king sent up a hurried prayer to Amun when he found himself surrounded by enemies and cut off from escape:

> What is this, father Amun?
> Is it right for a father to ignore his son?
> Are my deeds a matter for you to ignore?
> Do I not walk and stand at your word?
> I have not neglected an order you gave.
> Too great is he, the great lord of Egypt,
> To allow aliens to step on his path!
> What are these Asiatics to you, oh Amun,
> The wretches ignorant of god?
> Have I not made for you many great monuments,
> Filled your temple with my booty,
> Built for you my mansion of Millions-of-Years,

Given you all my wealth as endowment?
[...]
Do good to him who counts on you,
Then one will serve you with loving heart.
I call to you, my father Amun,
I am among a host of strangers;
All countries are arrayed against me,
I am alone, there's none with me![12]

When he is eventually rescued, he gives thanks by repeatedly using the verb "to find":

I found that Amun came when I called to him.
He gave me his hand and I rejoiced.

I found Amun helped me more than a million troops,
More than a hundred thousand charioteers.

I found my heart stout, my breast in joy.

I found the 2500 chariots that had encircled me
Scattering before my horses.[13]

This is no less far-fetched a tale than the rescue of the Israelites from their Egyptian pursuers. Amun himself lends the king a helping hand, endowing him with such overpowering strength and towering size that the Hittites and their allies flee in panic:

No man is he who is among us,
It is Seth great-of-strength, Ba'al in person.
Not deeds of man are these his doings,
They are of one who is unique,
Who fights a hundred thousand without soldiers and chariots,
Come quick, flee before him,
To seek life and breathe air![14]

That is the same alarm signal sounded by the Egyptians at the Sea of Reeds:

Let us flee from the face of Israel; for YHWH fighteth for them against the Egyptians! (Ex 14:25)

In a relief depicting the Battle of Kadesh, the following inscription accompanies the image of a division of Egyptian troops and chariots advancing in perfect battle formation toward the beleaguered camp:

> The coming of the *na'aruna* [crack troops] of Pharaoh from the land of the Amorites. They found that the host of the Hatti enemies hemmed in the camp of Pharaoh on its western side, while His Majesty sat alone, his army not with him [. . .]. The *na'aruna* broke into the host of the wretched Fallen One of Hatti as they were entering into the camp of Pharaoh, and the servants of His Majesty killed them and did not allow one of them to escape, their hearts being confident of the great strength of Pharaoh their goodly lord, he being behind them like a mountain of copper and like a wall of iron for ever and ever.[15]

What "really" happened was that an elite unit had been sent ahead by Ramesses II on a different route and now turned up unexpectedly on the battlefield, arriving just in time to rush to the king's aid. We can only assume that whatever may have transpired at the Sea of Reeds must have been similarly far removed from its poetic description. Ramesses II would surely have liked nothing better than for the poem he commissioned to commemorate his escape, like Moses and Miriam's song of thanksgiving, to have endured for thousands of years in popular memory. As it was, he had to make do with its monumental immortalization on the temple walls of Abu Simbel, Luxor, Karnak, and Abydos (as well as on many other memorials that have since disappeared, no doubt). Tourists may still marvel at these colossal wrecks today, but they are no longer understood in their religious significance.[16]

The contemporary records of the Battle of Kadesh show how realistic reporting, theological interpretation, and poetic stylization can exist side by side in the depiction of a single event; there is no need for them to represent distinct editorial stages spread far apart in time. At the same time, they indicate the extent to which the poetic and theological reshaping of an event can diverge from its realistic representation. We cannot rule out, therefore, that a group of fleeing Hebrew migrants may indeed have succeeded in evading their pursuers through a fortuitous chain of circumstances, which they went on to celebrate and commemorate as an act of divine intervention on their behalf and as a demonstration of God's awe-inspiring power.

Like the miracle at the Sea of Reeds, the ten plagues that precede it have always gripped the popular imagination, never ceasing to fascinate those who have read and heard about them. In the mind-boggling scale of their impact—natural catastrophes heaped on devastating epidemics—they raise two interrelated questions. First, might there be something in the biblical account—assuming that we are no longer willing to believe in miracles in our enlightened age—that reflects real, potentially still verifiable catastrophes such as volcanic eruptions, earthquakes, and tsunamis? And second, what traces might these traumatic experiences have left behind in the traditions of the other people they affected, particularly the Greeks and Egyptians? These questions have been given fresh impetus by Austrian excavations in the eastern Nile delta. Here the archaeologist Manfred Bietak discovered the ancient city of Avaris, capital of the Hyksos, the Canaanite migrants already associated by Flavius Josephus with the Israelites and Exodus. During the dig, Bietak came across pumice stone deposited at a certain layer by the massive volcanic eruption on the isle of Thera (now Santorini).

The breathtaking speculations sparked by this find and others like it have been explored in fictional form by Israeli author Zeruya Shalev in her novel *Thera* (2005). The novel's protagonist Ella Miller, who is writing an academic dissertation on the subject, may be considered representative of the vast literature (including various films and television series) devoted to understanding and explaining the Egyptian plagues. Ella Miller is an archaeologist. What fascinates her about Thera are not so much the remnants of a past civilization as the traces of its destruction, a scene of devastation and calamity:

> In the middle of the second millennium BCE, the worst recorded natural disaster in human history took place, and in the middle of the Mediterranean Sea the island of Thera was torn to shreds by unprecedented force. Unfathomable amounts of lava and ash leapt from the mountain that turned into a gaping maw, burying a wondrously developed ancient culture, leaving in its wake a crescent of smoking cliffs, a forlorn, craggy smile in the heart of the sea, and a desperate yearning for the sun, which would not show its face for many long years, [. . .] as the clouds of volcanic ash covered the light of the sun year after year, for seven consecutive winters.[17]

We know that the eruption of Tambora in Indonesia in 1815, the only recorded volcanic eruption of comparable size, caused a drastic transformation in the global climate lasting several years. The same can be assumed for the Thera eruption: even once the immediate aftermath, such as a tsunami and days of ash-darkened skies, had subsided, the Mediterranean basin must still have been plagued for years by unseasonably cold temperatures, poor harvests, and famine. Indeed, the after-effects of the Thera eruption have been demonstrated as far away as America and China. Layers of ash dating back to this eruption have also been found throughout the eastern Mediterranean.[18]

Ella Miller does not confine herself to the discipline of archaeology, however. She is intrigued by the long-term impact the catastrophe may have had on the cultural memory of the people living around the Mediterranean. The legend of Atlantis might seem the most obvious reference point here, but it plays no role in her speculations. Instead she investigates lamentations about natural disasters and civilizational collapses, a highly esteemed genre in Egyptian literature, the monotheistic revolution of King Akhenaten, and the Egyptian plagues described in the Book of Exodus. In some respects, Ella's theory recalls the arguments of the Russian-Jewish doctor and psychoanalyst Immanuel Velikovsky, who over seventy years ago linked the *Admonitions of Ipuwer* with the Book of Exodus, interpreting both as the report of a stellar catastrophe.[19] He doggedly set out to find traces of the memory of this catastrophe in all the great mythic traditions of the world. Tedious chronological obstacles were brushed aside by dispensing entirely with the conventional chronology: Akhenaten, Moses, and Oedipus all lived at the same time, he claimed. The fictitious Ella, by contrast, operates much more cautiously and rationally than her nonfictional predecessor, and she has a far more solid scientific foundation in the Thera eruption than did Velikovsky with his hypothesis of a meteorite impact. When Ella divorces her first husband, an archaeologist, and moves in with Oded, a psychotherapist, the psychoanalytical dimension also comes into play. Oded explains to her that, in his line of work, "it barely matters whether a story someone is telling me is true or made up. For the one who's telling it, it's the truth." The difference between historical and narrative truth could be no more succinctly expressed. Ella understands now that the point cannot be to use the Thera catastrophe or some tattered old papyri to prove the historicity of the Exodus story, as Immanuel Velikovsky had intended. The Exodus is simply not susceptible to archaeological verification. The truth of the tale is not to be found in its factual basis but in its significance for the teller.

Admittedly, there is a slim possibility that real-life experiences of catastrophe may inform the *Admonitions of Ipuwer*, the *Prophecies of Neferti*, and other examples of the genre of Egyptian wisdom literature. Such texts tend to be read by Egyptologists as politico-sociological treatises rather than as historical reports; they are vehicles for argument, not stories. These texts aim to impress upon the reader that the universe will fall into chaos if royalty is challenged or violated in any way. Then Ma'at—justice, truth, and order—will vanish from the face of the earth, anarchy will prevail, and nature itself will be in tumult. In the end, it little matters whether the texts are trying to keep alive the memory of a real catastrophe or an invented one; more important is the typically Egyptian idea of an intrinsic bond between royalty, justice, and the cosmos. If, given their clear political and didactic tendency, we have reason to doubt that the Egyptian lamentations have any basis in historical fact, then such skepticism is all the more warranted when it comes to the motives informing the account of the Egyptian plagues found in Exodus.

For her ingenious idea to combine archaeology, trauma, and memory in a way that illuminates Freud's psychoanalytical fascination with archaeology from a different angle, Zeruya Shalev could hardly have chosen a better example than Thera, the Pompeii of the Bronze Age. Even if the Thera catastrophe cannot be pressed into verifying the biblical account, it might nonetheless have influenced cultural schemata and psychic dispositions that left a deep and indelible mark on the experience and literary retelling of later catastrophes, and hence on the cultural memory of the people whose lives they affected.

The Egyptian-Hellenistic Tradition

There are extrabiblical reports of an Egyptian time of troubles that—unlike the Egyptian lamentations drawn on by Velikovsky and the fictitious Ella Miller—explicitly connect the country's woes with the departure from Egypt.

The oldest version of the story can be found in Hecataeus of Abdera (late fourth century BCE), whose history of Egypt has survived only in excerpts in Diodorus Siculus.[20] In his version, the story begins at a time of great distress: a plague is ravaging Egypt. The Egyptians interpret the plague as divine punishment for the presence of foreigners in their midst and the introduction of alien rites and customs. The foreigners are duly expelled. How they came to Egypt and where they came from remains unexplained. It is clearly unimportant; they were simply there. Some of the expelled foreigners, led by Cadmus and Danaus, colonize Greece, while others, led by Moses, move into Palestine. Moses forbids the making of divine images "because God does not possess a human shape. Rather, heaven alone who encompasses the earth is God and lord of all, and he cannot be depicted in images."[21]

Around thirty to forty years after Hecataeus's work, and surely influenced by his example, an Egyptian priest from Sebennytos named Manetho embarked on a similar project. Unlike Hecataeus, Manetho had mastered the different Egyptian writing systems and therefore enjoyed a quite different level of access to the sources. His work, like that of Hecataeus, survives only in isolated excerpts and citations. We have Flavius Josephus to thank for conserving the passages that interest us most about the departure of the children of Israel from Egypt. They are cited in his polemic, *Contra Apionem*, where he compiles the testimonies of pagan authors who wrote on the subject of the Jews.

Flavius Josephus presents the following extract from Manetho: King Amenophis (who can only be Amenophis III) wanted to see the gods, a wish that had earlier been granted to his ancestor, Hor. The sage Amenophis, son of Hapu,[22] tells the king that he may see the gods once he has cleansed the land of lepers. The king then rounds up 80,000 lepers, some of them priests, into the quarries in the eastern desert. Amenophis predicts divine punishment for this inhuman treatment of the sick. He foresees that they will receive help from outside, conquer Egypt, and rule for thirteen years. Not daring to tell the king this in person, he writes everything down and takes his own life.

The lepers are allowed to settle in Avaris, the ancient capital of the Hyksos. They choose Osarsiph, a Heliopolitan priest, to lead their leper colony. He makes laws for them prescribing all that is forbidden in Egypt and forbidding all that is prescribed there. The first and foremost commandment is not to worship the gods, the second not to spare any of their sacred animals (meaning that they must be eaten), nor to abstain from other forbidden food. The third outlaws association with outsiders. Upon promulgating these laws, Osarsiph takes the name Moses.

Osarsiph-Moses fortifies the city and sends out an invitation to the Hyksos, who had been driven out of Egypt some two or three hundred years earlier and are now living in Jerusalem, to join the lepers in their revolt. The Hyksos return. Remembering the prophecy, King Amenophis refrains from marching against the rebels, orders the images of the gods to be carefully hidden, and migrates to Ethiopia with sacred animals previously rounded up from all over the country. The lepers and Hyksos rule Egypt for thirteen years with such ferocious brutality that, in the collective memory of the Egyptians, the previous period of Hyksos rule seems almost like a golden age. Not only are the towns and temples laid waste and the holy images destroyed during this period, but the sanctuaries are turned into kitchens and sacred animals are roasted on the spit. Finally, Amenophis and his grandson Ramesses return from Ethiopia and drive out the lepers and their allies.

The enigmatic name Osarsiph could conceal an allusion to Joseph, particularly for a reader like Flavius Josephus.[23] The biblical four hundred years between Joseph and Moses would here be reduced to a time span within the biography of a single man, initially called Joseph (or Osarsiph), who renamed himself Moses upon stepping into his new role as leader and lawgiver. In the eyes of Josephus, who knew nothing of the links between the legend reported by Manetho and the Amarna period, the legend represents a polemical distortion of the biblical Exodus story. In a similar manner, Amos Funkenstein has also interpreted the legend of the lepers as a "counterhistory": a retelling of the past that, by consciously inverting the foundation story from which the Jews derived their self-image, sets out to destroy that image.[24] If we bear in mind the links to Amarna, however, there emerges the opposite possibility that the Egyptian legends of sacrilege and expulsion are older and may themselves have provoked the biblical Exodus story as a counterhistory. What both stories have in common is the idea that the presence of foreigners ushers in a time of troubles that only comes to an end with the expulsion or liberation of the aliens. That is made even clearer in subsequent variants of the story.

The account of the departure from Egypt given by Lysimachos was written two or three generations after Manetho.[25] Here the story begins with a famine in Egypt during the reign of King Bocchoris. An oracle orders the king to cleanse the temples of the "impure and impious" people who had settled there—a reference to the Jews, who were supposedly afflicted by leprosy and other diseases at the time and sought refuge in the temples. The measures then taken by Bocchoris are exceptionally cruel. He gives orders to drown the lepers and to drive the others into the desert. A "certain Moses" organizes the outcasts by giving them laws commanding them "not to think well of anybody and to destroy every temple and altar of the gods." He then leads them out of the country. Here, as in Hecataeus, the motif of a time of troubles functions as an initial situation that sets things in motion. In Hecataeus, the story begins with a plague, in Lysimachos with a famine. In both cases, an affinity to the biblical plagues can easily be recognized.

Chaeremon, an Egyptian who lived in the first half of the first century as a priest and pedagogue in Alexandria and after 49 in Rome as the tutor of Nero, gives yet another version of the story.[26] The goddess Isis appears to King Amenophis in a dream and reproaches him with the destruction of her temple in times of war. The priest and scribe Phritibantes (a rendering into Greek of the Egyptian title, "chief of the temple") advises him to propitiate the goddess by "purging" Egypt of the lepers. The king gathers 250,000 lepers and expels them from Egypt. Their leaders are Moses and Joseph, whose Egyptian names are Tisithen and Peteseph. In the city of Pelusium, they are joined by 380,000 would-be emigrants who have been refused permission to leave the country. At this point the story takes the same turn as in Manetho: the united forces of the lepers and the emigrants conquer Egypt and compel the king to seek refuge in Nubia. Only his son and successor, Ramesses, succeeds in reconquering Egypt and driving the "Jews" into Syria. Here, then, Joseph and Moses appear alongside each other as leaders of the outcasts; that could be a hint that the name Osarsiph in Manetho-Josephus should be read—as did Thomas Mann in his Joseph tetralogy—as an Egyptianized form of the name Joseph.

An especially interesting variant of the Exodus story can be found in
Pompeius Trogus's *Historicae Philippicae*. The reason for the Exodus is
the same in most of the other sources: an epidemic. "But when the
Egyptians had been exposed to the scab and to a skin infection, and
had been warned by an oracle, they expelled Moses together with the
sick people beyond the confines of Egypt lest the disease should spread
to a greater number of people." This hygienic reason for the expulsion
of the infected persons from Egypt also accounts for the exclusive character of Moses's legislation: "And because he remembered that they
had been expelled from Egypt due to fear of contagion, they took care
not to live with outsiders lest they become hateful to the natives for the
same reason. This regulation which arose from a specific cause, he
[Moses] transformed gradually into a fixed custom and religion."[27] The
"hygienic" explanation of the law corresponds to the extraordinary importance attached to leprosy in Leviticus chapters 13–14, particularly
to its early diagnosis and treatment. In this version, Moses appears as
the son of Joseph. Although Pompeius does not join Manetho in presenting him as an Egyptian priest, the cult he institutes in Jerusalem is
nonetheless characterized as *sacra Aegyptia*, Egyptian cult objects.
When leaving Egypt, Moses "secretly took with him the sacred objects
of the Egyptians. In trying to recover these objects by force, the Egyptians were compelled by storms to go home." Here we encounter a
number of biblical motifs that are missing in the other, extrabiblical
versions: the motif of gold and silver objects taken out of Egypt, which
lack all sacral significance in the biblical version and instead represent
gifts; the motif of the botched attempt to fetch back the emigrants; the
miracle at the Sea of Reeds from the biblical story, here presented as a
perfectly natural event; and the motif of public hygiene (leprosy).
Pompeius Trogus was clearly familiar with the biblical version and enriched the preexisting Hellenistic tradition with ingredients from this
source.

The classical account of the legend that has had the longest-lasting
impact is found in the *Historiae* of Tacitus, 5.3–5.[28] Egypt is stricken by
an epidemic that leads to bodily deformities; King Bocchoris consults
the oracle and learns that he must "purge" the country of this race
(*genus*) because the gods detest it (*ut invisum deis*). The Jews are driven
into the desert but find a leader in Moses, who brings them to Palestine

and founds Jerusalem. In order to consolidate his authority, Moses institutes a new religion that is the exact opposite of all other religions:
"The Egyptians worship many animals and monstrous images; the
Jews conceive of one god, and that with the mind only: they regard
those who make representations of god in man's image from perishable
materials as impious; that supreme and eternal being is incapable to
them of representation and is without end."[29] With typical concise-
ness, Tacitus defines the basic principle of this new religion as what
might be termed "normative inversion": "the Jews consider everything
that we hold sacred as profane and permit everything that for us is
taboo." In their temples they consecrate a statue of a donkey and sacrifice a ram "in order to ridicule the god Amun." For the same reason,
they sacrifice a bull because the Egyptians worship Apis.

In Egyptology there is now widespread acceptance that a displaced
memory of Akhenaten and the Amarna period lives on in Manetho's
account,[30] as Eduard Meyer proposed as early as 1904.[31] Akhenaten
committed the very sacrileges ascribed to Osarsiph in the legend: he
shut the temples, halted the rituals and feasts, dismissed the priests,
and installed a strict and exclusive monotheism. He lived in the time in
question as Amenophis III's successor, and his reign from the new
capital of Amarna did indeed last approximately thirteen years. This
reading of the legend of the lepers has recently been emphatically cor-
roborated by the Danish Egyptologist and demotist Kim Ryholt. He
was able to interpret a passage in Diodorus in a way that shed light on
this previously obscure passage while also demonstrating beyond a
shadow of a doubt that the memory of Amarna persisted into late- period Egypt. In chapter 64 of the first book of his *Bibliotheca historica*,
Diodorus speaks of the three great pyramids and reports two different
traditions about their builders (1.64.13).[32] The first ascribes them to
Khufu (Cheops), Khafre (Chephren), and Menkaure (Mycerinus). But
there is another tradition ascribing them to Harmaios (Horemheb),
Amasis (Ahmose), and Inaros (Inaros I), respectively. That can only
refer to the three most traumatic periods in Egyptian history and the
pharaohs who are credited with putting them to an end: Horemheb put
an end to the Amarna revolt, Ahmose drove out the Hyksos, and Inaros
I heroically led the resistance against the Assyrians.[33] The three great
pyramids appear, in this interpretation, as three monuments of trauma

and triumph, with the greatest of the three, the Khufu pyramid, serving to commemorate the Amarna trauma and its ending by Horemheb. The legend of the three historical traumas must have been strong enough, even at this late stage, for it to have been associated with the three pyramids at Giza.

In ancient Egyptian collective memory there thus existed a tradition about three periods of terrible suffering: the Hyksos domination, the abolition of the traditional religion in the Amarna period, and the four Assyrian invasions with their attendant destruction of temples, confiscation of sacred images, and loss of political sovereignty. That is not the same as an epidemic, to be sure, but that too was mentioned in connection with the Amarna period. It is very clearly expressed in the restoration stele of Tutankhamun:

> The temples of the gods and goddesses
> from Elephantine to the delta
> [had been neglected and] were about to collapse;
> their holy places were threatened by decay
> and had become ruin heaps,
> overgrown with weeds.
> The land was suffering a serious illness:
> the gods had turned from this land.
> If an army was sent to Palestine,
> to expand the boundaries of Egypt,
> it was not granted the slightest success.
> If one turned to a god in prayer
> to ask counsel of him, he did not draw nigh at all.
> If one went to a goddess, likewise,
> she did not draw nigh at all.
> For their hearts had become weak in their cultic bodies (statues).[34]

A plague actually broke out in the Middle East toward the end of the Amarna period, by far the worst epidemic in ancient history, comparable only to the Black Death of 1348 in the European Middle Ages.[35] The Egyptians called this plague "the Asiatic sickness."[36] The plague raged on for over twenty years; as the Hittite king Mursili reports, Egyptian prisoners brought it with them into Asia Minor:

> The storm-god of Hatti, my lord, by his verdict caused my father to prevail,
> and he defeated the infantry and the chariotry of Egypt and beat them. But
> when the prisoners of war who had been captured were led back to Hatti,
> a plague broke out among them and they began to die. From that day on
> people have been dying in Hatti.[37]

These lines are taken from a prayer sent up by Mursili to the Hittite
storm god entreating him to avert this pestilence that, having already
ravaged the country for a number of years and claimed the life of
his own father, Suppiluliuma, now threatened to carry off the entire
populace.

Like the Thera eruption, this event may well have left behind traces
in Egyptian and Canaanite storytelling traditions that found their way
into the Exodus story, particularly as the plague was interpreted at the
time as divine punishment: by the Hittites, for the breach of a treaty
with the Egyptians; in Egypt, as retribution for the crimes against religion committed in the Amarna period. It is even conceivable that the
expulsion of the Hyksos and the events of the Amarna period came
together, in the later cultural memory of the Egyptians and Canaanites,
into a common traumatic memory complex and condensed into the
overall image of "plagues."

The Institution of the Passover Feast and the Passover Haggadah

> He hath made his wonderful works to be remembered:
> YHWH is gracious and full of compassion.
>
> —*Psalm 111:4*

> Do this in remembrance of me.
>
> —*Luke 22:19; 1 Corinthians 11:24*

The first nine plagues almost all have an Egyptian complexion: Nile,
frogs, lice, vermin, diseased livestock, boils, locusts, even the more
rare cases of hail and darkness—during violent sandstorms, for example—are "plagues" that can easily be associated with Egypt. The tenth
plague—the one that finally prompts Pharaoh to give in—is the odd
one out. The killing of the firstborn is a biblical theme. It principally

brings to mind the story of the sacrifice of Isaac, demanded by God but
called off at the last minute. This story is generally understood as sig-
naling an end to the rite of firstborn male sacrifice. In Exodus 22:28 the
sacrifice is explicitly stipulated, while in Exodus 13:13 and 34:20 the
alternative possibility of "redeeming" the sacrifice with a sheep is provided. In Numbers 8:5–19 the Levites, who serve in the Temple, are
given up to God "instead of the firstborn of all the children of Israel":
"For all the firstborn of the children of Israel are mine, both man and
beast: on the day that I smote every firstborn in the land of Egypt I
sanctified them for myself" (8:17). The tenth plague, the death of the
(Egyptian) firstborn, is to be understood against this background, as a
specifically Israelite theme.[38] Whether in the form of a custom that was
once actually practiced (as clearly presupposed in Ex 22:28, Judges
11:29–40; Ez 10:26 and other passages) or that of a substitute for the
actual outstanding sacrifice (as in Ex 13:2, 11–13; 34:20), or that of a rite
that was explicitly rejected (Gen 22) or abhorred as pagan (Jer 19:5;
Deut 15:19–23), the sacrifice of the firstborn was mulled over almost
obsessively in the biblical and Phoenician-Punic imagination,[39]
whereas it played no role whatsoever in Egypt. Israel's role as God's
firstborn son should also be understood against this background. Passover lamb, firstborn, redemption, liberation: together, these themes
form an associative context that also includes the story and figure of
Jesus of Nazareth. As such, it numbers among the most influential focal
points in the Exodus narrative.

Between the ninth and tenth plagues, YHWH intervenes for the first
time in a way that relates to the institution of an eternal order rather
than serving merely to advance the plot. Here, long before all the statutes that will place the entire life of the community on an atemporal
normative footing are revealed, an initial structuring framework is established in the dimension of time. The month of departure is set as the
first month of the year, while the night of departure is fixed on the
fourteenth of that month. Because the months in the Israelite calendar
begin with the new moon day, the fourteenth—and hence the night of
departure—is a full moon. Nothing less is at stake here than the introduction of a new calendar. From now on, the year will no longer start
in fall, when plants are revived from months of summer heat by the first
cooling rains (just as, in more northerly climes, nature is awoken from

FIGURE 13. Preparation of the Passover feast. The upper section shows the matzot being distributed. Beneath, the doorposts are daubed with the blood of the sacrificed lamb. Illustration in the Passover Haggadah. Catalonia, mid-fourteenth century.

its winter sleep by the first warm touch of the sun). Instead, seemingly unrelated to natural rhythms, it will begin in the month when Israel drew out of Egypt. This intervention in the natural temporal order represents no less radical an innovation than the later introduction of the Christian and Islamic calendars, save that here, the innovation does not affect the *numbering* of the years (which was immaterial in sixth-century BCE Israel) but their *form*. The introduction of a calendar all its own represents a fundamental act of emancipation, sovereignty, and autonomy on Israel's part, announcing its intention to segregate itself from the institutions of its surroundings and its own past to stand on its own two feet:[40]

> And YHWH spake unto Moses and Aaron in the land of Egypt, saying, this month shall be unto you the beginning of months: it shall be the first month of the year to you. Speak ye unto all the congregation of Israel, saying, In the tenth days of this month they shall take to theme every man a lamb, according to the house of their fathers, a lamb for [each] house. [. . .] And ye shall keep it up until the fourteenth day of the same month: and the whole assembly of the congregation of Israel shall kill it in the evening.
>
> And they shall take of the blood, and strike it on the two side posts and on the upper door post of the houses, wherein they shall eat it. And they shall eat the flesh in that night, roast with fire, and unleavened bread; and with bitter herbs they shall eat it. Eat not of it raw, nor boiled at all with water, but roast with fire; his head with his legs, and with the inner parts thereof. And ye shall let nothing of it remain until the morning; and that which remaineth of it until the morning ye shall burn with fire. And thus shall ye eat it; with your loins girded, your shoes on your feet, and your staff in your hand; and ye shall eat it in haste; it is YHWH's Passover.
>
> For I will pass through the land of Egypt this night, and will smite all the firstborn in the land of Egypt, both man and beast; and against all the gods of Egypt I will execute judgment: I am YHWH. And the blood shall be to you for a sign upon the houses where ye are: and when I see the blood, I will pass over you, and the plague shall not be upon you to destroy you, when I smite the land of Egypt.
>
> And this day shall be unto you for a memorial; and ye shall keep it a feast to YHWH throughout your generations; ye shall keep it a feast by an ordinance for ever. Seven days shall ye eat unleavened bread; even the first day ye shall put away leaven out of your houses: for whosoever eateth leavened bread from the first day until the seventh day, that soul shall be cut off from Israel.

And in the first day there shall be an holy convocation, and in the seventh day [also] there shall be an holy convocation to you; no manner of work shall be done in them, save that which every man must eat, that only must be done of you. And ye shall observe the feast of unleavened bread; for in this selfsame day have I brought your armies out of the land of Egypt: therefore shall ye observe this day in your generations by an ordinance for ever. (Ex 12:1–17)

In the festival of commemoration instituted in chapters 12 and 13 in connection with the tenth plague, the death of the firstborn, three different festive rites are combined: (1) the Passover night, when the lamb is slaughtered, the doorposts are daubed with blood, and the meat is eaten in the prescribed manner; (2) the eating of unleavened bread (*maṣṣôt*) for seven days; and (3) the sacrifice of the male firstborn. All three rites are anchored, etiologically, in the events of the night of departure: (1) as a protective rite against the "destroyer" (*mašḥît*) who strikes the Egyptian firstborn dead; (2) to remember the haste of the exodus, and (3) in reference to the death of the Egyptian firstborn and YHWH's seigneurial right to all firstborn male children. This first normative or halachic insertion in the narrative is the work of the Priestly Source and post-Priestly redactors.[41]

The festival is a commemorative sign, a *zikkārôn* or memorial intended to hold fast the memory of this revelation of divine power for all time.[42] That is explicitly emphasized on two occasions: in 13:9 ("And it shall be a sign unto thee upon thine hand, and for a memorial between thine eyes, that YHWH's law may be in thy mouth: for with a strong hand hath YHWH brought thee out of Egypt") and 13:16 ("And it shall be for a sign upon thine hand, and for a memorial before thine eyes; for by strength of hand YHWH brought us forth out of Egypt"). The "signs" (*'ôt*), to be bound around the forehead and worn between the eyes, are "memorials" that serve to remind the wearer of this founding night throughout all generations: tefillin, in other words. At the same time, they are "signs of fellowship"[43] betokening affiliation to YHWH, and amulets ("phylacteries") shielding the wearer from harm.

The nighttime Passover feast is a ritual commemorative meal that forms the subtext and model for the Christian last supper. Yet there is a model for the Passover feast as well. The Assyrian king Esarhaddon had summoned his subjects and vassals to the capital to swear fealty to his designated heir and successor, Ashurbanipal. He instituted the ritual drinking of water in order to "make a memory" that would periodically refresh the memory of the oath each time the ritual was performed:

> They were given water to drink from a *sarsaru* jar by her [Ishtar of Arbela],
> She filled a drinking vessel of one *seah* [around six liters] with water from the *sarsaru* jar, and gave it to them, [saying]:
> "You shall say in your hearts thus: Ishtar is a narrow strait!
> And you will enter into your cities [and] you will eat bread in your districts,
> And you will forget this covenant [*adê*].
> But when you drink of this water, you will remember
> Once more and you will honor the covenant that I have made on account of Esarhaddon."[44]

Just as the *sarsaru* ritual involves the ritual drinking of water to remind drinkers of the oath they have sworn, so the Passover feast involves the ritual eating of unleavened bread to remind eaters of their hasty departure when there was insufficient time to leaven their dough with yeast. For the same reason, Passover is celebrated in the family and at home, not in the temple or synagogue, since the Israelites spent this night in their homes while YHWH's "destroyer" (*mašḥît*) stalked the houses of the Egyptians.

Later, in the diaspora, this regulation was elaborated in minute detail in the Passover Haggadah, the liturgy for the Seder night.[45] Moses is barely mentioned in this liturgy. That constitutes the biggest difference to the biblical story, where Moses is the protagonist. The Jewish Seder, the first night of the Passover week, is the ritual and liturgical execution of the commandment, "thou shalt teach it to thy sons, and thy sons' sons"—to wit, that we were slaves in Egypt and YHWH delivered us from bondage with a strong hand and an outstretched arm:

> In every generation [*běkol dôr wādôr*], a person is obligated to regard himself as if he had himself left Egypt. For it is stated: "And thou shalt shew thy son in that day, saying, This is done because of that which YHWH did unto me when I came forth out of Egypt" (Ex 13:8). It was not only our ancestors

whom he redeemed; rather, he redeemed us with them, as it is stated: "he brought us out from thence, that he might bring us in, to give us the land that he sware unto our fathers" (Deut 6:23).[46]

In every generation we are beholden to cast ourselves back in memory to an event that lies millennia in the past. A lamb is slaughtered, as when its blood was smeared on the doorposts so that the destroyer (Luther's "angel of death") would pass over, and unleavened bread is eaten, as when there was no time to leaven the dough before setting out. The ceremony seeks to engage the mind as well as the emotions and the body. The story must be narrated in first person: Why do we enact these rites and follow these commandments? Because we were slaves in Egypt. Just as this "we" encompasses all Jewish people, not just those who left Egypt at the time, so the concepts "Egypt" and "Pharaoh" relate to any form of oppression and violence, regardless of where they may occur. A Jew is someone who was freed from Egypt and who remains free to the extent that he honors the covenant and its commandments. In liturgical memory, history becomes myth, a repertoire of archetypal patterns against which every historical present appears transparent and legible. The Christians adopted this principle, and so we hear in a cantata composed by Johann Sebastian Bach for the second Sunday in Advent, an occasion very much taken up with thoughts of Christ's return on the day of judgment: "When will the day come when we leave the Egypt of this world?" Here the entire universe has become an "Egypt," a realm of suffering from injustice and oppression that will only be redeemed with the end of the world.

A few years ago an advertisement appeared in the *New York Times*, proclaiming:

> For thousands of years, Jews have affirmed that by participating in the Passover Seder, we not only remember the Exodus, but actually relive it, bringing its transformative power into our own lives.[47]

That is an excellent definition of liturgical memory. The Seder teaches identity through identification. It is concerned with transposing history into memory, making a particular past "ours" and inviting everyone in the community to take their own stake in that past. One could almost go so far as to speak of a transformation of semantic memory (what we have learned) into episodic memory (what we have experienced).

The Seder has the function of producing a framework for remembering the exodus, not just through recitation of the liturgy, the Haggadah, but also and especially through improvised storytelling, through "conversational remembering."[48] Framing devices organize our everyday lives, as Erving Goffman has shown.[49] By relieving us of the need to reflect for ourselves, they allow us to act spontaneously. With the Seder, we are moving away from the level of everyday conduct. This transition from everyday to holy-day behavior is explicitly thematized in the Haggadah. The festive arrangements have to be extraordinary enough to amaze the uninitiated, and the youngest child is expected to ask the question that sets in train the long sequence of explanations and stories: "Why is this night different from all other nights?"[50] It is a question expressing utter bewilderment: "What on earth is going on here?" By emphasizing the conspicuous difference between the Seder and every other night, the Seder begins with the festive staging of a change of frame.

Difference is a key concept in the Seder ceremony. God is praised for making a difference: between this night and all other nights, "between the sacred and the profane, between light and darkness, between the Sabbath and the six other days of the week, between Jews and gentiles"[51]—and between slavery (ʿăbōdâ) and freedom (ḥērût), the fundamental theme of the story that is to be remembered on this night.[52] All these distinctions can be experienced and understood due to an initial distinction by which the striking singularity of the scenery is marked off from the ordinariness of everyday life. Children pose questions, and the answers have the meaning of an initiation into a Jewish identity that derives from the exodus.

The Passover feast, like initiations into the ancient mysteries, plays with "what is shown" (deiknymenon), "what is done" (dromenon), and "what is said" (legomenon). "What is shown" is a plate or platter with six foods prepared and arranged in a ritually prescribed manner. "What is done" is that this plate, the items placed on it, and four cups of wine are handled in a certain way. There can be no doubt that we are dealing here with a festive meal, a commemorative feast.

After the introductory blessings, the drinking of the first cup of wine, and the blessing of the six ritual commemorative items, the plate is raised with the words "This is the bread of suffering that our ancestors ate in the land of Egypt." Then the second cup is poured out (but not yet drunk) and the youngest child asks the question "*mah ništanâ?*"

Why is this night different from all other nights?
In that on all other nights we don't dip things even one time, this night, two times.
In that on all other nights we eat leaven and matzah, this night, only matzah.
In that on all other nights we eat various vegetables, this night, bitter herbs.
In that on all other nights some eat sitting and others reclining, this night, we are all reclining.

At this point the story is told: We were slaves in the land of Egypt but YHWH, our god, led us from thence with a strong hand and an outstretched arm. There is discussion about how the story of the departure from Egypt should be told. The detail of posture is important: reclining and supported by the left arm. This too is a commemorative sign: it recalls the ancient symposium as a festive custom reserved for freemen and nobles, among whom the chosen people include themselves in celebrating the Seder.

There follows the "Midrash of the Four Children." In various passages of the Torah, it is set out how one should respond when a child inquires about the significance of a particular law or "the Law" itself. The passages are compiled in this Midrash and distributed over four types of children: one intelligent, one wicked, one simple, and one who does not yet know how to ask.

1. What does the intelligent child say?
"What mean the testimonies, and the statutes, and the ordinances which YHWH our God has commanded you?" (Deut 6:2). And you instruct him in the precepts of the Passover, to wit, "One may not eat anything after the Passover *'ăpîqômān.*

2. What does the wicked child say?
"What is this service to you?" (Ex 12:26; see 13:8)

"To you," and not to him. Since he removes himself from the group, and so
denies God, you in return must set his teeth on edge and answer him: "It is
because of that which YHWH did for me that I came forth from Egypt."
"For me," not for him. Had he been there, he would not have been
redeemed.

3. What does the simple child say?
   "What is this?" (Ex 13:14)
   And you shall say to him, "By strength of hand YHWH brought us out from
   Egypt, from the house of bondage."

4. And with him who does not know how to ask you must open and begin
   yourself. "And you shall tell your son in that day, saying, It is because of that
   which YHWH did for me when I came forth out of Egypt" (Ex 13:8).[53]

The "Midrash of the Four Children" is a minidrama about memory,
history, and identity. The question of identity is tackled by playing
with personal pronouns: I and me, we and us, you and he. The children
are taught to say "you" and "I" in reference to the three-and-a-half-
thousand-year-old story. "Back then we came from the east," a Jewish
visitor once told us when speaking of the often difficult migration path-
ways, mainly from the west and the north, by which Jews came to Palestine after the Second World War. "Back then": he was referring to the
Israelites who crossed the Jordan under Joshua's leadership.

Strangely enough, Moses plays no role in the Haggadah's tales of the
departure from Egypt. The recapitulation of the story of Israel's salvation begins with Abraham turning his back on both Haran and idolatry
(according to Joshua 24:2–4). Then the wine cup is raised and the matzot covered up with the redolent words: "For it was not one man only
who stood up against us to destroy us; in every generation they stand
up against us to destroy us, and the Holy One, blessed be he, saves us
from their hand."

Once more it is made clear that far more is at stake here than ancient
history. What is past is not over and done with.[54] Violence, persecution, and oppression are omnipresent—but so too is salvation. Recounting the exodus is not just an act of memory but also one of hope
and inspiration.

Then the cup is put back on the table and the matzot are uncovered. The recapitulation of the story continues with Jacob and the sojourn in Egypt (according to Deut 26:5ff., Gen 47:4; Deut 10:22; Ex 1:7ff., 16:7). Now the theme of liberation is introduced. All ten plagues are recalled with a keyword, and at each plague a finger is dipped in the cup of wine and a drop is spilled:

Blood (*dām*)
Frogs (*ṣĕpardĕʿîm*)
Lice (*kinnîm*)
Wild animals (*ʿārōb*)
Diseased livestock (*deber*)
Boils (*šĕḥîn*)
Hail (*bārād*)
Locusts (*ʾarbeh*)
Darkness (*ḥōšek*)
Death of the firstborn (*makkat bĕkôrôt*)

In the thanksgiving song *Dayyēnû* ("it would have sufficed"), God's acts of salvation are again brought to mind and continued from the plagues to the gift of land:

If he had brought us out from Egypt and had not carried out judgments against them—it would have sufficed.
If he had carried out judgments against them, and not against their idols—it would have sufficed.
If he had destroyed their idols and had not smitten their firstborn—it would have sufficed.
If he had smitten their firstborn and not given us their wealth—it would have sufficed.
If he had given us their wealth and had not split the sea for us—it would have sufficed.
If he had split the sea for us, and had not taken us through it on dry land—it would have sufficed.
If he had taken us through the sea on dry land, and had not drowned our oppressors in it—it would have sufficed.
If he had drowned our oppressors in it, and had not supplied our needs in the desert for forty years—it would have sufficed.

If he had supplied our needs in the desert for forty years, and had not fed us the manna—it would have sufficed.

If he had fed us the manna, and had not given us the Sabbath—it would have sufficed.

If he had given us the Sabbath and had not brought us before Mount Sinai—it would have sufficed.

If he had brought us before Mount Sinai and had not given us the Torah—it would have sufficed.

If he had given us the Torah and had not brought us into the land of Israel—it would have sufficed.

If he had brought us into the land of Israel and not built for us the Holy Temple—it would have sufficed.

There follow Midrashim on the three key concepts (or *deiknymena*) that need upholding: *pesaḥ*: the paschal lamb eaten by our ancestors in the temple; *maṣṣâ*: the unleavened bread eaten by our ancestors amid the haste of their departure; *mārôr*: bitter herbs recalling how the Egyptians embittered the lives of our ancestors. Psalms (113 and 114) and blessings ensue. Then the ritual meals are consumed, the two wine cups drained, and the *'ăpîqômān*, a previously hidden piece of matzah, is distributed among the guests. The third cup of wine is poured out and a prayer of thanksgiving offered. The wonderful Psalm 126 is recited and the period in Babylonian captivity is remembered—an ordeal that, like the Egyptian bondage, is past but not over and done with:

When YHWH will return the captives of Zion, we will be as dreamers.
Then our mouth shall be filled with laughter, and out tongue with praise.
Then shall they say among the gentiles:
YHWH has done great deeds for them!
YHWH has done great deeds for us; so we rejoice!
YHWH, bring back our captives, as you bring back the streams in the south.
They that sow in tears shall reap in joy.
Though they go on their way weeping, bearing the store of seed,
They shall come back with joy, bearing their sheaves.

There follow lengthy prayers of petition. The third cup is blessed and drunk. A fourth cup is poured out along with an additional cup for the prophet Elijah. The door is opened and a great liturgy of thanks made up of many psalms is recited (Pss 79:6–7; 69:25; Lam 3:66; Ps 115 *in toto*: against the heathen; Pss 116–118 as well as 136 and many more). The fourth cup is blessed and drunk. The concluding prayer looks forward to a return from the diaspora:

> Be merciful, Lord our God, on Israel your people, on Jerusalem your city, on Zion, the home of your glory, on your altar and your temple. Rebuild Jerusalem the holy city, soon and in our day, and lead us there.

The ceremony ends with the wish "Until next year in Jerusalem!"— *lĕšānâ habbā'â bîrûšālayīm.*

Excursus II: Moses's Song of Thanksgiving
and Handel's Oratorio *Israel in Egypt*

Trauma and triumph belong together in memory. In the Book of Exodus, triumph culminates in the miracle of the "Red Sea" (as it came to be called over the course of the book's reception) —more accurately, the safe passage of Israel through the Sea of Reeds, whose waters then rush back to engulf the pursuing Egyptian charioteers. Nowhere has this triumph found more overwhelming expression than in George Frideric Handel's oratorio *Israel in Egypt*.[55] Along with his dramatic oratorios, Handel wrote two nondramatic works in the genre, their libretti consisting entirely of collated passages from the Bible (a "scripture collection") without any additional commentary or reflection: *Israel in Egypt* (1738) and *Messiah* (1742). The choice of these two subjects—God's redeeming revelation as depicted in the Old and New Testaments, respectively—can hardly be fortuitous.

In the case of *Messiah*, we know who stands behind this choice of material and form: Charles Jennens, who also penned the texts for *Saul* and *Belshazzar*, those most dramatic of oratorios. He is also presumed to be the librettist of *Israel in Egypt*, since he claims in a letter to have put together another "scripture collection" for Handel besides *Messiah*.[56] This could only refer to *Israel in Egypt*. For this text, however, Handel did not actually need a librettist.

Handel began setting to music Exodus 15:1–21, "The Song of Moses," on October 1, 1738, only four days after putting the finishing touches to the score of *Saul*. He completed work on it on October 11. The song

gives voice to the Israelites' sense of triumph and gratitude after crossing the Red Sea and fleeing from Egypt at last. At the time, Handel may
have envisaged an anthem, an uplifting choral work to be sung during
a church service.

Unlike operas and oratorios, which in Handel's day were performed
in the theater before a paying public, anthems were generally commissioned for a specific ecclesiastical occasion. In October 1738, however,
no such official commission or occasion was forthcoming.[57] The suspi-
cion arises that personal motives may have played a role in his choice
of material. One reason may have been a feeling of happiness and gratitude occasioned by the successful completion of *Saul*, a work of epochal significance not just in the life of its composer but in the history
of music itself. Handel had just achieved a breakthrough to a completely new form of musical theater that, in creating a model for the
new genre of dramatic oratorio, would set the course for the following
decades of his composing career. Why should Handel have needed a
pre-text to guide him to the idea of setting to music Moses's song of
thanksgiving in the King James Version?

The immediately preceding years, 1737 and 1738, had been the absolute low point in Handel's life. In 1737, overworked and beset by professional conflict, he apparently suffered a stroke that left him paralyzed
in his right arm. In 1738 his opera company collapsed. He had his ox-
like constitution to thank for rescuing him from the first crisis: after
submitting to a drastic treatment in Aachen that might have killed a
lesser man, he made a surprisingly swift recovery. His muse rescued
him from the second. Returned from the cure, he immediately set
about composing the funeral anthem for Queen Caroline, the operas
Faramondo and *Serse*, and the dramatic oratorio *Saul*, a unique masterpiece that became acknowledged as the unsurpassed model for the
new genre. Handel had scored a triumph, not just over his illness, but
over his enemies as well, for the rival company that had brought about
his ruin by poaching his best talent, the Opera of the Nobility, had also
collapsed. Nobody could compete with him on the newly conquered
stage of the English oratorio. Setting to music Moses's song of thanksgiving can only have been Handel's idea; at any rate, neither a commission nor a complete libretto was available to him at the time he took the
project in hand.

FIGURE 14. The Israelites' song of thanksgiving after crossing the Red Sea. Jewish book illustration, 1740.

Given that an anthem could not be performed without an official occasion, Handel must soon have decided to expand the new work into a full-blown oratorio. On October 15 he continued setting biblical texts that related to the reasons for Moses's gratitude: the plagues by which God forced the Israelites' release, their nocturnal departure, and their passage through the Red Sea. In doing so, he relied less on the account given in the Book of Exodus than on Psalms 78, 105, and 106, which, like the Song of Moses, have the character of songs of thanks and praise. He introduced this part of the oratorio with a short recitative and a chorus relating to the suffering of the Israelites and Moses's calling. He finished it on October 20 and designated it as "parte seconda," with the previously composed "Song of Moses" now becoming part three. In selecting the texts for this part, he may well have sought counsel from Jennens.

As "parte prima," Handel prefaced everything he had written so far with his funeral anthem for Queen Caroline, composed in 1737. The anthem's text likewise consists of passages from the Bible that, through the substitution of the feminine third person for the masculine, could be inserted otherwise unchanged as "Lamentation of the Israelites for the Death of Joseph," notwithstanding that the biblical texts have nothing to do with either Joseph or Egypt.[58] The entire work was declared "fully complete" in a manuscript entry dated October 28.

Handel's oratorio *Israel in Egypt* is by far the most important musical treatment of God's saving deeds. Like the Jewish Passover Haggadah, Handel singles out the plagues and the Red Sea miracle as the key moments in the Exodus myth. Accordingly, the themes of triumph and salvation stand at the center. What seems to have stirred his creative imagination is, on the one hand, the depiction of the natural forces unleashed to bring about the Israelites' salvation and, on the other, the expression of triumphant jubilation on the part of the saved. In depicting the Egyptian plagues, he was enticed by the prospect of demonstrating the various painterly qualities of music.

In the plague of frogs (No. 3, Aria: "Their land brought forth frogs"), for example, he uses dotted rhythms and intervallic leaps to depict hopping frogs. In the plague of flies and lice (No. 4, Chorus: "He spake the word"),[59] the whirring insects are represented through demisemiquaver runs in the violins. The plague of locusts also features in this chorus; as soon as they are mentioned, from bar 31, the double basses and a second organ enter with semiquaver runs to raise the whirring and buzzing of the upper voices to a roaring din. The plague of hail (No. 5, Chorus: "He gave them hailstones for rain")[60] is captured in relentlessly pounding quaver beats and pelting semiquaver runs accompanied by intermittent blasts from the trombones, trumpets, and timpani. Of particular interest from a musical point of view is the depiction of the ninth plague, the plague of darkness (No. 6, Chorus: "He sent a thick darkness"). Here Handel produces an effect of tonal disorientation; listeners grope in the dark, unsure where the sequence of harmonies will take them. Time and again, hesitant progress gives way to

sharp dissonance, first in bars 3 and 4 with the D flat in the bass and the
C in the upper voice, then in bar 8, again in bar 12, and once more in
the diminished seventh chord at bar 14, the epitome of disorientation.[61]
The chorus begins in strict homophony and without a melodic line,
almost as if treading on the spot, before dissipating into a choral recitative.[62] In stark contrast, the tenth and final plague, the death of the
firstborn (No. 8, Chorus: "He smote all the firstborn of Egypt"), follows directly after.[63] Here the blows rain down inexorably, truly "sublime strokes,"[64] initially on the downbeats in the orchestra, then the
choir falls in with the rhythm of the blows.

From the last part of the oratorio, Moses's song of praise, I will mention only two numbers. The first, a wonderful example of musical
word-painting, is the chorus at No. 19: "The depths have covered them,
they sank into the bottom like a stone." As in the "darkness" chorus, the
music here glides slowly, gently, almost reverently on in the absence of
a pronounced melody, and the sinking of the drowned Egyptians is
depicted in steps of descending intervals. Equally remarkable is the
conclusion to the final chorus, No. 28, "Sing ye unto the Lord," where
the choir whips itself into a frenzy through constant repetition of the
formula, "the horse and his rider."

Driving tone painting to an extreme, Handel tells the story of the
exodus from Egypt almost exclusively from the chorus's point of view:
full of pathos and expression, triumphalist, and above all collective.
The protagonist is the people of Israel; the soloists must make do with
a subordinate role. Why is the story told, when is it told, by whom, and
for whom? The first impulse to write a song of praise and thanksgiving
may have arisen from Handel's personal circumstances, his near-
miraculous convalescence after a severe breakdown. The finished oratorio, however, stands in a more wide-ranging network of relations.
We are confronted with a work that is almost without parallel in the
repertoire: an oratorio made up almost entirely of choruses, among
them pieces for an eight-voiced double choir of a quite extraordinary
complexity. The oratorio's protagonist is the people of Israel. With this
oratorio, Handel appeals to the people of England, who since the Puritan Revolution had traced their descent from ancient Israel and the
people of the Exodus, with the same message used by prophets like
Hosea, Amos, Micah, Ezekiel, Jeremiah, and Haggai when they in-

voked the departure from Egypt: take heart, be true to the covenant, and you will be saved now and in the future as once you were saved from Egypt. In 1738 there were still no victories to report in the impending war with Spain, but that made it all the more necessary to take courage from the example of Israel's delivery from Egypt and England's own delivery from the Spanish armada in 1588.[65]

There is a place for Moses's song of praise not only in Handel's biography (as argued above) and in English history (as Ruth Smith has pointed out) but also in the liturgy of the Anglican Church (as has been shown by Hermann Goltz).[66] There the Quadragesima, the great period of Lenten fasting, is dominated by the Book of Exodus, the unevenly numbered chapters of which are read from at Evensong and the evenly numbered chapters at Matins. The first performances of *Israel in Egypt* fell into this period of the church year in April 1739. The interpretation of Lent and Easter in the light shed by the Book of Exodus goes back to early Christian, Byzantine, and West Roman Easter customs, and Moses's song of praise has a central place in those different traditions. That explains why Handel waited until the end of April before performing his oratorio; it also explains why, all theological concerns to the contrary, he received permission from the authorities to stage a purely biblical text in the theater. "Mr Handel has work'd a greater Miracle than any of those ascrib'd to Orpheus."[67]

PART THREE

THE COVENANT

To serve, to serve the idea of God, is the freedom for which
this people has been chosen.

—Arnold Schoenberg[1]

The Exodus story has become the master narrative of modern
constitutional thought. The covenant theology invented on
Sinai provided the blueprint for the social contracts of the
modern age.

—Rolf Schieder[2]

The cradle of modern democracy lies not just in Athens but in
Jerusalem, too.

—Eckart Otto[3]

CHAPTER SEVEN

THE CALLING OF THE PEOPLE

But ye are a chosen generation, a royal priesthood, a holy nation, a peculiar people; that ye should shew forth the praises of him who hath called you out of darkness into his marvelous light.

—*1 Peter 2:9*

The Jewish nation is to the whole inhabited world what the priest is to the state.

—*Philo of Alexandria*[1]

I am a stranger on earth: hide not thy commandments from me.

—*Psalm 119:19*

Holy People and Portable Fatherland

From the Sea of Reeds, the Israelites moved on to Mount Sinai. On the way, YHWH provided them with manna, quails, and water and gave them support in the fight against Amalek. Barely two months have elapsed since they turned their backs on Egypt. YHWH can say with some justice that he has borne his people "on eagles' wings" (Ex 19:4) in bringing them so speedily to the holy mountain. At Sinai, the mass of émigrés becomes a people, first from below and then from above. The first step is related in chapter 18. Jethro, Moses's father-in-law, comes to visit and witnesses firsthand how Moses spends all his waking hours settling the countless disputes that arise each day in such a large and disorganized community. He suggests to Moses that the populace should be organized along hierarchical lines:

And Moses chose able men out of all Israel, and made them heads over the people, rulers of thousands, rulers of hundreds, rulers of fifties, and rul-

ers of tens. And they judged the people at all seasons: the hard causes they
brought unto Moses, but every small matter they judged themselves.
(18:25–26)

This four-tiered structure of responsibility and representation is
based on a military chain of command yet serves the peaceful purpose
of resolving legal disputes. Each leader is responsible for his group—
numbering 10, 50, 100, or 1,000—which he represents to a higher level.
Moses shoulders responsibility for the entire community and represents it before God. Through responsibility and representation, the
amorphous mass is given a structure. The principle at work here might
be called an ascending "connectivism from below." The individual is
integrated into groups of increasing size and complexity all the way up
to the highest overarching unit, which might be called a "people" or
"nation" in the sense of a politically constituted entity.

Two points stand out in this episode. First, what we are witnessing
here could be described as the invention of bureaucracy. Bureaucracy
is a rational, abstract, and neutral principle that makes it possible to
organize, document, and administer a large group of people, in contrast to the smaller-scale power relations embedded in family, clan, and
tribal structures. In a bureaucracy, it is not the patriarch, headman, or
tribal chief who settles disputes and other questions, but qualified notables specially appointed by the authorities to rule on such matters.
Bureaucracy is the precondition for democracy; only a people constituted and administered on abstract, rational guidelines is capable of
deciding collectively on a rational course of action. In the wake of the
French Revolution, the evolution of legal culture (Code Napoleon) and
bureaucracy went hand in hand in France. It is thus only logical that the
momentous decision faced by the Israelites in what follows should be
preceded by their bureaucratic constitution.

It needs to be emphasized, second, that it is not YHWH who gives
Moses the idea for this measure but the Midianite Jethro. Bureaucracy
is not a divine institution but a secular one, based on the experience of
an older, foreign society. Egypt, where life was regulated and administered on all levels by bureaucrat scribes, would be the more obvious
model for emulation were it not for the fact that Egypt is far too negatively typecast throughout the story for it to serve as a model for any-

thing. At any rate, the introduction of bureaucracy is kept separate from the process of revelation. The bureaucratic neutralization of the complex social structures that the Israelites had evolved over time is a secularizing tendency in the further sense that, in tribal and high religions, these levels of society typically cohere around religious figures: ancestors, family gods, nome gods, civic deities, and the like. This step could be characterized, with Max Weber, as the turning point from charismatic to bureaucratic rule; yet Moses, practically the prototype of a charismatic ruler, loses nothing of his preeminence as a result. On the contrary, his rise to unequaled greatness only occurs in the final part of the narrative, the making of the covenant.

In the final version of the Book of Exodus, which is largely the work of the Priestly Source, the organization of the émigrés according to the principles of civil law and bureaucracy is related in the prelude to the "Sinai pericope." In a restricted sense, the pericope consists of chapters 19–24; conceived more broadly, it continues right up to Numbers 10. This section has all the signs of a later interpolation; indeed, from Numbers 10:11 the thread is taken up at exactly the point where it had been dropped in Exodus 18: with the departure en masse of the people of Israel, now organized along military lines and listed by the combat units or "hosts" to which they have been assigned.

Through the insertion of the Sinai pericope, we arrive instead at the third act and climax of God's revelation. It takes place at Sinai before the eyes of the people. The criterion of witnessing is constitutive for the concept of revelation. After all, we can speak of revelation only when we can identify someone to whom something has been revealed. In the first act, Moses had been the sole witness. His task was to communicate to others a revelation that had been granted him alone. In the sharpest possible contrast, YHWH then revealed his power for all to see in the form of the ten plagues. Everyone could witness what happened to Egypt. Yet he appeared there only in his works. By contrast to this highly public yet diffuse and basically mute revelation of his power, on Sinai he reveals himself in a targeted and specific form that represents something singular and new. This time the witnesses are the Israelites, whom YHWH addresses as his people and to whom he offers a covenant. Through their witnessing, they constitute themselves as a people in a wholly new, emphatic, and almost directly democratic sense. They—not Moses or the seventy elders or, as in later reprisals of the covenant idea, the church or a dynasty—are the partners of the covenant. What is revealed here is the "Law," the covenant's foundation and precondition. This revelation thus has a very precise content. It is the service for which the people has been chosen, the mission it has been called on from among all other nations to fulfill.

This section is in three parts. An introduction (chapter 19) outlines YHWH's plan to enter into a covenant with the people and recounts the preparations for it. Moses climbs the mountain three times. There God reveals to him his intentions in making the covenant, announces that he will appear before the people, and gives instructions on how they are to protect themselves. Each time Moses must come down from the mountain to secure the people's assent. Space must be created for the theophany on the third day. The people are therefore cordoned off to ensure that nobody sets foot in the sacred precinct. The main part is concerned with the handing down of the law, including the Ten Commandments and the "book of the covenant" (chapters 20–23). Chapter 19 (introduction) has its counterpart in chapter 24 (conclusion), where the covenant is sealed in a solemn ceremony and the laws are set down in writing.

The words Moses is told to use when announcing the covenant to the people refer back to YHWH's previous revelation of power:

> Ye have seen what I did unto the Egyptians, and how I bare you on eagles' wings,[2] and brought you unto myself. Now therefore, if ye will obey my voice indeed, and keep my covenant, then ye shall be a peculiar treasure[3] unto me above all people: for all the earth is mine. And ye shall be unto me a kingdom of priests, and a holy nation. (19:4–6)

The Israelites have already "seen" God reveal his power; now they are told to "obey"—that is, to understand, embrace, heed with "hearing hearts"—his "voice" as it reveals the Law, the Torah.[4] Seeing and listening draw attention to the Israelites' role as witnesses to YHWH's revelation. They were present as eyewitnesses when YHWH afflicted ten plagues on the Egyptians and destroyed their forces in the Sea of Reeds. Now they are called on to be earwitnesses to the new constitution God will reveal in his covenant.

FIGURE 15. Israel is chosen at Sinai: God speaks to Moses, Aaron, and the seventy elders. French book illustration, early fourteenth century.

Deuteronomy describes the steps leading up to the covenant under the same headings as the Book of Exodus while also directly appending the third step, the Law, which is to serve the covenant as its foundation and precondition.

1. *Election:*

For thou art a holy people [*'ām qādôš*] unto YHWH thy God: YHWH thy God hath chosen thee to be a special people [*'ām sĕgullâ*] unto himself, above all people that are upon the face of the earth.

YHWH did not set his love upon you, nor choose you, because ye were more in number than any people; for ye were the fewest of all people; but because YHWH loved [*'ahăbâ*] you, and because he would keep the

oath which he had sworn unto your fathers, hath YHWH brought you
out with a mighty hand, and redeemed you out of the house of bondmen,
from the land of Pharaoh king of Egypt.

2. *Covenant:*

Know therefore that YHWH thy God, he is God, the faithful God, which
keepeth covenant and mercy with them that love him and keep his
commandments to a thousand generations; and repayeth them that hate
him to their face, to destroy them: he will not be slack to him that hateth
him, he will repay him to his face.

3. *Constitution:*

Thou shalt therefore keep the commandments, and the statutes, and the
judgments, which I command thee this day, to do them. (Deut 7:6–11)

In the Book of Exodus, this step is taken in chapters 20–23, when the
laws are proclaimed and the people give their assent through acclamation; it is then ceremonially reaffirmed in chapter 24. With this step the
nation, having already been bureaucratically organized in chapter 18,
receives a constitution as God's chosen people. In contrast to the ascending "connectivism from below" outlined earlier, this step could be
termed a descending "collectivism from above" or "transcendental collectivism." By this I refer to the principle of a collective identity that is
transcendentally anchored, strictly delimited, and ordained from on
high, as opposed to a togetherness that has either emerged through a
quasi-organic process or been bureaucratically engineered.

I would venture to suggest that this "ethnogenetic stroke of genius"[5]
represents something new, something entirely without precedent in
the ancient world. The Egyptians called themselves simply "human beings" and believed their empire to be coextensive with the ordered universe. They felt a sense of togetherness that flowed from everything
they held in common: they all inhabited the same riverine oasis, which
was defined by natural boundaries (the Mediterranean to the north,
the first cataract to the south); they all spoke more or less the same
language; they all observed the same rites and worshipped the same
gods. Much the same can be said of all other empires. The Israelites, on
the other hand, derived their sense of togetherness from having been
chosen by YHWH to enter into the covenant and from having elected

to live by the Law, the constitution that qualified them as covenant partners. This constitution was bound up with the idea that the Israelites had a special task in the world. This is the second thing that makes the biblical idea of what constitutes a "people" or "nation" so unusual. As an avant-garde of piety and justice, the Israelites felt called on to practice the Law given them by YHWH. By accepting the terms of the covenant, they became not simply a "nation" but a nation unlike any other. The Book of Exodus defines this idea as "a kingdom of priests, and a holy nation" (*mamleket kōhănîm wĕgôy qādôš*). The Israelites were to behave toward all the other nations on earth as priests to the profane. The Egyptians saw themselves in much the same way during the final phase of their culture. Faced by their impending doom, they called their land the "temple of the entire universe."[6] By this they meant that Egypt was the land where the gods were at home, just as Israel understood itself as the people in whose midst YHWH dwelled. Here is formed an emphatic concept of people or nationhood that was probably just as important—if not more important—for the history of nation-building and nationalism in Europe than the ancient ideas of *polis* and *populus*.[7]

The story has now reached its climax, the point to which the whole story has been heading since the beginning and the reason why it was told in the first place. In order to arrive at this point, the people first had to be delivered from Egypt. In order to be delivered from Egypt, they first had to settle there, multiply, suffer oppression, and be saved. If we widen the scope to the Book of Genesis, the line leading up to the covenant can be traced—via the emigration of Jacob's clan to Egypt, Abraham's departure from Mesopotamia, and the emergence of the gentile nations following the flood (to which God alludes in Exodus 19:5) —all the way back to the creation of the universe. On the other hand, all subsequent history can be understood as the consequence or after-effect of the covenant made at Sinai. The covenant had to be made so that God's promises could be fulfilled, so that the land could be conquered and then lost again over the centuries, and so that the people of Israel could endure in the face of adversity, diaspora, and persecution. The covenant is the great turning point from prehistory to history. From now on, everything done within the covenant will have consequences according to whether it pleases or displeases God.

With that there emerges a new chronotope, a site with its own, linear temporality in which all causes inexorably give rise to their effects, no good deed is left unrewarded, and no evil deed remains unatoned; a context of meaning that allows even the worst catastrophes to be understood as just punishment and thus safeguards against chaos, senselessness, and despair. This idea of history is unprecedented and first comes into the world with covenant theology. The terrible suffering endured by the people in Egypt had nothing whatsoever to do with any sins they may have committed. This concept of sin first arises within the covenant made on Sinai and within the specific historical form—the framework of linear time—established by that covenant. All the ordeals that the people will have to undergo in the future will be attributable to sin. From now on, suffering is the unavoidable punishment for backsliding from the strict demands of the covenant made on Sinai.[8]

The history that God now undertakes to make in partnership with his people has the character of a project. It is directed toward the future and is based on three promises: the increase of Abraham's seed (taken to mean the people of Israel), the conquest of the Promised Land, and the fellowship with God, who will dwell among his people. The third promise is the decisive one and it comes to be fulfilled here, on Sinai. The first had already been fulfilled in Egypt and the second awaits the day when, after forty years wandering in the wilderness, the people will finally reach the banks of the Jordan.

The central concept defining the chosen people in both Exodus and Deuteronomy is "holiness" (*qādôš*): "And ye shall be unto me a [. . .] holy nation" (Ex 19:6), "For thou art a holy people unto YHWH thy God: YHWH thy God hath chosen thee to be a special people unto himself, above all people that are upon the face of the earth" (Deut 7:6 = 14:2; see also 26:18–19). Holiness implies segregation or isolation from the profane world. Through the covenant, Israel becomes a people that "shall dwell alone, and shall not be reckoned among the nations" (Num 23:9).

The new thing that enters into the world with covenant theology is the idea of a nation that is founded not on common descent, land, language, or sovereign rule but on divine law: the Torah. In his *Confessions* (1854), Heinrich Heine therefore called the Torah a "portable fatherland": a book that molds a mass of emigrated slaves into God's own people and endures for them as an inalienable homeland, existing independently of territory and borders, state institutions, temples, priests, and altars.[9] By creating the Torah, Moses created the people. Writing eighty years after Heine in a climate of National Socialist anti-Semitism, Sigmund Freud posed "the question as to what has really created the peculiar character of the Jew" and "came to the conclusion that the Jew is the creation of the man Moses."[10] With his book on Moses, Freud wanted to "explain the origin of the special character of the Jewish people, a character which is probably what has made their survival to the present day possible."[11] "We know that of all the peoples who lived round the basin of the Mediterranean in antiquity, the Jewish people is almost the only one which still exists in name and also in substance."[12] This very question had already preoccupied Heine, and he had arrived at the same result. He saw in Moses a

> gigantic figure! [. . .] How small Sinai appears when Moses stands on it! This mountain is only the pediment for the feet of the man whose head reaches to the heavens as he speaks with God.[13]

Heine identified Moses as a great artist:

> Unlike the Egyptians, however, he did not fashion his works of art from baked bricks and granite but built human pyramids; he carved out human obelisks; he took a tribe of poor shepherds and from it created a people that was also to defy the centuries, a great, eternal, holy people, a people of God that could serve as a prototype for all other peoples, all of mankind—he created Israel![14]

This act of creation takes place at Sinai. According to Jewish tradition, the souls of all Jews for all eternity were present at that moment. "Neither with you only do I make this covenant and this oath, but [. . .] also with him that is not here with us this day" (Deut 29:14–15), that is to say, with all generations to come. What emerges with covenant theology is Israel in the sense of an ethnic, political, and religious identity, and hence something completely new "that could serve as a prototype for all other peoples," as Heine astutely pointed out. For the idea of a religious identity based on a pact between God and a community to whom he has revealed his will, and that commits itself to live according to that will, did indeed become a prototype—if not for "all of mankind," then at least for the more than half of it who declare their allegiance to Christianity, Islam, and many other, more recent faiths.

This biblical concept of God's chosen people represents no less innovative and momentous an achievement than the biblical monotheism of loyalty. Monotheism (of loyalty) and a nation of the elect are two sides of the same novel idea: that of a covenant between God and human beings. The *one* God is the God of *one* people, and this *one* people is the people of the *one* God. What connects the two is the idea of the covenant that binds them together. This covenant is what first makes God one and the children of Israel his people. There are many different peoples in the world but only one has been chosen by YHWH to be his own, just as there are many different gods but only one to whom Israel has pledged its loyalty and obedience. Such loyalty would be meaningless in the absence of other gods. The covenant between creator and created does not admit alternatives; it cannot be rescinded. By contrast, the covenant between liberator and liberated has alternatives. The liberator can turn to other peoples, the liberated to other gods. That is why the idea of loyalty comes into play here, which the Bible illustrates by means of bridal, conjugal, and filial metaphors and fleshes out according to the model of a political alliance.

What is a covenant—*běrît* in Hebrew? A *běrît* is, first, a political alliance forged between partners who are not already "naturally" affiliated through ties of land, language, or blood. In political science, a distinction is made between organicist and voluntarist forms of community building. The covenant exemplifies a voluntarist association: a covenant is made between partners who freely decide on each other's suitability. In the ancient Near East, alliance treaties were sworn by gods who saw to it that they were upheld and that any infringements were punished.[15] What is altogether different and new, however, is the idea that a god could himself figure as partner in such an alliance rather than merely watching over it. In the Bible—at least in the reading suggested by the final version, if not in the genesis of the individual texts—the idea of a covenant with God is nothing new: God made covenants with Noah (Gen 9:9–17, with the rainbow as a sign) and Abraham (Gen 15:18; 17:2–14, with circumcision as a sign). Yet the Sinai covenant is something quite different. It combines the pledge of loyalty with the revelation of a collective constitution, way of life, and cultic organization. Further-

more, this revelation not only serves the people as a "portable fatherland"; it can also secure them God's lasting presence, practically
amounting to cohabitation. God does not make this pact with the
human race as a whole in his capacity as creator (as had been the case
with the Noah covenant) but with a particular group that he has brought
forth "from the midst of another nation" (Deut 4:34), "out of the iron
furnace, even out of Egypt" (Deut 4:20), and made his "peculiar treasure." With the motif of election, the idea of the biblical covenant takes
on the emotional resonance of a mutually binding love match in addition to the political dimension of a treaty. This covenant rests on strong
mutual devotion as much as it does on commandments and laws. The
chosen people are required to "love YHWH thy God with all thine
heart, and with all thy soul, and with all thy might" (Deut 6:5), while
YHWH "jealously" watches over the loyalty of his covenant partner and
explodes into fits of rage whenever Israel dallies with other gods.

That explains why at the Passover feast, the festival celebrating the
departure from Egypt and the making of the covenant at Sinai, the
Song of Solomon was read aloud from a parchment scroll (*mĕgillâ*). It
celebrates the pact as the consummation of a love match in the erotic
sense of a physical liaison between lovers.[16]

The Torah as Memory

> Only take heed to thyself, and keep thy soul diligently, lest
> thou forget the things which thine eyes have seen, and lest
> they depart from thy heart all the days of thy life: but teach
> them thy children, and thy children's children.
>
> *—Deuteronomy 4:9*

In the form of the Torah, the Israelites forge a memory for themselves
and so become a people that self-perpetuates over time. But what does
"forging a memory for oneself" actually mean? In his *Genealogy of
Morals*, Nietzsche differentiates between a quasi-natural memory that
embraces both remembering and forgetting and an artificially propa-
gated "memory of the will" that precludes all forgetting:

> How does one give the human animal a memory? How does one impress
> something on this [. . .] incarnated forgetfulness so that it remains present
> to mind? As we might imagine, the means employed to find a solution or

answer to this ancient problem have been far from tender; there is, perhaps, nothing more frightening and more sinister in the whole prehistory of man than his *technique for remembering things*: "Something is branded in, so that it stays in the memory: only that which *hurts* incessantly is remembered"— this is a central proposition of the oldest (and unfortunately also the most enduring) psychology on earth. [. . .] Things never proceeded without blood, torture, and victims, when man thought it necessary to forge a memory for himself. The most horrifying sacrifices and offerings (including sacrifice of the firstborn), the cruelest rituals of all religious cults (and all religions are at their deepest foundations systems of cruelty)—all these things originate from that instinct which intuited that the most powerful aid to memory was pain.[17]

These are impressive, unforgettable words. Nietzsche is clearly thinking here primarily of rites of initiation, which involved—and, in many tribal cultures, still involve—often gruesome tests of courage and endurance. Here too a memory is being forged. Such initiations always have to do with learning. The community into which the initiate is received defines itself by its collective memory, as set out in the canon of myths and norms that it passes on to the neophyte. In the same way, the Torah serves as a repository for all the historical knowledge and normative guidelines deemed important enough by the community to be handed down to future generations.

However, Nietzsche's ideas about the cruelty of archaic mnemonic techniques are based on an overly pessimistic anthropology. In his view, the "human animal" is a born egotist who is naturally predisposed to forget anything that does not serve his immediate interests. For that reason, anything reminding him of his fellow human animals and his obligations toward them must be painstakingly and painfully inculcated. Social civility is a straitjacket in which the human animal must be placed so that others may live with him. This pessimistic image of human society and culture was shared by Sigmund Freud, and if we go further back in history we could also mention Thomas Hobbes, who likewise envisaged human beings in their natural state as solitary, brutish, and asocial. Only the constant fear of being struck dead by their fellows drove humans to make a contract transferring all coercive force into the hands of a sovereign who would guarantee civil peace.[18] Today's anthropology sees things rather differently. It sees human beings as naturally predisposed toward interpersonal attachment, empathy, and sympathy, without which we could not even survive, let alone flourish. As human beings, we owe our entire mental and emotional make-up to our social bonds. *Homo naturalis* is inherently *homo civilis*; turning him into the lone wolf that Hobbes and Nietzsche picture him to be would take at least as much effort as transforming him into the responsible individual identified by Nietzsche as the end product of painful mnemonic drilling. Human beings live in social relations, feel a need to belong, and are generally prepared to shoulder the associated obligations and memories—perhaps not always willingly (as amply attested in the Torah; see chapter 9), but at least the compulsion to conform directed from outside is matched by a drive for sociality and solidarity coming from within. In any event, it is imperative that memory be stabilized in the form of ritual and hence also in the body. On this point Nietzsche is absolutely correct: the inclination to forget is always there, the human need for attachment does nothing to banish it, and memory therefore has need of stabilizing factors.

When considering "how one gives the human animal a memory," Nietzsche was thinking of how humans are socialized through a process he imagined to be painful and violent. For the Jews, however, the issue was how someone was to be Judaized, that is, initiated into the chosen people of Israel, a community living in covenant with God as well as with each other. This entailed a dual commitment: a vertical commitment to God and a horizontal commitment to one's fellows, as famously expressed in Jesus's double commandment, put together from two Torah passages (Deut 6:5 and Lev 19:18), to "love the Lord thy God with all thy heart" and to "love thy neighbor as thyself." Not only does the pact YHWH makes with Israel forge a bond between God and his people, it also binds together the individuals who make up that people. Remembering the covenant, staying true to YHWH, means staying true to one another. Such loyalty cannot persist without memory, since what is supposed to motivate it in perpetuity is the grateful memory of deliverance from Egyptian bondage.

Behind the Torah's function as the repository of national memory stands the experience of failure, total political collapse, the loss of kingship, land, and Temple. The covenant had broken down, and for that only one of the two partners, YHWH or Israel, could be at fault. The exiles preferred to take the blame themselves rather than abandon YHWH. They ascribed the breakdown to their failure to remember God and to honor the solemn commitments they had made him in the covenant. This motif can already be found in Hosea 8:14: "For Israel hath forgotten his Maker," and it subsequently runs through the Book of Deuteronomy from beginning to end. The book is founded on the fear of forgetting.[19] There are constant reminders that what Israel experienced during the exodus and swore in the covenant must not, under any circumstances, be forgotten:

> And it shall be, when the Lord thy God shall have brought thee into the land [...] to give thee great and goodly cities, which thou buildest not, and houses full of good things, which thou filledst not, and wells digged, which thou diggedst not, vineyards and olive trees, which thou plantedst not; when thou shalt have eaten and be full; then beware lest thou forget the Lord, which brought thee forth out of the land of Egypt, from the house of bondage. (6:10–12)

Many commandments can be summed up in the formula "Remember! Do not forget!" They relate to the procedures, institutions, and media of a memory culture, with priority placed on the institutions of transgenerational transmission.[20] Such education begins in the family and is continued in formal instruction and schooling. Next come the visible signs of memory, from physical and domestic reminders to public memorials. Third, liturgical and aesthetic forms of memory play a role as well: the great festivals of Passover, Shavuot, and Sukkot in addition to poetry, for Deuteronomy concludes with a song of Moses. From today's perspective, this can be extended to the role of the arts in memory culture: poetry, theater, film, music, painting, and so on. What is new is the absolutely binding force of this memory. Twice in the Book of Deuteronomy (4:2; 13:1) it is impressed upon the reader that nothing should be added to, subtracted from, or changed in this always-to-be-remembered, never-to-be-forgotten compendium of law, history, and confession.

There is a legend, associated with the original version of Deuteronomy, telling of its chance rediscovery after centuries of neglect.[21] According to the legend, the book was found in the course of restoration works on the Temple carried out in the reign of King Josiah. When it was discovered that the book was written by Moses and contained a summary of all the rules that must be observed in order for the land to prosper, there was widespread dismay: the book had been forgotten, the rules neglected, the covenant breached. The disaster that struck in 587, with the destruction of the Temple and the deportation of the elite into Babylonian exile, was thus inevitable. Deuteronomy presents itself as the forgotten codification of something that had to be remembered at all costs, and it gives grounds for the hope that now, with its definitive reappropriation, the covenant and salvation may once more be within reach. "Never again forget!": that is the motto that graces Deuteronomy and stands at the heart of the Torah, largely a product of the Babylonian exile.

In the form of the Torah, the deportees forged a memory that knit them together as a group and secured their collective identity even when abroad. It was this identity as God's people that prevented them from being absorbed into the polyglot Babylonian population. By staying true to their God, they stayed true to themselves, and they eventually succeeded, after an exile lasting fifty to seventy years, in returning to Jerusalem. Memory thus proved to be the most important foundation of the biblical idea of nationhood.

In the story of the departure from Egypt, we have before us the classic example of a group that forges a memory for itself, in Nietzsche's terms, with the help of an extraordinary cultural art of memory. This technique is designed to preserve in collective memory what under no circumstances must be forgotten: YHWH's saving deeds and the covenant commitments entered into at Sinai. It keeps alive the memory of a normative past by which the group defines itself and first constitutes itself as a nation in a religious sense.

Such a thing was unknown in Greece and Egypt. The Trojan War never figured as a normative past or provided a mythic foundation for Greek identity. For the Greeks, the past was replete with countless myths. Every city, every noble family had its own founding myth, and this very plenitude blocked the emergence of a collectively binding structure such as that characterizing the Exodus myth. In Egypt, myth was never bound up with the past. The Old Kingdom with its pyramids, for example, never played the role of a normative past in memory. So

far as the West is concerned, whatever normative force classical antiquity and biblical history may once have possessed is now much diminished. Certainly, they have nothing like the significance that the exodus
has for Judaism today. Germany, however, appears to have undergone
a decisive change in this respect, one that has spilled out into Europe
and even beyond. In various publications over recent years, Aleida Assmann has applied the concept of a normative past to the twelve years
of Nazi dictatorship in Germany, especially the Holocaust. She has argued that around thirty years ago, the memory of the crimes committed under Hitler belatedly brought about a fundamental shift in our
Western historical consciousness as well as in our memory culture.[22]
With the Shoah and the atrocities of the Second World War, the Ger-
mans, together with a significant part of the human race, have assumed
responsibility for a normative past that ought under no circumstances
to be forgotten—not just in the sense of ensuring that Auschwitz is
never repeated, but above all in the sense of asserting new norms of
humanity and justice that reveal their meaning and urgency only
against the background of those traumatic experiences. In much the
same way, ancient Israel had already elevated the departure from Egypt
into a normative past, since only by doing so could the liberating force
of the divine covenant and its laws be understood.

The Development of the Covenant Idea: Bridal and Filial Metaphors

Incipit exire qui incipit amare.
—*St. Augustine*[23]

The earliest texts to suggest the idea of a special relationship between
YHWH and Israel as his people are also the first to mention Moses and
the departure from Egypt: the books of the prophets Hosea and
Amos.[24] They clearly demonstrate the links between the motifs of departure, election, and commitment.

   In Hosea, the "monotheism of loyalty" is tangibly present for the
first time in literature. It represents the great innovation and the most
central element in biblical monotheism, remaining its dominant trait
through all the subsequent transmutations undergone by this religious

revolution. Like Amos, Hosea reproaches Israel with its sins, but in his eyes these do not consist primarily in injustice and oppression but in "whoredom" with alien gods. I collate here several of Hosea's most striking invectives against Israel's infidelity:

> They sacrifice upon the tops of the mountains, and burn incense upon the hills, under oaks and poplars and elms, because the shadow thereof is good: therefore your daughters shall commit whoredom, and your spouses shall commit adultery. I will not punish your daughters when they commit whoredom, nor your spouses when they commit adultery: for [the men] themselves consort with whores, and they sacrifice with harlots: therefore the people that doth not understand shall come to ruin. (4:13–14)

> I found Israel like grapes in the wilderness; I saw your fathers as the firstripe in the fig tree at her first time: but they went to *ba‘al pĕ‘ôr*,[25] and separated themselves unto that shame; and their abominations were according as they loved. (9:10)

A different image used by Hosea for the special bond between YHWH and his people is that of a father-son relationship:

> When Israel was a child, then I loved him, and called my son out of Egypt. But the more they were called, the more they went away from me: they sacrificed unto Baalim, and burned incense to graven images. (11:1–2)

More precisely, it is not so much the covenant itself that Hosea illustrates with the image of a father-son relationship as its breach. YHWH chose Israel for his bride when it was in a state of utter abandonment and neglect, adorning it and instructing it in his ways, but Israel proved unfaithful and dallied with other suitors, other gods. Such images have a tragic tinge to them; they befit a relationship that has already broken down. They are employed in exactly the same way by the prophets who preached a hundred to a hundred and fifty years later, Ezekiel (chapter 16) and Jeremiah (chapters 2–4):[26]

> But I said, How shall I set thee among my sons, and give thee a pleasant land, the most beautiful inheritance of any nation? And I said, Thou shalt call me, My father; and shalt not turn away from me. Surely as a wife treacherously departeth from her husband, so have ye dealt treacherously with me, O house of Israel. (Jer 3:19–20)

Only later, with the spiritual reinterpretation of the bridal imagery undertaken in the Song of Solomon, does the idea of an erotic relationship between God and his people appear in a more positive light.

Like the bridal metaphor, the father-son metaphor refers to a relationship based on choice, not on paternity and birth. YHWH chooses Israel in the same way a man would select a bride or adopt a son. Where Paul, in his Letter to the Romans 9:4, lists what defines "Israel" as a nation, he gives pride of place to sonship:

huiothesia	adoption as a son, sonship = election
doxa	glory (*kābôd* in Hebrew, God's presence in Israel)
diathekai	the covenants (made with Abraham, Moses, David)
nomothesia	the Law
latreia	worship
epangeliai	promises

Huiothesia means placing someone in the position of a son and does not imply any biological kinship. All six of Israel's distinctions stem from the idea of the covenant as a "voluntaristic" association resulting from mutual love and free choice, as opposed to a centuries-old, "organicist" togetherness arising from ancestry, cohabitation, and tradition.[27] While it is true that ancestry plays an important role in Israel's self-understanding, in the Book of Exodus it is explicitly stated that many people from other nations joined the Israelites on their departure as well ("And a mixed multitude went up also with them," 12:28; see also Num 11:4).[28] Considerable emphasis is placed on the fact that Moses married a Midianite and that Jethro, his Midianite father-in-law, actively assists him in his struggle to release his people from bondage. The key criterion for inclusion in the covenant is thus not ancestry; all that is required is a voluntary commitment to obey the body of laws ordained by God.

A brief comparison of this definition of Judaism with Herodotus's notion of Greekness (*to hellenikon*) may be informative:[29]

to homaimon	same blood (shared ancestry)
to homoglosson	same language
homotropa ethea	similar customs
koinai thusiai	common sacrifices

This organicist, nonvoluntaristic description of what it means to be Greek looks very much like a modern definition of Judaism. After all, a Jew today tends to be defined by common religion (including customs) and language as well as by matrilineal descent. Yet when Paul, in developing his own concept of "Israel," set out to abolish the ethnic qualifications for Judaism in order to accommodate gentiles, he could draw on the idea of the covenant and hence also the Exodus tradition.

This god who chooses Israel to be his bride or his son is one who, unlike all the other gods in the world at the time, has neither wife nor children. The partnership with Israel thus takes the place of the constellational relations that otherwise bind the gods together and form the main stuff of myth. No less novel than the idea of a cosmically isolated god who attaches himself solely to one nation is the idea of a politically isolated nation that attaches itself solely to one god. The partnership to which YHWH and Israel commit themselves is a highly exclusive, long-term relationship, fittingly expressed in metaphors of marriage, monogamy, and sonship.

The prophets who systematically deploy the metaphor of marriage for the covenant between YHWH and his people are Hosea, Ezekiel, and Jeremiah. All three are prophets of doom. They all foretell impending disaster for the people as divine punishment for their unfaithfulness: in the case of Hosea, the Assyrian conquest of Israel in 722 BCE; in that of Ezekiel and Jeremiah, the Babylonian invasion of Judah in 587 BCE. Adultery or "whoredom" is the keyword here, not marriage. Ezekiel devotes two whole chapters to this theme (16 and 23). The narrative underlying their prophecies supplements the four-act salvific drama of promise, liberation, covenant, and land grant with a tragic fifth act: YHWH finds Israel as an abandoned baby, lovingly cares for it through childhood, and weds the virgin once she has come of age, only to find himself serially cheated by her. He then spurns her on account of her incorrigible harlotry. What follows is only a short excerpt. In Ezekiel we read:

> Thus saith the Lord, YHWH, unto Jerusalem: Thy birth and thy nativity is of the land of Canaan; thy father was an Amorite, and thy mother a Hittite. And as for thy nativity, in the day thou wast born thy navel was not cut,

neither wast thou washed in water to supple thee; thou wast not salted at all, nor swaddled at all. None eye pitied thee, to do any of these unto thee, to have compassion upon thee; but thou wast cast out in the open field, to the loathing of thy person, in the day thou wast born.

And when I passed by thee, and saw thee polluted in thine own blood, I said unto thee when thou wast in thy blood, Live; yea, I said unto thee when thou wast in thy blood, Live. I have caused thee to multiply as the bud of the field, and thou hast increased and waxen great, and thou are come to excellent ornaments: thy breasts are fashioned, and thine hair is grown, whereas thou wast naked and bare.

Now when I passed by thee [again], and looked upon thee, behold, thy time was the time of love; and I spread the corner of my garment over thee, and covered thy nakedness: yea, I sware unto thee, and entered into a covenant with thee, saith the Lord, YHWH, and thou becamest mine. Then washed I thee with water; yea, I thoroughly washed away thy blood from thee, and I anointed thee with oil. I clothed thee also with broidered work, and shod thee with fine leather, and I girded thee about with fine linen, and I covered thee with silk. I decked thee also with ornaments, and I put bracelets upon thy hands, and a chain on thy neck. And I put a jewel on thy forehead, and earrings in thine ears, and a beautiful crown upon thine head. Thus wast thou decked with gold and silver; and thy raiment was of fine linen, and silk, and broidered work; thou didst eat fine flour, and honey, and oil: and thou wast exceeding beautiful, and thou didst prosper into a kingdom.

And thy renown went forth among the heathen for thy beauty: for it was perfect through my comeliness, which I had put upon thee, saith the Lord, YHWH. But thou didst trust in thine own beauty, and playedst the harlot because of thy renown, and pouredst out thy fornications on every one that passed by; his it was. And of thy garments thou didst take, and deckedst thy high places with divers colours, and playedst the harlot thereupon: the like has never been, nor ever shall be. Thou hast also taken thy fair jewels of my gold and of my silver, which I had given thee, and madest to thyself images of men, and didst commit whoredom with them.

And thou tookest thy broidered garments, and coveredst them: and thou hast set mine oil and mine incense before them. My bread also which I gave thee, fine flour, and oil, and honey, wherewith I fed thee, thou hast even set it before them for a sweet savor: and thus it was, saith the Lord, YHWH. Moreover thou hast taken thy sons and thy daughters, whom thou hast borne upon me, and these hast thou sacrificed unto them to be devoured. Is this of thy whoredoms a small matter, that thou hast slain my children, and delivered them to cause them to pass through the fire for them? And in all thine abominations and thy whoredoms thou hast not remembered the days of thy youth, when thou wast naked and bare, and wast polluted in thy blood. (16:3–22)

And in Jeremiah:

He says, If a man put away his wife, and she go from him, and become another man's, shall he return unto her again? Shall not that land be greatly polluted? But thou hast played the harlot with many lovers, and wouldst thou now return to me? saith YHWH. Lift up thine eyes unto the high places, and see where thou hast not been defiled. In the ways hast thou sat waiting for them, as the Arabian in the wilderness; and thou hast polluted the land with thy whoredoms and with thy wickedness. Therefore the showers have been withholden, and there hath been no latter rain; and thou hadst a whore's forehead, thou refusedst to be ashamed.

Wilt thou not from this time cry unto me, My father, thou art the guide of my youth? Will he reserve his anger for ever? Will he keep it to the end? Behold, thou hast spoken and done evil things as thou couldest.

YHWH said also unto me in the days of Josiah the king, Hast thou seen that which backsliding Israel hath done? She is gone up upon every high mountain and under every green tree, and there hath played the harlot. And I said after she had done all these things, Turn thou unto me. But she returneth not. And her treacherous sister Judah saw it.

And I saw, when for all the causes whereby backsliding Israel committed adultery I had put her away, and given her a bill of divorce; yet her treacherous sister Judah feared not, but went and played the harlot also. And it came to pass through the lightness of her whoredom, that she defiled the land, and committed adultery with stones and with stocks. And yet for all this her treacherous sister Judah hath not turned unto me with her whole heart, but feignedly, saith YHWH. (3:1–10)

Both prophets deploy a metaphorical language for a covenant more often breached than observed, likening Israel's serial backsliding to adultery and harlotry. Like Hosea, they target the officially condoned religion that must have been practiced in public and at court, which they believe to be all too similar to the religions found in neighboring countries: the worship of YHWH as chief god and civil deity, alongside other gods like Asherah, Anat, and Ba'al, in city temples and hilltop shrines. It is striking that the prophets who invoke the idea of the covenant and call for a monotheism of loyalty do so under the impression of infidelity and failure, sin and betrayal. Presumably this tragic grounding of the Exodus story already characterized the *Exodus narrative, which may have belonged to the Hosean-Deuteronomi(sti)c tradition and was combined with the Book of *Genesis and expanded in the Priestly Source.

If we cast a glance at other parts of the world at the time, we see that bridal and filial metaphors for the relationship between gods and kings were commonplace. In Mesopotamia, for instance, the king and the goddess Inanna-Ishtar were joined together each year in sacred marriage.[30] The image found by Israel's prophets for the bond of love and election between God and his chosen people likewise stands in the mythic tradition of a sacred marriage between farmers and their fields, the king and his land, or heaven and earth. Here the image no longer symbolizes fertility but fidelity (or rather infidelity). The prophets draw on it to castigate the religious practices that flourished in Israel during the entire monarchical period, from its beginnings until Babylonian exile, when deities such as Asherah and Ba'al were worshipped alongside YHWH. But the image of a loving relationship between God and his people was to resonate far beyond this pattern of prophetic argument, ensuring that the love songs collected in the Song of Solomon, for example, could be interpreted in this light and admitted into the canon.[31] Just as Israel reinterpreted the figure of the king who weds Inanna-Ishtar, the divine personification of the land, by replacing the king with God and the goddess with the people, so Christianity reinterpreted the figure of the people chosen by God to be his bride by replacing the people with the soul.[32] "Behold! Whom? The bridegroom! Behold him! How? As a lamb!" cries the "Daughter of Zion" in Bach's *St. Matthew Passion*. She no longer represents the people—she is imploring them to behold their savior, after all—but the individual soul, devoutly bound to Christ in love, longing, and compassion.

In Egypt, the pharaoh was regarded as the son of the supreme deity and given the title "son of Ra." In religious ceremonies, he played the role of son to all the gods and goddesses in the Egyptian pantheon, his putative mothers and fathers.[33] The Jerusalem monarchy also adopted the model of the king's divine sonship from Egypt. "Thou art my son; this day have I begotten thee," God tells the king in Psalm 2:7.[34] God chooses the king to be his son, a transformation that takes place the instant he is crowned. In Psalm 89:27, God pledges: "I will make him my firstborn, higher than the kings of the earth."

The image of Israel's divine sonship is firmly anchored in the Exodus myth. Unlike the bridal metaphor, which always has tragic connotations in the prophets Hosea, Jeremiah, and Ezekiel and looks backward to the adulterous violation of the covenant, the image of sonship in Exodus has positive connotations and looks forward to Israel's election and the fulfillment of God's promises.

> Thus saith YHWH, Israel is my son, even my firstborn. And I say unto thee: let my son go, that he may serve me. And if thou refuse to let him go, behold, I will slay thy son, even thy firstborn. (Ex 4:22–23)

Rather than looking back in anger at the broken covenant, the image of sonship here looks forward in hope to the liberation of Israel, soon to be compelled by the death of the Egyptian firstborn, as well as the making of the covenant, which will see the freed Israelites become God's chosen people and hence his adopted son.[35]

TREATY AND LAW

The Deconstruction of Kingship: Treaty and Law
as the Constitution of God's People

The original version of Deuteronomy dates from around a century after the prophet Hosea. Whereas Hosea had resorted to bridal and filial metaphors when describing the covenant between God and his people, Deuteronomy codifies the covenant in a formal treaty of alliance, thereby giving it the status of an institution recognized under international law. The covenant is now no longer metaphorical but the real thing. The first version of the Sinai pericope must have arisen around the same time and in the same tradition. In the context of the Priestly Exodus narrative, it "conveys the impression of an enormous parenthesis."[1] The guiding concern of the Priestly Source is compositional in nature. It sets out to provide a chronologically ordered narrative framework extending all the way from the creation of the universe to the consecration of the Temple. It also inserts older documents into this framework such as the Sinai pericope, which, like Deuteronomy, links the motifs of revelation, covenant, and law with the Exodus-Moses narrative. That accounts for the relatively abrupt shift from narrative mode to normative mode that occurs in Exodus 19 and continues all the way through to Numbers 10:10, where there is an equally abrupt switch back to narrative. At this point, as Lothar Perlitt remarks, "the people have no inkling of the great covenant made with God at Sinai" and start grumbling "just like they did before, that is, in Ex 17."[2]

Today there is widespread acceptance that the two key elements that come together in the Sinai-Torah—the Exodus story and the idea of the law as Israel's constitution—were originally separate. In the liturgical recapitulations of salvational history (Deut 26; Jos 24; Ps 78; Pss 105–107), the covenant and the giving of the law go unmentioned. Only in Nehemiah 9 and in Stephen's speech to the Sanhedrin in Acts 7 are

both elements, Exodus and the law, brought together.³ In Hosea, however, it is already clear from the outset that the motifs of departure,
election, and covenant belong together, even if the idea of the covenant has not yet taken the form of a treaty of political alliance first given
it in Deuteronomy.⁴

The authors of Deuteronomy borrowed the model of a political contract from Assyria. The loyalty oath that King Esarhaddon had his subjects and vassals swear to his designated successor, Ashurbanipal, in
672 BCE makes its influence felt right down to the wording of the biblical text. One of those vassals must have been King Manasseh of Judah,
so it may be assumed that a copy of the succession treaty and oath was
stored in the royal archive in Jerusalem.⁵ When applying this Assyrian
template to the covenant between YHWH and the people, the biblical
authors adopted and adapted it in two ways. First, God does not make
this treaty with the king, in his capacity as the people's representative
before the gods, but directly with the people themselves; and second,
the loyalty clauses are not between the people and the king, in his capacity as the gods' representative before the people, but between the
people and God. In a startling innovation, the king's position as representative and intermediary is thus bypassed. Through the "transference"⁶ of the king-god relationship and the king-people relationship to
the relationship between God and his people, Assyrian state ideology
is converted into Israelite covenant theology. The fact that God makes
his covenant with the people as a whole, rather than through the intercession of royalty, priesthood, or some other representative authority,
becomes the basis for a new, specific, emphatic, and to some extent
"democratic" conception of the people. The people—not Moses, not
the seventy elders, not Aaron, not the Levites—assume the role of a
sovereign partner in the covenant. This directness of access to God is
what lends the biblical concept its democratic force.

When God speaks of Israel as his "son" in Hosea and Exodus, the
people are stepping into the position traditionally occupied by the
king. The institution of sacral kingship—whether in Egypt or in Jerusalem—is thereby done away with. The covenant dispenses with the
need for a king, whose role is now taken over by the people. In Old
Testament covenant theology, royalty is conspicuous by its absence.⁷
In 2 Samuel 7:17, God says to Samuel in relation to David: "I will be his

father, and he shall be my son." God uses similar terms when speaking
to the people in Leviticus: "And I will walk among you, and will be
your God, and ye shall be my people" (26:12). Here, too, a son is adopted rather than born. An entire people is elected by YHWH in order
that they may take up the office of divine sonship otherwise reserved
for kings. Accordingly, the traditional role of the sacred king is split in
half and the two parts arising from the division are assigned to God and
the people. In relation to the world of the gods, the king traditionally
appeared in the role of son (Egypt) or groom (Mesopotamia) as their
alliance partner of choice; in relation to the world of humans, he was
the source and guardian of law and justice. In the new model of covenant theology, God himself becomes the king and rules his people
through justice and good laws, while the people attain sovereignty as
God's chosen covenant partner, a "kingdom of priests and a holy nation" (Ex 19:6). This part of the royal office is, therefore, transferred to
the people. Other parts are ascribed to God.

The theologization of the law—the idea, that is, of making God the
legislator, not just the judge and guardian of the law—is a revolutionary
step. To be sure, the law had been closely associated with the gods
throughout the ancient Near East for millennia. The gods saw to it that
laws were obeyed and contracts honored. Law as a sphere of orderly,
civilized conduct and the idea of justice were divine institutions, the
essential framework within which kings promulgated their laws and
judges pronounced their verdicts. The sun god as an all-seeing judge to
whom the unjustly persecuted might appeal for redress was a familiar
idea in Mesopotamia, Egypt, and also the Kingdom of Israel.[8] For all
that the gods might exercise oversight, however, the actual making of
laws was the preserve of kings and their legal advisers, since the laws
of the land had to be adapted to changing historical circumstances and
royal sovereignty would not brook any restrictions in this regard. The
notion that there might be such things as eternal, timelessly valid laws
was simply inconceivable. Yet the theologization of the law envisaged
nothing less. With this step, God took on the same function that Egyptian, Near Eastern, and surely also Davidian monarchs guarded as the
most important of their prerogatives. When God is ascribed legislative
powers in this way, the law becomes *ius divinum*, divine law.

The most significant innovation in this step, however, is not that the previously royal function of lawgiving is transferred to God but that from now on, entirely different areas of human communal life, areas that ancient Near Eastern or Egyptian legal traditions had left untouched, are made the subject of divine legislation. I refer to the norms of charity and almsgiving, of empathy with the proverbial widows and orphans, with the suffering, weak, and needy, with slaves and foreigners. In Egypt and Mesopotamia, such precepts pertain to "wisdom," a moral initiation into the kind of rules that make for a harmonious society but fall outside the remit of the law, which is only concerned with enforceable laws. This means, on the one hand, that most of the relevant biblical commandments have their counterparts in ancient Near Eastern and Egyptian wisdom literature; the principle of a moral order undergirding social relations cannot be chalked up to biblical monotheism.[9] On the other hand, though, the inclusion of morality into the *ius divinum* means that these norms now command incomparably greater authority than ever before, since they are now enforceable before God. With that, a vertical axis has been drawn into the moral structure of interpersonal relations.

That has led many theologians—but not just theologians—to conclude that without this vertical axis, without this personal God before whom humans are called to justify themselves and to whom they can appeal in the event that they have been wronged, a moral order for human society cannot possibly function. It has further been claimed that biblical monotheism first brought such an order into the world. This claim is justified to the extent that God first appears as a lawgiver in the Sinai pericope, whereas he otherwise only appears in the religions of the ancient world as a judge and upholder of law and order. The vertical axis in the moral structure of interpersonal relations was already given with the idea of divine justice, but it is considerably strengthened once God is made lawgiver as well. Above all, it makes an enormous difference whether this vertical axis is represented by a king or some other organ of secular rule, or whether its status as a divinely revealed document takes it entirely out of the hands of worldly authorities.

Another crucial aspect of kingship is likewise transferred to God in the context of covenant theology. When offering the people partnership in the covenant, God calls himself "YHWH, thy God, who brought thee forth out of the land of Egypt, from the house of bondage." In other words, he defines himself through this story as Israel's savior. He is not offering a pact to the entire human race in his capacity as their creator (as he had done with Noah), but to those he has freed in his capacity as their savior. We are dealing here with a specific and historical covenant between a particular—not a universal—god and a particular people that first constitutes itself *as* a people by entering that covenant. As covenant partner, God takes on the role of a national deity and "the children of Israel" acquire the status of a divine people. This is not the impersonal God who dwells beyond the cosmos but the living, inner-worldly, engaged God who resolves to dwell among his people. God's inner-worldly, historical presence is another factor that makes kingship unnecessary—this, too, a revolutionary and potentially democratic element in the new covenant theology.

In the context of Egyptian and Babylonian sacral kingship, the king was also responsible for the link to the world of the gods. As an Egyptian text puts it, it was his task to provide humans with law and justice, and the gods with sacrifices. As the sole earthly inhabitant empowered to have dealings with the gods (even if he habitually delegated this task to the priests), he maintained the ongoing ties between heaven and earth, nature and society. When YHWH himself now takes things in hand, chooses a people, sets them free, and allies with them so that he may dwell in their midst, he supplants the role of the king, whose services as lord of history and mediator between gods and mortals are no longer required. History as the stage on which royalty struts its stuff makes way for *historia sacra*, the salvational history that God has in mind for his people. This revolutionary conception could only emerge once Israel was no longer ruled by kings.

From this transposition of a political model—the treaty of alliance—onto the relation between the human world and the world of the divine, something entirely new arises that was to set the trend for the modern world religions. With this step, Israel turns its back on the traditional orders of religious and political life, and there is no more fitting symbol for this exit than Exodus, the tale of the departure from Egypt.

The Ten Commandments

Only one who studies the Torah is free.
—*Mishnah Avot 6:2*[10]

And only the law can give us freedom.
—*Johann Wolfgang von Goethe*[11]

The proclamation of the law between the framing chapters 19 (theophany) and 24 (covenant ceremony) proceeds in two parts. In the first part, YHWH makes an appearance, heralded by thunder and lightning, smoke, fire, and a trumpet blast, to proclaim the Ten Commandments to all the people (20:1–21). Because the people cannot long endure God's voice, everything that follows is conveyed by Moses. A sharp break thus separates the Decalogue and what has come to be known as the "Covenant Code" (Ex 20:22–23:33). The Ten Commandments are thereby clearly set apart from the main body of all the laws and commandments issued on Sinai. Only the Ten Commandments have been heard by all the people with God's own voice; everything else has been relayed by Moses. This makes them even more authoritative, lending them the character of absolute, eternally valid truth. Unlike experiential truths, which rest on insight or "wisdom," revealed truths are incontrovertible and immutable. I am well aware that "truth" and "revelation" are anachronistic concepts when applied to the mindscape and historical context of the Sinai pericope. There is no precise equivalent to "revelation" in biblical Hebrew: the law is not revealed at Sinai but "given," and the Hebrew word *'ĕmet*, which means "truth" as well as "faith" or "trust," blurs the line between knowledge and belief. The "truth" or trustworthiness of the law revealed or given at Sinai resides in the absolute authority of its transcendent source. If Hobbes ascertains that *auctoritas non veritas facit legem* ("authority, not truth, makes the law," *Leviathan* ch. 26), then at Sinai, *auctoritas* and *veritas* are one and the same. That is the meaning of revelation, and even if the word is lacking in biblical Hebrew, this precise meaning nonetheless informs the story from start to finish. We should refrain from assuming that concepts can only ever be expressed through an exactly matching word. The word "revelation" (Latin *revelatio*, Greek *apokálypsis*) literally means "uncovering" and refers to the unveiling of a future cur-

FIGURE 16. Moses and the revelation of the law on Sinai. The 51 altar images in Klosterneu-burg are arranged into three rows of 17 images each. Scanned horizontally, each row reflects one of the three epochs in the Augustinian understanding of history; scanned vertically, each scene is typologically linked to the scenes placed directly above and beneath it. Top row: *ante legem*, scenes from before the revelation of the law at Sinai. Middle row: *sub gratia*, scenes from the New Testament. Bottom row: *sub lege*, scenes from the Sinai revelation to Christ's birth. In the panels above the scene shown here, Noah's ark (top) and the Pente-cost miracle (middle) are depicted. The scroll quotes the Shema prayer (Deut 6:4: D[ominu] tu[us] D[ominu]s Unus: "The Lord your God is one Lord"). Nicholas of Verdun, 1181.

FIGURE 17. *Moses Receiving the Tablets of the Law*. Marc Chagall, 1960–1966.

rently hidden from human sight: specifically, the end of the world. That is not what the Sinai "revelation" is about. Here the text draws on a more general concept of "revelation," referring to a truth that is not already known (in the manner of an empirically verifiable truth) but must first be disclosed to the believer. The narrator of the events at Sinai takes great pains to bring out the otherworldliness, the binding authority, and the founding singularity with which God reveals the covenant and the law, and the concepts "revelation" and "truth" mean nothing else here.

The writing on the stone tablets records the commandments revealed to all the people by YHWH himself, not the entire corpus of laws. "And he gave unto Moses, when he had made an end to communing with him upon mount Sinai, two tables of testimony, tables of stone, written with the finger of God" (Ex 31:18).[12] Since ancient times, these two tablets have been imagined and depicted as steles with plain rounded tops. In other words, they have been given the Egyptian form of the "royal command" as the prototype of performative textuality. The fact that God inscribes the Ten Commandments on *two* tables points to the inner division of these supreme norms. The first group consists of the commandments relating to one's obligations toward God, while the second regulates one's obligations toward the community. In the "double commandment of love," in which Jesus distills the essence of the divine law, this distinction between a vertical and a horizontal axis finds the clearest possible expression:

> "Thou shalt love the Lord thy God with all thy heart, and with all thy soul, and with all thy mind." [Deut 6:5] This is the first and greatest commandment. And the second is like unto it: "Thou shalt love thy neighbor as thyself." [Lev 19:18] On these two commandments hang all the law and the prophets. (Matt 22:37–40)

There was only ever uncertainty concerning how the commandments were to be divided between these two groups and how they were to be enumerated. The Ten Commandments appear twice in the Bible: once in Exodus and a second time in Deuteronomy. There are slight discrepancies between the two passages in both wording and numbering. The Exodus version counts the ban on foreign gods and the ban on images as two commandments, condensing the two prohibitions on desire into one to arrive at the number ten:

Exodus 20:1–17	Deuteronomy 5:6–21
I am YHWH thy God, which have brought thee out of the land of Egypt, out of the house of bondage.	I I am YHWH thy God, which brought thee out of the land of Egypt, from the house of bondage.

Exodus 20:1–17	Deuteronomy 5:6–21
I Thou shalt have no other gods before me.	Thou shalt have none other gods before me.
II Thou shalt not make unto thee any graven image, or any likeness of any thing that is in heaven above, or that is in the earth beneath, or that is in the water under the earth. Thou shalt not bow down thyself to them: for I, YHWH thy God, am a jealous God, visiting the iniquity of the fathers upon the children unto the third and fourth generation of them that hate me, and shewing mercy unto thousands [of generations] of them that love me, and keep my commandments.	Thou shalt not make thee any graven image, or any likeness of any thing that is in heaven above, or that is in the earth beneath, or that is in the waters beneath the earth. Thou shalt not bow down thyself unto them, nor serve them; for I, YHWH thy God, am a jealous God, visiting the iniquity of the fathers upon the children unto the third and fourth generation of them that hate me, and shewing mercy unto thousands [of generations] of them that love me and keep *his* commandments.
III Thou shalt not take the name of YHWH, thy God, in vain; for YHWH will not hold him guiltless that taketh his name in vain.	**II** Thou shalt not take the name of YHWH, thy God, in vain; for YHWH will not hold him guiltless that taketh his name in vain.
IV Remember the sabbath day, to keep it holy. Six days shalt thou labor, and do all thy work, but the seventh day is the sabbath of YHWH, thy God. In it thou shalt not do any work, thou, nor thy son, nor thy daughter, thy manservant, nor thy maidservant, nor thy cattle, nor thy stranger that is within thy gates. For in six days YHWH made heaven and earth, the sea, and all that in them is, and rested the seventh day: wherefore YHWH blessed the sabbath day, and hallowed it.	**III** *Keep* the sabbath day to sanctify it, *as* YHWH, thy God, hath commanded thee. Six days thou shalt labor, and do all thy work, but the seventh day is the sabbath of YHWH, thy God. In it thou shalt not do any work, thou, nor thy son, nor thy daughter, nor thy manservant, nor thy maidservant, *nor thine ox, nor thine ass*, nor *any* of thy cattle, nor thy stranger that is within thy gates; *that thy manservant and thy maidservant may rest as well as thou. And remember that thou wast a servant*

Exodus 20:1–17	Deuteronomy 5:6–21
	in the land of Egypt, and that YHWH, thy God, brought thee out thence through a mighty hand and by a stretched out arm. Therefore YHWH, thy God, commanded thee to keep the sabbath day.
V Honor thy father and thy mother: that thy days may be long upon the land which YHWH, thy God, hath given thee.	IV Honor thy father and thy mother, *as YHWH, thy God, hath commanded thee*; that thy days may be prolonged, *and that it may go well with thee*, in the land which YHWH, thy God, giveth thee.
VI Thou shalt not kill.	V Thou shalt not kill.
VII Thou shalt not commit adultery.	VI *Neither* shalt thou commit adultery.
VIII Thou shalt not steal.	VII *Neither* shalt thou steal.
IX Thou shalt not bear false witness against thy neighbor.	VIII *Neither* shalt thou bear false witness against thy neighbor.
X Thou shalt not covet thy neighbor's house, thou shalt not covet thy neighbor's wife, nor his manservant, nor his maidservant, nor his ox, nor his ass, nor any thing that is thy neighbor's.	IX *Neither* shalt thou *desire* thy neighbor's *wife*. X *Neither* shalt thou covet thy neighbor's *house*, his *field*, or his manservant, or his maidservant, his ox, or his ass, or any thing that is thy neighbor's.

Judaism, Calvinism, and the Anglican Church all teach the Exodus version, whereas the Catholic and Lutheran churches opt for the version found in Deuteronomy.[13] The third commandment by Jewish (and Calvinist, etc.) reckoning thus corresponds to the second commandment as calculated by Catholics and Lutherans, who therefore have to split up the ban on desire in order to arrive at the number ten. The traditions diverge further in how they treat God's words of self-introduction: in Judaism they are counted as the first commandment (the bans on foreign gods and graven images then being combined in the second commandment); among the Reformed churches, Anglicans, and Orthodox, they are grouped with the ban on foreign gods; whereas Catholics and Lutherans treat them as a separate preamble to the commandments:[14]

	Judaism (Exodus) 5 + 5	Catholics, Lutherans (Deuteronomy) 3 + 7	Reformed, Anglicans, Greek Orthodox (Exodus) 4 + 6
Preamble		Self-introduction YHWH's emancipatory deeds	
1	Exclusivity commandment YHWH's rule	Foreign gods	Exclusivity commandment and ban on foreign gods
2	Foreign gods, images	Name	Images
3	Name	Sabbath	Name
4	Sabbath	Parents	Sabbath
5	Parents	Murder	Parents
6	Murder	Adultery	Murder
7	Adultery	Theft	Adultery
8	Theft	False testimony	Theft
9	False testimony	Desire: neighbor's wife	False testimony
10	Desire	Desire: house, etc.	Desire

In Jewish depictions of the tables of the law, the Ten Commandments are divided equally between the two tablets. In Christianity, four are inscribed on one and six on the other, or—most frequently—they are split into groups of three and seven. This difference stems from how Jews view the fifth commandment (by their count: "honor thy father and thy mother"). Whereas they categorize it as a religious commandment, for Christians it belongs among the social commandments.

It is even unclear which commandment should appear in first place. For Judaism it is the opening statement: "I am YHWH thy God, which have brought thee out of the land of Egypt, out of the house of bondage." What, we might ask, is the subject and what is the predicate of this sentence? If "YHWH thy God . . ." is the predicate, then the sentence is an answer to the question "Who are you?" and can in no way be construed as a commandment. Rather, it emphasizes the authority lying behind the commandments that follow: "I, who led you out of Egypt, have the right to demand of you the following." If the divine name YHWH is understood as the predicate, however, then it responds to the question "Who is our God, who led us out of Egypt?" Understood in this way, the formula does indeed have the character of a commandment: "You should recognize and worship me, and no other, as YHWH, your savior."[15] On this reading, the ensuing ban on alien gods, along with the ban on graven images, constitutes the second commandment. Yet the ban on alien gods cannot be split off from God's words of self-introduction, understood as a claim to exclusiveness. This is shown in Hosea 13:4, for example: "Yet I am YHWH thy God from the land of Egypt, and thou shalt know no God but me: for there is no savior beside me." God's self-revelation as Israel's savior from Egyptian captivity is the prefatory justification for the ban on alien gods, which therefore must count as the first commandment: "Thou shalt have no other gods before me."[16]

Tellingly, God does not say that there are no other gods besides him. On the contrary, such gods exist, but Israel is forbidden from having anything to do with them. In the words of Benno Jacob, "the gods are not denounced as 'idols,' nor are other nations dissuaded from following them. All that matters here is the relationship between YHWH and Israel, and YHWH takes Israel into his heart: you are mine! No-one else's! I betroth myself to you forever! It is the image of a *marriage* that lies behind this expression [i.e., "no other gods," J. A.]. Whatever the circumstances may be, the wife belongs to *one* man alone. For her, everyone else is an *'îš 'aḥēr*. This is not to say that there are no other men out there, only that they do not exist *for her*."[17]

In the first commandment we have before us the central tenet of biblical monotheism. It is not a statement of the "monotheism of truth," which denies the existence of other gods. Instead, it explicitly attests to the "monotheism of loyalty." When referring to this form of an exclusive commitment to God, some scholars therefore prefer to speak of "monolatry" rather than "monotheism." By this they mean the exclusive (or "monogamous," to stick with Jacob's metaphor) worship of a single god that simultaneously acknowledges the existence of other gods. The problem with this terminology, however, is that it obscures the fact that we are dealing here with a completely unique conception in the history of religion. Monolatry may crop up here and there, and Israel's exclusive worship of YHWH may indeed have arisen from an original monolatry. But there is an absolutely crucial additional factor in play here: the covenant theological foundation. What is called for here is loyalty. The "other gods" do not simply go unheeded when the Israelites turn in reverence to face their one and only lord; rather, they are expressly prohibited and their worship is anathematized as a breach of the covenant. A covenant is made here between one god among many and one nation among many, and this covenant is based on an act of salvation that connects the people freed from Egypt, and this people alone, with the god who freed them, and this god alone.

The second commandment, the ban on images, is to be understood as prohibiting cultic images, in particular. In this sense it goes hand in hand with the ban on foreign gods. It is both impossible and forbidden to make a likeness of YHWH since no mortal eye has ever seen his form (Deut 4:12; 15). All (cultic) images of something therefore *eo ipso* represent other gods. The commandment has been variously interpreted throughout the ages, in a narrower and a broader sense. In the narrower sense, it was taken to refer only to images depicting gods or God. This means that images are permissible so long as one does not bow down before them in adoration. That is the opinion expressed in the Mishnah tractate Avodah Zarah ("foreign worship"), so it is hardly surprising that a great many depictions of mythological and other scenes

FIGURE 18. Moses with the Ten Commandments, divided equally between the two tablets according to Jewish custom and enumeration. Joos van Gent, panel in the Palazzo Ducale in Urbino, fifteenth century.

have been found in the synagogues and villas of ancient Judaism. Christianity got around the ban on images by arguing that God (or the "word") became visible flesh in Christ, although this iconophilic stance periodically unleashed violent iconoclastic countermovements, first in Byzantium and then in Protestantism. What is decisive is the covenant theological idea of immediacy. The covenant God makes with Israel dispenses with intermediaries. Any form of representation would destroy the directness of the link to God established by the covenant.

The first part of the Ten Commandments (Ex 20:2–6), up to the words "and keep my commandments," is stylized as a first-person address from God. After that point he is referred to in the third person. This switch—already made in Deuteronomy 5:10 with the words "keep *his* commandments"—draws attention to the first two commandments in the Exodus version. This first part is also characterized by the lengthy commentary that justifies the ban on foreign gods and images with reference to God's "jealousy."[18] God's jealousy and punitive wrath are the flip side of the love and mercy he shows in offering his partnership to Israel; they logically belong together in his engagement for Israel. By entering into the covenant with Israel, God must distinguish between friend and foe, between those who stay true to the covenant and those who betray it, between those who keep his commandments and those who break them. God's singularity thus inheres in the exclusiveness of the bond he shares with Israel rather than in any existential oneness.

The ban on images polarizes the world into friend and foe. No other commandment does such a thing. Taking YHWH's name in vain, failing to keep the Sabbath, dishonoring one's father and mother, killing, fornicating, stealing, lying, and coveting—these may all be deadly sins, but the commandments they violate do not polarize the world in the same way as the ban on images, nor do they provoke God's jealous wrath and make the sinner God's declared enemy. The world cannot be divided up into murderers and nonmurderers, adulterers and faithful spouses, or suchlike categories for the other commandments. It can, however, be split into the opposing camps of iconophobes and iconophiles, Team YHWH and the apostates. More starkly than any other commandment, the question of images reveals who stands with God and who stands against him. That is why the ban on images is the quintessence or signature of the new religion founded

on Sinai, a religion which, since the seventeenth century, has gone
under the name of "monotheism." Monotheism draws a line between
itself and other religions, excluding them as heathen. The ban on images defines those excluded in this way as idolaters. Anyone who
makes images joins the ranks of the idol worshippers and hence automatically stands against God.

The ban on taking God's name in vain, like the ban on images, ad-
mits a broader and a narrower interpretation. Whereas the narrower
interpretation restricts the ban to the unnecessary or unseemly use of
the divine name (*laššāw'* = in vain, literally "worthlessly" or "for nothing"), the broader one extends it into a general taboo on naming. In
Orthodox Judaism, not only is the tetragrammaton avoided in spoken
discourse and replaced with "Adonai" (Lord) or "ha-Shem" (the
name), the pronunciation of *'ĕlōhîm* (God) is deliberately distorted
into *'ĕlōkîm* as well. When Orthodox Jews are writing in English, "God"
becomes "G-d." In such practices, an original, essentially magical view
of naming is perpetuated or revived. According to this view, naming or
depicting someone can potentially expose that person to malign influence by bringing him or her to renewed presence. The God of Israel
cannot be subjected to such influence, control, or manipulation via
iconic or verbal representation. Once it is forbidden to make an image
of God, all that remains for humans to venerate is his name. It is therefore imperative that it be kept holy.

The most important difference between the versions of the Decalogue found in Exodus and Deuteronomy lies in the justification for the
Sabbath commandment.[19] Deuteronomy justifies the commandment
with reference to the sojourn in Egypt: never again shall humans and
animals be enslaved and exploited so mercilessly. The Sabbath becomes the paragon for the new model of society offered here as a coun-
termodel to Egypt. At the head of the charter of human rights proclaimed at Sinai is the right to rest and recuperation. The Exodus
version grounds the Sabbath in God's rest on the seventh day of creation. This justification is far more grandiose than that given in Deuteronomy. By honoring the Sabbath, the new society secures its place in
the cosmic order of things. Resting on the seventh day is interpreted as
imitatio Dei, and the working week is correspondingly understood as

the microcosmic emulation or even continuation of the drama of creation.

A Priestly tendency is at work in the justification of the Sabbath commandment in terms of creation theology. The Priestly Source begins with the mythical depiction of creation as a seven-day affair, and nothing could accord more with its guiding intention than to base the Sabbath—and hence the entire complex of human action and inaction—on God's own action and inaction at the start of all things. That is entirely in keeping with mythical thinking, as Thomas Mann showed more clearly in his Joseph novels than any scholar of religion. Life gains meaning and dignity when it is based on the "primal forms and norms" of myth. These belong on a different temporal plane to the past of historical events, an "absolute past," to use Ernst Cassirer's term, from which the continually advancing present never increases its distance and which is brought to presence in acts of festive celebration.

Deuteronomy's foundation of the Sabbath commandment in terms of liberation theology points in the opposite direction. The inhumane oppression and enslavement suffered in Egypt belongs in a historical past rather than a mythical one. Having been delivered from this past once and for all, the Israelites are enjoined to remember what happened (rather than "make it present") in order that it may never be repeated and so they never lose sight of the emancipatory meaning of God's commandments and prohibitions. Different constituencies stand behind the two different versions: the Jerusalem priesthood is responsible for the creation theological version found in Exodus, the Deuteronomist lay theologians for the liberation theological version provided in Deuteronomy.

Because the Priestly Source is considerably more recent than Deuteronomy, the Priestly version of the Decalogue must be considered the later one. It suits the Priestly agenda of stitching together Genesis and Exodus, cosmogenesis and ethnogenesis, creation and Temple. In the long run, the Priestly interpretation of the Sabbath has proven the more influential. The Jewish liturgy at the beginning of Shabbat emphasizes the creation theological justification.[20] Jesus, however, evidently had the Deuteronomy version in mind when he said, "The sabbath was made for man, and not man for the sabbath" (Mark 2:27).

The Sabbath is to be "sanctified," that is, kept separate from the remaining days of the week. This is to be achieved by strictly abstaining from anything that resembles work. The taboo on working on the seventh day is unique in the entire ancient world.[21] The Hebrew word *shabbat* is cognate with the Babylonian-Assyrian word *shab/pattu*, meaning "full moon festival." In Israel, too, it only appears in the Bible in this meaning prior to the Babylonian exile. The shift in meaning from "full moon day" to "seventh day" only takes place in exile. Exemption from normal work duties on feast days naturally occurs in other religions and cultures as well. Yet the Sabbath commandment does not involve a temporary release from labor but an outright ban on it. Permission to rest from work has become a duty to abstain from it. That is something altogether new.

The Sabbath commandment and the commandment to honor one's parents are the only ones expressed in positive terms (Remember/keep . . . , Honor . . .). All the rest are negatively worded ("Thou shalt not . . ."). On the Jewish reading, the commentary to the commandment on parental authority—"that thy days may be long upon the land which YHWH, thy God, hath given thee"—relates to all five commandments listed in the first table, under which it draws a line. They define the conditions for living in the Promised Land. Whoever breaks these commandments must disappear. The bans on foreign gods and images as well as the Sabbath commandment are definitional commandments: they spell out what it means to be a Jew, meaning that whoever trespasses them must be eliminated. That holds equally true for the commandment on parental authority; and it is telling that, whenever in the Bible zeal and loyalty toward YHWH demand that not even next of kin be spared, brothers and children may be threatened but never parents. Today's readers are surely not the first to find the cruelty of such provisions hard to stomach.

Of all the Ten Commandments, the Sabbath commandment exerted the most far-reaching influence on Judaism during the crucial formative years of exile and the postexilic years in Judea. "It is difficult to find another example," Benno Jacob writes, "where a single and so simple rule, in the absence of all secular compulsion, has so profoundly and lastingly influenced the education of a people. [. . .] It [the Sabbath, J. A.] has been preserved, under the most trying circumstances imaginable, as the purest, most secure and most enduring vessel for monotheism, the one least susceptible to contamination by gentile ideas and customs. In short, it has been largely responsible for helping the people of Israel weather the storms of history."[22] "If Heine was to call the Torah the 'portable fatherland' of Judaism," remarks Alexandra Grund, "then the Sabbath has been a kind of 'portable temple' since the very beginning."[23]

In Judaism, as previously mentioned, the commandment to honor one's father and mother is numbered among the divine commandments, first because one's relationship with God is mediated by one's parents and second because this "honoring" originally included a funerary cult and hence also a connection beyond the grave. In a society without an old age pension scheme, one of the duties of the oldest son was to care for his parents in their old age, bury them upon their death, mourn them, and ensure they were sent off with all due ceremony. That this should be considered one of the divine commandments is made clear in Sirach 3:15:

> Whoever deserts a father is no better than a blasphemer, and whoever distresses a mother is accursed of the Lord.

In Christianity, by contrast, the commandment to honor one's father and mother is reckoned among the social commandments.

The second table with the social commandments does without commentary and is therefore shorter. That also gives rise to the usual Christian division into commandments 1 to 3 (or 4) on one table and 4 (or 5) to 10 on the other.

The ban on killing uses the word *rāṣaḥ*, which only appears in the sense of "murder" and never refers to death in combat, execution, or the slaughter of animals. The Noahide law, "Whoso sheddeth man's blood, by man shall his blood be shed: for in the image of God made he man" (Gen 9:6), is much more general and also contains a rationale.

In Israel, the conditions for adultery are met only when a man sleeps with a woman who is betrothed to another or already married. A man cannot break his own marriage, only the marriage he disrupts. The commandment is not aimed at safeguarding conjugal fidelity but at keeping the family—and the family inheritance along with it—intact. The ban on theft protects property just as the ban on adultery protects the family. Commandments 6–8 (or 5–7) all have to do with misdeeds. They are further linked by reference to one's "neighbor": it is morally reprehensible to kill or rob those close to you or ruin their marriage.

The bans on false witness and coveting in commandments 9–10 (or 8–10) relate to "neighbors" who could be envied or calumniated on account of their all too tempting proximity.[24] The former commandment regulates what may be said, the latter what may be thought and desired. The three categories into which the sins listed on the second table may be grouped play a dominant role in other ancient Near Eastern civilizations, particularly in ancient Egypt. They may be characterized as sins of deed, word, and thought.[25`]

The Covenant Code and the Solemnization of the Covenant

The actual work of lawgiving gets underway in Exodus 21:1 with the sentence "Now these are the judgments [*mišpāṭîm*] which thou shalt set before them." This collection (21:1–23:33) is named the "book of the covenant" in 24:6–8. The Book of the Covenant (or Covenant Code) is artfully structured in the form of a ring:[26]

Prologue: Ex 20:22–23 Backward glance at the theophany and the bans on foreign gods and idolatry

A 20:24–26 Altar law

  B 21:2–11 Manumission of Hebrew slaves in the seventh year

   C 21:12–22:19 Criminal laws

    D 21:12–17 Capital offenses (murder and manslaughter, assaulting one's parents, theft)

      E 21:18–31 Physical injury; 21:32–22:15 *yĕšallēm* laws (compensation for wrongdoing)

      E' 22:16–17 Physical injury (deflowering an unwed girl)

    D' 22:18–20 Capital offenses (witchcraft, bestiality, idolatry)

   C' 22:20–23:9 Social commandments

     F 22:21 Protection of aliens

      G 22:22–27 Protection of the weak (widows and orphans, debtors, pawnbrokers)

       H 22:28–31 Laws of piety

     G' 23:1–8 Laws of justice and charity

F' 23:9 Protection of aliens
    B' 23:10–11 The Sabbath year
A' 23:13–19 Feast arrangements
Epilogue: 23:20–33 Forward glance at settlement in the Promised Land,
commandment to drive out the inhabitants, and ban on making an alliance
with the Canaanites

The prologue and epilogue correspond in two points: just as the
prologue looks back to the theophany, so the epilogue looks forward
to the continuation of the Israelites' migration and their eventual settlement,[27] and both place renewed emphasis on the ban on foreign
gods: "Do not make any gods to be alongside me" (20:23) and "Thou
shalt not bow down to their [i.e., the Canaanite] gods, nor serve them,
nor do after their works; but thou shalt utterly overthrow them, and
quite break down their images" (23:24). A (altar law) and A' (feast arrangements) mirror each other in their connection to God. These are
ritual laws, much like the ban on seething a kid in its mother's milk that
concludes the Priestly Source Dodecalogue in 34:26. They form the
framework (B—B') within which no more ritual laws are to be found,
only criminal laws (C) and social commandments (C'). The regulations
on the Sabbath year (B and B') mediate between the ritual laws and the
social commandments. They link to the Sabbath—and hence to the
fourth commandment, which is again repeated at 23:12 in its social
meaning (and not in its cosmic meaning, as at 20:11)—by referring to
God; otherwise they deal with the poor, who must either give themselves up to slavery and then spend no longer than six years in servitude or else endure hunger and then be fed at public expense in the
seventh year.

Three types of prescriptions are thus clearly distinguished from each
other in the Covenant Code: ritual laws for interactions with God,
criminal laws for indictable offenses, and social laws. These last may
not be enforceable in any earthly court of law, but God is perpetually
vigilant and assesses Israel's claim to righteousness on whether they are
obeyed.[28] These three types correspond to the distinction between
ḥuqqîm (ritual laws), mišpāṭîm (criminal laws), and miṣwôt (social
commandments). I have already pointed out that, in my eyes, the ju-
ridification of the social commandments, and hence morality (C'), rep-

resents the truly revolutionary innovation in the biblical theologization of the law. It undoes the distinction between law and morality that
emerges with all desirable clarity in the difference between legal literature and wisdom literature in the ancient Near East and Egypt. In this
regard, the theologization of the law entails dedifferentiation. Through
this act of transference, morality—that is, the rules for harmonious coexistence, the "art of community"[29]—is transformed into a dimension
of divine proximity. By acting morally, one moves closer to God.

The capital offenses (D–D') are divided into violent crimes against
other human beings (D) and sins that cause nobody harm but are an
abomination to God (D'):

> D
>
> > He that smiteth a man, so that he die, shall be surely put to death. And
> > if a man lie not in wait, but God deliver him into his hand; then I will
> > appoint thee a place whither he shall flee.
> > But if a man come presumptuously upon his neighbor, to slay him with
> > guile; thou shalt take him from mine altar, that he may die.
> > And he that smiteth his father, or his mother, shall be surely put to
> > death.
> > And he that stealeth a man, and selleth him, or if he be found in his hand,
> > he shall surely be put to death.
> > And he that curseth his father, or his mother, shall surely be put to
> > death. (21:12–17)
>
> D'
>
> > Thou shalt not suffer a witch [*mĕkaššēpâ*] to live. Whosoever lieth with
> > a beast shall surely be put to death.
> > He that sacrificeth unto any god, save unto YHWH only, he shall be
> > utterly destroyed. (22:18–20)

It can all too easily be imagined just how fateful the injunction to kill
witches was to prove. To cite just one example, it plays a prominent
role in the witch-hunting manifesto, "The Hammer of Witches" (*mal-
leus maleficarum*), by Heinrich Institoris and Jacobus Sprenger (1486–
1487).[30] The commandment may have made sense when the new religion was still struggling to assert itself—through violent means, if
necessary—in the hostile "cultural space" of Canaan. From the vantage
of its reception history, however, it must be counted among the "stat-

utes that are not good" (Ez 20:25), like so much else in the Bible that
can now be discarded without regret. After all, the speech about the
"statutes that are not good" is *also* the word of God, and in the strict
sense at that. It ought not to be forgotten that the principle of critical
self-review is already built into the Hebrew Bible (Jer 31; Ez 18).

A special place is taken up by the social commandments regarding
aliens (F, F'), which are influenced by the memory of Egyptian bondage (see chapter 4):

> F = 22:21: Thou shalt neither vex a stranger, nor oppress him: for ye were
> strangers in the land of Egypt.
> F' = 23:9: Also thou shalt not oppress a stranger: for ye know the heart
> [*nepeš*] of a stranger, seeing ye were strangers in the land of Egypt.

The centerpiece of the social commandments (C'), formed by the
commandments enjoining piety, strikes a discordant note in this context (H):

1. Thou shalt not revile the gods, nor curse the ruler of thy people.
2. Thou shalt not delay to offer the first of thy ripe fruits, and of thy
   liquors.
3. The firstborn of thy sons shalt thou give unto me.
4. Likewise shalt thou do with thine oxen, and with thy sheep: seven days
   it shall be with his dam; on the eighth day thou shalt give it me.
5. And ye shall be holy men unto me: neither shall ye eat any flesh that is
   torn of beasts in the field; ye shall cast it to the dogs.

At the heart of these commandments is the order to sacrifice the
firstborn son (the word "give" cannot be construed in any other way),
which we have already briefly discussed in the context of the tenth
plague. This is the commandment that Ezekiel explicitly cites as an
example of the "statutes that are not good" (*ḥuqqîm lō' ṭôbîm*):

> And I polluted them in their own gifts, in that they caused to pass through
> the fire all that openeth the womb, that I might make them desolate, to the
> end that they might know that I am YHWH. (20:26)

This commandment is all the more puzzling given that other passages
expressly order the firstborn son (on whom God has a proprietary
claim) to be released (e.g., Ex 34:20).

This example offers valuable insight into how the Priestly Source operates with preexisting materials. The framework functions to transform originally secular or state law into divine law. That also explains the composition's cyclical structure. Through the expanded Sabbath commandments (B, B'), and ritual laws (A, A'), an older body of statutes (C and perhaps also C') is included in God's revelation of the law at Sinai. The external parameters (prologue and epilogue), combined with the ban on other gods and the order to make war on the Canaanites, integrate this foreign body into the setting of the Exodus story. What results is the body of laws that, as the "Covenant Code," forms the basis of the pact concluded between YHWH and Israel.

The parallel that the external framework produces between the ban on foreign gods and images, on the one hand, and the commandment to expel the Canaanites and shun them as treaty partners, on the other, is quite remarkable. In the prologue we read:

> And YHWH said unto Moses, Thus thou shalt say unto the children of Israel, Ye have seen that I have talked with you from heaven. Ye shall not make alongside me any gods of silver, neither shall ye make unto you gods of gold. (20:22–23)

And in the epilogue:

> For mine Angel shall go before thee, and bring thee in unto the Amorites, and the Hittites, and the Perizzites, and the Canaanites, the Hivites, and the Jebusites: and I will cut them off. Thou shalt not bow down to their gods, nor serve them, nor do after their works: but thou shalt utterly overthrow them, and quite break down their images. [...]
> And I will set thy bounds from the Sea of Reeds even unto the sea of the Philistines, and from the desert unto the river: for I will deliver the inhabitants of the land into your hand; and thou shalt drive them out before thee. Thou shalt make no covenant with them, nor with their gods. They shall not dwell in thy land, lest they make thee sin against me: for if thou serve their gods, it will surely be a snare unto thee. (23:23–24; 31–33)

Liberation and invasion, revolution and colonization belong together as two sides of the same story. Just as the Israelites' exodus from Egypt forms the primal scene of revolutionary freedom movements, so too their conquest of Canaan, with the permission and indeed duty to drive out and destroy the original inhabitants, forms the primal scene of colonialism. Emigrant Puritans and Boers who saw themselves as God's chosen people identified Native Americans and Africans, respectively, with the Canaanites, as did the Spanish conquistadors upon encountering the Incas. Charles V "eased his royal conscience" by having chapter 20 of Deuteronomy read to him,[31] where this dark theme is given even harsher treatment:

> But of the cities of these people, which YHWH, thy God, doth give thee for an inheritance, thou shalt save alive nothing that breatheth:
> But thou shalt utterly destroy them; namely, the Hittites, and the Amorites, the Canaanites, and the Perizzites, the Hivites, and the Jebusites; as YHWH, thy God, hath commanded thee:
> That they teach you not to do after all their abominations, which they have done unto their gods; so should ye sin against YHWH, your God. (20:16–18)

Another passage in Deuteronomy should be cited in this context:

> When YHWH, thy God, shall bring thee into the land whither thou goes to possess it, and hath cast out many nations before thee, the Hittites, and the Girgashites, and the Amorites, and the Canaanites, and the Perizzites, and the Hivites, and the Jebusites, seven nations greater and mightier than thou;
> And when YHWH, thy God, shall deliver them before thee; thou shalt smite them, and place them under the ban [ḥērem]; thou shalt make no covenant with them, nor shew mercy unto them:
>
> Neither shalt thou make marriages with them; thy daughter thou shalt not give unto his son, nor his daughter shalt thou take unto thy son.
> For they will turn away thy son from following me, that they may serve other gods: so will the YHWH's anger be kindled against you, and destroy thee suddenly.
>
> But thus shall ye deal with them; ye shall destroy their altars, and break down their images, and cut down their groves, and burn their graven images with fire.
> For thou art a holy people unto YHWH, thy God: YHWH, thy God, hath chosen thee to be a special people unto himself, above all people that are upon the face of the earth. (7:1–6)

Brutality toward the original inhabitants of the Promised Land is here openly endorsed as a sacred duty and given a religious rationale. The Canaanites' gods and rites provide sufficient grounds for their annihilation. As a sacred, chosen people, the Israelites are forbidden from making contact with the natives lest they be infected by their religion; the heathen must be destroyed and driven out. In this regard, the Book of Deuteronomy is far more explicit than the Priestly Book of Exodus, but the idea of waging a holy war of extermination (*ḥērem*, "ban") is the same in both.

The long shadow cast by the Exodus story should not be passed over in silence. It furnished Christian conquerors, invaders, and colonizers with arguments to legitimate their own mistreatment of indigenous people, while at the same time providing anticlerical proponents of the Enlightenment—and, later, anti-Semites as well—with ammunition for their attacks on the Old Testament. The reactions of Christian apologists to those who denounced their legitimation of violence were often no less dubious than the attacks themselves. The apologists pointed out that God himself gave the orders for destruction, making the Israelites nothing more than the executors of a divine command that brooked no opposition. As such, they could not be held accountable for the acts they committed in God's name, as if the assumption of a bloodthirsty god were easier to accept than that of a bloodthirsty nation. Other apologists (such as Johann David Michaelis and Johann Gottfried Herder) asserted—notwithstanding scriptural evidence to the contrary—that the Israelites had an older claim to the land, which had been opportunistically settled by the Canaanites while its rightful occupants were held up in Egypt.[32]

With the making of the covenant—and only now—the third "Mosaic distinction" comes into effect: the distinction between friend and foe. Following the passage cited earlier about God choosing Israel to be his "holy people" (*'ām qādôš*), Deuteronomy continues:

> Know therefore that YHWH thy God, he is God, the faithful God, which keepeth covenant and mercy with them that love him and keep his commandments to a thousand generations; and repayeth them that hate him to their face, to destroy them: he will not be slack to him that hateth him, he will repay him to his face. Thou shalt therefore keep the commandments,

and the statutes, and the judgments, which I command thee this day, to do
them. (7:9–11)

YHWH is the "faithful God" (*hā'ēl hanne'ĕmān*) and "loyalty"
(*'ĕmûnâ*) is the keyword in this new relationship, founded on the
model of the covenant (*bĕrît*) between YHWH and the children of Israel: the monotheism of loyalty. The monotheism of loyalty is unique
to the Moses covenant, which the Israelites can either make or break
depending on their level of commitment to the commandments. The
Abrahamic covenant was made between the creator god of Genesis
and an individual; the semantics of loyalty was alien to it, as was its
corollary, the distinction between friend and enemy. In Genesis, the
tribes occupying the Promised Land are listed as well. Here there are
even ten of them, not seven:

> Unto thy seed have I given this land, from the river of Egypt unto the great
> river, the river Euphrates: the Kenites, and the Kenizzites, and the Kad-
> monites, and the Hittites, and the Perizzites, and the Rephaims, and the
> Amorites, and the Canaanites, and the Girgashites, and the Jebusites.
> (15:19–21)

But nothing is said about driving these people from their homes and
wiping them out. Strict and aggressive exclusivism is reserved for Deuteronomy and also, in a scarcely attenuated form, the pre-Priestly
Book of *Exodus. This stance needs to be understood in the context of
the ban on foreign gods and idolatry. What we have before us is a
purely religious conflict. The monotheism of loyalty to the one YHWH
posits an inflexible opposition between itself and the religious customs
of its environment. Those customs, however, are not to be identified
with the archaic tribal religions of the indigenous Canaanites. Rather,
they have three reference points: first, the preexilic religion of the
court and the broader populace of Israel itself, denounced as adulterous by prophets like Hosea, Ezekiel, and Jeremiah; second, the rites
that the returning exiles found being practiced by those who had
stayed behind; and third, the Babylonian religion they encountered in
exile, which was to be avoided at all costs lest contact lead to assimilation. Behind the semantics of violence stands the exiles' resolute will
to maintain their cultural and religious identity under the pressure of

FIGURE 19. Moses receives the tables of the law. French book illustration (Noyon), c. 1210.

Assyrian and Babylonian oppression, as well as their energetic, ultimately successful attempt to give Israel a new foundation after the catastrophe.

The friend-enemy distinction, along with the associated sacred violence toward God's enemies, is the price paid by this new form of religion. The "faithful" God is the "jealous" God (*'ēl qannā'*). Anyone who inquires into the enormous historical impact of these texts cannot afford to indulge in apologetics if it means turning a blind eye to the intolerance that has been a necessary part of that impact. Within the framework of the semantics of loyalty that underpins the Hoseanic and Deuteronom(ist)ic tradition, the opposite of intolerance is not tolerance but indolence. From this point of view, an indolent god, a god unmoved by the fidelity or infidelity of his people, would be of no use to Israel in times of trial, such as when faced with persecution or exile. The violence invoked here is "sacred" violence, the violence of a "holy people" that must defend itself against the pressure to assimilate exerted by its surroundings and remain true to its lord—and hence to itself—in the face of temptation and persecution. This called for the strictest possible form of self-segregation: sanctification. Such violence may once have had its day, but that day has long since passed.

The ceremony for solemnizing the covenant was conducted very differently from the procedure usually followed in vassal treaties. Normally a covenant was "cut" (*kārat bĕrît*, likewise in Greek: *spondas* or *horkia temnein*).[33] One or more animals were sacrificed. The slaughtered animals were then cut into two pieces and the parties to the covenant walked between the divided pieces. It is thought that, in submitting to this rite of passage, the treaty-maker was placing a curse on his head: "The fate that befell these animals will befall me if I ever break the covenant."[34] The ceremony probably had an additional meaning tied to the cutting of the animal into two pieces. Passing through the divided pieces symbolized the union of the two partners in the treaty, just as the Greek idea of the *symbolon* (from *symballein*, to bring together) refers to the halves of a previously broken clay ring, retained for purposes of identification by the parties to a contract and their descendants. YHWH performs a ritual of this kind with Abraham:

> And he said unto him, Take me a heifer of three years old, and a she goat of three years old, and a ram of three years old, and a turtledove, and a young pigeon. And he took unto him all these, and divided them in the midst, and laid each piece one against another. [...] And it came to pass, that, when the sun went down, and it was dark, behold a smoking furnace, and a burning lamp that passed between those pieces. In the same day YHWH made a covenant with Abraham. (Gen 15:9–10, 17–18)

Astonishingly, YHWH is the one who makes a solemn commitment here, passing through the animal halves in the form of a fiery flame, whereas Abraham has fallen into a deep sleep and experiences everything as in a dream. Indeed, in the Abrahamic covenant it is YHWH who binds himself to Abraham, not the other way around. Abraham is unfettered by any laws or obligations apart from the rite of circumcision, and even this "sign of the covenant" is not mentioned until Genesis 17. YHWH pledges him the Promised Land (Gen 15:18–21) before sealing his promise with the rite. The covenant with Abraham, founded on God's promise rather than any law, goes beyond even the Moses covenant, which stands and falls with the law.

The covenant made on Sinai calls for a new, quite different form of ceremony, which I have already touched on earlier. Its most striking characteristic is the emphasis it places on free will: far from appearing in the role of an overlord imposing a contract and constitution on his vassals, God makes his people an offer that they are free to accept or refuse. Moses sets out the conditions to the Israelites on two occasions, first by reciting them from memory, and then, once they have been written down, in a public reading of the "Covenant Code." On each occasion the people give their assent. The same emphasis on free will characterizes the ceremony to renew the covenant that Moses conducts at Moab, just before the people move into Canaan (Deuteronomy 29), as well as the ceremony that Joshua holds at Shechem after they have occupied the land (Joshua 24).

Two ceremonies are combined when the covenant is solemnized at Sinai. Moses conducts the first ceremony at the foot of the mountain:

1. Moses conveys all of YHWH's words to the people, who give their assent.
2. Moses codifies the statutes in the "Covenant Code."
3. Moses builds an altar and calls for animals to be sacrificed.
4. "Moses took half of the blood, and put it in bowls; and half of the blood he sprinkled on the altar" (24:6).
5. "And he took the book of the covenant, and read in the audience of the people: and they said, All that YHWH hath said will we do, and be obedient" (24:7).
6. "And Moses took the blood, and sprinkled it on the people, and said, Behold the blood of the covenant, which YHWH hath made with you concerning all these words" (24:8).

The other ceremony is orchestrated by YHWH, who summons Moses, Aaron, Nadab, Abihu, and the seventy elders to the mountaintop to reveal himself to them:

1. And YHWH said to Moses, Come up . . .
2. Then Moses, Aaron, and the rest rose up . . .
3. "And they saw the God of Israel: and there was under his feet like a pavement of sapphire as clear as the sky itself" (24:10).
4. "And upon the nobles of the children of Israel he laid not his hand: also they saw God, and did eat and drink" (24:11).

The description of this dual ceremony to solemnize the covenant is also cyclically structured, with YHWH's ceremony (Y) framing that of Moses (M):

Y 1   24:1–2   YHWH invites the delegation up to the mountaintop
M 1–6   24:3–8   Moses's ceremony at the base of the mountain:
                              First reading of the law
                              Animal sacrifices, division of the blood
                              Second reading: recital of the Covenant Code
                              "Blood communion": sprinkling of the altar with
                              half of the blood, sprinkling of the people with the
                              other half
Y 2   24:9–11   YHWH's ceremony on the mountaintop: revelation and
                              feasting

Moses devises the rite of "blood communion" so that every individual in the community will be physically included in the covenant, which connects them with each other as much as it binds them to YHWH. The rite takes up the motif of the divided animal parts, with one half of the blood being sprinkled on the altar and the other half on the people. Insofar as it recalls the rite of priestly consecration (Ex 29:20–21), where priests are sprinkled with the blood of sacrificed animals, the "blood communion" also has the function of ritually consecrating the entire people as a "kingdom of priests, and a holy nation" (Ex 19:6).[35]

The "blood communion" was subsequently adopted by Christianity in the drinking of the wine, proclaimed by Jesus as "the blood of the new covenant":

Drink ye all of it; for this is the blood of the new covenant, which is shed for many for the forgiveness of sins. (Matt 26:27–28; Mark 14:23–24; see also Luke 22:30 and 1 Cor 11:25, which draw on the motif of the new covenant in Jer 31:31ff.)

The letter to the Hebrews draws the parallels between the blood rituals of the Old Testament and the blood of the new covenant. The sprinkling of blood in the Old Testament has been superseded in the New Testament by the drinking—albeit symbolic—of blood both human and divine, a completely unthinkable proposition in the context of Old Testament semantics:

Neither by the blood of goats and calves, but by his own blood, [Christ] entered in once into the holy place, having obtained eternal redemption for us. For if the blood of bulls and of goats, and the ashes of a heifer sprinkling the unclean, sanctifieth to the purifying of the flesh, how much more shall the blood of Christ, who through the eternal Spirit offered himself without spot to God, purge your conscience from dead works to serve the living God? (Hebr 9:12–14)

For when Moses had spoken every precept to all the people according to the law, he took the blood of calves and of goats, with water, and scarlet wool, and hyssop, and sprinkled both the book, and all the people, saying: "This is the blood of the covenant, which God hath enjoined unto you." (Hebr 9:19–20)

Sprinkling something or someone with sacrificial blood is a purification ritual. According to Leviticus 16:14–16, it is to be carried out in the "holy place" on the day of atonement, when the high priest will sprinkle the *kappōret* seven times with the blood of a bull and a goat: "And he shall make an atonement for the holy place, because of the uncleanness of the children of Israel, and because of their transgressions in all their sins." By linking the "blood communion" of the Sinai covenant with these rituals of purification through blood and ashes, the letter to the Hebrews presents the sprinkling of the people with sacrificial blood as a rite of purification, and hence sanctification. That is surely a key aspect to the ceremony. Purified and sanctified, Moses and the seventy elders are now suitably prepared to endure the awe-inspiring sight that awaits them at the summit of Mount Sinai.

Excursus III: "Excarnation" and Theologization of the Law

There must have been law codes in Israel long before the first version of the Covenant Code, just as there were in Mesopotamia. Unlike the biblical texts, however, the Mesopotamian codes make no attempt to derive the laws from expressions of divine will. They do not even claim normative validity. They amount to a body of legal literature that gives scholars and rulers the knowledge of the legal tradition they need in order to draft and promulgate new laws; they do not provide judges with normative guidelines to consult when making their judgments.

The best known such collection, the Codex Hammurabi, was certainly intended by this king to claim normative validity. As such, Hammurabi had the laws engraved on a stele immortalizing him as a great lawgiver. The stele was meant to provide guidance to all who sought legal advice in the future. It was thus not made to serve as a model for future legislators but to offer orientation for plaintiffs and defendants. But the Codex never really functioned in this form, mainly because the kings who followed Hammurabi were understandably reluctant to have their legislative powers curbed in any way by preexisting legal codes.[36]

In Egypt there were no law codes comparable to those in Mesopotamia. The legal literature consisted primarily of documentation of legal transactions, such as the famous records of the tomb robbery trial and the trial of those involved in the harem conspiracy against Ramesses III, papers recording sales of properties, houses, offices, and other valuable assets, testaments, tax lists, and administrative documents of all kinds. The kings occasionally augmented this living legal and bureaucratic tradition by issuing decrees that were then promulgated through monumental inscription, somewhat like the Codex Hammurabi but without its commemorative character. The purpose of these texts was not to immortalize the king but to make binding provisions for cases that had no precedent in the legal tradition. The edicts therefore also never refer to the whole of political and civil life, only ever to limited areas, especially endowments. As the personal creation of an individual benefactor, these could lay claim to statutory protection that even future kings would be obliged to uphold. The king's role as creator and founder, particularly of buildings and religious institutions, encompassed the duty to extend legal protection to what had been created. That explains why the genre of the legal inscription in the form of an edict or decree—the Egyptian term for the genre *wedj nisût*[37]—is so well documented.

The term *wedj nisût*, "royal command," designates at once the speech act of the royal fiat and its written form, typically inscribed on a round-topped stele, the form in which the two tablets of the law with the Ten Commandments are traditionally depicted.[38] This form of inscription is best captured with Aleida Assmann's concept of "excarnation."[39] The decree—that is, the gift of the lawgiving, reality-creating word—is incarnated in the king, and this word is excarnated in the form of the stele on which the decree is inscribed. In the process, the reality-creating, "performative" quality of the speech act "command" also enters into the stele and its inscription. The stele does not protocol or record the speech act as an event belonging to the past; rather, it performs that event in the medium of writing. Writing is both the expression of the reality-creating, lawgiving decree and its pronouncement by the king himself, but given lapidary permanence through its medium. That distinguishes the inscribed royal decree from the various forms of legal literature.

What the "incarnation" of law in the king entails is illustrated most clearly by the Egyptian conception of legal kingship. Justice, legality, and the law are incarnated in the king. He has at his command the two crucial qualities of "knowledge" (*Sia*) and "utterance" (*Hu*), both of which are hypostasized as distinct deities. Both also lend their assistance to the sun god in his work of creating and maintaining the universe. In this context, we also encounter the idea that the sun god himself dwells in the heart of the king and speaks through his mouth, just as YHWH uses Moses as his mouthpiece. In a hymn to Amun-Ra, we read:

> Your being [*djet=ek*] is what dwells in the heart of the king of Upper Egypt:
> against your enemies he turns his anger [*ba'uw*].
> You sit on the mouth of the king of Lower Egypt:
> his words match your instruction.
> Both lips of the lord are your sanctuary,
> Your Majesty is inside him:
> He speaks on Earth what you have decided.[40]

Another text addresses the king (Ramesses II):

> Hu is your mouth,
> Sia is your heart,
> your tongue is a shrine for Ma'at,
> the god sits on your lips.[41]

Pharaoh embodies justice (Ma'at). Through his decisions and actions, he realizes the ideal of a just order. He is an example of what Plato, as well as the ancient political philosophers who followed in his footsteps, would call the "living law" (*nomos empsychos, lex animata*).[42] The concept of *nomos empsychos* takes back the step of excarnation.

Having been externalized in writing, monumentalized in stone, and so made impervious to further change, even at the hands of the king, the law is now to be moved back to where it came from and where, according to Hellenistic political theology and metaphysics, it has its sole legitimate place: the ruler's "soul."[43] The Egyptian equivalent to the idea of the "living" *nomos*, the law incarnated in the ruler, can be found in the richly developed phraseology concerning the three divine hypostases made flesh in the Pharaoh: law (Ma'at), legal investigation (*Sia*), and pronouncement of judgment (*Hu*).[44] Two samples have already been cited above.

In Egypt, the law incarnated in the king is only occasionally "excarnated" in the form of written edicts on a strictly limited range of matters. In this it differs from a codex, which has a much wider remit. A codex shares with royal edicts the quality of performative textuality. Unlike the edicts, however, it aims to provide a comprehensive codification of the law, even if this ambition is not always fully realized. The entire sphere of social and political life is to be regulated by the laws collected, decreed, and promulgated in the form of the codex. In contrast to the edict, which creates only a local legal sphere for the protection of a particular endowment or group, the codex lays down the law for all society. In Egypt and in the ancient Near East, the king was expected to safeguard this legal sphere in the broadest possible sense. A codification of the law would have taken away his most vital role and deprived him of his chief source of legitimacy. The gods themselves decreed no laws, instead creating the king (or rather the institution of kingship) to carry out this task.

From a political viewpoint, the theologization of the law thus means nothing less than the abolition of royal sovereignty over the law. The Torah takes the place of kingship, which from now on can be tolerated, at best, as a concession to the people's political immaturity.[45] The collection of laws that forms the basis of the older Covenant Code (Ex 21:12–23:9) is of royal rather than divine provenance, since it undoubtedly dates back to the period of monarchy.[46] Only after the fall of the monarchy, in exile, does the Covenant Code acquire a framework (Ex 20:22–21:11; 23:10–33) that transforms it into *ius divinum*.

The performative character of this transformation of law into scripture is highlighted in the story of the forgotten book told in 2 Kings 22–23. During restoration works on the Temple, a book is unearthed that turns out to contain the laws written down by Moses. The king and his people are appalled and devastated by what they read: due to their ignorance of the book, the laws have not been observed and punishment is unavoidable. It is impossible to imagine that the discovery of the Codex Eshnunna or the Hammurabi stele could have provoked similar reactions in Mesopotamia. One can only react in this way to valid law. Since de Wette's *Critical and Historical Introduction to the Canonical Scriptures of the Old Testament* (1806–1807), there has been widespread agreement that the legend of the rediscovered book must refer to Deuteronomy. That does not mean that Deuteronomy (or a proto-Deuteronomy) must date to 622 BCE. The date could be as fictitious as the story itself. In any event, Deuteronomy represents the definitive, authoritative version of Israel's legal tradition, elevated to the status of revealed truth and thereby theologized. With this book, the step from *ius regium* to *ius divinum* is taken. The law is canonized and released from the vicissitudes of time: from now on, nothing may be deleted, added, replaced, or modified (Deut 4:2; 13:1). Whereas the validity of laws in the ancient Near East rarely outlived the reigning monarch, God's laws are everlasting. That makes it all the more important that they be remembered and preserved as accurately as possible. Just as the Book of Exodus is devoted to the eternal memory of the departure from Egypt, prescribing the liturgical form of this remembrance in the Passover feast and the Festival of Matzah, so the Book of Deuteronomy is devoted to the eternal memory of the commandments and laws revealed on Sinai, prescribing highly differentiated and elaborate mnemonic techniques to this end.

Excursus IV: The Decalogue and Egyptian Norms for Judging the Dead

In 1672 John Marsham published a work, titled *Canon chronicus Aegyptiacus, Hebraicus, Graecus*, in which he proposed an intellectual history as well as a chronology for the ancient world. His aim was to show how wisdom and knowledge branched out from their source in Adam to circulate among the nations of the earth and thence flow down to the West. In this text, written 150 years before the hieroglyphs were deciphered and 170 years before the publication of the Egyptian Book of

the Dead, Marsham compares the Decalogue with what he calls the
"Apologia Funebris" of the ancient Egyptians. His source is the text *De
abstinentia*, by the Greek philosopher Porphyry (third century CE),
who describes there the Egyptian mummification rituals. In an aristo-
cratic burial, he writes, the entrails were separately removed and
placed in a chest (*kibotos*). After all the other funerary rites were carried out, the embalmers took hold of this chest and called the sun god
as witness. One of the embalmers then raised his voice on behalf of the
deceased:

> He says something like this, as Euphantos translated it from the language
> of his homeland: "O Lord Sun and all the gods who give life to humans,
> receive me and present me to the eternal gods to reside with them. The
> gods of whom my parents told me I have reverenced for all the time I lived
> under their rule, and I have always honored those who begot my body. I
> have neither killed any other human being, nor stolen from any what he
> had entrusted to me, nor done any other unpardonable act. And if during
> my life I have been at fault by eating or drinking something forbidden, I did
> not do it myself, but through these," showing the box which contains the
> stomach. Having said this he throws it into the river, and embalms the rest
> of the body as being pure. In this way they thought that a speech for the
> defense was owed to the divinity about what they had eaten and drunk and
> any other wrongs they may have committed.[47]

That leads Marsham to the following commandments, which we here
compare to the Decalogue in the Jewish enumeration:

Apologia funebris Aegyptiorum	Decalogus Hebraeorum
1. Honor the gods	1. No other gods
	2. No graven images
	3. Take not the Lord's name in vain
	4. Keep the Sabbath holy
2. Honor your father and mother	5. Honor your father and mother
3. Do not kill	6. Do not kill
	7. Do not commit adultery

continued

Apologia funebris Aegyptiorum	Decalogus Hebraeorum
4. Do not steal	8. Do not steal
5. Do no other wrongs	9. Do not bear false witness
	10. Do not covet

For Marsham, this "Pentalog" was not only the common denominator of the Egyptian "Funeral Apology" and the biblical Decalogue but
also the origin of the latter. It is the ethics that the Hebrews learned
during their sojourn in Egypt and took with them when they left. The
comparison also shows how correct Jewish tradition was in counting
the fifth commandment ("honor your father and your mother") among
those that concerned the relationship between man and God and were
engraved on the first tablet, and not among the commandments concerning interpersonal relations, which were engraved on the second.

It is tempting to take up this comparison again today, now that the
hieroglyphs have been deciphered and the Egyptian Book of the Dead
has been published, translated, and annotated in multiple versions. The
"Funeral Apology" is found in chapter 125, better known as the "Negative Confession." The prohibitions listed here are not expressed in the
form "Thou shalt not . . ." but in the confessional mode of "I have
not . . ." It is not simply a matter of denying all guilt, since while the
deceased is delivering his defense his heart is being weighed against the
symbol of truth, growing heavier with each lie. These prohibitions
must therefore be observed so that the deceased can appear before the
judges of the dead to deny any wrongdoing without visibly perjuring
himself.

The 82 denials of guilt in chapter 125 of the Book of the Dead are
divided into two lists that the deceased reads out to the chair of the
court (A) and the 42 judges (B). Only List A is structured according to
a clearly discernible thematic order. List B, by contrast, takes its structure not just from the 42 transgressions but also from the 42 divine
judges and their places of origin, the capitals of the 42 administrative
districts (or "nomes") into which Egypt was organized. Naturally, what
results from the mutual interference of several ordering principles is

FIGURE 20. The weighing of the heart ceremony in the Judgment of the Dead. Book of the Dead of Hunefer, c. 1280 BCE.

something of a hodgepodge. Both lists begin with the blanket assurance that "no *jzf.t*" (untruth, injustice, chaos) has been done; expressed positively, Ma'at has been done.

The sins itemized in B may be categorized into those of thought, word, and deed:

Sins of thought (failures to "say" Ma'at—for the Egyptians, "saying" and "thinking" were synonyms):
3 I was not covetous; 18 I have only desired what is my own; 16 I have not secretly listened to others; 26 nor winked my eye at them; 39 I have not puffed myself up; 40 nor raised myself above my station; 23 I was not heated (or: "hot-mouthed"); 31 not choleric; 30 not violent; 24 I have not turned a deaf ear to the words of truth.
Sins of word (failures to say Ma'at):
9 I have not lied; 11 not scolded; 25 I have not quarreled; 29 sued; 21 terrorized; 33 spoken unnecessary words; 37 raised my voice; 35 I have not uttered blasphemies; 38 I have not uttered curses against the king; 17 I have not spoken rashly.
Sins of deed (failures to do Ma'at):
2 I have not robbed with violence; 4 I have not committed theft; 5 I have slain neither man nor woman (A is more general: I have not killed, nor given orders to kill [A 15–16]); 13 I have not killed the "divine cattle" (= people); 7 I have not acted deceitfully; 8 not taken the things belonging to the temple; 10 not stolen food; 15 not robbed portions; 14 not practiced

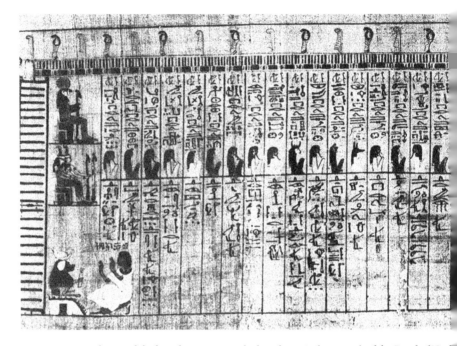

FIGURE 21. The deceased declares his innocence before the 42 judges. Book of the Dead of Nach

grain usury; 12, 22 I have not transgressed; 19 I have not lain with the wife of another man; 20 I have not committed fornication; 27 I have not committed sodomy.

The theme of "causing conflict" that is developed in B is supplemented by the theme of "causing harm" in List A:

12 I have inflicted no pain; 13 I have not let others go hungry; 14 I have not caused tears; 15 I have not killed; 16 I have not given orders to kill; 17 I have done no one any harm.

Just as B places emphasis on social norms, so A places emphasis on offenses toward the gods. Above all, these include the cardinal offenses against sacrificial offerings and temple goods that are frequently documented in other sources as well:

18 I have not plundered the offerings in the temples; 19 I have not diminished the offerings of bread in the temples; 20 I have not carried away the cakes from the spirits of the dead.

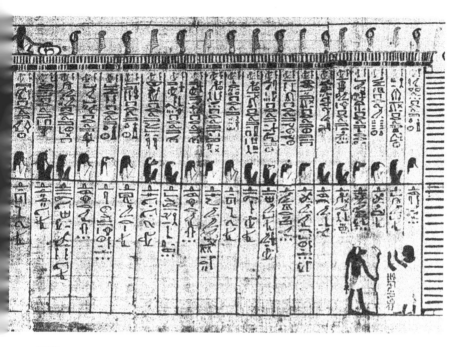

, 1400 BCE.

More specific taboo violations that B barely bothers to mention (at most 36: *I have not waded in water*?) are spelled out in A:

> 30 I have not snared the birds in the swamplands of the gods; 31 I have not fished in their pools; 32 I have not stopped the floodwaters in their season; 33 I have not dammed running water; 34 I have not quenched fire when burning; 35 I have not neglected to offer choice meats on the days (of the feasts); 36 I have not driven off the cattle of the temple estates; 37 I have not stood in the way of a god at his procession.

In A, various misdemeanors involving weights and measures are listed that B dispatches in a single sentence (6: *I have not trimmed the measure*):

> 23 I have not added to nor diminished the measures of grain; 24 I have not diminished the palm measure; 25 nor falsified the cubit of land; 26 I have not added to the weights of the balance; 27 I have not lightened the weight of the scales.

All that the two lists have in common are the sexual offenses, which appear in exactly the same wording:

I have not copulated,
I have not ejaculated.

(A 20–21 = B 27 and 20)

In A, and in A alone, the general claim to have done no *isfet* is extended to ten sentences, perhaps offering something like a general summary:

I have not treated others unjustly
nor have I mistreated animals;
I have not wrought injustice (*iuiit*) in the place of Ma'at,
I have not known what has no existence,
I have brought about no evil,
I did not raise the daily work quota in the morning,
my name did not reach (through accusation) the controller of the bark (the sun god),
I have not blasphemed against any god,
I have not defrauded the poor of their property,
I have not done what the gods abhor.

If we place the Decalogue alongside the Egyptian lists, the similarities are immediately apparent. These are confined to the second half of the commandments: do not kill, do not commit adultery, do no steal, do not lie, do not covet. On the Egyptian side, what is striking is the specificity with which sins of thought and sins of word are itemized. For example, the ban on winking is intended to prevent the bribing of judges or witnesses by an interested party, who might signal at them during court proceedings to make sure they do his bidding. In the Bible, such rules have their place in the more secular books of wisdom literature but not in the God-given Torah:

A naughty person, a wicked man, walketh with a crooked mouth.
He winketh with his eyes, he speaketh with his feet, he teacheth with his fingers;
Deceit is in his heart, he deviseth mischief continually; he soweth discord.

Therefore shall his calamity come suddenly; suddenly shall he be broken without remedy.

These six things doth the Lord hate: yea, seven are an abomination unto him:

A proud look, a lying tongue, and hands that shed innocent blood,

A heart that deviseth wicked imaginations, feet that be swift in running to mischief,

A false witness that speaketh lies, and he that soweth discord among brethren. (Prov 6:12–19)

The taboo on naming decreed in the second (or third) commandment, "Thou shalt not take the name of YHWH, thy God, in vain," is nowhere to be found in the "Funeral Apology." There was something similar to this in Egypt, however. It appeared in connection with oath-taking, which was also the original context of the biblical commandment, as Leviticus 19:12 indicates: "And ye shall not swear by my name falsely, neither shalt thou profane the name of thy God." In his confession to Osiris, engraved on a stele in Abydos, Ramesses IV declares:

I have not sworn by the goat of Mendes in the house of the gods,
I have not uttered the name of Tatenen.

In the same inscription, we also find an equivalent to the commandment to honor one's father and mother:

I have not repudiated my father,
I have not rejected my mother.[48]

Sins of thought and sins of word, which play such a dominant role in Egyptian thought, are expanded on in the "holiness code" of Leviticus:

Thou shalt not defraud thy neighbor, neither rob him: the wages of him that is hired shall not abide with thee all night until the morning.

Thou shalt not curse the deaf, nor put a stumblingblock before the blind, but shalt fear thy God: I am YHWH.

Ye shall do no unrighteousness in judgment: thou shalt not respect the person of the poor, nor honor the person of the mighty: but in righteousness shalt thou judge thy neighbor.

CHAPTER EIGHT

Thou shalt not go up and down as a talebearer among thy people: neither shalt thou stand against the blood of thy neighbor: I am YHWH.
Thou shalt not hate thy brother in thine heart: thou shalt in any wise rebuke thy neighbor, and not suffer sin upon him.
Thou shalt not avenge, nor bear any grudge against the children of thy people, but thou shalt love thy neighbor as thyself: I am YHWH. (19:13–18)

The theme of dealing fairly with weights and measures is explored in the Book of Deuteronomy:

Thou shalt not have in thy bag divers weights, a great and a small.
Thou shalt not have in thine house divers measures, a great and a small.
But thou shalt have a perfect and just weight, a perfect and just measure shalt thou have: that thy days may be lengthened in the land which YHWH, thy God, giveth thee.
For all that do such things, and all that do unrighteously, are an abomination unto YHWH, thy God. (12:13–16)

If we compare the Decalogue with the "Funeral Apology," we find only three commandments that, for structural reasons, lack an Egyptian counterpart: no other gods, (and therefore) no graven images, keep the Sabbath holy. The Egyptians had no qualms about worshipping "other" gods; on the contrary, they were far more concerned about inadvertently neglecting deities and omitting them from their religious ceremonies. In order to worship and stay in touch with the gods, the Egyptians needed images. The Egyptian divine laws dictate that the gods should not be scorned and the taboos not broken. Needless to say, there was no shortage of feasts and holidays in Egypt. But there was no commandment to honor them and keep them holy. It is not by chance, therefore, that these three commandments (1, 2, 4) appear at the beginning of the Decalogue. They form the revolutionary core of the Israelite religion, what distinguishes it from all other religions of its environment and sets it apart from its own prehistory. Everything that follows has numerous parallels in the religions of the region as well as in the Egyptian "Funeral Apology." Indeed, at times the apology explores the relevant themes with a more refined moral sensibility, as in the commandments to cause no tears, to do no harm, to spare animals unnecessary suffering, not to speak without thinking,

and not to turn a deaf ear to words of truth, not to mention the still
baffling ban on knowing what has no existence.

These are the precepts of a worldly wise, experiential knowledge
that teaches the art of harmonious coexistence and is handed down
from one generation to the next. They stand under the sign of Solomonic wisdom, not Mosaic revelation. Two commandments are para-
mount here: not to be covetous and not to turn a deaf ear to words of
truth. These are the twin pinnacles of Egyptian wisdom. While the ban
on covetousness is placed at the end of the Decalogue, hearing is nowhere mentioned in the law. It does appear at the apex of wisdom in
the books attributed to Solomon, though, when he prays that God
will grant him a "listening heart" as the highest humanly attainable goal
(1 Kings 3:9).

In their combination of legal principles, moral norms, and ritual taboos, the laws governing the Judgment of the Dead correspond to a certain extent to the Torah, which contains moral norms (*miṣwôt*) and ritual
prescriptions (*ḥuqqîm*) alongside laws (*mišpāṭîm*). The Egyptian bans
are not decreed by God, however; the gods function here only as judges,
not legislators. This difference is so massive that one could ask whether
any meaningful parallels can be drawn here. The parallel lies in the idea
of justification. The Torah not only forms the basis for life in the covenanted community but also offers vindication before God. That is also
the function performed by chapter 125 in the Book of the Dead. Both
texts, the Torah and chapter 125, could be called a codex of justification.
They provide human beings with guidelines for leading a life that is both
pleasing before God and righteous in the eyes of the community.

In Egypt, too, a promise is bound up with this justification, but it is
a promise that goes far beyond anything found in the Old Testament.
It is one that seems almost to anticipate Christian ideas: the promise of
entry into paradise and the community of the gods, redemption from
the dominion of death, and eternal life in the world to come. Anyone
justified by the divine tribunal passed through to the "field of rushes,"
the Egyptian Elysium. Whether this codex of justification had a comparable influence to the Torah on the way Egyptians went about their
daily lives is an open question, however. Here there are no mnemotechnical instructions such as we find framing the Torah: keep reading God's word, keep discussing it, keep transcribing it, never lose

sight of it, never stop thinking about it. To what extent did ordinary
Egyptians even have access to the Book of the Dead before they crossed
into the beyond? We cannot know for sure; nonetheless, we have the
testimony of a certain Baki from the fourteenth century BCE, who
claims to have made the laws of the Judgment of the Dead the basis of
his conduct during life:

> Ma'at is an excellent protective wall for the one who speaks it,
> on that day when he arrives at the court
> that judges the wretch and uncovers his character,
> and punishes the sinner [*isfeti*] and cuts off his *ba*.
> I existed without blame,
> so that there is no complaint against me and no sin of mine before them,
> and so that I might emerge vindicated
> and praised among those provided with a tomb,
> who have gone to their *ka*. [...]
> I am a worthy [...] who emulated the laws of the Judgment of the Dead
> [literally: the "Hall of the Two Ma'at"],
> for I intended to reach the realm of the dead
> without my name being attached to any meanness,
> without having done anything evil to any man,
> or anything that their gods censure.[49]

Similar declarations to those appearing in chapter 125 of the Book of
the Dead can be found in many tomb inscriptions.

This chapter draws on an established model for codifying laws in
writing that may be significant for the idea and wording of the Torah as
well. This is the genre of statutes that a particular group sets for itself,
for example, a priesthood or some other religious community. Chapter
125 of the Book of the Dead maintains the closest connections in both
form and content to the oaths sworn by novices when they were inducted into the priesthood. Here they must swear never to have committed certain offenses, or never to commit them in the future:

> I shall eat nothing that is forbidden to priests.
> I shall cut nothing with a knife [...] nor ask anyone else to do what is
> forbidden.
> I have cut off the head of no living being,

I have killed no man,
I have nothing to do with unclean men,
I have slept with no youth,
I have not slept with the wife of another, [...]
I shall not eat or drink what is forbidden or is listed (as forbidden) in the books.
Nothing will stick to my fingers.
I shall weigh out no grain on the threshing floor.
I shall take no scale in my hand.
I shall measure no land.
I shall visit no unclean place.
I shall touch no sheep's wool.
I shall seize no knife, to the day I die.[50]

These rules can be summed up as the "*nomos* of the temple," a set of rules that—like all statutes binding a community—also has the characteristics of a contract. Whoever sticks to these rules belongs in the covenant; whoever breaks them will be cast out. In this case, members of the covenant or religious order are helped out by a mnemonic device: the rules of the *nomos* are written on the walls of the passageways that the priests pass through each morning on their way to carry out their duties:[51]

Lead (no one) into falsehood,
enter not into impurity,
tell no lies in his house!
Do not be greedy, slander not,
take no bribes,
make no distinction between rich and poor,
add nothing to the weights and measures and detract nothing,
do not tamper with the bushel [...].[52]

The idea of the Judgment of the Dead translates this idea into the hereafter. The afterlife—the sphere of eternal life known as the "house of Osiris," in contrast to the realm of the dead—here forms the social space into which the dead are inducted, in keeping with the template of novices inducted into the temple and its priesthood. Chapter 125 of the Book of the Dead codifies the quasi-priestly *nomos* of the afterlife.

In this sense, the Torah may also be regarded as the quasi-priestly *nomos* of a divine covenant that required the Israelites to be "a kingdom of priests, and a holy nation," as stipulated in the introduction to the revelation of the law. The Promised Land is a temple, God's people its priesthood, the Torah its statute book, just as in Egypt the hereafter can be seen as a temple, the community of justified dead as its priesthood, and chapter 125 its statute book.

For all that they have in common, the crucial differences separating the two traditions should not be overlooked. First, the covenant is a communal agreement; it concerns the chosen people and their collective resolution to lead a life in conformity with the Torah. The Judgment of the Dead, by contrast, concerns the individual and his or her personal resolution to lead a life in conformity with Ma'at. By turning away from the law (with the exception of the Decalogue) and by no longer defining itself in terms of ethnicity, Christianity opened its doors to gentiles, on the one hand, while making the individual soul a partner in the divine covenant, on the other. Second, the divine covenant has nothing to do with royalty and the state. The idea of a covenant first arises in exile and is realized under conditions of substatehood, when the formerly independent kingdom of Judah was a province in the Persian Empire. Here, the foundation is laid for the idea of an otherworldly kingdom of God that competes with the worldly state, the *civitas terrena*. The Egyptian afterlife, by contrast, is the extension of the pharaonic state into the realm of the gods, according to the principle: as on earth, so in heaven. The house of Osiris is imagined as a welfare provider governed by the same laws as the house of Pharaoh. Third, the great historical turning point of the "Axial Age," already implicit in the concept of revelation, separates Egyptian ethics from Jewish law. Unlike the laws of Ma'at, the law of the Torah rest on revelation. They cannot be gleaned from any kind of experience; in them, the absolute intrudes into the realm of the given, the conditional, and the contingent. Whereas Egyptian Ma'at stands and falls with the pharaonic state, Israel's divine covenant makes a decisive break with this grounding of ethics in the state. Biblical ethics stands and falls with the idea of the covenant with God, and this holds true for both the Old Testament and the New, for Judaism and Christianity.

CHAPTER NINE

RESISTANCE

Moses and the Violent Fate of the Prophets

The authentic, only and deepest theme in the history of the
world and humanity, to which all others are subordinated,
remains the conflict between faith and unbelief.

—*Johann Wolfgang von Goethe*[1]

Murmuring in the Desert

The Israelites' passage from the Sea of Reeds to Sinai, and then on
through the desert to the land of Canaan, is periodically interrupted by
outbreaks of mutiny and rebellion. These did much to contribute to the
later stereotype of the fiercely recalcitrant, "stiff-necked" Jew. What
could be the meaning of so unflattering a self-description? What sense
can we make of these constantly repeated scenes of popular revolt?
These scenes, to be subjected to closer examination in what follows,
express a dual form of resistance. The first is the resistance to the message of the One God and the covenant from those who, having entered
the covenant of their own free will, now shrink from the excessive demands it places on them. The second is the resistance put up by the
covenant and the One God to everything the people used to believe
and practice. This religion of an exclusive pact with God *is* resistance
and it *encounters* resistance.

Unlike the Abrahamic covenant in Genesis, which knows neither
loyalty nor disloyalty, blessing nor curse, the Mosaic covenant stipulates strict adherence to the law. It therefore has a dark side as well as a
light one. The dark side makes its presence felt as soon as the covenant
has been made. It consists in the curse that is no less a part of the institution of political alliances than the blessing. The curse is particularly
evident in the strongly emphasized jealous and "choleric" tempera-
ment of the divine overlord. The unsparing relentlessness with which

the Bible dwells on this dark side is truly astonishing. Time and again, emphasis is placed on how much must be sacrificed in order to stay true to the covenant and, conversely, how much fear and suffering the Israelites must endure when they face historical catastrophe knowing they stand under a curse for having squandered God's blessing. The other covenants reported on in the Bible, those with Noah, Abraham, and David, are unshadowed by any hint of divine malediction, and it may safely be assumed that at least the first two of these covenants represent conscious Priestly alternatives to the Deuteronomic idea of the covenant.

The Exodus narrative reaches its climax in the covenant with God, which motivates both the departure from Egypt and the entry into the Promised Land. In the context of this narrative, the dark side of the covenant is expressed in the scenes of "murmuring" as well as in the fits of divine rage they provoke as soon as the covenant has been concluded. Michael Walzer has given this theme particular prominence in his book *Exodus and Revolution*. According to his political interpretation of the Exodus story, this motif expresses the difficulties and dilemmas typically encountered whenever an ancien régime is overthrown: there are deserts to cross after every revolution. Having thrown their weight behind the revolutionaries in their initial enthusiasm for the cause, the people turn against the revolutionary elite or vanguard party once they are expected to endure privation, coercion, and violence on the long and arduous march to a new order. Such counterrevolutionary resistance is given querulous voice in the scenes of "murmuring," and it is in these scenes—whose truthfulness has been confirmed by countless subsequent historical experiences—that we find one important reason for the enduring vitality of the Exodus story.

Walzer is right to stress the importance of these recurring scenes of "murmuring," in which the people revolt against Moses's leadership and the entire project of emigration.[2] Undoubtedly, his political interpretation of these scenes as an expression of counterrevolutionary resistance captures a central aspect of their reception history. In this chapter, I would like to take a different approach by focusing on their religious significance, examining how they reflect what Goethe called "the conflict between faith and unbelief."

The first of these scenes takes place before the passage through the Sea of Reeds, when the Israelites take fright upon seeing the Egyptian forces in hot pursuit. Foreseeing this reaction, YHWH had directed them to avoid the heavily patrolled coastal route, lest they lose heart and return to Egypt upon catching sight of enemy troops (Ex 13:17). Now, in their protest speech, Egypt is mentioned five times in seven lines:

> Because there were no graves in *Egypt*,
> hast thou taken us away to die in the wilderness?
> Wherefore hast thou dealt thus with us, to carry us forth out of *Egypt*?
> Is not this the word that we did tell thee in *Egypt*, saying,
> Let us alone, that we may serve *Egypt*?
> For it had been better for us to serve in *Egypt*,
> than that we should die in the wilderness. (Ex 14:11–12)[3]

These scenes are already reprised in Exodus 15, after Moses has led his people through the Sea of Reeds, even though YHWH had just demonstrated his superior power and loving kindness toward Israel in the most miraculous, awe-inspiring, and—one would have thought—unforgettable manner. But at Marah, where the parched Israelites cannot drink the bitter waters after three waterless days in the wilderness of Shur, they have already started to "murmur" (*wajillonû*).[4] God instructs Moses to make the water sweet by throwing in a piece of wood. In the wilderness of Sin, they longingly recall the fleshpots of Egypt and renew their complaints; this time God provides them with quail and manna.

In Rephidim (chapter 17) there is again no water, and the people protest so vehemently that Moses fears they will stone him to death. God tells Moses to strike the rock at Massah-Meribah with his staff, causing water to gush out.

In these scenes en route from the Sea of Reeds to Sinai, there is still no word of divine wrath and punishment. The people grumble and God immediately comes to their aid. Only once they have pledged him their unconditional trust and loyalty—only, that is, with the covenant at Sinai—does their grumbling provoke God's righteous indignation, which he proceeds to vent in a variety of punishments.

FIGURE 22. Moses and Aaron (left) supervise the gathering of manna. Ercole de' Roberti, c. 1490.

These scenes are described in the Book of Numbers.⁵ When the people once again start murmuring upon setting out from Sinai, "his anger was kindled, and the fire of the Lord burnt among them," and they "called the name of the place Taberah, because here the fire of the Lord burnt among them" (Num 1:1–3). While still in Taberah, the people resume their litany of complaints, yearn for the delicacies of Egypt, and grow weary of their unvarying diet of manna: "and the anger of the Lord was kindled greatly" (11:10). Now Moses, too, finds the burden of the perennially grumbling people too much to bear and complains before God. Rather than taking offense, YHWH advises Moses to appoint seventy elders to a kind of war council. In addition, he promises and delivers plentiful supplies of quail meat. But then, "while the flesh was yet between their teeth [. . .], the wrath of the Lord was kindled against the people, and the Lord smote the people with a very great plague" (11:33). At the next station it is Aaron and Miriam, Moses's siblings, who quarrel with him on account of the "Ethiopian woman" he had married, and because he presumes to act alone as God's mouthpiece: "Hath YHWH not spoken also by us?" (12:1–2) At this point we read the remarkable sentence, presumably intended to counter the charge of arrogance: "Now the man Moses was very meek, above all the men which were upon the face of the earth" (12:3). Here too God's wrath is kindled and Miriam is afflicted with leprosy. Although God immediately heals her upon Moses's in-

FIGURE 23. Moses strikes water from the rock. Copperplate engraving of Exodus 17 by
Matthäus Merian, 1630.

tercession, she still has to spend seven days in quarantine outside the
Israelite camp.

The next occasion, when the scouts sent ahead by Moses to "spy
out" the Promised Land return to the wilderness of Paran, sees the
worst crisis since the episode with the Golden Calf. This time the cause
for complaint is no longer hunger and thirst but rather the central values of covenant theology: faith and unbelief, loyalty and apostasy, trust
and distrust in the sense of the whole undertaking. For the first time,
YHWH himself (and not Moses) is held responsible for the departure
from Egypt with all its dangers:

> Would God that we had died in the land of Egypt! or would God we had
> died in this wilderness!
>
> And wherefore hath YHWH brought us unto this land, to fall by the sword,
> that our wives and our children should be a prey? were it not better for us
> to return into Egypt?
>
> And they said one to another, Let us make a captain, and let us return into
> Egypt. (14:2–4)

FIGURE 24. The scouts return from the Promised Land. Copperplate engraving of Exodus
13 by Matthäus Merian, 1630.

Several of the scouts spread the rumor that the Promised Land is
settled by a race of giants whom the Israelites stand no chance of de-
feating. The people rise up against Moses, clamoring for a new leader
to take them back to Egypt. They threaten to stone Moses and Aaron,
along with Joshua and Caleb, who had tried to talk them out of returning. "And the glory of the Lord appeared in the Tabernacle of the congregation before all the children of Israel." Once again God wants to
destroy the entire people; once again Moses succeeds in deflecting him
from his purpose. God pardons his wayward flock, but he also punishes
them: the entire generation of those who emigrated from Egypt,
"which have seen my glory, and my miracles [. . .] and have tempted
me now these ten times, and have not hearkened to my voice, surely
they shall not see the land which I sware unto their fathers" (14:22–23).
The faithless Israelites are condemned to wander forty years in the wilderness until "they shall be consumed, and there they shall die."

The symbolic character of the narrative is evident throughout this
episode. The forty years refer to the time it will take for the generation

of inveterate grumblers to die out in the wilderness. Only those born after the exodus will enter the Promised Land:

As truly as I live, saith YHWH, as ye have spoken in mine ears, so will I do to you: Your carcases shall fall in this wilderness; and all that were numbered of you, according to your whole number, from twenty years old and upward, which have murmured against me, doubtless ye shall not come into the land, concerning which I sware to make you dwell therein, save Caleb the son of Jephunneh, and Joshua the son of Nun. But your little ones, which ye said should be a prey, them will I bring in, and they shall know the land which ye have despised. But as for you, your carcases, they shall fall in this wilderness. And your children shall wander in the wilderness forty years, and bear your whoredoms, until your carcases be wasted in the wilderness. After the number of days in which ye searched the land, even forty days, each day for a year, shall ye bear your iniquities, even forty years, and ye shall know my breach of promise. I, YHWH, have said, I will surely do it unto all this evil congregation, that are gathered together against me: in this wilderness they shall be consumed, and there they shall die. (14:28–35)

God justifies the length of the sentence with reference to the forty days the scouts were abroad. Moses also spent forty days on Sinai, leading those waiting at the foot of the mountain to give up hope of his eventual return and fashion a substitute in the idolatrous form of the Golden Calf. In the New Testament, God's spirit leads Jesus into the wilderness to be tempted by the devil for forty days. With that, the motif of the forty years spent wandering in the wilderness is taken up in modified form, as Jesus himself acknowledges. When the devil advises him to satisfy his hunger by turning stones into bread, he replies with reference to Deuteronomy 8:3: "Man does not live by bread alone." For the Israelites, the forty years in the wilderness are what the forty days in the desert are for Jesus—a time of trial and temptation:

And thou shalt remember all the way which YHWH, thy God, led thee these forty years in the wilderness, to humble thee, and to prove thee, to know what was in thine heart, whether thou wouldest keep his commandments, or no. And he humbled thee, and suffered thee to hunger, and fed thee with manna, which thou knewest not, neither did thy fathers know; that he might make thee know that man doth not live by bread only, but by ever word that

FIGURE 25. The punishment of Nadab and Abihu. Copperplate engraving of Leviticus 10:1–2 by Matthäus Merian, 1630: "And Nadab and Abihu, the sons of Aaron, took either of them his censer, and put fire therein, and put incense thereon, and offered a strange fire before YHWH, which he commanded them not. And there went out fire from YHWH, and devoured them, and they died before YHWH." Many "grumblers" came to a similar end in the desert.

proceedeth out of YHWH's mouth doth man live. Thy raiment waxed not old upon thee, neither did thy foot swell, these forty years. Thou shalt also consider in thine heart, that, as a man chasteneth his son, so YHWH, thy God, chasteneth thee. (Deut 8:2–5)

Did the people pass the test? In the light of what follows, one would have to conclude that they did not, for there is still no end to their murmuring even after they have been rebuked and harshly punished. Shortly after, Korah and his clansmen among the Levites launch a rebellion, supported by two hundred and fifty notables who resent Moses and Aaron's privileged access to God. The rebellion occurs immediately after God had introduced a new mnemotechnical institution for preserving the covenant in everlasting memory: the knotted fringes or tassels (ṣîṣīt) the Israelites are instructed to attach to their upper garments:

And it shall be unto you for a fringe, that ye may look upon it, and remember all the commandments of YHWH, and do them; and that ye seek not after your own heart and your own eyes, after which ye use to go a whoring: that ye may remember, and do all my commandments, and be holy unto God. I am YHWH, your God, which brought you out of the land of Egypt, to be your God: I am YHWH, your God.

Now Korah, the son of Izhar, the son of Kohath, the son of Levi, and [with him] Dathan and Abiram, the sons of Eliab, and On, the son of Peleth, sons of Reuben, took men, and they rose up before Moses, with certain of the children of Israel, two hundred and fifty princes of the assembly, famous in the congregation, men of renown. And they gathered themselves together against Moses and against Aaron, and said unto them, Ye take too much upon you, seeing all the congregation are holy, every one of them, and YHWH is among them. Wherefore then lift ye up yourselves above YHWH's congregation? (Num 15:39–16:3)

The rebellion involved members of the Levite aristocracy. The Korahite rebels had just heard Moses again enjoining all Israelites to "holiness"; on what possible basis, then, could he and his brother claim a monopoly over ritual contacts with God? Dathan and Abiram go so far as to substitute Egypt for the Promised Land, praising it as the fabled land of milk and honey:

Is it a small thing that thou hast brought us up out of a land that floweth with milk and honey, to kill us in the wilderness, except thou make thyself altogether a prince over us? Moreover thou hast not brought us into a land that floweth with milk and honey, or given us inheritance of fields and vineyards: wilt thou put out the eyes of these men? We will not come up. (Num 16:13–14)

The Korahites demand the right to offer incense to God. Moses lets God decide, and the rebels are promptly swallowed up by the earth along with their censers. The following morning, this shocking incident sets off a fresh round of complaints as the people accuse Moses and Aaron of killing the Korahites and their supporters. The glory of the Lord again appears above the Tabernacle to unleash a plague on the grumblers. By the time Aaron puts a stop to it by fumigating the congregation with incense, it has claimed some 14,700 lives.

FIGURE 26. *Moses strikes water from the rock.* Tintoretto, 1577.

When the people resume their trek and strike camp in the wilderness of Sin, the same complaints about the "waters of Meribah" break out that had already been heard in Exodus 17:

> And there was no water for the congregation; and they gathered themselves together against Moses and against Aaron. And the people chode with Moses, and spake, saying, Would God that we had died when our brethren died before YHWH! And why have ye brought up YHWH's congregation into this wilderness, that we and our cattle should die there? And wherefore have ye made us to come up out of Egypt, to bring us in unto this

evil place? It is no place of seed, or of figs, or of vines, or of pomegranates; neither is there any water to drink.

And Moses and Aaron went from the presence of the assembly unto the door of the tabernacle of the congregation, and they fell upon their faces; and the glory of YHWH appeared unto them. And YHWH spake unto Moses, saying, Take thy rod, and gather thou the assembly together, thou, and Aaron thy brother, and speak ye unto the rock before their eyes; and it shall give forth his water, and thou shalt bring forth to them water out of the rock: so thou shalt give the congregation and their beasts drink. And Moses took the rod from before YHWH, as he commanded him.

And Moses and Aaron gathered the congregation together before the rock, and he said unto them, Hear now, ye rebels; must we fetch you water out of this rock? And Moses lifted up his hand, and with his rod he smote the rock twice: and the water came out abundantly, and the congregation drank, and their beasts also. And YHWH spake unto Moses and Aaron, Because ye believed me not, to sanctify me in the eyes of the children of Israel, therefore ye shall not bring this congregation into the land which I have given them.

This is the water of Meribah, where the children of Israel quarreled with YHWH and where he was proved holy among them. (20:2–13)

The scene is evidently included here as a freestanding episode rather than as a reworked version of Exodus 17. On this occasion, however, Moses and Aaron are punished, not the grumbling Israelites: they will not be the ones to lead their people into the Promised Land.

What offense have they committed? Moses struck the rock with his staff rather than commanding it with words. The rock would have yielded water at the behest of its creator; instead, it obeyed the blow due to magical compulsion. Moses performed magic tricks, playing the sorcerer, instead of giving God the opportunity to demonstrate his holiness by working a miracle. That is why Aaron must die in the desert and Moses on Mount Nebo. In the account of the same scene in Exodus 17, there is no word of such a conflict:

And all the congregation of the children of Israel journeyed from the wilderness of Sin, after their journeys, according to YHWH's commandment, and pitched in Rephidim; and there was no water for the people to drink.

FIGURE 27. Moses strikes water from the rock. Jewish book illustration, northern France, late thirteenth century.

Wherefore the people did chide with Moses, and said, Give us water that we may drink. And Moses said unto them, Why chide ye with me? Wherefore do ye test YHWH? And the people thirsted there for water; and the people murmured against Moses, and said, Wherefore is this that thou hast brought us up out of Egypt, to kill us and our children and our cattle with thirst?

And Moses cried unto YHWH, saying, What shall I do unto this people? They be almost ready to stone me. And YHWH said unto Moses, Go on before the people, and take with thee of the elders of Israel; and thy rod, wherewith thou smotest the river, take in thine hand, and go. Behold, I will stand before thee there upon the rock in Horeb; and thou shalt smite the rock, and there shall come water out of it, that the people may drink. And Moses did so in the sight of the elders of Israel.

And he called the name of the place Massah, and Meribah, because of the chiding of the children of Israel, and because they tested YHWH, saying, Is YHWH among us, or not? (17:1–7)

The punishment seems excessively harsh, the explanation forced. The biblical narrators were clearly hard put to explain why exactly Moses should not be permitted to enter the Promised Land. This already provoked Goethe to suspect that another, more tangible motive for Moses's disappearance at the threshold to the Promised Land was being covered up here.

Moses's biography requires that he should die in Moab and not lead his people into the Promised Land. Otherwise, there would be no occasion for his great valedictory address with its recapitulation of the law and renewal of the covenant, the subject of Deuteronomy. The Deuteronomistic conception of the exodus dictates that Moses must die before reaching the Promised Land, casts around for a reason for this death, and finds it in the story of Meribah (Exodus 17), reworked in Deuteronomistic form in Numbers 20. Moses cannot reach the Promised Land because the lawgiver must disappear from the scene once his work is done, frustrating calls for his laws to be amended or revised. For the same reason, Solon went abroad for ten years after legislating his reforms in Athens and Laozi disappeared traveling westward after having finished his Tao-Te-Ching. Second, Moses must be denied a gravesite and funerary cult. Now that the people have entered into a community with the God who dwells in their midst, his role as an intermediary is played out. The motif of Moses dying before reaching the Promised Land is further linked to the decision to reserve the story of the occupation for the Book of Joshua and end the Torah with the death of Moses. The Torah concludes with the sentence "And there arose not a prophet since in Israel like unto Moses, whom the Lord knew face to face." With that, Moses has become what the Islamic tradition calls "the seal of the prophets." The phase of foundation and gestation is over, an eternally valid order has been created, and whatever happens from now on can unfold only within the bounds of that order.

The final scene of murmuring is told in the following chapter (Num 21:4–9), preceded by an opening skirmish in the style of a holy war.[6] The king of Arad has attacked Israel and taken several captives. "Then Israel vowed a vow unto YHWH and said, If thou wilt indeed deliver this people into my hand, then I will utterly destroy their cities" (Num 21:2). That means relinquishing all claims to booty, killing anything that lives, burning everything in the marketplace, and laying waste to the city. YHWH heard their vow "and delivered up the Canaanites." Upon continuing their journey, however, the people become "discouraged." They suffer hunger and thirst and have lost all taste for manna. This time, an enraged God sends them venomous snakes rather than quails. The people repent of their sins and God instructs Moses to fashion an antidote: a "serpent of brass" that heals any snakebite victim who beholds it.

This episode already exceeds the ten scenes of "murmuring" about the adversities of emigration that God in his omniscience had foretold after the eighth such scene, the return of the scouts:

1	Ex 14:11–12	Panic upon catching sight of the Egyptian forces at the Sea of Reeds. Back to Egypt! Cf. Ex 13:17, where YHWH himself foresees this crisis.
2	Ex 15:22–24	Thirst. Marah: transformation of the bitter waters into water that is fit to drink.
3	Ex 16:1–3	Hunger. Longing for the fleshpots of Egypt. Back to Egypt! God sends quails and manna.
4	Ex 17:1–3	Thirst. Why did we ever leave Egypt? Moses strikes water from the rock at Massah-Meribah.
5	Num 11:1–3	Discontent. The people complain, and God sends fire that consumes "the uttermost parts of the camp" (Taberah).
6	Num 11:4–35	Longing for fish and meat. Back to Egypt! The "mixt multitude" contaminates the Israelites with their discontent, and God sends a plague to punish them ("graves of the people who lusted").
7	Num 12:1–13	Miriam and Aaron criticize Moses on account of his Kushite wife and his privileged access to God. God punishes Miriam with leprosy.

8	Num 14	Fear. The people panic and clamor to return to Egypt after hearing the scouts' false rumors. God punishes them with forty years in the wilderness.
9	Num 16:12–14	Rebellion of the Korahites, who demand the same cultic rights as Moses and Aaron. God punishes the rebels, who are swallowed up by the earth, and sends a plague that claims 14,700 victims. Dathan and Abiram: back to Egypt as "a land that floweth with milk and honey."
10	Num 17	The people grumble on account of the fatalities. God wants to destroy them but Aaron quickly makes amends.
11	Num 20	Thirst. Back to Egypt! Moses strikes water from the rock at Massah-Meribah (= no. 4). God punishes Moses and Aaron, who were only meant to address the rock, not strike it. They will die before entering the Promised Land.
12	Num 21	Hunger. Back to Egypt! The people grow sick of manna. God afflicts them with venomous snakes but shows Moses the remedy (the bronze serpent).

The number ten is emphasized by God himself. However it may have been arrived at, it lends the motif of murmuring a particular weight, equating these "ten" scenes with the ten plagues visited on Egypt.[7] In eight of these scenes (1, 3, 4, 6, 8, 9, 11, 12), the wish to return to Egypt is expressed: better a slave in Egypt than a corpse in the desert. On one occasion Egypt is even called a "land that floweth with milk and honey" (9: Num 16:12–14). No more forceful rebellion against YHWH's plan for salvation can be imagined than this longing for Egypt and the desire to return there. In Hosea (11:1; 8:13; 9:3) and Deuteronomy (28:68), conversely, it is YHWH himself who threatens to send the people back to Egypt and hence revoke his special plan for them.[8]

These eleven or twelve episodes of "murmuring" are complemented by two scenes in which the people, rather than resisting YHWH, are led astray when they take an initiative that sins against his jealous and wrathful love: the scene with the Golden Calf (Ex 32), where they flout the ban on graven images, and the scene in Shittim (Num 25), where they flout the ban on worshipping other gods. In making the Golden

Calf, they are not so much taking *another* god as creating an image of their *own* god to carry before them, since they have given up all hope of ever again seeing Moses, who has now been away on Sinai forty days. Yet an image of the unimaginable god is automatically (albeit unintentionally) the image of a different god. In this scene, God reveals for the first time the jealous love that the first and second commandments had already warned against. YHWH reacts so violently to this transgression that he resolves to wipe out the entire people, a course of action from which Moses dissuades him only with great difficulty.

God's wrath appears most prominently in the scene in Shittim, since now jealousy in the proper sense of the term has been aroused. Here the Israelites actually worship *another* god, Baʿal-Peor (*baʿal pĕʿôr*). Located on the east bank of the Jordan in Moab, Shittim was the Israelites' last stop before crossing the Jordan. Here the people struck camp "and began to commit whoredom with the daughters of Moab. And they called the people unto the sacrifices of their gods; and the people did eat, and bowed down to their gods" (Num 25:1–2).

The link between sexual impropriety and idol worship is a central topos in the Hebrew Bible. Beginning with the early prophets, especially Hosea, and continuing above all in Ezekiel and Jeremiah and throughout the entire Deuteronomistic history, contact with alien gods is regularly castigated as "whoredom." Worship of alien gods begins with the love of foreign women, who seduce their partners into following their religious rites. That is why we read in the Book of Exodus:

> I will deliver the inhabitants of the land into your hand; and thou shalt drive them out before thee. Thou shalt make no covenant with them, nor with their gods. They shall not dwell in thy land, lest they make thee sin against me: for if thou serve their gods, it will surely be a snare unto thee. (23:31–33)

And similarly in Deuteronomy:

> Thou shalt make no covenant with them, nor shew mercy unto them. Neither shalt thou make marriages with them; thy daughter thou shalt not give unto his son, nor his daughter shalt thou take unto thy son. For they will turn away thy son from following me, that they may serve other gods: so will YHWH's anger be kindled against you, and destroy thee suddenly. (7:2–4)

At Shittim God's anger is kindled, and he has Moses impose a punishment no less draconian than the one inflicted after the dance around the Golden Calf:

> Take all the leaders of the people, and hang them up before YHWH against the sun, that YHWH's fierce anger may be turned away from Israel. And Moses said unto the judges of Israel, Slay ye every one of his men were joined unto Ba'al-Peor. (Num 25:4–5)

God further gives vent to his fury in a plague that claims 24,000 lives. There then occurs a scene that dispels God's anger at a stroke:

> And behold, one of the children of Israel came and brought unto his brethren a Midianitish woman in the sight of Moses, and in the sight of all the congregation of the children of Israel, who were weeping before the door of the tabernacle of the congregation. And when Phinehas, the son of Eleazar, the son of Aaron the priest, saw it, he rose up from among the congregation, and took a javelin in his hand; and he went after the man of Israel into the tent, and thrust both of them through, the man of Israel, and the woman through her belly. (Num 25:6–8)

This act brings a sudden end to the plague:

> And YHWH spake unto Moses, saying: Phinehas, the son of Eleazar, the son of Aaron the priest, hath turned my wrath away from the children of Israel, while he was zealous for my sake among them, that I consumed not the children of Israel in my zeal. Wherefore say, Behold, I give unto him my covenant of peace; and he shall have it, and his seed after him, even the covenant of an everlasting priesthood, because he was zealous for his God, and made an atonement for the children of Israel. (Num 25:10–13)

The root *qn'*, "zeal" or "jealousy," appears four times in this short passage. The text expresses the mirror-image relationship between God's jealousy and human zeal with particular clarity: "because his zealousness (*bĕqan'ô*) reflected my own zeal (*'et qin'ātî*)," "that I consumed them not in my zeal (*bĕqin'ātî*)." The words *qānā'*, (human) zealousness, and *qin'â*, (divine) "jealousy," are derived from the same root. Phinehas is commended for butchering the couple in the tent and his memory is sanctified.[9]

In the First Book of Maccabees, for example, the outbreak of the Maccabean revolt is told with reference to this scene. Antiochus IV

Epiphanes, the Seleucid king who ruled over Judea at the time, had proclaimed an edict abolishing the Jewish religion and introducing pagan sacrificial rites. When the high priest Mattathias refused to carry out the prescribed sacrifice, a Jew stepped forward to do it for him.

> Which thing when Mattathias saw, he was inflamed with zeal, and his reins trembled, neither could he forbear to shew his anger according to judgment: wherefore he ran, and slew him upon the altar. Also the king's commissioner, who compelled men to sacrifice, he killed at that time, and the altar he pulled down. Thus dealt he zealously for the law of God, like as Phinehas did unto Zambri the son of Salom. And Mattathias cried throughout the city with a loud voice, saying, Whosoever is zealous of the law, and maintaineth the covenant, let him follow me. So he and his sons fled into the mountains, and left all that ever they had in the city. (2:24–28)

Two scenes of the Exodus story are invoked in this passage: in his murderous zeal, Mattathias follows the example of Phinehas, and with his cry, "Whosoever is zealous of the law, follow me," he takes his cue from Moses, who rallied the Levites following the dance around the Golden Calf: "Whosoever is on YHWH's side, let him come unto me" (Ex 32:26). In Shittim, a primal scene of proverbial "whoring" with other gods thus makes way for a no less influential primal scene of violent zeal for God.

When we cast an eye over all the crises brought about by popular discontent ("murmuring"), open rebellion, and flagrant violations of the covenant, we arrive at a grand total of fourteen scenes. They make the departure from Egypt look like a project that is constantly imperiled by resistance and can only be completed with recourse to considerable violence. Among these scenes, three stand out due to the length accorded them in the narrative, the harshness with which they are punished, and the theological and political importance they thereby assume: the episodes of the Golden Calf, the scouts (no. 8) and Baʿal-Peor in Shittim. All three place the covenant in jeopardy through the severity of the offenses committed: idolatry (the Golden Calf), worship of other gods (Baʿal-Peor), and unbelief, in the sense of a lack of faith in God's promises (scouts). The covenant that YHWH concludes with the Israelites requires both loyalty—no other gods!—and faith: faith that God will keep the promises he made to the patriarchs and then renewed to Moses. This very faith in a future, more benign dispensation is abandoned by the Israelites when they hear the terrible rumors spread by the scouts. Faith, accompanied by a shift in temporal awareness from a fixation on the primordial templates furnished by myth to the future-oriented temporality of salvation history, forms the basis of the new religion and covenant that the Jews are called on to embrace. The tremendous gravity of their conversion, a process spanning more than a generation and requiring nothing less than the creation of a new type of human being: that is the dominant theme of this fourth act in the Exodus drama. It can be schematized as follows:

Egypt: Border		Sinai				Moab: Border
1	2, 3, 4		5, 6, 7	8	9, 10, 11, 12	
		Golden Calf		Scouts		Shittim
Panic	Thirst, hunger	Betrayal	Hunger 7: Miriam and Aaron	Panic	Thirst, hunger 9: Korah's clan	Betrayal
Faith		Loyalty		Faith		Loyalty

The Murder of Moses?

From time to time, suspicions have been raised that these scenes of mutiny and rebellion cover up a crime so terrible that it had to be expunged from the cultural memory of Israel: the lynching of Moses. In what follows, I examine three proponents of this thesis: Johann Wolfgang von Goethe, Sigmund Freud, and Ernst Sellin. In his essay "Israel in the Wilderness" (1819), Goethe contended that Moses was murdered during the exodus from Egypt.[10] Goethe set out in this essay, first, to distinguish narrative from legislation in the books from Exodus to Deuteronomy and, second, to limit the story to what might plausibly have occurred. He did so by stripping away anything that smacked of the miraculous. For example, the biblical forty years spent wandering in the wilderness become a mere two-year voyage. Toward the end, shortly before crossing the Jordan, Moses "disappeared […] and we should be very much in error, if Joshua and Caleb had not considered it a good deed to terminate the regency of a limited man they had suffered for a number of years, and to send him the same way that he before had sent so many unfortunate people. Thus they would bring this affair to an end, in order to pursue in all seriousness the occupation of the entire right bank of the Jordan and of the country located on that side." Accordingly, Goethe sees the motive for the murder not in the new religion proclaimed by Moses but in his hapless, indecisive, and autocratic leadership. This murder forms the climax in a series of mutinies that had accompanied and dogged the exodus from the outset; indeed, Goethe goes so far as to identify this resistance to his leadership as the general theme of the last four books of Moses (although, strictly speaking, the relevant scenes are only found in books 2 and 4). Goethe's decision to foreground this motivic thread stems from the extraordinary opening claim to his investigation of the Exodus story:

> The authentic, only and deepest theme in the history of the world and humanity, to which all others are subordinated, remains the conflict between faith and unbelief. […] While the first book of Moses records the triumph of faith, the last four take as their theme the triumph of unbelief, which, in the pettiest manner, […] does not openly confront and attack faith, but instead obstructs its progress with each step, […] such that it threatens to wreck at the beginning a great and noble purpose undertaken upon the most glorious promises of a trustworthy national god, and prevents its ever being fully consummated.[11]

When he refers to "faith," Goethe has in mind monotheism, the religious conviction common to East and West, Islam and Christianity. That is why the essay appears in the *Notes and Essays for a Better Understanding of the West-Eastern Divan*. Conflict is an essential part of monotheism and forms the secret engine of history, at least in those parts of the Western and Eastern world that have been shaped by it. The idea that monotheism brought intolerance, conflict, resistance, and its violent suppression into the world had already been defended by David Hume;[12] Goethe draws on it here. In the Abrahamic covenant of Genesis, he discerns the "triumph of faith." In his view, the history of unbelief already begins with the departure from Egypt. We would see things differently today. It is precisely the exodus that performs the decisive step into belief, celebrating its supreme triumph in the miracle at the Sea of Reeds. Only then, immediately after the passage through the sea, does conflict break out.

A very different interpretation of the same motif was offered when Sigmund Freud read it in the light of psychohistory and the psychology of religion. Freud showed as little interest as Goethe in analyzing the ten or twelve scenes of "murmuring," instead condensing and sharpening them into the claim that Moses was murdered by his disgruntled followers. In his book *Moses and Monotheism,* completed in 1938, shortly before he went into exile in London, he argued that Moses was killed by the Hebrews he had led out of Egypt because they could no longer endure the heightened moral demands and imageless, disembodied abstraction of his God. Freud identifies Moses as an Egyptian devotee of the monotheistic solar religion introduced by Akhenaten. Following the death of the heretic king and restoration of the traditional religion, Moses joined up with the Jewish community settled in the Delta to emigrate to Canaan, where they hoped to escape persecution and salvage monotheism. On the way there, he tightened the strictures of the new religion by rejecting the image of the solar deity; from now on, only the purely intellectual idea of a transcendent god would be permitted. By murdering him, the "Jews" repeated the killing of the "primal father" by the "primal horde." According to Freud, the unconscious memory of this great prehistoric crime is indelibly inscribed into the human psyche as an "archaic legacy." The Hebrews thereby renewed the trauma of that primordial crime to instigate a process diagnosed by Freud as a collective neurosis:

Early trauma—defense—latency—outbreak of the neurosis—partial return of the repressed: such is the formula which we have laid down for the development of a neurosis. The reader is now invited to take the step of supposing that something occurred in the life of the human species similar to what occurs in the life of individuals: of supposing, that is, that here too events occurred of a sexually aggressive nature, which left behind them permanent consequences but were for the most part fended off and forgotten, and which after a long latency came into effect and created phenomena similar to symptoms in their structure and purpose.[13]

The murder of Moses was repressed, leading the Mosaic message to enter a centuries-long latency phase. That is how Freud accounts for the time lag between his Moses, who lived in the fourteenth century BCE as a contemporary of Akhenaten, and the appearance of the prophets in the historical record from the late eighth century on. The memory of the monotheism proclaimed by Moses gradually returned and reasserted itself among the people with irresistible momentum, as typically occurs whenever the repressed returns: "each portion which returns from oblivion reasserts itself with peculiar force, exercises an incomparably powerful influence on people in the mass, and raises an irresistible claim to truth, against which logical objections remain powerless: a kind of *credo quia absurdum*."[14]

Freud had delivered his myth of the primal father's murder in his book *Totem and Taboo* (1913), the anthropological foundation of the Oedipus complex (the "archaic legacy") and a general model for the genesis of religion. This was a heuristic myth that Freud synthesized from ideas he found in Charles Darwin, James George Frazer, and William Robertson Smith. In the primal horde, humans lived in extended families or clans; the strongest man, the "primal father," claimed all women for himself and threatened any son who challenged his sexual monopoly with castration or expulsion. Eventually, the primal father was beaten to death by the strongest of his sons, who then claimed the same position for himself—and the process began again. The cycle lasted thousands of years, leaving behind indelible traces in the human psyche, until at last the patricidal system was put to an end and the murdered primal father was made the object of religious worship as the totemic animal of his clan. A screen memory intervened and the gruesome memory of what happened was pushed down into the unconscious. Totemism evolved into polytheism, further concealing the true core of religion, until it resurfaced more strongly in monotheism—with pathogenic results.

Heuristic myths are constructions that are among the legitimate tools of psychoanalysis.[15] Their truth lies not in their paleoanthropological verifiability but in their power to explain the present, that is, the illness with its treatable and potentially curable symptoms. Freud draws on the patricidal origin of religion to explain the central position taken in all religions by the motifs of guilt and atonement. Every religion is dominated by a diffuse sense of guilt, and they all set out to appease the divine world through sacrifices and rituals that involve some measure of cruelty and pain.

In *Moses and Monotheism*, Freud applied the same model to the genesis of biblical monotheism, which did indeed represent something entirely unprecedented and revolutionary in the history of religion.[16] This time, though, he did not have the option of grounding his speculations in a mythical, scientifically unverifiable prehistory. Instead, he had to erect his construction in the glaring light of a history amply attested in the archaeological, epigraphic, and philological record. With that in mind, Freud chose the era of the Egyptian heretic king, Akhenaten.

According to Freud, the murder of the primal father repeats itself in the killing of Moses. Now it is no longer the human psyche in general but the specifically Jewish soul that receives the imprint it has retained to this day. That was the starting point for Freud's investigation: "We wanted to explain the origin of the special character of the Jewish people, a character which is probably what has made their survival to the present day possible."[17] With the murder of Moses, the Hebrews unwittingly reenacted the patricide in the primal horde and underwent a process of retraumatization. Freud's theory entails a dual form of resistance: one conscious, leading to the death of Moses; another unconscious, causing both the crime and the Mosaic (monotheistic) message to be repressed. The postulate that this resistance had an unconscious dimension, one that defined both the early history of Jewish monotheism and the "special character" of this nation, sheds light on the psychohistorical implications of monotheism. These are of great interest even if we disregard the contentious allegation of murder.

Freud borrowed the thesis that Moses was killed before entering the Promised Land from the unjustly neglected Old Testament scholar Ernst Sellin. The scene at Shittim serves as the point of departure for Sellin's reconstruction of an alternative line of biblical tradition, one centered on the violent fate of the prophets.[18] Behind Phinehas's slaughter of Zimri and the Midianite woman Cozbi, whose princely origin is stressed in Numbers 25:14–15, stands the suppressed murder of Moses and his Midianite wife. In Sellin's view, the murder occurred when Moses sought to implement God's cruel command to hang or

impale the leaders of the people in broad daylight. In his interpretation, the scene at Shittim, which comes at the end of the scenes depicting the rebellious and recalcitrant "murmuring" of the "stiff-necked"
people on their forty-year trudge through the wilderness, in fact marks
the beginning of a different tradition extending from Moses to Jesus of
Nazareth.

Sellin posits an original version of Numbers 25 that was still known
to Hosea:

> Hosea is still familiar with what came after Num 25:3–5 in its original form.
> He knows that in Shittim, in the holy place of his God, Moses fell victim to
> a trick played on him by his own people after they turned to Baʻal-Peor and
> Moses had called on them to repent or in any event had called down pun-
> ishment upon them. Perhaps his sons had to be killed alongside him. It all
> amounts to an incomparably tragic and harrowing tale.[19]

Like Freud, whom he would influence in this regard, Sellin is driven
by archaeological pathos to search for a concealed historical truth lying
beneath the sugar-coated surface of a falsified textual tradition. He has
in mind the tragic fate of the *historical* Moses. Yet his observations are
no less applicable to the *literary* Moses, considered as a tragic variant
or even earliest version of the Exodus myth that later redactors of the
material found intolerable and which they therefore felt duty-bound to
censor.[20]

The Violent Fate of the Prophets

> But he was wounded for our transgressions, he was bruised
> for our iniquities: the chastisement of our peace was upon
> him; and with his stripes we are healed.
> —*Isaiah 53:5*

> O Jerusalem, Jerusalem, which killest the prophets, and
> stoneth them that are sent unto thee!
> —*Luke 13:34*

In contrast to how he was understood or at least quoted by Freud, Sellin's chief concern was not to return to the scene of the crime but to

reconstruct a tradition that runs through the entire Bible, both Old Testament and New. Sellin places Moses's tragic fate in the broader context of servants who suffered and died for the sins of their people, as attested in the prophets and especially in the Servant Songs of Deutero-Isaiah. In doing so, he draws a line from Moses to Jesus, whose Passion was understood by the apostles in the light of the Servant Songs. Even if the murder of Moses is nowhere explicitly mentioned in Hosea, and even if his name does not appear in the Servant Songs of Deutero-Isaiah, there are nonetheless passages that refer to the violent, deadly fate of the prophets. In Nehemiah's great historical summation, we read:

> But they were disobedient, and rebelled against thee, and cast thy law behind their backs, and slew thy prophets which testified against them to turn them to thee, and they wrought great provocations. (9:26)

And in Luke, Jesus cries out: "O Jerusalem, Jerusalem, which killest the prophets, and stoneth them that are sent unto thee!" (Luke 13:34 = Matt 23:37). In Luke and Matthew, Jesus lingers particularly on the killing of Zechariah:

> Therefore also said the wisdom of God, I will send them prophets and apostles and some of them they shall slay and persecute, that the blood of all the prophets, which was shed from the foundation of the world, may be required of this generation: from the blood of Abel unto the blood of Zacharias, which perished between the altar and the temple; verily I say unto you, it shall be required of this generation. (Luke 11:49–51, cf. Matt 23:34–36)

Luke returns to this topic in the Acts of the Apostles, reporting the question posed by Stephen in his sweeping overview of Jewish history:

> Which of the prophets have not your fathers persecuted? And they have slain them which predicted the coming of the Just One; of whom ye have been now the betrayers and murderers; who have received the law by the disposition of angels, and have not kept it. (7:52–53)[21]

Here, then, the violent deaths of the prophets are openly proclaimed. On this basis, Sellin sees in Moses the first victim of this murderously antiprophetic and antimonotheistic tradition. Unlike for Freud, who adopted from him the murder theory, for Sellin the hypothetical murder of Moses does not create a spiritual trauma—that is Freud's own, psychoanalytical contribution to the debate set off by his predecessor—but rather establishes a cultural and biographical template. As we will see, however, Sellin also operates with notions of collective pathology that Freud would subsequently distill in his diagnosis of a neurotic illness.

Sellin by no means confines himself to an isolated passage in the prophet Hosea that in his view alludes to the murder of Moses, as Freud would have us believe. Instead, he follows a motivic strand that runs all the way through the Bible from the Book of Exodus (which mentions Moses's near stoning in chapter 17) to the gospels: the motif of the prophets' martyrdom. Sellin speculates that knowledge of Moses's teaching as well as of his death was restricted to "a small circle":

> We cannot expect to find it [Moses's monotheistic message, J. A.] from the start in the official cult, in the popular religion. All we can expect is that here and there a spark flew up from the spiritual fire he had kindled, that his ideas were not entirely extinguished but here and there quietly influenced beliefs and customs, until sooner or later, conveyed by special experiences or by persons singularly moved by his spirit, they broke out with renewed vigor and gained influence on broad swaths of the population.[22]

Sellin has in mind a small oppositional group that had to contend with fierce and occasionally deadly resistance from the court and the general populace. Those who belonged to this group not only kept alive the Mosaic message, they also remained keenly aware of the obstacles that had been put in its way.[23] In Sellin's account, they even pinned on the murdered Moses the same messianic hopes of return that Judaism later placed on Elijah. This is hinted at in the scene of Christ's transfiguration on Mount Tabor, where Moses and Elijah appear to the disciples alongside the transfigured Christ. Sellin even goes a step further: not only did the people tend the memory of Moses, they also remembered the terrible sin of his murder, along with all the other crimes committed against his followers. As a result, they eventually succumbed to a kind of collective psychic malaise. For Sellin, it is an indisputable fact that in the third century BC [Sellin is referring to Deutero-Zechariah], despite all the priestly cover-ups, the tradition of Moses' martyrdom had still been kept alive; that this murder, together with their own apostasy, was perceived by the people to be the great sin that was making them deathly ill; and that they would need to atone for that sin before the day of salvation could break. Their rejection of the man who had founded their own religion, the prophet who had brought them the plain belief in the one holy God and his clear and simple moral will, had been the people's downfall, and only by returning to him could they recover their health.[24]

Today Sellin's book has all but fallen into oblivion.[25] Like a mosquito trapped in amber, it lives on only in the footnotes to Freud's book on Moses, even though that book was far more strongly influenced by Sellin than has previously been appreciated. Freud appropriated not only Sellin's hypothesis of murder but also his idea of a tradition that had been marginalized before later—following the return from exile, with Ezra and Nehemiah—finding widespread acceptance. Finally, he was able to find in Sellin the theory of a psychohistorical pathology, although the diagnosis he offered differed considerably from that of his predecessor. What he missed, however, is the line drawn by Sellin from numerous other biblical passages to the Servant Songs in Deutero-Isaiah and from there to the New Testament.[26]

The point is not whether Moses was actually murdered, as Freud assumed, and whether Hosea alludes to this crime, as Sellin claimed, two theses that nobody would seriously defend today. The point is rather that there is a rich tradition in the Old and New Testaments concerning both the persecution inflicted on the prophets by their contemporaries for the monotheistic message they preached and the feelings of guilt that arose as a result. In the circles of the prophetic and Deuteronomistic opposition there was an acute awareness, not just that serious offenses had been committed in breach of the covenant, but also that the messengers sent by God to judge the people and warn them of their inevitable punishment had been persecuted and, on occasions, killed. It is the merit of Sellin's forgotten book to have brought this tradition to light and drawn attention to its psychohistorical dimension. His audacious attempt to link the theme of the recalcitrant people and the violent fate of the prophets with Moses and the Exodus story warrants serious consideration.[27]

Two motifs connect Moses with the tradition of God's suffering servant. One is the motif of vicarious suffering. When God resolves to destroy the people following the sacrilege of the Golden Calf and to recommence salvation history on a new footing with Moses, Moses volunteers to take God's punishment in their stead.[28] Moses's role as intercessor for Israel, to which Erik Aurelius has drawn attention, also belongs in this context, particularly in his aspects of accused and accusing intercessor.[29] The other motif is the murderous hatred that repeatedly confronts Moses and twice almost leads to his stoning. With that, the people have already sinned more than enough against their prophet, even if they did not go so far as to kill him.

Sellin and Freud concur in arguing that the Jewish people have a heightened awareness of their own sinfulness, although they part company in tracing its etiology. Sellin traces it back to their resistance against the prophets, who never tired of reproaching them with their sinful ways. Freud saw in this guilty conscience the psychohistorical sign of monotheism as a "father-religion," interpreting it as a reactive formation to the "murderous hatred" toward the father:

> An essential ingredient of the father-relationship is ambivalence; it was inevitable that, as time went by, another feeling should seek to find expression, namely the hostility that had once driven the sons to kill the father they so admired and feared. In the context of the Moses religion there was no room for direct expression of murderous father-hatred; only a powerful reaction to that hatred was able to come out, the feeling of being at fault because of that hostility, the guilty conscience at having sinned against God and doing so still, unceasingly.[30]

> The reinstatement of the primal father in his historic rights was a great step forward, but it could not be the end. The other pieces of the prehistoric tragedy also pressed for recognition. What this process set in motion is not easy to guess. Apparently, a growing sense of guilt seized the Jewish people, and possibly the entire civilized world of the time, as a precursor of the return of the repressed content [. . .]. Paul, a Roman Jew from Tarsus, seized on that sense of guilt and correctly traced it back to its prehistoric source. He called it "original sin," a crime against God that could be atoned

for only by death. It was through this original sin that death had entered the world. In reality, the crime worthy of death had been the murder of the subsequently deified primal father. However, the murder was not remembered; instead, its atonement was fantasized.[31]

The concept of ambivalence that Freud introduces here is not just essential to the father-relationship, but also to the covenant-relationship founded on Sinai and put to the test during the trek through the wilderness. The covenant promises the chosen people the unimaginable happiness of partnership with God while at the same time threatening them with the most terrible punishments should they break their word, such as those painted in Deuteronomy 28 and Leviticus 26:14–39. The covenant is ambivalent in that it can be both a blessing and a curse. This ambivalence brings with it the problem of violence, which we have already identified in the idea of loyalty and its distinction between friend and enemy. The problem of violence comes to the fore in the scenes of murmuring and also, with particular virulence, in the story of the Golden Calf, to be discussed in more detail in chapter 10.

The motif of violent resistance pervades the story of the divine covenant from its beginnings to the catastrophe of exile. Freud condensed that long story into a single dramatic event, the hypothetical murder of Moses. For Freud, the great puzzle was not so much the resistance encountered by the prophets but rather, on the contrary, what he believed to be the irresistible force with which their monotheistic message gripped the popular imagination after centuries of "latency." He saw a solution to this puzzle in the "return of the repressed." That interpretation clashes with the Deuteronomistic account of the preexilic period, and we have no reason to take Freud's side in this matter.

Sellin, by contrast, placed the hypothetical murder of Moses at the beginning of a chain of attacks on the prophets, extending all the way to the confession of sins in Nehemiah and Christ's admonition of Jerusalem in Luke 13. Above all, he located the Deutero-Isaian Servant Songs (Isa 52–53) in this context, reading them as the high point of liturgical confessions of guilt. In Moses, he claimed to see the representative of all persecuted prophets, the archetype of the servant of God who must take on ridicule, violence, and ultimately death for the sins of his people. To my knowledge, only Klaus Baltzer has followed him down this path. In his book *Das Bundesformular*, first published in 1960 and translated into English eleven years later as *The Covenant Formulary*, Baltzer had already worked through the tradition of admissions of guilt in ancient Near Eastern, biblical, and postbiblical sources. Thirty-five years later, in his monumental commentary to Deutero-Isaiah,[32] he found in Sellin's favor, offering a range of fresh arguments to link the four Servant Songs to Moses.[33]

The resistance that Moses's leadership and message encountered among the Israelites was, if anything, only intensified once they entered the Promised Land and found themselves castigated by the prophets. The Israelites at least lacked the opportunity to abandon YHWH for other gods while they were still wandering in the wilderness, before arriving in Moab. Besides, they had God's promise and goal before their eyes to remind them, through all their tribulations, of their journey's higher end. Yet instead of remembering God's saving deeds, they opted to serve the gods of their new country and pile one sin on top of the other. It is important to make clear that resistance to the new, exclusive form of the YHWH religion heralded by the prophets did not come from the side of a secular, profane orientation, from the fools who say "there is no god" (*'ên 'ĕlōhîm*, Ps 14:1; 53:1), but from the traditional, popular, state-sanctioned version of inclusive or "syncretistic Yahwism."[34]

The people themselves could not have been more adamantly or comprehensively opposed to the religious revolution recounted in the Exodus story, and the excessive demands imposed by their reluctant conversion to this new form of religion are shown with the utmost clarity. Serving YHWH emancipates from service to Pharaoh, the Egyptian house of bondage (*bêt 'ăbodîm*), but it does not entail freedom as such. Instead, it merely substitutes one form of service for another, albeit the true divine service that brings freedom from human oppression. In the scenes of murmuring, the monotheism of loyalty and the covenant proclaimed by Moses is presented as unappealing, inconvenient, and unpopular. This new religion can only win through against stubborn resistance and with occasional recourse to violence. That is "the eternal conflict between faith and unbelief" (although it actually only gets underway with the covenant at Sinai), in which Goethe discerned "the authentic, only and deepest theme in the history of the world and humanity."

This aspect of the story undoubtedly has a historical background. It should not be imagined that the monotheism of the divine covenant— which, without denying the existence of other gods, demands exclusive loyalty to the One Savior and his laws—was the dominant religion in Israel in the time of the First Temple. Far from it: we are dealing here with an oppositional movement made up of a few trouble-making prophets and their supporters, a small minority that was continually and sometimes violently opposed by both the courtly elite and the general populace. In Amos, God scolds the Israelites for "command[ing] the prophets, saying, Prophesy not" (2:12). Jeremiah is told to "prophesy not in the name of the Lord, that thou die not by our hand" (Jer 11:21), and he reports the execution of the prophet Urijah (26:20–24). We should also not assume that the exiles who ended up in Babylon were unanimously enthused by the prospect of abandoning their new homes and undertaking the arduous journey back to Jerusalem, now a city in rubble where their houses, even if they were still standing, had long since been occupied by others. Many would have stiffly resisted the call to return, and this resistance would also have found an echo in the scenes of murmuring.[35]

The line from Nehemiah to Luke suggested by Sellin was drawn out more fully by Odil Hannes Steck in his dissertation on Israel and the violent fate of the prophets. Drawing on a trove of biblical (Old and New Testament) and extrabiblical (Qumran, Midrash, Talmud) sources, Steck argues that, according to a widely attested tradition, Israel not only turned a deaf ear to the prophets sent it by God but did all it could to kill them. He sees the ideological context of this idea in the Deuteronomistic history, which tends to interpret the disasters that befell Israel (first in 722 BCE, with the fall of the Northern Kingdom, then in 586, with that of the Southern Kingdom) as God's punishment for Israel's permanent disobedience. The authors of the history preferred to accept blame for every imaginable transgression rather than having to assume that God had turned away from Israel, repealed its election, and broken off the project of a joint history. That resulted in the formation of a recurring narrative schema, what Steck calls the "Deuteronomistic prophetic message":

A The stubborn, disobedient people,
B warned by the prophets to change their ways,
C remain unrepentant / C[1] kill the prophets,
D so incurring God's punishment.

In the form ABCD, this pattern pervades the entire Deuteronomistic history and the books of the prophets of judgment, especially Jeremiah. In its intensified form ABC[1]D, we first encounter it in Nehemiah
and then, in a remarkable efflorescence, in a host of intertestamental,
New Testament, and rabbinic sources, as well as in Flavius Josephus.
By this stage, all hope for a renewal of the covenant in the sign of salvation history seemed lost. As a province of the Persian, Seleucid, and
finally Roman empires, Israel continued to stand under God's judgment, "weighed down by all the guilt the people had accrued over the
course of their history."[36] Steck is right to deny that the schema's continuing presence attests to the literary dependence of these late works
on the Deuteronomistic history. The schema persisted instead as the
expression of a "living idea" or mentality: a pervasive sense of guilt akin
to that which Sellin and Freud once attributed to the murder of Moses.
This sense of guilt was indebted to the Deuteronomistic view of history, which "has been kept alive in confessions of sin and penitential
prayers"[37] and thus remains embedded in an everyday liturgical
context.

The Deuteronomistic view of history may be termed a "posttraumatic" one. The trauma in question is the catastrophe of 587 BCE, understood as the realization of the curses for breaking the covenant
threatened in the covenant terms cited in Deuteronomy. What lay behind the catastrophe, on this account, was YHWH's fury at the Israelites' constant violation of his commandments and their violent intran-
sigence toward the prophets he had sent to chastise and warn them. In
this situation, Israel saw itself as cursed. Only by radically changing its
ways could it hope to regain God's blessing. In liturgical confessions of
sin and penitential prayers, the Deuteronomistic view of history has
continued to make its guilt-inducing presence felt in the postexilic centuries and into the post-Christian era.[38]

Steck, who appears not to be familiar with Sellin's book on Moses,
never entertains the possibility that the sometimes violent resistance

faced by Moses might be linked with the "violent fate of the prophets."[39] Nothing lies further from his purposes than to connect the figure
of the "suffering Moses"[40] with the suffering servant of God in Deutero-
Isaiah.[41] It is unclear, however, why this connection could not have
been made in the associational space of collective memory, particularly if we follow Steck in starting out from the "history of mentalities"
rather than from any literary affiliation. Jesus, who was seen by his disciples as the successor to Moses, Elijah, and the prophets and identified with the figure of the suffering servant of God, attests to this connection. His death was meant to lift the curse under which the people
believed they still stood in a situation of ongoing foreign rule and
oppression.

The extraordinary prominence accorded the theme of resistance in
the biblical texts—not just in the Deuteronomistic history, but already
in the Exodus narrative itself—is explicable only from the posttraumatic situation in which those texts came to be written. If the narrative
was intended simply as a founding myth for Israel, it would be hard to
say why the people whose genesis it relates are made to appear in such
a poor light. Why must the Israelites be forced to accept the happy
outcome of freedom from Egyptian oppression and partnership with a
God who will settle down with them in a fertile land? Why do they not
gratefully accept the monotheistic package offered them by their
leader? The narrative owes its gloomy tone solely to the fact that it has
to cover the downfall of Israel along with its rise. If it wants to salvage
the idea of God's covenant with Israel as his chosen people, the only
idea that can alleviate the ongoing ordeal of the present, then it must
interpret that ordeal as God's ongoing judgment for their sins. At least
God can then remain in the covenant to castigate and punish—but also
stay true to—his wayward people. The idea of God's righteous anger
and judgment is a figure of theodicy. We see now that the distinction
between blessing and curse is just as much a part of the covenant as
that between friend and enemy.

When the exiled elite returned from Babylon around 520 BCE,
bringing with them the original texts of what would later become the
Torah, they set out to win over to the new religion all those who had
stayed behind in the land. Whereas the old religion had largely been a
matter of ritual observance, this new religion, based on the ideas of

covenant, law, and loyalty, demanded total commitment extending across all areas of life. There can be no doubt that it would have met with considerable resistance. These experiences are reflected in the scenes of "murmuring." Above all, they influenced how one particular motif came to be developed in the narrative: that of the "sins of the fathers," which God takes out on their children and their children's children. It was indeed the second and third generation of those deported in 587 who could gradually come back after the conquest of Babylon in 539, resolving to turn away from the guilt-laden past to realize a completely new vision of God's people and his religion. Much as in Germany after 1945, it seemed that this fresh start could only succeed through an elaborate memory culture that held fast to an awareness of past transgressions in order to break their grip on the present.

CHAPTER TEN

THE
INSTITUTIONALIZATION
OF DIVINE PRESENCE

> If thou wilt walk in my statutes, and execute my judgments,
> and keep all my commandments to walk in them; then will I
> [. . .] dwell among the children of Israel, and will not forsake
> my people Israel.
>
> *—1 Kings 6:12–13*

> For where two or three are gathered together in my name,
> there am I in the midst of them.
>
> *—Matthew 18:20*

> For ye are the temple of the living God; as God hath said, I
> will dwell in them, and walk in them; and I will be their God,
> and they shall be my people.
>
> *—2 Corinthians 6:16*

YHWH Comes to Dwell among His People

The powerful scene of theophany and feasting ends when Moses is
called up to the mountain and into the fiery cloud to be given the tables
of the law. At this point, both the waiting Israelites and the reader expect him to return soon after with the stone tablets. Instead he remains
in the cloud for forty days and nights, where he receives detailed instructions on how to build the desert tabernacle. Only then does
YHWH hand down the long-awaited tables of the law (31:18). These
seven seemingly never-ending chapters, covering every conceivable
aspect of tabernacle construction and design, represent one of the longest catalogs in any literary tradition, ancient or modern.[1] By comparison, the otherwise similar description of the building of the Temple
under Solomon takes up only two chapters (1 Kings 6–7). Even more

FIGURE 28. In the cloud on Sinai, Moses is given instructions for building the Tabernacle. Copperplate engraving of Exodus 25–31 by Matthäus Merian, 1630.

remarkably, practically the same catalog is repeated—albeit in a somewhat different order —in the last six chapters of the third part of Exodus, where surely a single sentence would have sufficed: "And the Israelites did everything YHWH had told Moses that they should do."[2] The fact that the whole list is rolled out on two occasions, first in the form of instructions to Moses and then as actions carried out at his behest, underscores the enormous importance given this section in the Priestly Source. For there is scholarly consensus that the section comes from "P," the source that for the first time combined primordial history, patriarchal history, and the Exodus-Sinai tradition into a comprehensive historical work.

Although the duplicated catalog refers to the component parts of the portable tent shrine, not its external appearance, this can be inferred with some certainty from the inventory. The courtyard enclosure, made up of wooden panels and curtains, was 100 cubits long, 50 cubits wide, and 5 cubits high. The Tabernacle itself was 12 cubits wide, 30 cubits long, and 10 cubits high, one cubit equaling around one and

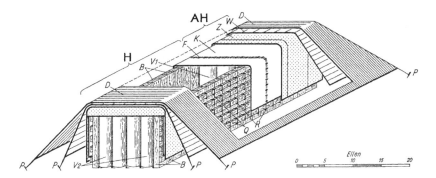

FIGURE 29. The Tabernacle according to Exodus 26, modern reconstruction. A temple-like space for worship framed by gold-covered acacia wood boards was contained in the original tent. It was initially covered with valuable carpets then roofed with three waterproof layers. The interior was divided by curtains into the Holy Place and the Holy of Holies; its layout recalls the Jerusalem temple in other ways as well.
   K A magnificent ceiling embroidered with cherubim. The ceiling is divided into two sections (each consisting of five curtains), connected by golden clasps (**F**). **Z** Goat-hair tent covers consisting of two parts (with six and five panels, respectively), connected with bronze clasps above the curtain to the Holy of Holies. **W** Ram-skin and **D** dolphin-skin protective covers, held in place by tent pegs (**P**). **B** Wooden walls with five crossbars (**Q**), attached by golden "rings" (**R**) to the beams. **V1** Cherubim-embroidered curtain in front of the Holy of Holies (supported by four columns). **V2** Curtain in front of the Holy Place (supported by five columns). **H** Holy Place (20 × 10 × 10 cubits). **AH** Holy of Holies (10 × 10 × 10 cubits).]

a half feet. Those are unexceptional, realistic, and workable dimensions. They match the measurements of the First Temple at a ratio of 1:2 (60 x 20 cubits, according to 1 Kings 6:2–3, cf. Ez 41:1–14), while the tent was one-tenth as long as Noah's mythical ark (300 cubits, according to Gen 6:15–16).

The tent is divided front and rear by a curtain. The whole area is termed a "sanctuary" (*miqdāš*); the Tabernacle is called the "tent of encounter" (*'ōhel mô'ēd*), while the back part of the tent is referred to as the "dwelling place" (*miškān*). There are thus three zones of graduated holiness: the enclosed courtyard (*ḥāṣēr*), the space in front of the curtain, and the area behind it. Such a layout is familiar from Egyptian or Near Eastern temple design. Even though the tent sanctuary may never have existed in historical reality, it is still described as a real, tangible object, not as an imaginary, utopian one like the New Jerusalem (Rev 21:10–27). A monumental building in stone would hardly be described in terms of its materials and fittings; instead, emphasis would

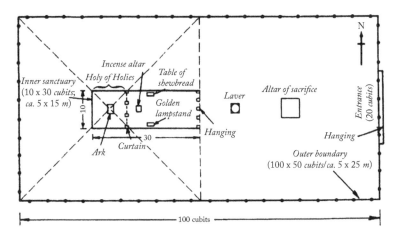

FIGURE 30. Floor plan of the desert sanctuary, modern reconstruction.

fall on its external appearance and architectonic structure. The point is that we are dealing here with a portable, demountable building. The impressive monumentality associated with a temple makes way for the abundance and costliness of the individual parts, which are described here so precisely that a vivid image arises in the mind's eye.

The catalog of instructions begins with the sacred objects:[3] the ark of the covenant (*'ārôn*) with the tables of the law (*'ēdût*) and the *kappōret* with the two winged cherubim (*kĕrūbîm*), which are to be displayed in the "dwelling place" (*miškān*) behind the curtain, the seven-branched lampstand (*mĕnōrâ*), the offering table with the "shewbread" and an incense altar placed in front of the curtain. The *kappōret* is not the lid of the ark but a golden object resting upon it. The Septuagint renders the word with *hilasterion*, the Vulgate with *propiti-atorium*, and William Tyndale, following Luther, offers "mercy seat" (Luther: *Gnadenstuhl*). The Hebrew word *kāpar*, "to cover," also has the sense of "to purify, atone, reconcile," whence the "day of atone-ment," *yôm kippûr*.[4] The *kappōret* is a means of atonement, an instru-ment for restoring the divine presence in the face of the people's inevi-table sinfulness and alienation from God. At any rate, this is how St. Paul understood this ritual item when he called the crucified Christ the *hilasterion* sent forth by God (Rom 3:25).[5]

The *kappōret* makes it possible to draw close to God under condi-tions of human imperfection; as such, it is a gift of divine grace. The

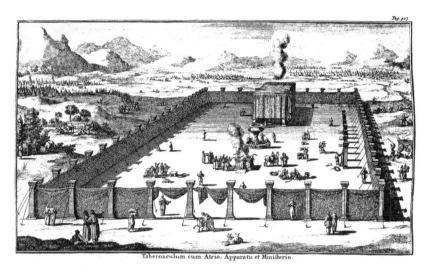

Tabernaculum cum Atrio, Apparatu et Ministerio.

FIGURE 31. The desert sanctuary, reconstruction. Copperplate print, 1695.

two cherubim are to be imagined as winged hybrids similar to griffins or sphinxes.[6] If placed facing each other at opposite ends of the *kappōret* with wings outstretched, as stipulated, then they mark the borders of an unoccupied space directly above the *kappōret*. YHWH wishes to address Moses from out of this vacant, cherubim-fringed space. Several texts such as 1 Samuel 4:4 or Psalm 18:10 (cf. 2 Sam 22:11; Isa 37:16) praise God as the one "who dwelleth between the cherubim" (*yōšēb hakkĕrūbîm*).[7]

The ark thus has two functions: it serves as both a receptacle for the tables of the law and a throne. Its rings and supporting poles allow it to be easily transported when the tent sanctuary is dismantled and the Israelites move on or when they take it out on a procession, much as the Assyrians and Babylonians paraded their processional images or the Egyptians their divine barks. During the war against the Philistines, for example, the ark was taken from Shiloh, where it was kept in the period of the Judges, to the battlefield at Eben-Ezer, where it was captured by the Philistines and removed to the temple of Dagon at Ashdod (1 Sam 4–5). The ark brought the Philistines no luck, however; they gave it back and it was taken to Kiriath-Jearim, where it remained for the next twenty years.

King David eventually has the ark moved to Jerusalem following his conquest of the city. Along the way, a man is struck dead when he puts

Pag: 425.

Arca cum Cherubinis,Urna Mannæ Lege et Virga Aaronis.

J.v.d.Arda f.

FIGURE 32. The ark of the covenant with the cherubim. Copperplate engraving, 1695.

his hand out to stop it from falling off the cart. David is so spooked that
he initially stores the ark with a private citizen, taking possession of it
only when he sees the blessings it brings the man and his household.
The entire transport takes the form of a festive procession with music
and dancing, offerings of thanksgiving and feasting (2 Sam 6). David

reassembles the tent and places the ark back inside, but he would much rather build YHWH a temple. Then one night YHWH appears to the prophet Nathan with a message for David: although he will provisionally stay in the Tabernacle, he will establish David's throne forever and anoint a successor who will build the temple in his stead (2 Sam 7). All the motifs associated with God's dwelling are reprised in this story: pledge, election, covenant, but also taboo and a magically charged holiness requiring the utmost caution.

The description of the tent sanctuary dates from the period of the reconstruction of the Temple in Jerusalem (520–515). The ark of the covenant and the golden lampstand formed the central symbols in the imageless cult of the Second Temple. They survived even the plundering and desecration of the Temple under Antiochus IV Epiphanes in 167 BCE and, through a miracle that the Jews still celebrate at Hanukkah, the eternal light burned on in the lampstand without having to be refueled. The menorah was finally brought to Rome with the destruction of the Temple under Titus and Vespasian in 70 CE, as depicted on the Arch of Titus.

Empty throne, cherubim, lampstand: these are images of inextinguishable splendor that went on to inspire Christian art, particularly in the form in which they figure in prophetic visions and psalms.

The list of holy objects and their precious materials is followed by a description of tent fittings such as carpets, ceilings, hangings, supports, rings, sockets, hooks, pins, and so on, as well as equipment like basins, bowls, and a bronze washbasin with washstand. The whole ensemble is at once extraordinarily opulent and readily transportable; it is thus purpose-built for accompanying the people on their long trek. The following chapters concern sacerdotal garments,[8] rites having to do with priests and the consecration of the altar, regular morning and evening sacrifice and burnt offerings, levies for the upkeep of the sanctuary, ingredients for anointing oil and incense, as well as the appointment of workmen. The highest standards of craftsmanship and unrelenting labor are enjoined, but then YHWH adds an emphatic reminder to keep the sabbath rest:

Verily my sabbaths ye shall keep:
for it is a sign between me and you throughout your generations;

FIGURE 33. Relief from the Arch of Titus depicting the plundered menorah. Forum Romanum, late first century CE.

that ye may know that I am YHWH that doth sanctify you.
Ye shall keep the sabbath therefore; for it is holy unto you.
Every one that defileth it shall surely be put to death:
for whosoever doeth any work therein,
that soul shall be cut off from among his people.

Six days may work be done;
but in the seventh is the sabbath of rest, holy to YHWH:
wherefore the children of Israel shall keep the sabbath,
to observe the sabbath throughout all generations, for a perpetual
covenant.
It is a sign between me and the children of Israel for ever:
for in six days YHWH made heaven and earth,
and on the seventh day he rested, and was refreshed. (Ex 31:13–17)

This again makes clear that the sacralization of time surpasses anything
that can be accomplished in space. Not even work on YHWH's sanctuary may be allowed to infringe on the sabbath rest. Sabbath and Temple are both grounded in the act of creation, but whereas experience has shown that the Temple can always be destroyed, the sabbath endures forever as a temple in time.[9]

Like the first revelation scene that precedes it (Ex 3:1–4:17), the story of the Golden Calf is of non-Priestly origin and goes back either to an interwoven source or to a later interpolation. It is followed in the concluding chapters (35–40) by a second run-through of the inventory of items contained in the tent sanctuary. This time, though, they are presented as a report of how Moses faithfully carried out God's commands. The report deviates from God's speech in its ordering of the individual building phases. God had started out by listing the sacred objects—the ark of the covenant, the table for the shewbread, and the seven-branched candelabrum—before turning to the "dwelling place" (*miškān*) where those objects were to be housed: the ark with the *kappōret* and the cherubim in the innermost area, separated by a curtain from the rest of the sanctuary, with the table and lampstand in front. Now, sensibly, the *miškān* is built first; then come the ark, *kappōret*, offering table, and lampstand, together with an incense altar that God had only mentioned afterward and that he had also instructed to be placed inside the *miškān*, just in front of the curtain. Finally, the altar of burnt offering is erected in the forecourt, along with the external tent wall separating the *miškān* and the forecourt from their profane surroundings. The staggering quantities of precious metals required for the Tabernacle are given at the end of chapter 38: 29 talents (*kikkār*) and 730 shekels of gold (around 970 kilograms), 100 talents and 1,775 shekels of silver, 70 talents and 2,400 shekels of bronze.

Chapter 39 is devoted to the production of priestly vestment and regalia and concludes with Moses giving his blessing to the work that has been carried out so far. In chapter 40, God sets a date for setting up and consecrating the Tabernacle. Clearly, at this stage in the construction process the Tabernacle has not yet been fully assembled; only the individual components have been manufactured. The assembly is scheduled for the first day of the first month, that is, the beginning of the second year after the exodus. God had earlier established the first month as the month of the departure from Egypt (Ex 12:1). The journey to Sinai had lasted two and a half months, the Israelites arriving there on the first day of the third month (Ex 19:1). Nine months thus remained for God to reveal the commandments, make the covenant,

FIGURE 34. Aaron in the Tabernacle. View from the rear wall of the Holy of Holies. Copperplate engraving by Matthäus Merian, 1630.

and give instructions for building the Tabernacle, as well as for Moses to put those instructions into effect. The erection of the tent sanctuary in time for the New Year was evidently the work of a single day.

God again briefly recapitulates the whole inventory, this time in the order of assembly rather than that of manufacture: first the *miškān* divided by a curtain—the ark with the *kappōret* behind the curtain, the table, lampstand, and incense altar in front—with a laver for washing the priests and finally the "holy garments" for Aaron and his sons. Moses does as told, then the sanctuary with all its components is run through, again in brief, for the fourth time.

The chapter—and with it the Book of Exodus—closes with God's entry into his dwelling place:

> Then a cloud covered the tent of the congregation, and the glory of YHWH filled the tabernacle.
> And Moses was not able to enter into the tent of the congregation, because the cloud abode thereon, and the glory of YHWH filled the tabernacle.
> (40:34–35)

This situation is taken up again in Numbers 9, shortly before the people set out on their forty years of wandering in the wilderness:

And on the day that the tabernacle was reared up the cloud covered the tabernacle, namely, the tent of the testimony: and at even there was upon the tabernacle as it were the appearance of fire, until the morning. So it was always: the cloud covered it by day, and the appearance of fire by night. And when the cloud was taken up from the tabernacle, then after that the children of Israel journeyed: and in the place where the cloud abode, there the children of Israel pitched their tents. At YHWH's commandment the children of Israel journeyed, and at YHWH's commandment they pitched: as long as the cloud abode upon the tabernacle they rested in their tents. And when the cloud tarried long upon the tabernacle many days, then the children of Israel kept the charge of YHWH, and journeyed not. And so it was, when the cloud was a few days upon the tabernacle; according to YHWH's commandment they abode in their tents, and according to YHWH's commandment they journeyed. (9:15–20)

The Tabernacle serves a dual purpose: it serves YHWH as a "dwelling place" and the Israelites as a place of worship and divine contact. God is now no longer encountered only in occasional dream visitations, sightings, and revelations; he has become a constant and reliable presence: an institution. This dual function is expressed in the terms *miškān*, "dwelling place," and *'ōhel mô'ēd*, "tent of meeting" (or "tent of testimony"). Each appears around twenty-seven times in these chapters. Phrases like "the dwelling place of the tent of meeting" make clear that *miškān* refers to the Holy of Holies behind the curtain and *'ōhel mô'ēd* to the tent as a whole, whereas the entire complex, including the enclosed courtyard, is termed *miqdāš*, sanctuary.

The verb *šākan*, the root of *miškān*, originally means "to tent," not "to dwell." From there it makes its way into Greek as the Semitic loanword *skēnē*, "tent," "hut," "stage," "scene." In Hebrew, "dwelling" in the sense of a permanent abode is called *môšāb*, from *yāšab*, to dwell or be enthroned,[10] as in Psalm 132:

For YHWH hath chosen Zion,
he hath desired it for his habitation:
this is my rest for ever,
here will I dwell [*yāšab*], for I have desired it. (132:13–14)[11]

The contrast between the civic deity enthroned on Zion and the god who freed his people from Egyptian bondage and journeys in their midst may reflect that between the Northern Kingdom, where the Exodus myth prevailed, and the Southern Kingdom, where Zion theology had its seat. More plausible than this geographical division, however, is a temporal one. Although the biblical narrative gives the impression that the portable tabernacle was older and more original than the immovable temple where YHWH dwells as a civic deity, the opposite appears in fact to be true, at least so far as the genesis of the relevant texts is concerned: whereas Zion theology dates back to the early monarchy, around the tenth or ninth century, the "Shekinah theology" of the God who dwells among his people as they wander from place to place works through the experience of the loss of state, city and Temple. It thus represents something entirely new.[12]

The world of the narrative introduces a further, quite different innovation: the replacement of sporadic, epiphanic contacts with God, such as had been the case from the tales of the patriarchs to the revelation on Sinai, with a permanent divine presence in the form of an institutionalized religion, complete with shrine, priesthood, and divine worship. This essentially brings Israel into line with how other nations dwell with their gods. These, too, build temples to accommodate their deities amid their cities, so providing a fixed framework and setting for human contact with the divine. The dwelling place of the gods—the sanctuary with the cultic shrine—is clearly demarcated from the sacrificial altar, albeit through shrine doors that normally conceal the cult image and are opened only during the ritual sacrifice and then closed again, not through a curtain. The establishment of a religion with shrine, priesthood, and divine worship is thus at once an innovation in Israel from the perspective of the Exodus story and a normalizing act with regard to other nations, just as, several hundred years later in the time of the narrative, the institution of royalty "such as all the other nations have" (1 Sam 8:5) is depicted as both an innovation and a return to normality.

With an institutionalized religion, Israel becomes more like other nations (*gôyīm* = heathen). This was unprecedented to this point in the narrative. The patriarchs occasionally build altars in Canaan. Abraham builds one at Sichem (Gen 12:7), between Bethel and Ai (13:4), after

YHWH appears to him there to promise land to his descendants. Isaac builds an altar at Beersheba when YHWH visits him in a dream, likewise promising land (26:25). And Jacob goes a step further upon waking from his awe-inspiring dream of the ladder: he erects a stone pillar, calls the place Bethel ("God's house"), and vows to make it a house of God if he receives divine protection (28:22). Upon his return from Mesopotamia, he too erects an altar at Sichem (33:20) but is commanded to continue to Bethel and build an altar there. God reappears to him there with pledges of land and prosperity, and he sets up another stone pillar (35:14–15, clearly a duplicate of 28:22). No evidence of a religion institutionalized in temples and rituals can be gleaned from these passages. Every move to establish contact had previously come from God, with the single exception of Jacob's prayer to God before his meeting with Esau (32:10–13). None of these altars is associated with any ritual activity that might have endured beyond the occasion of its establishment. The narrative discontinues this tradition (if such it may be called) in Egypt, and Moses has no dedicated place from which to make contact with God until the tent sanctuary is built.[13] Only once the law has been revealed and the covenant established has the time come to create such a place, establish a liturgy, and give the covenant the form of a religion.[14] From the perspective of the Priestly Source, God's creation is completed in this institutionalization of religion; the narrative arc that began with the opening words of Genesis here reaches its appointed end. With that, as Bernd Janowski writes, "a process gets underway that is aimed at transforming the world as a space of tangibly experienced divine presence. This creation-theological dimension of the Sinai story is the specific contribution of the Priestly history."[15]

There are striking parallels between creation and Tabernacle. Moses had to wait six days on the mountain before being called into God's presence. In these six days, medieval commentators concluded, God created a model of the tent sanctuary, just as he had created the world in six days. Attention is frequently drawn to the fact that Moses was shown a model on the mountain:

> According to all that I shew thee, after the pattern of the tabernacle, and the pattern of all the instruments thereof, even so shall ye make it. (25:9)

And look that thou make them after their pattern, which was shewn thee on the mount. (25:40)

And thou shalt rear up the tabernacle according to the fashion thereof which was shewed thee in the mount. (26:30)

As it was shewed thee in the mount, so shall they make it. (27:8)

On the seventh day Moses was called to inspect the work.[16] Creation story and building report are connected in seven parallel formulations:

God made . . .	Make me . . .
For in six days . . .	And the cloud covered it six days . . .
And he rested on the seventh day	The seventh day he called unto Moses out of the midst of the cloud
Thus the heavens and the earth were finished	Thus was all the work of the *miškān* complete
And God saw everything that he had made	And Moses saw the work
And, behold, it was very good	And saw they had made it just as YHWH had commanded
And God blessed the seventh day	And Moses blessed it

With the building of the Tabernacle—that is, with the institutionalization of divine presence in the form of an established religion—God's creation of the world is complete.

The nonritualized, or at any rate noninstitutionalized, relationship with God depicted in the Priestly Source, as well as in the other sources that went into it, was thus wholly atypical for the time. This was a deliberate innovation on the part of the Priestly Source. The Israelite religion is henceforth founded and grounded on Sinai. The religion practiced by other nations—or, put differently, religion in the previous sense of the term (including preexilic Israelite religion itself) —is heathenism. True religion is first created here.

How is it possible, though, that this "true" religion differs so little from the "heathen" religions of its environment and comes across as more than a touch heathen itself, at least in its Priestly version? What baffles us most is this so concretely imagined, physical, and yet somehow magical idea of God "dwelling" among his people. This direct contact between God and his people should not be depicted too idyllically. The more closely they dwell together, the more testily God reacts to every perceived transgression. These reactions have the character of an almost automatic, uncontrollable emotional discharge. The divine tent is stretched too tight, as it were, such that the perennially sinful Israelites complain to Moses: "Behold, we die, we perish, we all perish. Whosoever cometh any thing near unto the Tabernacle of YHWH shall die: shall we be consumed with dying?" (Num 17:12–13) God solves the problem by appointing the Levites to serve in the Tabernacle: "Neither must the children of Israel henceforth come nigh the tabernacle of the congregation, lest they bear sin, and die" (Num 18:22). The orderly cohabitation of God and his people thus requires that a hierarchical principle be introduced into the egalitarian ideal of a "kingdom of priests." For all that, this idea of the sacred still smacks of the archaic or "heathen" in its proximity to "mana" and the "taboo."

When we think of "heathenism," we tend to envisage a religion of immanence, one of material, this-worldly, place-bound divine presence: a religion that thinks of its gods as visibly present in the world, approachable, and in need of care. In the form of their cultic images, the gods must each day be woken up, washed, dressed, swathed with incense, worshipped, and nourished with sacrificial offerings. The Priestly religion sketched here is surprisingly similar to this idea (which, to be sure, is not entirely fair to "heathen" understandings of the gods and religious practices). In the form of the cloud that covers the sanctuary and the "glory" (*kābôd*) that fills it, YHWH is palpably and visibly present here on earth, and the demands he makes of his priestly servants exactly match those made by the "heathen" gods. What particularly jars, not just with today's notions of biblical monotheism, but also with the ideas of God and the possibility of a human connection with him set forth, say, in Deuteronomy, is the idea that one can live in an almost physical sense with God, who—as is repeatedly emphasized—proposes to dwell "among the children of Israel [*bĕtôk bĕnê yiśrā'ēl*]"[17] rather than, say, in heaven or on Sinai. This description has little in common with our usual ideas of an imageless cult of an invisible, transcendent God. On the contrary, the text teems with images and materials. Time and again, emphasis is placed on sight, imagery, vision. Where, then, lies the difference?

The all-deciding difference to heathen religion lies in the conditions that YHWH attaches to his offer to dwell among his people. There are two. The first is that they lead an upright, "holy" life and follow his statutes: "Ye shall do my judgments, and keep mine ordinances, to walk therein" (Lev 18:4). The whole complex of moral commandments (*miṣwôt*), statutes (*mišpāṭîm*), and religious laws (*ḥuqqîm*) revealed on Sinai is designed to lay the foundations for this community of God and people. "And ye shall be unto me a kingdom of priests [*mamleket kōhănîm*], and a holy nation [*gôy qādôš*]," God says before proclaiming the commandments and laws (Ex 19:7). Priests are members of the community who have sanctified themselves for contact with the sacred by strictly observing the purity laws; now the entire nation is enjoined to sanctify itself by keeping God's commandments. Only under this condition will God

> set my tabernacle among you: and my soul shall not abhor you. And I will walk among you, and will be your God, and ye shall be my people. (Lev 26:11–12)

The Holiness Code introduced in the third book of Moses captures this principle in the oft-repeated formula "Ye shall be holy, for I am holy." There is something utopian about the ideal of a sacred, almost mystical communion between God and people. This ideal goes beyond the vision of a land "flowing with milk and honey" and is fundamentally botched and betrayed in Canaan itself, as the subsequent history, related in the books Judges to 2 Kings, never tires of pointing out.

The second condition for God and people coming to dwell together is absolute loyalty. What that means is made clear in the middle section, the story of the Golden Calf, which elucidates the institutionalization of divine presence—the theme of the third part of Exodus—from its polar opposite.[18]

The Golden Calf: The Original Sin against the Covenant

> The threat hanging over the people who made a covenant with God
> is breach of covenant. What that signifies, however, is betrayal.
> —*Klaus Heinrich*[19]

The story of the Golden Calf shows the subject of the concluding chapters of Exodus to be the production of divine presence. God has voiced

FIGURE 35. Worship of the Golden Calf, Moses breaking the tables of the law. French book
illustration (Noyon), c. 1210.

the wish to dwell among his people and thereby set the whole process
in motion. And what do the people do? Are they equally keen to have
God dwell in their midst? They are: just as the Tabernacle expressed
God's longing to be close to his people, so the Golden Calf reflects the
people's yearning to be close to their God. The people have no interest

FIGURE 36. Worship of the Golden Calf. In the upper-left corner Joshua approaches Moses, who is just about to break the tables of the law. Fresco by Raphael in the Vatican Loggia, 1515–1518.

in forsaking YHWH for other gods. It is just that they have lost all hope of ever seeing Moses alive again during the forty days he spends on the mountain. They watched him enter the fiery cloud, and now he is nowhere to be seen. All contact with God has been lost with him too, since Moses had always been the intermediary. In this state of chronic disorientation, they forget the ban on making images, even though they had heard it with their own ears as the second of the Ten Commandments, and beg Aaron: "Up, Make us gods, which shall go before us; for as for this Moses, the man that brought us up out of the land of Egypt, we know not what is become of him" (Ex 32:1).

In the speech he made when awarded the Lucas Prize in Tübingen on May 24, 2011, the Jewish philosopher Avishai Margalit distinguished "between apostasy and idolatry, between worship of a false god and false worship of a true god. The latter is a betrayal of God, the former

FIGURE 37. *The Adoration of the Golden Calf.* Nicolas Poussin, 1633–1634.

that of a religious community."[20] YHWH and Moses do not recognize this distinction. In their eyes, idolatry and apostasy are the same thing, regardless of whether the object of worship was the false god or the true. Since the true god forbids images, worshipping *any* image is tantamount to apostasy. The Israelites are not crying out for different gods; all they need is a substitute for Moses, who had led them and kept them in touch with the true god. Aaron, who really should have known better, is strangely compliant and agrees without demur, organizing the collection of gold earrings and melting them down into the statue of a calf. The Israelites exclaim: "These be thy gods, O Israel, which brought thee up out of the land of Israel!" Aaron makes the calf an altar and proclaims a great feast for the next day.

> And they rose up early on the morrow, and offered burnt offerings, and brought peace offerings; and the people sat down to eat and drink, and rose up to play. (Ex 32:6)

The Israelites could not have sinned more grievously. All this was happening at the foot of the mountain even as Moses was taking pre-

FIGURE 38. Moses breaking the tables of the law. Rembrandt, 1659.

cise instructions at the summit about how the promised community between God and his people was to be realized: the tables of the law were to be handed out, the "dwelling" (*miškān*) erected according to the God-given specifications—but now the people have taken matters into their own hands and are doing everything wrong.

YHWH is determined to annul the covenant and annihilate the people. "Go, get thee down," he says to Moses,

for thy people, which thou broughtest out of the land of Egypt, have cor-
rupted themselves. [...] I have seen this people, and behold, it is a stiff-
necked people: now therefore let me alone, that my wrath may wax hot
against them, and that I may consume them: and I will make of thee a great
nation. (Ex 32:7–10)

In the first of three pleas in total, Moses uses two arguments to dis-
suade God from his murderous intention: would not the Egyptians
conclude that God brought them out only to kill them in the desert?
And did he not promise their forefathers prosperity and land? And at
that, "YHWH repented of the evil which he thought to do unto his
people" (32:14).

Upon descending from the mountain with the stone tablets and witnessing their goings-on, however, Moses delivers a terrible verdict. He
breaks the tablets in his rage and calls out:

> Who is on YHWH's side? Let him come unto me. And all the sons of Levi
> gathered themselves together unto him. And he said unto them, Thus saith
> YHWH, God of Israel, Put every man his sword by his side, and go in and
> out from gate to gate throughout the camp, and slay every man his brother,
> and every man his companion, and every man his neighbor. And the chil-
> dren of Levi did according to the word of Moses: and there fell of the people
> that day about three thousand men. For Moses had said, Consecrate your-
> selves [literally: "fill your hands"[21]] today to YHWH, for every one of you
> was against his son and against his brother, so that he might bestow upon
> you a blessing this day. (32:26–29)

This text, one of the most frequently cited pieces of evidence for an
intrinsic link between monotheism and violence, makes clear that the
commitment to God which the people entered into in the covenant
takes precedence over all other relationships, even the closest blood
ties. By murdering "son and brother" (the most terrible deed imaginable, including in biblical semantics), the Israelites follow God's bidding and declare their overriding loyalty to the covenant.

This is a truly "horrific text"[22] and is meant to be read that way:
cruel, upsetting, and painful. It is supposed to hurt, since "only something that continues to hurt us stays in the memory."[23] Therein lies the
mnemotechnical function of this story, hence the repeated emphasis
on the element of pain: "slay every man his brother, his companion,

FIGURE 39. Moses orders that the Golden Calf be destroyed and its worshippers punished.
Andrea Celesti, 1682–1685.

his neighbor"; "every one of you against his son and against his
brother" (just not "his father," which would have been all too unbearable even in this context). While these verses may well belong to a
later redactional stage,[24] they have found their way into the canon and
must be understood in this setting. The Levites, who had inherited a
legacy of violence (Gen 34) and were cursed by Jacob on that account
("Cursed be their anger, for it was fierce; and their wrath, for it was
cruel: I will divide them in Jacob, and scatter them in Israel," Gen
49:7), are now held up as paragons of loyalty. Loyalty and violence are
not mutually exclusive. Whoever stands "for YHWH" and holds true
to the covenant must be prepared to make the ultimate sacrifice, even
if that means slaying his own son and brother. Those who do so have
"consecrated" themselves as holy warriors and brought blessings on
their apostate nation. In Deuteronomy 33:8–9 Moses and the Levites
are blessed for a loyalty that knows nothing of brothers, fathers, and
sons:

> Let thy Thummim and thy Urim be with thy holy one, whom thou didst
> prove at Massah, and with whom thou didst strive at the waters of Meribah;
> who said unto his father and to his mother, I have not seen him; neither did
> he acknowledge his brethren, nor knew his own children: for they have
> observed thy word, and kept thy covenant.

The characteristic ambivalence pertaining to the idea of the divine covenant encompasses both blessing and curse, loyalty and betrayal, friend and foe. Through their backsliding, the worshippers of the Golden Calf have shown themselves to be traitors and enemies of God. Just as the story of the sacrifice of Isaac (Gen 22) symbolically renounces the archaic custom of sacrificing the firstborn male, so the story of the Golden Calf symbolically renounces the archaic worship of YHWH in the form of a golden statue. We are confronted here with one of those cases where a once-sacred practice appears abhorrent to a later generation. In the second of his Joseph novels, Thomas Mann sheds light on this phenomenon in relation to the example of Pesach festival: merely thinking about the festival is enough to make Jacob almost physically ill because the slaughtered ram whose blood is sprinkled on the doorposts involuntarily reminds him that the firstborn son was once sacrificed in place of the ram.[25] The formerly sacred custom is attested in the Book of Kings, where it is said of King Jeroboam I:

> Whereupon the king took counsel, and made two calves of gold, and said unto them, It is too much for you to go up to Jerusalem: behold thy gods, O Israel, which brought thee up out of the land of Egypt.
> And he set the one in Bethel, and the other he put in Dan.
> And this thing became a sin. (1 Kings 12:28–30a)

It became a sin as a result of the revolutionary change in perspective, the sweeping conversion experience, called for by Hosea and carried out first by the community in exile and then, with the building of the Second Temple, by the populace at large. Christoph Uehlinger is certain "that for decades, perhaps for centuries, a cultic image—more precisely, the image of a bull: the bull of Bethel—could and did function as an iconic condensation of the [...] 'experience' of freedom bestowed on Israel by YHWH."[26] The close connection between the bull calf statue and the Exodus myth is confirmed in the wording used by Jeroboam when unveiling the statue, which repeats the phrasing of Exodus 32:4 almost verbatim. I find no reason to doubt either the historicity of the bull cult in Bethel and Dan or its links with the Exodus myth. As Henrik Pfeiffer writes: "In the bull, Yahweh found a congenial presence symbol. It allowed him to appear as a god who could be experienced, not just in the cosmic phenomena of storm and thunder, but also as the overlord of state, king and country."²⁷ Above all, YHWH in bull form was seen as the liberator from Egyptian captivity. Just as we can plausibly assume that such a statue could be found in each of the sanctuaries of the Northern Kingdom, Dan and Bethel, and that it represented neither Ba'al nor Hadad but YHWH, the god of the exodus, so it makes sense to assume that this instrument of bringing YHWH to living presence had forfeited its place in the Deuteronom(ist)ic-Priestly religion of the Second Temple. Quite the contrary, "this thing became a sin" and was all but demonized. The God of early Judaism cannot be experienced in cosmic phenomena nor does he lord over "state, king and country," all of which had been exposed in their historical contingency and vulnerability by the experience of exile. The Persian king holds sway over state and country, but YHWH is lord of the earth and Israel's covenant partner.

As figures of renunciation, the ban on images and the episode of the Golden Calf pertain to the semantics of the conversion demanded by the early prophetic opposition and particularly by Hosea, the prophet of the Northern Kingdom. Hosea never tires of castigating those who worship "idols," cultic images made of precious metals and especially the "calf of Samaria":

> Of their silver and their gold have they made idols for their own destruction. I have spurned thy calf, O Samaria; mine anger is kindled against them: how long will it be ere they attain to innocence? For from Israel was it also: the workman made it; therefore it is not God: but the calf of Samaria shall be broken into pieces. (8:4b–6)

> Ephraim is joined to idols: let him alone. When their drink is gone, they give themselves to whoring: their rulers with shame do love. (4:17–18)

> The inhabitants of Samaria shall fear for the calf of Beth-aven: for the people thereof shall mourn over it, and the priests thereof that rejoiced on it, for the glory thereof, because it is departed from them. (10:5)

> And now they sin more and more, and have made them molten images of their silver, and idols according to their own understanding, all of it the work of the craftsmen: they say of them, Let those who offer human sacrifice kiss calves! (13:2)

Only by renouncing images and converting to the imageless worship of YHWH can the Israelites hope to avert disaster:

> Asshur shall not save us; we will not ride upon horses: neither will we say any more to the work of our hands, Ye are our gods: for in thee the fatherless findeth mercy.
> Ephraim shall say, What have I to do any more with idols? I have heard him, and observed him: I am like a green fir tree. From me is thy fruit found. (14:4, 8)

By installing his two golden calves, Jeroboam had drawn upon himself a curse that led to the downfall of the Northern Kingdom (1 Kings 14:7–16). According to the Priestly Source, the same curse had already weighed on those who fled from Egypt, but Moses had lifted it through his intercession. Now, however, in the time of the narrative, it had been realized.

The forgiveness Moses had secured from YHWH does not entail freedom from punishment; it only—but also crucially—ensures the continuation of the covenant. Under the terms of the covenant, sin must still be punished. Moses shoulders this responsibility with help from the Levites, who thereby prove themselves to be paragons of covenant fidelity. In the event of an emergency—and breach of covenant constitutes just such an emergency—this fidelity encompasses zealotry, a fanatical, murderous militancy on God's behalf. The verses Exodus 32:27–29 form the primal scene of such divine zeal, an inherent part of the monotheism of loyalty that no apologetics can fully gloss over. The scene's affinity to Deuteronomy 13 has often been remarked on. There it is pronounced a sacred duty to denounce anyone, even your own brother or son, who follows other gods and incites you to renege on the covenant. The origin of this rule in Esarhaddon's loyalty oaths on behalf of Ashurbanipal has also been established. It is evident that Assyrian state loyalism stands behind the requirement of a loyalty to YHWH overriding all natural bonds and obligations. Yet it is hardly by accident that the text found its way from Assyrian state ideology into the canon. It also belongs there, since the idea of an unconditional, self-abnegating commitment to YHWH, a militant engagement for God and the covenant that transcends all claims made by kith and kin, is bound up with the concept of loyalty that lies at the heart of this monotheism. Here we are not dealing with dogmas and questions of truth but with the honor of an offended god, and in this matter there can be—even today—no tolerance.

Anyone who worships images breaks the covenant that God made with Israel through the law. Moses makes that symbolically clear by breaking the tables of the law when he descends from Sinai and sees the people dancing around the Golden Calf. This story defines how the friend-enemy distinction, on which the first and second commandments in the Decalogue are based, is to be applied. It does not separate "us" and "them"; rather, it splits one's own group down the middle, pitting brother against brother, friend against friend, neighbor against neighbor. In the light of this distinction there are no longer any natural bonds.

When YHWH draws Moses's attention to the people's breach of covenant, he announces his intention to destroy the people and make a fresh start with him, Moses. Moses is able to make him change his mind: that is the first test he has to pass in this crisis. The next morning, after his terrible verdict, Moses reascends the mountain and pleads with YHWH for a second time to forgive the people their sinful ways. "If not, blot me, I pray thee, out of thy book which thou hast written" (Ex 32:32) —the book of life containing the names of the pious. No offer could be more dreadful, since it means taking on the sins of the people and suffering the most terrible fate that can be imagined in the context of biblical semantics: not just to die but to be wiped forever from God's memory. Moses appears here as God's suffering servant, of whom it is said in Isaiah 53:5: "But he was wounded for our transgressions, he was bruised for our iniquities: the chastisement of our peace was upon him; and with his stripes we are healed."[28] God refuses the bargain and rejects outright the possibility of substitutionary atonement: "Whosoever has sinned against me, him will I blot out of my book" (Ex 32:33). This scene echoes in Judaism in the prayer recited during the ten "High Holy Days" between Rosh Hashanah and Yom Kippur: "Remember us for Life, King who delights in Life, inscribe us in the book of Life, for you, God of Life!"[29] Moses's willingness to make a sacrifice that far surpasses any conceivable martyrdom retains its power to impress.

God grants his forgiveness but with the proviso that, "when my time comes, I will visit their sins upon them"—foreshadowing the fall of Jerusalem and the Babylonian exile. "And YHWH plagued the people," the passage concludes, "because of what they did with the calf which Aaron had made" (Ex 32:35).

Loyalty is not the only value, however, that the story of the Golden Calf helps illustrate. The story is interlinked with the theme of the Tabernacle, and in this connection something else is at issue: YHWH's presence among his people. God brings that presence to an abrupt end when he proposes to send an angel to go before the Israelites rather than escorting them himself. In doing so, he goes back on the building of the Tabernacle, which he had earlier shown and described to Moses at great length. The theme of God's presence forms the centerpiece of the story of the Golden Calf, chapters 32:30–34:9.

Moses is unhappy with the solution proposed by God of sending an angel ahead of the Israelites but not accompanying them himself. He dares a third petition. If God fails to recognize "that this nation is thy people" and refuses to go with them himself, then Moses too will not go with them—and God relents: "I will do this thing also that thou hast spoken" (33:17). This is the third test in the ongoing crisis, and Moses passes it as brilliantly as he did the other two. His success emboldens him to make the daring request: "I beseech thee, show me thy face." While that is impossible, for "no man shall see me, and live" (33:20), YHWH promises to pass by Moses and show himself from "behind" ('āhôr). Philo interpreted this passage allegorically:

> "Thou shalt see my back parts, but my face shall not be beheld by thee": It is sufficient for a wise man to know God a posteriori, or from his effects; but whosoever will needs behold the naked essence of the deity, will be blinded with the transcendent radiance and splendor of his beams.[30]

Following on from this allegorical reading, the Enlightenment then made the connection to the veil of Isis, which simultaneously conceals and reveals itself in nature.[31]

First, though, Moses is commanded to chisel out two new stone tablets and return with them early next morning to the mountain. He does as he is told, and as God passes him by he repeats the double-

edged self-definition on which the ban on images was based. This so-
called Grace Formula[32] is one of the key texts of biblical theology:

> YHWH, YHWH,
> merciful and gracious God,
> longsuffering, and abundant in goodness and loyalty,
> keeping mercy for thousands,
> forgiving iniquity and transgression and sin,
>
> and that will by no means clear the guilty,
> visiting the iniquity of the fathers upon the children, and upon the chil-
> dren's children, unto to the third and to the fourth generation. (Ex
> 34:6–7)

"Abundant in goodness and loyalty" (*rab-ḥesed we'ĕmet*)—in this
self-description, the crucial keyword "loyalty" appears. The Hebrew
word *'ĕmet* may be translated into English as both "loyalty" (or "faithfulness") and "truth." The Septuagint gives *alēthinos*, "truthful," while
the Vulgate offers *verus*, "true." In the semantics of covenant theology,
"loyalty" and "truth" are one and the same. Something is true if it has
been tried and tested. The fact that the word is missing from all the
other passages where the "Grace Formula" is invoked—Numbers 14:18,
Psalms 86:15, Psalms 103:8, Jonah 4:2, Joel 2:13—makes its presence in
this passage all the more significant. God stays true to the covenant and
keeps faith even with those who have betrayed him. Whereas YHWH
had made the first covenant with the freed, now he renews it with the
fallen. In the post-Priestly final version of the Book of Exodus, the description of the Tabernacle as a second creation (chapters 25–31) is
immediately followed by the story of the Golden Calf as a second fall
from grace (chapters 32–34). This relapse, however, does not result in
an expulsion from the promised paradise of divine presence. YHWH
solemnly renews the covenant and reiterates its conditions:

1. No alliances with the inhabitants of the Promised Land.
2. Destroy their altars, serve no other gods: for YHWH is a jealous God.
3. No mixed marriages with the inhabitants of the land.
4. No idolatrous images.
5. Keep the Feast of Unleavened Bread.

6. All firstlings belong by rights to God; the firstborn ass and the firstborn son should be redeemed.
7. Keep the Sabbath holy.
8. Observe the Feast of Weeks.
9. Go on a pilgrimage to Jerusalem three times a year.
10. Do not offer the blood of the sacrifice with leaven, nor leave any of the paschal lamb until the morrow.
11. Give up the best of the firstfruits.
12. Do not seethe a kid in its mother's milk. (34:10–26)

This Dodecalogue is not inscribed on stone tablets by God himself; instead he instructs Moses: "Write thou these words: for after the tenor of these words I have made a covenant with thee and with Israel" (34:27).

The first four commandments are dedicated to sanctifying the nation by segregating it from the Canaanites; the following seven refer to festivals and the Sabbath, and the conclusion is formed by the puzzling prohibition on cooking a young goat in its mother's milk. This directive is similarly intended to distance Israel from the customs of the land,[33] and it owes its central importance in Judaism to its prominent position here in covenant law. Conspicuously absent from the Dodecalogue are the commandments regulating interpersonal conduct. Its primary concern is not to establish a just society but to lay the ground rules for "sanctification" and hence for divine presence, the dominant theme of the last sixteen chapters of Exodus.

With the renewal of the covenant after the crisis brought on by the "stiff-necked" people, the circle is complete. The story of the Golden Calf is structured in three parts:

1. Breach of the covenant: chapter 32:1–29
2. Divine presence: chapter 32:20–34:9
3. Renewal of the covenant: chapter 34:10–35

The middle section refers to the general theme of the third part of the Book of Exodus (chapters 25–40), while the sections framing it deal with the theme of the covenant in its aspects of loyalty: first from the human perspective (the nation's infidelity and the zealous faithfulness of the Levites), then from the divine perspective (God's mercifulness

FIGURE 40. Moses with horns. Michelangelo's sculpture from the tomb of Julius II in Rome, S. Pietro in Vincoli, 1513–1515, final revision in 1542.

in maintaining his commitment to the covenant while still punishing the guilty).

With his third plea, by which he succeeds not only in moving God to renew the covenant but also in glimpsing God himself, at least from behind, Moses attains the larger-than-life, heroic stature we see in the depictions of Michelangelo, among others, as well as in the cultural memory of the Jews, Christians, and Muslims. When he descends from the mountaintop, his face is shining so brightly from God's reflected glory that he has to cover it with a veil so that Aaron and the Israelites can bear to look at him.

In the Hebrew it is written: *qāran 'ôr pānāyw*. That can only really be translated as "the skin of his face shone"; *qāran* means "to send out rays." That is how—admittedly rather ponderously—the Septuagint translates the passage into Greek. Translated literally, then, the passage reads: "the sight of the skin on his face shone forth." In the Latin Vulgate, by contrast, we read: *cornuta esset facies sua*, "his face was horned." Is this a simple translation error? In fact, *qeren* also means "horn," and our English word "horn," like *cornu* in Latin and *qurn* in Arabic, comes from the same root. Mesopotamian and Canaanite deities typically wear a horned helmet that makes it look as if horns are growing out of their foreheads. Horns are clearly also an archaic visual metaphor for the sacred. To that extent, the Vulgate translation is not as far-fetched as it may at first appear.

No other scene from the Book of Exodus or the following three books of Moses has exerted so great an influence on how Moses figures in the cultural memory of the human race as this one. This is the scene Heine had in mind when he wrote: "How small Sinai appears when Moses stands upon it!"

Excursus V: The Golden Calf in Schoenberg's Opera *Moses und Aron*

From the scant few verses devoted to the story of the Golden Calf in Exodus 32, Schoenberg forges the entire second act of his opera *Moses und Aron*. The orgiastic "dance around the Golden Calf," merely hinted at in verse 6 with the verb *lĕṣaḥēq*, "to indulge in revelry," is expanded into an almost forty-minute sequence that represents an incontestable high point in the history of opera.[34] Unlike in the Bible, where the people merely grumble and complain, the making of the calf is here preceded by open rebellion: the people threaten to kill Moses, Aron, and the seventy elders if they refuse to restore their old gods to them. The old gods took care of law and order; now lawlessness, greed, and robbery run riot in the camp and the new law has yet to be unveiled. Perhaps Moses is dead, killed by his intractable god or by the old gods he abandoned. The people hanker after these old gods, and Aron delivers them in the form of the Golden Calf: "People of Israel! I'm returning your gods to you and you to them, just as you have demanded. Leave the eternal one in his remoteness! Gods who will be near you every day befit you more."[35]

Schoenberg's point is that the adoration of idols is pure regression. The people yearn to break away from the new invisible god and go back to their old visible gods. They want to rescind their pact with YHWH. The Bible tells a different tale. Here, as shown earlier, the Israelites have no interest in rejecting YHWH and turning to other gods. They only want to find a replacement for Moses, whom they had relied on to establish contact with God and to lead them in the wilderness. Even King Jeroboam, who "made two calves of gold" so that the people of the Northern Kingdom could worship without having to undertake the trip to Jerusalem, wanted to represent YHWH rather than to fall into apostasy (1 Kings 12). In both cases, their subjective intentions were of no help to the idol-makers. Every image, regardless of what its maker may have meant by it, is automatically an "other god" in God's eyes and incites his jealous wrath. Schoenberg's interpretation of the ban on images targets a key point. The problem with images does not lie in their impotence, their constitutive incapacity to represent the unrepresentable; quite the contrary, it lies in their dangerous power to bring other, false gods to living presence. In a note in his sketches for the opera, Schoenberg remarks: "A false god is contained in all that surrounds us, it can assume the image of anything, it originates in everything, just as everything has its origin in it; it is like the nature that encompasses it and is also contained in it, as in everything else. This god expresses a worship of nature and makes every living thing equal to god."[36] To depict is to deify, to make what is depicted an object of idolatrous desire. Nothing living should be depicted since, in Aron's words, "in all things that are, a god lives."[37] Each time an image is made, a god is produced: a false god.

The god produced as a result of Aron's action is the People itself: "you gave the gods substance from out of your innermost being," that is, the secular, "everyday" longing for happiness and security. "Worship yourselves in this symbol!"[38] Aron's sin—and that of his people, too—is "ethnotheism," self-deification of the people, worship of one's own collective self and the dreams that give it "substance." These dreams become visible in the Golden Calf.

The almost overwhelming power of the image to bring something divine (albeit a "false god") to living presence is conveyed in the people's reactions in the third scene of act 2. This is the opera's centerpiece and, at 659 bars, its longest scene. "I went very far in the execution of this scene," Schoenberg writes in a letter, "because it goes to the heart of my thinking, and here my piece is at its most *operatic*—which it should be, after all."[39] The image seems spontaneously to provoke the people to react with displays of ritual behavior. Under its spell, they perform rites that we, schooled by the polemical denunciations of the Bible and the church fathers, tend to imagine as typically "pagan." In the highly nuanced, formally complex elaboration of this scene, its purpose becomes evident: to present paganism as a false religion and hence to provide a vividly sensuous illustration of the Mosaic distinction. Because sacrifice is so central to pagan ritual, the stage is initially filled with offerings brought in from all sides. The ritual character of animal slaughter is made clear in the "Dance of the Butchers."[40] The three entrances that follow draw attention to other aspects of image worship: the miraculous healing of a sick woman,[41] the beggars who cast off their last belongings,[42] and the old men who offer themselves in sacrifice.[43] Death, appearing here for the first time, remains present in the following entrances, first as murderous violence—the tribal leaders strike down the youth who, in his zeal for the one true God, had opposed the idolaters[44]—then in the ritual human sacrifice of the four naked virgins, and finally in ritual suicide, in the ecstatic excess of an orgy that obliterates the boundaries between *eros* and *thanatos*, sexual frenzy and bloodlust.[45] The presence of the old gods in image form unleashes primal urges of abandonment and violence, demonstrating to the audience what the destruction of images entails: liberation from the false gods that hold us captive to the transient realm of carnal fears and desires, drives, compulsions, cravings, and needs. At stake here is what Freud calls an "advance in spirituality," the sublimation of instinct into intellect, the "triumph of spirituality over sensuality." In *Moses and Monotheism*, Freud had this to say about the ban on images:

Among the precepts of the Moses religion there is one that is of greater significance than at first appears. It is the ban on making an image of god—the
compulsion, in other words, to worship a god one cannot see. [. . .] If the ban
was accepted, it had to be far-reaching in its effects. For it meant that sensory
perception was now given second place to what may be called an abstract
idea, a triumph of spirituality over sensuality—strictly speaking, a renunciation of instinct with all its inevitable psychological consequences.[46]

Schoenberg's Moses stands for this spirituality or intellectuality
(*Geistigkeit*). It would be too simple to place Aron on the opposing side
of sensuality. In Schoenberg's opera, Moses takes up a position whereas
Aron represents a process: the process of distanciation and alienation.
Schoenberg uses musical means to make this clear. The thematic material moves ever further away from the tonal symbols that stand for the
idea of God as the symphonic exuberance and rhythmic verve of the
increasingly independent orchestra whip the revelers to a pitch of self-
intoxicating ecstasy.

When Moses descends from the mountain with the tables of the law,
the orgy has already dissipated. He does away with the calf with a mere
verbal gesture: "Away, you image of impotence to hold the limitless in
an image!"[47] Confronted by his brother—"Aron, what have you
done?"—Aron presents the calf as yet another of the "marvels" he produced "when your idea brought forth no word, my word brought forth
no image."[48] Moses, too, performed sorcery when he destroyed the
image with his word. Moses brandishes the tablets in riposte: "That is
no image, no miracle! That is the Law."[49] Just as the tablets proclaim
God's eternal law, so Aron's mouth should proclaim his brother's ideas:
"perishable, in the speech of your mouth!" Like Moses himself, Aron
and the people must live only for the idea: "It must grasp the idea! It
lives only for that!" In grasping the idea, the people justify their having
been chosen by God. Aron, ethnotheist that he is, lives only for the
people, and the people live only "if they can see, hear, touch." To live
for the idea means to be "a lamentable people, a nation of martyrs."
Aron wants to dissolve the idea in commandments and prohibitions.
Since the people are incapable of grasping it consciously, "your will"
shall be "done unknowingly." "I would not want to experience that,"
Moses replies.[50]

Schoenberg reprises here the key idea of a dialogue from his drama *The Biblical Way* (1928). Its hero, Max Aruns (as the name indicates, a combination of Moses and Aaron), aims to establish a Jewish state in Africa, "New Palestine," and win the rabbi David Asseino as its spiritual leader. Aruns fails in his endeavor, and Asseino comments on his death with words that anticipate Moses's position: "The idea resists any material realization, in the same way that God does not tolerate any representation of himself. Whoever dedicates himself to the idea must either renounce the attempt to realize it, or make do with a reality which he would not want to experience. Therefore whoever is compelled to live out an idea inevitably becomes its martyr."[51] Moses, too, comes close to failure. The conflict with Aron escalates when Aron plays his last trump card: even the tables of the law "are only an image, a part of the idea." On hearing these words, Moses shatters the tables.[52]

The tables are shattered in the Bible as well, when Moses sees the Golden Calf and the dancing multitude. They are replaced, however. Moses returns to the mountaintop and comes back with new tables. The people are punished, Aaron gets off lightly, and the story resumes its familiar course with the tables and the pillars of cloud and fire. Schoenberg offers an altogether different scenario: the tables remain broken and the pillars of cloud and fire are now presented as further Aaronite idols, which the people follow as blindly and deliriously as they had earlier followed the Golden Calf, only now singing pious songs of the favor they have found in God's sight. Instead of reascending the mountain, Moses now despairs of his mission: "So all that I thought was madness, and can and must not be said. O word, you word that I lack!"[53] Here Moses breaks the tables of the law not from his fury at seeing the calf and as a symbolic expression of the broken covenant, but in his despair at the insight that even the Torah is only an image, "false as an image can only be."

Confronted with this insight, Moses sinks into an abyss of negative theology that is latent in the biblical ban on images but held in check by the positive theology of the revelation. The biblical ban does not stipulate that God tarries in absolute transcendence, beyond all human imagining and therefore also beyond all representation. The reason we may not depict him is because he has *spoken* to us but not *shown* himself to us. Images are not rejected in view of God's undepictability but in view of his word. Images must disappear to make room for that word, the Torah.[54] The task is not just to disenchant the world by doing away with images but also, and above all, to install something else in their place: the Torah. The Torah replaces images and makes them redundant. Where once there were images, now there is Torah. Where images still prevail, there can be no Torah.

A "Book of the Temple"?

The Priestly Source, which probably emerged in its earliest form following the return from exile around the end of the sixth century BCE,[55] culminates and concludes in the third part of the Book of Exodus. Let us recall the structure of the first two books of Moses, that is, the Priestly Source including its non-Priestly portions:

Genesis			Exodus		
I	II	III	IV	V	VI
1–11	12–36	37–50	1–15a	15b–24	25–40
Creation and primal history	Patriarchs	Story of Joseph	Exodus	Covenant, law, contract	Religion as symbiosis of God and people

Franziska Bark has devoted a substantial monograph to the comparatively neglected sixth part of the Priestly Source (and third part of Exodus),[56] analyzing its literary form and investigating the Jewish exegetical history. The conclusion she arrives at is that "the reader finishes the book with no firm idea of what the desert sanctuary actually looks like."[57] Reading the text as if it were a deliberately unperformable score, she argues that a visualization of the sanctuary is almost programmatically undermined at each step. As convincing as I find the idea that the text is meant to cause a sanctuary to arise in the reader's mind, I cannot agree that the text simultaneously prevents such a picture from emerging. It seems obvious to me that the authors had a very concrete image in mind and that they sought to convey this image to their readers with the utmost attention to detail. Bernhard Lang is probably right to suggest that this image is modeled on a Persian royal tent.[58] Undoubtedly, the attempt to describe an imperfectly imaginable space or object has a long literary pedigree, from the description of the New Jerusalem in Revelation 21 and the dimensions of God in the Jewish Shi'ur Qomah tradition all the way to Kafka's *Trial*. But the chapters devoted to the desert sanctuary seem to me to be written with the aim of reconstructing the ideal protosanctuary in the medium of language. At the time, readers familiar with Phoenician craftsmanship and Persian royal tents would have received a fairly precise idea of what the sanctuary looked like, even if later readers were left with a rather sketchier idea.

An Egyptologist's mind immediately turns to the ancient Egyptian counterpart to such an imagined protosanctuary: a reed hut that all late Egyptian temples, in their archaizing longing to return to the origins, sought to emulate in stone through the typically Egyptian temple features of inward-sloping walls, torus and corvetto cornice. These temples also generally contain lengthy inscriptions (or "monographs") recounting the legend of the temple's origin as a reed hut on the "primal hill." The last fifteen chapters of the Book of Exodus represent just such a "monograph."

There is an even closer connection between these chapters (along with Leviticus and Numbers 1–10) and the "Book of the Temple" that Joachim Quack is collating and editing from the thousands of tiny fragments he has found scattered among various museums and collections.[59] This book, which survives in remnants of more than forty copies in classical Egyptian, Demotic, and Greek, presumably dates from the restoration period following the Assyrian catastrophe of the seventh century BCE, a time when plans were underfoot to renovate and rebuild the temples laid waste by the Assyrian invaders. A historical introduction depicts a similar catastrophe long ago (in the first half of the third millennium) and goes on to describe the ideal temple—its ground plan, decoration, paraphernalia, priesthood, rites, and duties—as the blueprint for an ambitious program of temple building, albeit one that would only be systematically implemented under the Ptolemies. The order of the day in Egypt was to describe the "canonic"

temple on which the country's many religious centers could model
their own temple building.

In Israel, where after the normatively binding Josianic cult reform
(whether literary or historical in origin) there could be only one temple, the Temple in Jerusalem, what mattered was to place the Temple
in a line of tradition that reached back via the Solomonic temple to the
protosanctuary at Sinai. That is why the history set out in the Priestly
Source culminates in an Israelite "Book of the Temple." It unfolds a
narrative arc that extends, in its first part, from the creation of the
world to the abyss of Egyptian captivity before leading out of that
abyss, in its second part, to the creation of a new order in which God
communes with his people in his tent sanctuary.

The prophet Ezekiel also wrote a "Book of the Temple" in the form
of a reported vision (Ez 40–48). Franziska Bark compares this report
with the depiction of the tent sanctuary in Exodus 25–40, identifying
it as another "unperformable score," a text that deliberately frustrates
the reader's efforts to visualize what it describes.[60] Here too, however,
the realism of the Temple description is striking, even if in this case it
is confined to the floorplan and the third dimension is missing. Ezekiel
dates his vision to the twenty-fifth year of Babylonian captivity, around
570–560 BCE. It seems evident to me that this text—the only one that
can be compared with Exodus 25–40 in its comprehensiveness and
wealth of detail—fulfills exactly the same function as the third part of
the Book of Exodus: to provide a "Book of the Temple" that could
serve as a model and foundation for restoring the Temple, the Temple
cult, and in this case even the monarchy after the longed-for return to
Jerusalem. Perhaps we can almost speak of a common literary genre in
relation to Exodus 25–40, Ezekiel 40–48, and the Egyptian "Book of
the Temple."[61] The common denominator of these three compositions
is their function of laying the literary and normative basis for a complete renewal of temple building and ritual life in the aftermath of catastrophic destruction. In Egypt, this situation arose on three occasions:
after the foreign rule of the Hyksos (1620–1510), after the Amarna period (1360–1340), and after the four Assyrian invasions (720–670). If,
as seems most likely to me, we can date the Book of the Temple to the
period of restoration following the Assyrian depredations, we are faced
with a historical constellation corresponding to the traumatic experi-

ences of Israelite history with the downfall of the Northern Kingdom in 722 BCE and the Southern Kingdom in 587 BCE. Toward the end of the sixth century, the Israelites returning from exile found themselves in a situation comparable to that of the Egyptians after the Assyrian invasions, although the plight of the Israelites, forced to start anew after total destruction, was considerably more dire.

The Priestly Source thus has its roots in a historical situation where the priority was to rebuild the Temple from the ground up, complete with priests, regular offerings, and ritual ordinances. Its concluding section provides a model for this refoundation. We are dealing here with a dual relationship to the divine model: on the mountaintop, clouded in glory, God showed Moses the model of a tent sanctuary and its furnishings,[62] and this protosanctuary in its textual form in turn provided the model for Solomon's temple and now for the new Temple. The Israelites are thus enjoined, not to reconstruct the Solomonic temple, but to realize the shared prototype of the tent sanctuary in the medium of stone architecture and on a larger scale. That prototype exists solely in the medium of language.[63]

As mentioned previously, neither a sanctuary nor a religion of the kind portrayed here actually existed in Israel at the time narrated. Indeed, from the viewpoint of the Deuteronomist history, the same could be said of religion during the later period from the occupation of the Promised Land to Babylonian captivity. The condition YHWH attached to his pledge to dwell with Israel—holiness in the sense of justice, purity, and loyalty—had been betrayed in the most ignominious manner. The official state religion, no less than the regional popular religion, had been irremediably sullied by worship of other gods, however much YHWH may have been exalted as head of the pantheon, while the justice prescribed by the revealed law had been neglected and trodden underfoot. That had already been the position of the early prophets who foresaw the Assyrian catastrophe. Now, with both the Priestly and Deuteronomist schools embarking on a thoroughgoing reconstruction of the past in a bid to salvage meaning, hope, and purpose from the wreckage of the salvational project, the burning question was that of guilt. Under no account could the blame for Israel's downfall lie with YHWH; his faithfulness and justice had to be preserved at all costs. The people, not God, had broken the covenant.

Whereas the Deuteronomist tradition assigned guilt (or rather "sin") primarily to the people's failure to live by the law, the Priestly tradition—first Hosea and then Ezekiel in particular—placed priestly idolatry, disloyalty to the cult of YHWH, in the foreground. Like Hosea, the Priestly Source saw the goal of salvational history in the living community with God instituted on Sinai, and it commended this goal to the generation returning from exile as a religious ideal. This spirit animates the previously cited vision of the prophet Haggai, who dates it to October 17, 520 BCE, right at the time the Priestly Source was being compiled:

> In the seventh month, in the one and twentieth day of the month, came the word of YHWH by the prophet Haggai, saying:
> Speak now to Zerubbabel the son of Shealtiel, governor of Judah, and to Joshua the son of Josedech, the high priest, and to the residue of the people, saying, Who is left among you that saw this house in her first glory? And how do ye see it now? It is not in your eyes in comparison of it as nothing? Yet now be strong, O Zerubbabel, saith YHWH; and be strong, O Joshua, son of Josedech, the high priest; and be strong, all ye people of the land, saith YHWH, and work: for I am with you, saith YHWH of hosts. According to the word that I covenanted with you when ye came out of Egypt, so my spirit remaineth among you: fear ye not! [...]
> The glory of this latter house shall be greater than of the former, saith YHWH of hosts: and in this place will I give peace, saith YHWH of hosts. (Hag 2:1–5, 9)

This prophetic utterance explains why the departure from Egypt is remembered at precisely this moment, the "zero hour" of a radical new beginning after the catastrophe. After centuries mired in guilt, sin, and suffering, the time had come to return to the origins, to God's promises and saving deeds, in the hope that the ideal of communion with God would finally be realized in the Second Temple.

CONCLUSION

Narrative, Historical, and Performative Truth

"To deny a people the man it calls its greatest son is not to be undertaken lightly"—with these words Freud began *Moses and Monotheism*, a book that set out to unmask the greatest of Jews as an Egyptian.[1] For all that, Freud did his best to prove that Moses had really existed. Freud had his sights set on the *historical* Moses, seeking to strip away the layers of biblical varnish that in his view had obscured his original greatness. Today, Moses is typically treated as a "fictional" or "literary" character. Perhaps there once was a man called Moses—perhaps he was even an Egyptian—but that man has so little in common with the Moses of the tradition, the "greatest son" of the Jewish people, *rabbēnû*, "our teacher," that it seems unnecessary to ask whether he ever really lived and, if so, which nation he belonged to.[2] He lives on in the hearts and minds of the Jewish people (among others), and that is enough.

Much the same could be said of the tale of the departure from Egypt. To deny all historical reality to a tradition celebrated to this day as the founding event of a people's existence—to vary Freud's sentence—is not to be undertaken lightly, especially since this is a story with which many non-Jewish people have also identified: Armenians, Ethiopians, English, Dutch, Americans, Boers, as well as such diverse movements as Protestantism, Pietism, Puritanism, the Civil Rights movement, Latin American liberation theology, and revolutions like the Puritan Revolution of Oliver Cromwell.[3] Here too, however, we encounter the same situation as with Moses: today we tend to see this tradition as a fictional or literary composition, without ruling out the possibility that something may have happened in the thirteenth or twelfth century BCE around which memories then began to cluster, possibly in the context of an annual commemorative ceremony. Perhaps a persecuted minority took flight and was miraculously saved from pursuing forces; yet this historical event would have as little in common with the Exodus story of the Bible as the historical Moses does with the Moses of the tradition, so the matter can be laid to rest there. The hypothetical origins of the story are less important than the historical conditions of its literary growth into the monumental, truly world-changing dimensions it has come to assume over the millennia.

Anyone who declares Moses and the story of the departure from Egypt to be "fictitious" (or "literary," which amounts to the same thing) rather than historical must first explain how these terms—historicity, fictionality, literariness—are to be understood. In my view, they are all equally unsuited to this context. The concept of fiction disqualifies itself for a story that claims the utmost binding force and explanatory power—and in that sense "truth" —for the time in which it is being told. Fictions are stories that invite the reader or listener to sit back and relax because they have no impact on his or her current actions. That is emphatically not how the story of the departure from Egypt works. It has, or claims to have, enormous consequences for the present. It tells a tale of liberation from relations that have always prevailed, and prevail to this day, into a new state promising freedom and prosperity provided certain conditions are met in the here and now. That is hardly what literary scholars have in mind when they speak of fictionality.

It would be more appropriate to invoke the concept of performativity here. Texts or speech acts are performative if they produce the very reality they represent. The truth resides in their enactment or implementation. The Exodus story does not write history; it makes history. The world to which the story refers arises with that narrative as its foundation. There probably never was a pharaoh who oppressed the Israelites and drowned in the Red Sea while pursuing them, but identifying one of today's Arab rulers with that pharaoh by calling him a "fira'un" can still be devastating. The Exodus story is performative in the sense that it provides those telling it with an identity. It is just as real as the people who define themselves in relation to it and who, uniquely among the peoples of the ancient world and despite all the persecution they have had to face, have survived to this day by virtue of that identification and self-definition. No less problematic than the concept of fictionality is that of literature, understood as an aesthetic category ("fine writing," belles-lettres). Literature in this sense plays a significant role in the Hebrew Bible, the TaNaKh (for Torah, Nevi'im, Ketuvim). The canonic part of the hagiographies (Ketuvim) is literary through and through. It contains love poetry, poems of prayer and ritual, moral and philosophical works, novellas and stories. The second subdivision, Prophets (Nevi'im), is already quite different, however. That is made clear in Ezekiel 33:32, where God says to his prophet: "And lo, thou art unto them as a very lovely song of one that hath a pleasant voice, and can play well on an instrument: for they hear thy words, but they do them not." Not to mention the first section, the Torah, which presents itself as God's revelation to Moses and the direct notation of his divine will! This text is as true and real as Judaism and the other religions based on the Torah. The truth of the Bible is not to be confirmed by archaeological discoveries ("so the Bible *is* right after all!") but by the existence of the people founded upon it and by the religions that emerged from it. In short, concepts like "fictionality" and "literature" are out of place when applied to texts of such world-changing, reality-shaping effect. Their truth should not be reduced to their historical verifiability.

Revelation

The overarching and most important theme in the Book of Exodus has proved to be the idea of revelation, albeit in a completely new sense of the word: not as the occasional expression of divine will, whether articulated spontaneously or mediated through cultural techniques such as divination, but as a binding instruction from God, issued once and for all time, encompassing and regulating all aspects of human and social existence. Revelation in this sense has no parallel in other religions and appears for the first time in the Book of Exodus. The revealed character of the events narrated there should not be contested on the grounds that there is no word for "revelation" in Hebrew. After all, there is no word in the Hebrew of the Torah for "freedom" either, and yet the story is self-evidently about liberation from the direst oppression. There are concepts that lack matching lexemes while still being realized at the level of discourse. Only later—for example, in the process of interpreting the Exodus story—are they distilled in a word.

Let us recapitulate the five steps in which the concept of revelation is developed in narrative form; the witnesses or addressees are placed within brackets:

1. Revelation of the name and Moses's calling at the burning bush (Moses)
2. Revelation of God's power in the form of the ten plagues and the Red Sea miracle (Pharaoh, the world)
3. Revelation of the law and covenant at Sinai (the people)
4. Revelation of the Tabernacle (Moses)
5. Revelation of the divine nature and renewal of the covenant after the crisis (Moses)

The first two steps can be linked to similar phenomena in Egypt and Babylonia. Egyptian deities also reveal themselves to kings, addressing them in long speeches to advise them of their intentions, and the dead take on divine roles to make such speeches in the afterlife. The Babylonians and Hittites also interpreted natural catastrophes, epidemics, and crushing defeats as divine interventions, displays of power on the part of the gods they had angered. The transition to a completely new understanding of the world based on revelation does not take place until the third act in the unfolding drama. Here a secular law code, together with an equally secular set of rules for living together in society, is transposed into the mode of revelation. Through this "theologization of the law," the constitution of a people, its entire way of life, has bestowed on it the status of absolute, eternal truth. That is without parallel in the ancient world. When Hammurabi, as depicted on a stela in the Louvre, appears before the sun god, Shamash, to dedicate his code to him as the god of law and justice, that is something quite different to God appearing before Moses to hand down his divine law in the form of the stone tables and dictate everything else to him.

In decreeing the Decalogue, moreover, YHWH bypasses Moses to address the people as a whole, communicating his will to them in quasi-democratic openness, without the need for any royal or prophetic intermediary. That is not only without precedent in the history of religion; it is also unparalleled in the Hebrew Bible. God's proclamation of the Decalogue accordingly lies at the heart of the theme of revelation. This act also stands at the center of the Sinai pericope. It requires the volcanic theophany, the people's assent to the covenant by acclamation and the written record of the two tables. The three great codices—Covenant Code, Holiness Code (in Leviticus), and Deuteronomic Code—were all tacked on to this primary act of revelation in order that they might partake of its prestige as *ius divinum*. As legal codes conveyed by Moses, they should not have required a theophany. In its creative affirmation of God's devotion to the world in the medium of language, the proclamation of the Ten Commandments can only be compared to the creation of the world through the word. This reality-creating word is what, from the Christian (Johannine) point of view, became flesh in Jesus Christ (John 1:14).

Where does this step belong, historically speaking? That is a question that may meaningfully be asked of Exodus, unlike the quest for the historical origins of the departure from Egypt. This step has the downfall of the Kingdom as its precondition. God and his people fill the vacuum left by the collapse of state authority, royalty, and sovereignty. The pre-Priestly Exodus narrative is no longer extant and can only be reconstructed from allusions and summaries in psalms and prophetic books, but we can be sure it lacked the Sinai pericope. It must have traced the Israelites' path from departure and liberation via election and covenant to entry into the Promised Land. These three narrative threads are inextricably intertwined. The revelation of the law at Sinai was missing from the original version of Exodus. This section, with its theologization of the law as *lex divina*, belongs to a compositional stage that presupposes the fall of the monarchy and comes to grips with it in the medium of theology. The new idea of revelation initially protected the community against loss of religious and ethnic identity in Babylonian exile. Later, it secured the redefined and reorganized Judaism of the Second Temple a measure of autonomy as a province in the Persian Empire.

The theologization of the law is a step of such breathtaking audacity and far-reaching consequences that it must have taken several decades to establish and consolidate. Two distinctions are essential for understanding the innovative significance of this step: first, the distinction between royal law, monitored and enforced by secular authorities, and divine law, which stands outside the purview of all human institutions; and second, that between justice (or law) and morality (or wisdom). The idea of a tribunal of gods administering divine law was commonplace in the ancient world. In Mesopotamia and Egypt, it was primarily connected with the idea of an all-seeing sun god, and in Egypt also with the Judgment of the Dead (see Excursus IV). In Israel, it was above all the early prophets such as Isaiah, Amos, and Micah who championed God's calls for justice. Here it is not predominantly law that is at stake but morality, social responsibility, care for the under-privileged (widows and orphans, strangers, the poor), covenant faith-fulness, and solidarity: in short, the kind of behavior that cannot be mandated or policed by any earthly judiciary and must therefore be referred to a higher power, to divine omniscience, vigilance, and jus-tice. Everything else—whatever can be mandated, executed, en-forced—is the prerogative of royal law. With the loss of state and mon-archy, however, royal law is integrated into divine law and declared sacrosanct as divinely authorized *ius divinum*. This act of authorization presumably occurred in exile, with the development of the Deutero-nom(ist)ic tradition, and it forms the third, vitally important stage in the drama of revelation. The Covenant Code reveals the traces of this integration in its literary structure. A document of originally profane royal law is framed by socioethical and cultic statutes of divine law and thereby transformed in its entirety into divine law. With that, the ideal of an order of law that transcends state institutions and the vagaries of history comes into being.

The driving force and goal of this transformation is the preservation of autonomy in Babylonian exile and under Persian suzerainty. The so-lution to this problem lay in redefining "ancestral laws" (*patrioi nomoi*) as divine laws, as *lex divina*. Autonomy is realized as theonomy, and liberation from human servitude—from slavery—is realized by serving God. In this way, it was still possible to live in the freedom of divine law while remaining a vassal of the Persian Great King.

Out of Egypt

If the (real) theme of the Book of Exodus is "revelation," why is this theme represented by the departure from Egypt? Whenever an exodus is undertaken, a border is crossed; in the act of crossing, moreover, it is first drawn and defined as the border between the old (which has to be left behind) and the new (which is to be entered and possessed).

333

This new order is the subject of the monumental five-act drama of revelation narrated in the Book of Exodus. By contrast, Egypt stands for the old, abandoned order, the epitome of all that is forevermore to be despised and rejected. Just as a newly liberated Israel defines itself against Egypt, which now becomes the old world of slavery, so too it defines itself against its new environment as the designated addressee of God's revelation. By following the revealed law, Israel becomes the "holy"—that is, the isolated—nation. Egypt offers itself as a multifaceted symbol for what Israel had to leave behind in the course of the revolution recounted in Exodus. This revolution has three distinct dimensions:

1. In the *political* dimension, it appears as a revolt against the political system of ancient Near Eastern sacral kingship and as the birth of God's chosen people, Israel, in a completely new form of political community.

2. In the *religious* dimension, it means abandoning the polytheist—or rather, cosmotheist—system of ancient Near Eastern and Mediterranean religions, which rested on the symbiotic integration of gods and humans in the world, in favor of a completely new form of symbiosis between the one world-transcending God and the one people he has chosen among all the nations.

3. On the level of *intellectual* and especially *temporal orientation*, it means leaving behind a mythic order of time for a historical order of time. Where once the past lay in front of people and the future behind them, with guidance for the present being sought in the timeless patterns of myth, now the past lay behind them and the future ahead of them. This shift takes the form of a pledge: the Promised Land for the forefathers, Paradise for the Christian faithful. The shift can be understood as the transition from *historia divina*, myth as stories about gods, to *historia sacra*, salvational history, a history the god of Israel shares with his chosen people. It involves, first, the founding narrative of the people of Israel, second, the creation of monotheism—the monotheism of loyalty— and third, the radical reorientation for humans in the world, from myth to history in the sign of promise (and disavowal) and loyalty (and apostasy).

In all three dimensions, ancient Egypt is the polar opposite to the new order set out in the Book of Exodus. In no other polity in the ancient world was the principle of sacral kingship realized so comprehensively as in Egypt. The same goes for the principle of cosmotheism, the congruence of god and world, the immanence of the divine and the holy in nature and the cosmos. In no other religion was this principle expressed and theologically reflected in so vast an array of texts and images, such that it continued to exert an influence even after the ancient Egyptian world had passed away and remains to this day indissolubly associated with Egypt. In no other culture's history, finally, were the temporal patterns of mythic thinking—the dominance of cyclical time, the ideal of regeneration, the retrospective orientation to primordial mythic patterns—applied with such consequentiality. Egypt was the clearest manifestation of what had to be left behind if the Israelites were to gain entry into the world of the Bible, with its completely new ideas about God and the universe, humankind and society, time and history. And since these ideas have profoundly shaped the world we live in today, the vitality of the Book of Exodus as the founding myth of that world remains undiminished.

Exodus as Political Myth

In the political dimension, the Exodus story has become the epitome of political myth and a model for ethnogenesis in three respects: first, as "emigration," that is, revolutionary secession from an imperialist or colonial union to form a distinct, independent entity; second, as "election" over other nations in the sense of a special mission; third, as occupation of a "Promised Land" and hence as a primal scene of colonialism. In all three points, the Exodus story became the founding myth of the United States of America: the seventeenth-century Puritans set out for their own Promised Land in the New World in the awareness that, as a new Israel, they had inherited God's promise and the God-given mission to create a righteous society that would be pleasing in his sight. Even today, the USA remains guided by the missionary impulse to spread democracy and the free market to all four corners of the earth. The Boers likewise made the Exodus myth their own when they broke away from the British Cape Colony to found their own state in the interior.

The pathos of exclusiveness and self-separation that animates the Exodus myth also lies behind all the nationalist movements and nation-state creations of the nineteenth century, although here the element of emigration is missing. These were all sustained by an awareness of being unique and having a special mission in the world to fulfill.[4] Max Weber noted that the idea of the chosen people is "somehow" present each time a nation is created.[5] Many of these national myths go back to the Middle Ages. Here, the motif of allochthony or foreign origin also plays a conspicuous role. The Romans had already located their origins elsewhere, in Troy. They identified Aeneas, whose path took him from burning Ilium to Latium (with many detours along the way), as their progenitor. On the same model, the medieval Franks and Normans traced their ancestry back to the Trojans.[6] The name Scotland comes from Scota, supposedly a daughter of the very pharaoh who reigned during the Exodus and came to grief in the Sea of Reeds. As legend has it, she was the ancestral matriarch of the Scots, who migrated to Scotland via Spain.[7] The Polish nobility traced their descent from the Sarmatians on the Persian Black Sea coast.[8]

In its political dimension, the Exodus myth founds a concept of the *people* as a religious idea and thus here too stands opposed to Egypt, which established the *state* as a religious idea. Just as there is no word in Egyptian that could be translated as "people" or "nation," whereas Hebrew offers two candidates, '*ām* und *gôy*,[9] so too the theocratic idea of the divine covenant contains an anti-Egyptian element, critical of the state and all its works, that first comes to expression in Deuteronomy 17 and subsequently plays a recurring role in history, above all in the Puritan Revolution in seventeenth-century England.[10]

Exodus and Monotheism

The religious dimension of Exodus as a founding myth has, if anything, proved even more significant than its political dimension. In this aspect, it presents itself as the founding myth of monotheism. Here it is important to bear an important distinction in mind. Monotheism, as founded by the Exodus myth, does not deny the existence of other gods; on the contrary, it presupposes them. The guiding idea of this monotheism is loyalty: loyalty to the One Liberator from Egyptian captivity, in contrast to the many other gods who seek to seduce the Israelites into bowing down before them. This specific monotheism results from the interlinked ideas of election and the covenant. God chose this one nation among the many nations in order to make a covenant with it, while the Israelites pledge their fealty to this One God among the many gods by entering into a covenant with him. What holds this covenant together is not the natural and indissoluble bond between creator and created but God's fierce love for his people, which he demands that they reciprocate. The covenant is primarily an emotional, affect-based connection, which is why it is expressed primarily in bridal and conjugal metaphors. Entering the covenant requires first having exited something else; in this sense, exodus and divine covenant go together. That is also the meaning of St. Augustine's wonderful saying, "Incipit exire qui incipit amare."

Love and loyalty are inseparably shadowed by their opposites, anger and sinful betrayal. The loving God of the covenant is equally "the jealous, wrathful God" (*'ēl qannā'*), and abandoning him for other gods is the original sin against the covenant. Therein lies the ambivalence of the covenant idea and its grip on the human psyche. This new and unprecedented idea of the divine covenant is what lends the Exodus myth its extraordinary power. The monotheism of loyalty has endured through all subsequent developments and interactions as the dominant element in all Abrahamic religions.

This idea contrasts with the creation-theological belief in the One God by whom all things were made and on whom they all depend in their being. While creation myths would certainly have arisen at an early stage in the Israelite religion, such traditions only took their definitive form with the Priestly version of the Book of Genesis. The Babylonian myths that found their way there attest to the influence of Babylonian and Iranian ideas met with in the exilic and postexilic periods. There is no mention of loyalty and wrath in the Book of Genesis. These motifs relate instead to the semantics of covenant theology and are thus a central part of the Exodus tradition. In Egyptian religion, belief in the One God from whom the whole world arose is bound up with the conviction that this world is home to many other gods, who are no different from everything else in owing their existence to their creator. The "cosmogonic" monotheism we are dealing with here is allied with polytheism. Which one comes into view at any given time depends on whether we are looking at the origin of the world or the existing world. The Israelites, however, transformed the cosmogonic monotheism they encountered among the Babylonians, Egyptians, and Persians into an absolute monotheism that could be made compatible with their monotheism of loyalty. For this new form of monotheism, which I call the "monotheism of truth," the other gods simply do not exist, and worshipping the One God is not a matter of loving faithfulness but of enlightened insight, just as worshipping the other gods signifies folly and blindness.

The Book of Exodus runs the gamut from the most abject misery to the highest calling, from captivity in Egypt to emancipation in God's service, from separation from God under conditions of oppression to union with God under conditions of freedom. The further steps in the Exodus story—the Israelites' wandering in the wilderness and their eventual arrival in the Promised Land—are omitted from the Book of Exodus and reserved for later books (Numbers and Joshua). Entry forms the narratological counterpart to exodus, but in the context of the Priestly Source it takes place with the building of the tent sanctuary, not in Canaan. Strictly speaking, it is God who enters here into a symbiotic relationship with his people. Here, too, an inversion of Egyptian and Babylonian custom is apparent. In these, as in all other cultures of the "pagan" world, gods and goddesses reside in cities and preside over them as tutelary deities. Made manifest in their cult images and statues, they form the stationary centers of a spatial order that is at once local and social. This form of access to the divine, mediated by temples and cult images, is replaced in the Priestly Source by the idea of God's immediate presence. Temple and city make way for tent and camp, while mobility, transience, and fixity of purpose (with the goal of the Promised Land) appear instead of spatial order and fixity of place. Above all, cult images are replaced by God's direct, indwelling presence in the form of his *kābôd* (his "glory") in the cloud, his word, and his instruction (Torah). This form of divine presence is not communicated by images, as in Egypt and Babylon; on the contrary, it is destroyed by them and requires that they be destroyed in turn.

The Priestly Source added this conception of an entrance marking the fulfillment of the departure from Egypt to the Exodus story, simultaneously linking it back to the Book of Genesis. In doing so, it created a far more grandiose narrative arc, extending all the way from the creation of the world to the institution of the Temple and its religion, now elevated to the rank of a second creation (or completion of the first). The Temple of the Priestly Source has assimilated the experience of exile in two key respects. First, in the form of a tent it can be pitched anywhere and is not tied to any sacred site. More precisely, the sacred site is the people themselves: by keeping God's laws and commandments, they make themselves holy, readying themselves for God to dwell in their midst. Second, in the form of the canonic texts the Temple can also be erected in the imagination of the reading and listening community. In this spiritualized form, it safeguards the religion established here against the existential threats and temptations of diaspora. This helps to account for the miraculous fact that the Jews—uniquely among the peoples of the ancient world—succeeded in preserving their ethnic and cultural identity despite two millennia spent scattered over the face of the earth.

With that, there arises an idea of religion that has come to dominate much of the world and has irreversibly transformed it. Founded on revelation, it asserts the liberating force of the truth against time-honored customs and traditions. It demands of believers a commitment that, no longer confined to ritual dealings with the sacred, extends across all aspects of life: justice, everyday routines and practices, holidays and workdays, state and family. Religion now becomes something distinct from "culture," to which it stands opposed as a critical voice, while at the same time claiming sovereignty—at least potentially—over all other "spheres of value" (Max Weber) such as politics, law, the economy, science, and art.

It is in this sense, to return to our starting point, that the Exodus story can be understood as "the most grandiose and influential story ever told." It tells of a radical shift that it itself brought about in the course of its various retellings and reinterpretations, and it has become the narrative template and symbol for fundamental intellectual, religious, and political changes.

NOTES

1. See now Schieder, ed., *Die Gewalt des Einen Gottes.*
1. Freud, *Moses and Monotheism,* 53.
2. Winkler, *Geschichte des Westens,* 25.
3. A. Assmann, *Ist die Zeit aus den Fugen?,* 94.
4. Schramm, *Fünf Wegscheiden der Weltgeschichte,* 50–82.
5. Jacob, *Das Buch Exodus,* divides the book into two halves, each consisting of three parts:
   First Half
      Part One: Ex 1–7:13: From the oppression of Israel to God's call to Moses
      Part Two: Ex 7:14–11:10: The Ten Plagues of Egypt
      Part Three: Ex 11:11–18:27: From Egypt to Sinai
   Second Half
      Part Four: Ex 19–24: Revelation of the law and covenant
      Part Five: Ex 25–34: The sanctuary
      Part Six: Ex 35–40: Construction of the sanctuary
6. Walzer, *Exodus and Revolution.*
7. Koschorke, "Exodus," draws attention to this and many other resonances of the Exodus story.
8. Jaspers, *The Origin and Goal of History.*
9. Metzler, "A. H. Anquetil-Duperron (1731–1805) und das Konzept der Achsenzeit"; Metzler, *Kleine Schriften zur Religion und Geschichte der Antike.*
10. See Eisenstadt, ed., *The Origins and Diversity of Axial Age Civilizations,* as well as the numerous other edited collections in the field.
11. J. Assmann, "Cultural Memory and the Myth of the Axial Age."

CHAPTER ONE: THEME AND STRUCTURE OF THE BOOK OF EXODUS

1. Pope Leo the Great, cited in Tück, "Verborgene Menschheitsreligion?"
2. Tück, "Verborgene Menschheitsreligion?" Tück's sentence refers to God's revelation in Jesus Christ; in my opinion, however, it may equally be applied to Exodus as an act by which God turns to face the world.
3. Görg, " 'Der starke Arm Pharaos' "; Hoffmeier, "The Arm of God."
4. The covenant on Sinai is a matter of covenant theology, not creation theology, even if the Priestly Source gives a creation-theological framework and support to the covenant-theological Exodus story by constructing a narrative arc from Genesis 1 to Exodus 25

and beyond. That emerges with all clarity from God's self-description as the one "who brought you out of the land of Egypt, the house of bondage." Covenant and law presuppose liberation and election, but not creation.

5. Hinduism is also based on sacred texts and differentiates here between "what is heard" (*smrti*), which is of greater canonicity, and "what is remembered" (*śruti*), which is of lesser. The Hindu concept of "what is heard" has nothing in common with the biblical idea of a one-off, all-surpassing revelation, however.

6. See Bark, *Ein Heiligtum im Kopf.*

7. "Within the Priestly Source, the form of God's presence becomes ever more differentiated over the course of the narrative. In the primal history, God speaks directly with the actors, in the tales of the forefathers he descends from heaven and then reascends (e.g., Gen 17), and from Ex 16 he appears in the mode of the *kābôd.*" Letter from Konrad Schmid; see also Schmid, "Der Sinai und die Priesterschrift."

8. The chapter division goes back to Stephen, Bishop of Canterbury, 1205, and was adopted by the Jewish Masoretes. The verse breaks are the work of the Humanist publisher Henri Estinenne, 1551. The Masoretes organized the Bible into divisions (Parashijot Petuchot, Abk: Pe) and subdivisions (Parashijot Stumot, Samech). These are not identical with the conventional verse breaks of Christian origin. Information from Daniel Krochmalnik.

9. In Babylon, Marduk built the great temple Esangila as the crown of all creation. In Egypt, temples stand on the "primal mound," the first hill to appear once the great floodwaters started to recede.

CHAPTER TWO: THE HISTORICAL BACKGROUND

1. H. Blumenberg, *Lebensthemen*, 95.

2. A source frequently cited in this context is the letter of an Egyptian border official: Pap. Anastasi VI 51–61 (Gardiner, *Late-Egyptian Miscellanies*, 76–77; Helck, *Beziehungen Ägyptens zu Vorderasien*, 274; Weippert, *Textbuch*, 171–173); see also the "journal of a border official," pap. Anastasi III 6:1–5:9 (Weippert, *Textbuch*, 165–168). There it is a question of groups of nomads who migrate to Egypt with their cattle as a result of drought or famine.

3. Freud, *Moses and Monotheism.*

4. Krauss, *Das Moses-Rätsel.*

5. Knauf, *Midian.*

6. Finkelstein, *The Bible Unearthed*; Dever, *Who Were the Early Israelites?*

7. See in particular Keel, *Göttinnen, Götter und Gottessymbole.*

8. See van Seters, *Hyksos*; Bietak, *Avaris, the Capital of the Hyksos*; Schneider, *Ausländer in Ägypten.*

9. Stadelmann, "Die 400-Jahr Stele"; Stadelmann, "Vierhundertjahrstele."

10. Redford, "The Hyksos Invasion in History and Tradition," has argued for a connection between the four- hundred-year stele and Genesis 15:13 as well as the Hyksos invasion. Stadelmann has argued against it, unconvincingly in my view.

11. Pap. Sallier 1 (Apophis and Sekenenre) 1:2–3, in Gardiner, *Late-Egyptian Stories*, 85; Goedicke, *The Quarrel of Apophis and Seqenenre*, 10–11.

12. Urk VI, 7:15–16.

13. The "marriage" with his sister Nephthys is an apocryphal tradition that plays no special role in either cultic practice or mythology.

14. Brinkschröder, *Sodom als Symptom*, 199.

15. See Gager, *Moses in Greco-Roman Paganism*, 30–31.

16. See Stern, *Greek and Latin Authors*, 1:97–98. On the imputation of a donkey cult, see Stricker, "Asenarii I," "Asenarii II," "Asenarii III," "Asenarii IV"; Bickerman, "Ritualmord und Eselskult"; Bori, *The Golden Calf, and the Origins of the Anti-Jewish Controversy*, 102–113; Schäfer, *Judenhass und Judenfurcht*, 56–57.

17. *Aegyptii pleraque animalia effigiesque compositas venerantur, Iudaei mente sola unumque numen intellegunt: profanos, qui deum imagines mortalibus materiis in species hominum effingunt; summum illud et aeternum neque imitabile neque interiturum*: Tacitus, *Historiae* 5.5.4 = Stern, *Greek and Latin Authors*, 2:19–20.

18. Plutarch, *De Iside et Osiride* 31.9, 363 C–D = Babbitt, *Plutarch's Moralia V*; Griffiths, *Plutarch's De Iside et Osiride*, 418–419.

19. Veltri, *Eine Tora für den König Talmai*.

20. Stern, *Greek and Latin Authors*, 1:66–77.

21. Manetho apud Josephus, *Contra Apionem* 82–83. Waddell omits this passage as a later gloss and thereby arrives at the bizarre idea that Josephus held the equation of the Hyksos with the "Arabs" to be more probable than that with the Jews (196–197)—which would disqualify his entire chronological argument. Bernhard Lang has alerted me to the fact that the most recent English translation of Josephus, *Contra Apionem*, which contains a detailed commentary on this section, also treats *C. Ap.* 83 as an interpolation; see Flavius Josephus, *Against Apion*, 56–57.

22. J. Assmann, "Akhanyati's Theology." In his opera *Akhnaten*, Philip Glass has his chorus sing verses from Psalm 104 in Hebrew after Akhnaten (countertenor) sings the Great Hymn.

23. Here I follow Q (11QPsᵃ frag. E), where *rûḥākā*, "thy breath," appears instead of the Masoretic text's *rûḥām*, "their breath." *Rûḥām* can be translated as "thy breath" as well, however, according to Dahood, *Psalms III*, 101–150, if the *m* is understood as an "enclitic mem," which frequently replaces the suffix –*k* in the parallelism membrorum so as "to avoid parallelistic monotony."

24. See recently Krüger, *Das Lob des Schöpfers*. For a contrasting view, see Keel, *Geschichte Jerusalems*, 1:281–284.

25. That must be emphasized against Heinrich August Winkler, who begins his history of the West with Akhenaten. In principle, however, the idea of starting a history of the West with the prophetic monotheism of the Bible, rather than with Homer and Plato, is splendid.

26. Loretz, *Habiru-Hebräer*; Jericke, *Hebräer/Ḫ'apiru*.

27. See Dever, *Who Were the Early Israelites?*; Donner, *Geschichte des Volkes Israel*, 70–71.

28. Hendel, "The Exodus in Biblical Memory"; Hendel, "The Exodus as Cultural Memory."

29. See Lang, "Von der kriegerischen zur nativistischen Kultur."

30. See Finkelstein, *Das vergessene Königreich*, 31–32.

31. Hornung, "Die Israelstele des Merenptah"; Fecht, "Die Israelstele des Merenptah"; Weippert, *Textbuch*, 168–171.

32. Finkelstein, *The Bible Unearthed*; Keel, *Geschichte Jerusalems*. To be sure, this statement stands in need of modification. There are significant differences between the material culture of those who settled the hill country of northern Judea (in whom we can discern the beginnings of Israel in the 12th and 11th centuries) and the other inhabitants of Canaan. In particular, there are significant discrepancies in their pottery, domestic architecture, and burial rites. This does not suggest, however, that they originated elsewhere, only that they differentiated themselves culturally from their neighbors.

33. Pfeiffer, *Jahwes Kommen von Süden*, takes issue with this interpretation, arguing for an origin in the Northern Kingdom. However, convincing objections are offered by Leuenberger, "JHWHs Herkunft aus dem Süden."

34. Othmar Keel has drawn my attention to the fact that, although there are numerous Palestinian place names containing divine names like Baʿal, Astarte, Shemesh, etc., there is none associated with YHWH. This further suggests that YHWH was not an indigenous god and that the motif of his foreign origin has more than symbolic significance.

35. See Becker, "Von der Staatsreligion zum Monotheismus." With regard to Persian-era Judea, Becker prefers to speak of "post-statehood" rather than "sub-statehood." The concept of poststatehood does not quite capture the situation, however. The parallel between the Theban and Jerusalem theocracies lies precisely in their substatehood. Both function within the bounds of an overarching state organization: the Persian Empire and the Transeuphratene satrapy in Judea and the Tanitic or Saitic kingdom in Egypt. I have Konrad Schmid to thank for the reference to Oswald, "Auszug aus der Vasallität."

36. In ancient Near Eastern warfare, horses were not used for riding but were harnessed to chariots instead. That is why, in recent times, the phrase *sûs wĕrōkĕbô* has generally been translated as "horse and charioteer." For all that, equestrian figures were very popular in Israelite-Jewish craftwork during Ice Age II C (last third of the 8ᵗʰ century to early 6ᵗʰ century). Some 119 exemplars have been found in Jerusalem alone! See Keel, *Göttinnen, Götter und Gottessymbole*, 390–401.

37. Luiselli, *Die Suche nach Gottesnähe*.

38. Berlin Stele 20377, ÄHG No. 148.

39. Bergson, *Materie und Gedächtnis*, 148.

40. The story of the northern tribes' secession is told in 1 Kings 12–14.

41. 1 Kings 14:25–26; see Schipper, *Israel und Ägypten*, 117–132; Keel, *Geschichte Jerusalems*, 1:339–344.

42. Crüsemann, *Bewahrung der Freiheit*, 108; Kessler, *Ägyptenbilder*.

43. Finkelstein, *Das vergessene Königreich*, 52–56; Tilly and Zwickel, *Religionsgeschichte Israels*.

44. On the purely literary character of the Jeroboam narrative, see Galvin, *Egypt as a Place of Refuge*, 92–114.

45. See Särkiö, *Exodus und Salomo*; Särkiö, "Concealed Criticism of King Solomon."

46. Debus, *Die Sünde Jerobeams*.

47. Keel, *Geschichte Jerusalems*, 2:1002–1027; Lux, "Der Zweite Tempel," 158–159.

48. See also Schramm, *Fünf Wegscheiden der Weltgeschichte*, 50–82.

49. See Lang, "Die Zahl Zehn und der Frevel der Väter."

CHAPTER THREE: TEXTUAL HISTORY AND THE HISTORY OF MEANING

1. See the excellent overview of the situation in Weimar, "Priesterschrift." Weimar favors the first interpretation. See also Nihan and Römer's overview in Römer, ed., *Einleitung in das Alte Testament*, 138–164. Gertz, *Tradition und Redaktion*, would also prefer to understand P as a "source" rather than as a redactional stage. However, he also shows that, in the text we have before us, P offers a continuous narrative whereas the non-P sources are only present in fragments. What could be more logical than to assume that P itself incorporated these preexisting sources?

2. See, for example, the construction of a "Jerusalem History" in Zenger, *Einleitung in das Alte Testament*, 120–129.

3. See Römer, ed., *Einleitung in das Alte Testament*, 148–151. Israel Finkelstein also contends "that both blocks—Patriarchs and Exodus—were combined at a relatively late stage by a Priestly author." Finkelstein, *Das vergessene Königreich*, 168.

4. Voegelin, "Historiogenesis", in *Anamnesis*, 79–116.

5. See A. Assmann and J. Assmann, eds., *Kanon und Zensur*, 11–15.

6. Much the same holds true for aesthetic texts—poetry and belles-lettres—whose beauty is inseparable from their textual form.

7. See van den Toorn, *Scribal Culture*, and especially Carr, *Writing on the Tablet of the Heart*.

8. See Fishbane, *Biblical Interpretation*.

9. See Oz, *Jews and Words*.

10. Yerushalmi, *Usages de l'oubli*, 15.

11. Keel, *Geschichte Jerusalems*, 2:1125.

12. Josephus, *Contra Apionem* 2.22.

13. A. Assmann, "Im Dickicht der Zeichen."

14. This discovery by Julius Wellhausen is widely accepted today; see Becker, "Julius Wellhausens Sicht des Judentums."

15. Becker ("Das Exodus-Credo," 83) writes: "references to Exodus in the prophetic literature cannot be dated to preexilic times with any certainty. The relevant passages in Amos (2:10; 3:1; 9:7) have since been found to be later additions, and Hos 11; 12:10 and 13:4 (cf. 8:13; 9:3–4) should probably also be excised from the preexilic testimony." Yet Becker equally holds that the Exodus myth had "its home in the Northern Kingdom of Israel [. . .], where it arose as a national founding myth" ("Das Exodus-Credo," 86). In my opinion, then, there are no good reasons for abandoning the early dating of references to the Exodus myth in Hosea and Amos.

16. Becker, "Das Exodus-Credo," 88–89, makes this case particularly strongly.

17. This was already impressively demonstrated by von Rad, "Das formgeschichtliche Problem des Hexateuch."

18. Linked to this in Hosea is the threat that the people will have to return to slavery in Egypt due to their unrighteousness, disobedience, and disloyalty to the covenant (8:13; 9:3; 11:5).

19. Lang, "Leviten."

20. In the form (Pa'-di-'El) the name is attested in a papyrus from Saqqara (pSQ FAM, 395). Further Egyptian names among the Levites include Merari, Hophnui, Hanamel, and Pashhur.

21. Eckart Otto ("Mose und das Gesetz") and Jan Christian Gertz ("Mose und die Anfänge") advocate dating it to the Assyrian period.

22. See Assmann, J. "Fünf Stufen zum Kanon."

23. See Keel, *Geschichte Jerusalems*, 1:476–504.

24. Karin Finsterbusch, *Deuteronomium*, dates Deuteronomy to the period of exile, taking the Josianic reform and the tale of the chance discovery of the book (2 Kings 22) to be works of fiction. See, however, Keel, *Geschichte Jerusalems*, 1:519–598, who presents historical, archaeological, and philological arguments for the historicity of the measures to purify religious practice introduced by Josiah and, more generally, adduces a religious and cultural transformation under his rule.

25. I have Bernhard Lang to thank for referring me to Moberly, *The Old Testament of the Old Testament*. In Moberly's view, Genesis represents the "Old Testament" of the Pentateuch, with the remainder (Exodus through Deuteronomy) forming the "New Testament." The analogy is a suggestive one, albeit unsatisfactory so far as the compositional

history of the text is concerned. With Exodus, the real history anticipated and promised in the Book of Genesis commences, just as (from a Christian point of view) the Old Testament comes to fulfillment in the New. I join Albert de Pury, Thomas Römer, Konrad Schmid, Bernhard Lang, and others, however, in understanding Genesis as a response and alternative to Exodus rather than as its precursor.

26. Galvin, *Egypt as a Place of Refuge.*

27. See Schmid, *Erzväter und Exodus.*

28. It also sticks out owing to the fact that it is Moses who seeks to establish contact here, not God (as in all other instances): after his failed first appearance before Pharaoh, Moses "returned unto the Lord" (5:22). Where did he go? Not back to Sinai, surely? The "tent of meeting" that could allow Moses to make contact with God does not yet exist.

29. Douglas, *In the Wilderness; Thought Styles; Jacob's Tears.*

30. See Morton Smith, *Palestinian Parties and Politics,* 102. In the conflict between the "pious layman" Nehemiah and the Priestly establishment, Smith sees the origins of a conflict that continues with the Maccabees, Essenes, Pharisees, early Christians, and Reformers.

31. Kristeva, *Revolution in Poetic Language,* 86–88.

32. H. Blumenberg, *Lebensthemen,* 95.

33. On the theory of cultural memory, see A. Assmann, *Erinnerungsräume;* J. Assmann, *Religion and Cultural Memory.* On the side of Old Testament theology, this approach has been ventured by Carr, *Writing on the Tablet of the Heart,* and Hendel, *Remembering Abraham.*

34. Sanders, *From Sacred Story to Sacred Text,* 43–44. Sanders distinguishes between *ethos* (= Halacha) and *mythos* (= Haggadah).

35. See Theissen, *Der Schatten des Galiläers;* Lang, *Jesus der Hund;* Türcke, *Jesu Traum.*

36. The Latin word *biblia* is the plural of the Greek *biblion,* "book."

37. Janowski, "Die kontrastive Einheit der Schrift."

38. See Borchmeyer's presentation of the reception history of Thomas Mann's Joseph tetralogy in his commentary to the New Frankfurt Edition: T. Mann, *Joseph und seine Brüder.*

39. I thank my friend Daniel Krochmalnik for enlightening me on these important points.

40. Hartwich, *Die Sendung Moses;* Goldstein, *Reinscribing Moses.*

41. On Martin Luther King and Barack Obama as Moses figures, see Schieder, ed., *Die Gewalt des Einen Gottes,* 150–174, esp. 165–167.

42. On the "difference between a dialectic of knowing and not-knowing and a dialectic of loyalty and betrayal," see Heinrich, *Parmenides und Jona,* 63–126 (citation on p. 69).

43. Schäfer, *Judenhass und Judenfurcht,* 242–259.

44. Schäfer, *Judenhass und Judenfurcht;* Bloch, *Antike Vorstellungen vom Judentum;* Yavetz, *Judenfeindschaft in der Antike.*

45. Lang, "Der Mann Mose," 66.

46. Jubilees 22:16, in Rießler, *Altjüdisches Schrifttum,* 597; see also Lang, "Der Mann Mose," 66–67.

47. Letter of Aristeas, 139 and 142, in Delling, *Die Bewältigung der Diasporasituation,* 9; Rießler, *Altjüdisches Schrifttum,* 210–211.

48. All too freely translated in Rießler, *Altjüdisches Schrifttum,* 1061: "It is good to combine study of the law with worldly affairs." The saying is ascribed to the famous rabbi Gamaliel, a man of such wisdom that even the apostle Paul sat at his feet (Acts 22:3).

49. Sloterdijk, *In the Shadow of Mount Sinai,* speaks of a "singularization strategy" that separates the One National God from the assembly of gods and the One Holy Nation from the assembly of nations. This is the very strategy that Rousseau recommended to

the Poles so that they might constitute and assert themselves as a national identity. The laws and traditions of ancient Israel were designed "so they could not be blended with those of the other nations; he [Moses] weighed it down with distinctive rites and ceremonies; he constrained it in a thousand ways in order to keep it constantly alert and to make it forever a stranger among other men, and all the bonds of fraternity he introduced among the members of his republic were as many barriers which kept it separated from its neighbors and prevented it from mingling with them." See Rousseau, "Considerations on the Government of Poland," 180. This strategy made it possible for the Jewish people to maintain their identity even under conditions of diaspora.

50. Sloterdijk, *In the Shadow of Mount Sinai*, calls this "total membership."
51. Janowski, *Ein Gott, der straft und tötet?*; Assmann, "Monotheismus und die Sprache der Gewalt"; Schieder, ed., *Die Gewalt des Einen Gottes*.
52. See Lang, "Der Mann Mose," 62-64. The traditional translation, "jealous," is fitting where the covenant is understood as a love contract, as in Hosea, Jeremiah, Ezekiel, and others. See also Lang, "Le dieu de l'Ancien Testament est-il un dieu jaloux?"
53. We need not be overly concerned here by the fact that the Priestly Source, which in linking the books of Genesis and Exodus also brought together creation and covenant theology, then explicitly refers to the creation in justifying the Sabbath commandment and in erecting the tent sanctuary. The genuinely monotheist statement at Deuteronomy 4:35, "YHWH is God; there is none else beside him" (see also 4:39; 7:9), likewise originates in a postexilic textual stratum while still making sense in the context of a semantics of loyalty.
54. On this political notion of love as covenant fidelity and loyalty, see Moran, "The Ancient Near Eastern Background." Moran is able to show that this concept originates in the language of international law and state loyalism, especially as such language characterizes neo-Assyrian texts of the eighth and seventh centuries. Moran emphasizes the striking distinction between Hosea's idea of love and the Deuteronomic conception. In Hosea, YHWH's love for Israel is central, whereas in Deuteronomy Israel's love for YHWH, expressed in faithful adherence to the law, stands in the foreground. In Hosea, love is a sexual metaphor, whereas in Deuteronomy it designates the thing itself: fidelity to the covenant. On the basis of strong affinities with the loyalty oath texts of Esarhaddon, several scholars (including Otto, *Das Deuteronomium*; Steymans, *Deuteronomium 28*; Steymans, "Die literarische und historische Bedeutung"; C. Koch, *Vertrag*, have pushed the first version of Deuteronomy back into preexilic (Josianic) times, in keeping with the legend of the discovery of the book of Moses during Josiah's reign (see 2 Kings 22–23). By contrast, Finsterbusch, *Deuteronomium*, places even the original version in the period of exile. See also Rüterswörden, *Deuteronomium*.
55. Othmar Keel has drawn particular attention to the theological problem that, through the transposition of the Assyrian loyalty oath model onto YHWH, the cruel, intolerant features of Assyrian royal ideology were also added to the Deuteronomist image of God (see Keel, *Geschichte Jerusalems*, 1:562–563, with reference to Deut 13). In Deuteronomy 13:7–12 it is stipulated that a man should denounce his own brothers, his own children, his own wife, if they secretly incite him to abandon YHWH. See the corresponding passage in the Assyrian template: "Should you hear a wicked, bad, inappropriate word, that is not fitting, not good, for Ashurbanipal, the crown prince [...], from the mouth of your brothers, your sons, your daughters [...] and keep quiet about it [...]" (Otto, *Das Deuteronomium*, 3–4). These are cruel texts that cannot be glossed over by recalling instances of YHWH's goodness and mercy.
56. This important observation was made by Westermann, "Boten des Zorns."

57. Lactantius, *L. Caelii Firmiani Lactantii De Ira Dei Liber.*
58. Lactantius, *De ira Dei* 11.15.
59. See, above all, Keel, "Die Heilung des Bruchs"; Keel, *Geschichte Jerusalems,* 1:575; Staubli, "Antikanaanismus."
60. Lohfink, "Gewalt und Monotheismus," is representative of the many who have disagreed with me on this point.
61. "Holy war" is not a biblical concept. For this reason Albertz, ed., *Geschichte und Theologie,* 122–127, favors the term "Yahweh war."
62. Sa-Moon, *Divine War in the Old Testament;* von der Way, *Göttergericht und "heiliger Krieg";* Lang, *Buch der Kriege—Buch des Himmels;* R. Schmitt, *Der "Heilige Krieg" im Pentateuch.*
63. Molke, *Der Text der Mescha-Stele;* Weippert, *Textbuch,* 242–248.
64. Keel, *Geschichte Jerusalems,* 1:573.
65. Keel, *Geschichte Jerusalems,* 1:575, with reference to Levenson, "Is There a Counterpart?"
66. I am not certain whether it is appropriate to speak of anti-Canaanism in Hosea. Hosea does not turn against Canaanite religion as such but against the religion of Israel insofar as it has been tainted or contaminated by Canaanite influence. He has no interest in driving out or annihilating the Canaanites themselves, even if he will have no truck with their deities. Authentic, fierce anti-Canaanism first appears in Deuteronomy and the *Exodus narrative (stage 2), influenced by Deuteronomy and the Deuteronomist school. According to Hosea, the Israelites should return to the wilderness in order to recover the lost purity of their religion.
67. Keel refers to Ferdinand Deist, "The Dangers of Deuteronomy."
68. Keel has drawn particular attention to this point; see esp. Keel, "Der zu hohe Preis der Identität."
69. Keel, "Der zu hohe Preis der Identität," 96–97; Keel, "Leben aus dem Wort Gottes?"

PART TWO: THE EXODUS

1. J. S. Bach, Cantata 70 ("Watch! Pray! Pray! Watch!"), words by Salomon Franck, 1716.
2. Walzer, *Exodus and Revolution,* 149.

CHAPTER FOUR: THE TRIBULATIONS OF THE ISRAELITES
AND THE BIRTH OF THE SAVIOR

1. "Les deuils valent mieux que les triomphes, car ils imposent des devoirs, ils commandent l'effort en commun"; Renan, "Qu'est-ce qu'une nation?"
2. This description of the Hebrew population explosion has something animalistic about it and makes the Egyptians' increasing alarm seem understandable. Because the text offers six words at this juncture (*pārû, yišrĕṣû, yirbû, ya'aṣmû,* and twice *mĕ'ōd,* "very"), the medieval Jewish commentaries concluded that the Hebrew women all bore sextuplets. The commandment to go forth and multiply given in Genesis 1:28 and 9:1 uses the imperative, *pĕrû ûrĕbû ûmil'û 'et-hā'āreṣ,* "be fruitful, and multiply, and replenish the earth." Here God is keeping the promise made to Abraham in Genesis 17: *wĕ'arbeh 'ôtĕkā,* "and I will multiply thee" (17:2), *wĕhiprētî 'ōtĕkā,* "and I will make thee fruitful" (17:6) each time with the addition, *bim'ōd mĕ'ōd,* "exceedingly." In 35:11, the same promise is renewed to Jacob: "I am El Shaddai, be fruitful and multiply," *pĕrēh ûrĕbēh.* In 28:14, we read, "And thy seed shall be as the dust of the earth." On *šāraṣ,* "teem" or

"multiply," Konrad Schmid writes (in a letter): "*Šāraṣ* is applied to human beings only in Gen 9:7, where God says to Noah and his sons, 'And you, be ye fruitful, and multiply; bring forth abundantly (*šāraṣ*) on the earth.' If you compare the situation of Noah's family after the flood with that of Jacob's clan of seventy when they move to Egypt, it's easy to see how the flow of the narrative calls for a rapid increase in population. The whole earth has to be replenished from Noah's family (Gen 10), just as Jacob's small brood has to become a great and mighty people within just a few verses. The increase in the Israelite population in Egypt is no less divinely ordained a process than the earth's repopulation following the flood."

3. This translation, instead of "more and mightier than we," following Leibowitz, *Studies in Shemot*, 1:25.

4. "Let us be wise together" (*nithakkĕmâ*). Wisdom, in this context, consists in taking measures that conceal their genocidal intent and only resorting to outright violence once these measures have proven ineffective. In her commentary, Nehama Leibowitz reads this text in the light of the Holocaust.

5. *'ālâ min-hā'āreṣ*, "get up out of the land," not "take control of the land."

6. See Leviticus 25:43: "Thou shalt not rule over him [a Hebrew slave] with rigor [*bĕpārek*]." This is the only other occurrence of the word *pārek* apart from Exodus 1.

7. My thanks to Daniel Krochmalnik, who drew my attention to the fatal echo of Nietzsche's "slave morality" in the word "slavery." "We need," he writes, "to imagine a form of service that is ennobling, not degrading—and the right expression for this is not 'slavery'."

8. See Hardmeier, "Die Erinnerung an die Knechtschaft." Sarna has collated the key passages in *Exploring Exodus*, 4–5.

9. See also Deuteronomy 10:19: "Love ye therefore the stranger: for ye were strangers in the land of Egypt."

10. See von Rad, "Das formgeschichtliche Problem des Hexateuch," 11–20.

11. Allochthony is the opposite of autochthony and refers to immigration and foreign origin. "Homeland" is taken here to be a question of self-determination, not origin.

12. Van Houten, *The Alien in Israelite Law*; Bultmann, *Der Fremde im antiken Juda*; Ramirez-Kidd, *Alterity and Identity*; Otto, *Gottes Recht als Menschenrecht*, 239–247.

13. J. Assmann, ed., *Gerechtigkeit*; Janowski, *Die rettende Gerechtigkeit*; Smit, "Justification and Divine Justice."

14. Dörrie, *Leid und Erfahrung*.

15. For this concept and its counterpart, "remediation," Aleida Assmann refers to Bolter, *Remediation*; Grusin, "Premediation."

16. A. Assmann, "Impact and Resonance."

17. Leibowitz, *Studies in Shemot*, 1:8.

18. Rifkin, *The Empathic Civilization*.

19. Presumably a term for the pair of bricks on which Egyptian women squatted while giving birth.

20. *kî-ḥāyôt* implies that there is something animalistic about the Hebrew women, as captured in Martin Buber's translation, *tierlebig*.

21. Verses 20–21 relate how God rewarded the midwives with prosperity and "houses" (= descendants). Given that the narrative otherwise has God enter the story only in chapter 3, I take these two verses to be a later addition intended to emphasize the good deed of the two midwives. In doing so, however, it interferes with the significant motif of God's silence during the long period of Egyptian captivity, as well as the breaking of that silence in chapter 3.

22. On the discussion of this question in the Jewish tradition, see Leibowitz, *Studies in Shemot*, 1:31–38. Josephus assumes the midwives to be Egyptian, and a Midrash includes them among the holy women among the heathen, along with Hagar, Zipporah, Pharaoh's daughter, Ruth, and Jael. These commentators read "midwives of the [= for the] Hebrews" instead of "Hebrew midwives." Konrad Schmid writes: "Ex 1:22 makes clear that the execution order would be carried out by Egyptians. It is also highly unlikely that 'Hebrew midwives' would be entrusted with the task of murdering their own people's children. Moreover, Ex 1:19 suggests that the midwives ordinarily tended to Egyptian women."

23. In honor of their good deeds, the Brandeis Hillel Foundation set up the Shiphrah and Puah Award. "Fear of God" (*yirat 'ĕlōhîm*) is precisely what Abraham assumed the Egyptians lacked when he took the precaution of presenting Sarah to them as his sister.

24. Sloterdijk, *In the Shadow of Mount Sinai*, chapter 4.

25. See Albertz, *Exodus 1–18*, 48–52.

26. *ṭôb*, actually "good."

27. The Hebrew word *tēbâ* is a loanword from the Egyptian (*db'.t*), where it means "box, coffin, sarcophagus." In the Bible it appears only here and in Genesis as a term for Noah's ark. *Tēbâ* is reserved for Noah's ark and Moses's casket; see also the Greek *thibis*? It is probably no coincidence that both Noah's ark and Moses's ark of bulrushes are buoyant containers. In Plutarch's version of the Osiris myth, moreover, his coffin (*db'.t*) becomes a floating vessel.

28. *gōme'*, "papyrus"—this too an Egyptian loanword (*qm'*).

29. The Hebrew *sûp* is linked with the Egyptian *twfy*, "reed."

30. *śĕpat hay'ōr*. *śāpâ* = actually "lip," like the Egyptian *sp.t*, which is likewise used for "edge, bank." *Yĕ'ōr*, "Nile, river," comes from the Egyptian *jtrw*, "river, Nile." The accumulation of Egyptian words in this passage is striking. This too is a resonance phenomenon.

31. In ancient Egypt, as in the ancient Near East more generally, infants were breastfed for three years; this age is probably what is designated by the formula *wayyigdal hayyeled*, "and when the child had grown up."

32. Cited in Otto, "Mose und das Gesetz," 52–53 (with the transliteration of the neo-Assyrian text) and Otto, *Mose*, 37. See Lewis, *The Sargon Legend*.

33. Konrad Schmid remarks (in a letter): "So much for the current context of Ex 1. Ex 2, however, can also be read as a self-contained narrative, in which case the reason would be that Moses was born out of wedlock." Schmid refers to Otto, "Mose und das Gesetz," 50–59. It seems to me that the textual basis for an extramarital birth is shaky; see Albertz, *Exodus 1–18*, 57. Otto is correct insofar as the meaning of an original *Vita Mosis* is concerned. But if we consider instead the mnemohistorical resonance of the tale of Moses's birth, there can be no doubt that the link between infanticide and rescue has been of seminal importance. Thomas Mann and Sigmund Freud allege that Pharaoh's daughter bore Moses out of wedlock and then passed him off as a foundling.

34. Redford, who in "The Literary Motif" has collected some thirty-two examples of the "exposed child" motif in ancient literature, categorizes them according to the reasons for exposure: (1) scandal, (2) threat to the ruler, and (3) the threat of massacre. The fact that the Sargon legend belongs in the first category while the Moses story (in his opinion) belongs in the third indicates, for Redford, that there is no connection between them. According to Otto, however (see note 33), the Moses story could equally be assigned to the first category.

35. Pap. Berlin 3033 (Westcar Papyrus); see Lepper, *Untersuchungen zu pWestcar*.
36. The motif of prophecy is also found in the Targum Pseudo-Jonathan; see McNamara, *The Aramaic Bible*, cited in Langston, *Exodus through the Centuries*, 18. Here Pharaoh dreams that Egypt is weighed against a lamb and the lamb is found to be heavier. Jannes and Jambres interpret the dream: a child will be born to the Israelites who will one day destroy Egypt.
37. Willi-Plein, "Ort und literarische Funktion," contends that the root *wld*, "to give birth," which recurs throughout Exodus 1:15–2:10, surreptitiously hints at the Egyptian meaning of "Moses" (which would have been familiar to readers). This theory strikes me as farfetched.
38. Diodorus, *Bibliotheca historica* 3.3; see A. Assmann and J. Assmann, eds., *Hieroglyphen*, 33.
39. On Spencer, see J. Assmann, *Moses the Egyptian*, 55–90; J. Assmann, "Das Geheimnis der Wahrheit"; Stroumsa, "John Spencer and the Roots of Idolatry."
40. Spencer, *De legibus*, 157: "Deum voluisse ut Moses mystica rerum sublimiorum simulacra scriberet, eo quod huiusmodi scribendi ratio, literaturae, qua Moses institutus erat, hieroglyphicae non parum conveniret."

CHAPTER FIVE: GOD REVEALS HIS NAME

1. Leibowitz, *Studies in Shemot*, 1:17–19, also links God's silence in the opening two chapters with his naming on five occasions in 2:22–25, even declaring the latter to be grammatically erroneous. As Utzschneider and Nitsche show in *Arbeitsbuch*, 79–80, words of sensory perception (such as seeing, looking, recognizing, hearing) predominate throughout this section, suggesting the sensual immediacy of God's revelation.
2. Janowski reads *yāda'* and translates "manifested himself" (*tat sich kund*), referring to Exodus 6:3, where it says that YHWH "was unknown" to the patriarchs (*Die Welt als Schöpfung*, 183). Likewise Propp, *Exodus*, 1:178, with reference to Ezekiel 20:5 and LXX. This reading would interfere with the parallelism of hearing—remembering and seeing—knowing. Martin Buber also translates "and God recognized" (*und Gott erkannte*).
3. Staubli, "Eines Tages trieb er das Vieh," 10.
4. *Šal nĕālêkā mē'al raglêkā.*
5. *Wayyîrā*', "fear overcame him"—just like Moses in the "burning bush" scene, the same word. It is the terror that grips someone when they know themselves to be in the immediate presence of the sacred. The same word is also contained in the expression *manôrā*', "how fearful."
6. Pascal, *Pensées*, 178–179; translation modified. The text of Pascal's "Mémorial" usually appears as an appendix to his *Pensées*.
7. The motif of fertility appears on only one further occasion: no woman shall have a miscarriage or be infertile (Ex 23:26).
8. *Sinuhe* B81–86; see Weippert, *Textbuch*, 55.
9. Brunner-Traut, *Altägyptische Märchen*, 36.
10. See J. Assmann, *Tod und Jenseits*, 204–212, 299–318.
11. Riedweg, "Initiation—Tod—Unterwelt"; Zuntz, *Persephone*.
12. See J. Assmann, "Myth as 'historia divina.'"
13. See Steck, *Moses und Aron*; Kerling, "O Wort, du Wort"; Strecker, *Der Gott Arnold Schönbergs*.
14. When using the name "Aron," I am referring to the character in Schoenberg's opera; "Aaron" refers to the biblical figure.

15. An addition of the Priestly Source to create a link to Genesis 15 and 17.

16. See Exodus 3:12, *kî-'ehyeh 'immāk*, "I will be with thee"; 4:12, *'ehyeh 'im-pîkā*, "I will be with thy mouth," similarly 4:15; see also Jeremiah 11:4: *wihyîtem lî lě'ām wěānōkî 'ehyeh lākem lē'lōhîm*, "so shall ye be my people, and I will be your God," or in negative form Hosea 1:9: *kî 'attem lō' 'ammî wěānōkî lō'-'ehyeh lākem*, "for ye are not my people, and I will not be your God." That is also how the Talmud interprets the formula: "I will be with you in this trial, just as I will be with you in the trials still to come" (Berakhot 9b, cited in Mosès, "Ich werde sein, der ich sein werde," 75).

17. See Mosès, "Ich werde sein, der ich sein werde." Benno Jacob remarks trenchantly: "God is to be understood historically, not metaphysically" (*Das Buch Exodus*, 73).

18. Nicolaus Cusanus, *De docta ignorantia*, 96–99.

19. Lactantius, *Div. Inst.*1.6; English translation by Fletcher, *The Works of Lactantius*, 15.

20. *Corpus Hermeticum*, Nock and Festugière ed. and trans., 2:321.

21. Plutarch, *De Iside et Osiride* 9 (354C) 9–10 = Griffiths, *Plutarch's De Iside et Osiride*, 130–131, 283–284; Hani, *La réligion égyptienne*, 244–245; Harrauer, " 'Ich bin, was da ist,' " 337–339.

22. Reinhold, *Die hebräischen Mysterien*, 42. In his strange duplication of the inscription at Sais, Reinhold appears to be following Voltaire; see Voltaire, "Essai sur les moeurs et l'esprit des nations," §XXII: "Des rites égyptiens," 103: "Il se serait fondé sur l'ancienne inscription de la statue d'Isis, 'Je suis ce qui est'; et cette autre, 'Je suis tout ce qui a été et qui sera; nul mortel ne pourra lever mon viole.' "

23. Schiller, "Die Sendung Moses." On Reinhold's influence on Schiller, see Hartwich, *Die Sendung Moses*, 29–47, and J. Assmann, *Das verschleierte Bild*. I have edited Schiller's essay together with Reinhold's text and cite them from this edition (Reinhold, *Die hebräischen Mysterien*).

24. Kant, "Kritik der ästhetischen Urteilskraft," 417. Kant's book appeared in the same year as Schiller's essay (1790).

25. Schiller, "Die Sendung Moses," 150.

CHAPTER SIX: SIGNS AND WONDERS

1. The opposite trick—casting a spell to immobilize a snake—is widespread among Egyptian magicians to this day and has often been described and photographed. See Sarna, *Exploring Exodus*, 67–68.

2. Quaegebeur, "On the Egyptian Equivalent"; Quaegebeur, "La designation."

3. The Hebrew phrase *'eṣba' 'ĕlōhîm* (literally: "with the finger of God") is reprised by Jesus: "If I drive out demons by the finger of God [*en daktylō theou*], then the kingdom of God [*basileia theou*] has come upon you" (Luke 11:20). Like the "signs and wonders" that God commands Moses and Aaron to perform before Pharaoh, the miracles performed by Jesus reveal the presence of the kingdom of God. "The Lord shall reign for ever and ever" (Ex 15:18), we read at the end of the demonstrations of divine power in and against Egypt. That is what is being displayed here.

4. The motif of the magic contest is confined entirely to P. See van Seters, "A Contest of Magicians?"; Römer, "Competing Magicians." On the Egyptian background to the contest, see Noegel, "Moses and Magic."

5. Lichtheim, *Ancient Egyptian Literature*, 142–151.

6. Lichtheim, *Ancient Egyptian Literature*, 125–151.

7. See Lepper, *Untersuchungen zu pWestcar*; Simpson, ed., *The Literature of Ancient Egypt*, 14–16.

8. On the categorization of the plagues into three groups of three plus one (the tenth plague), see Greenberg, "Redaction of the Plague Narrative."

9. The Hebrew word *makkāh*, "blow, plague," is postbiblical (e.g., the passage from Pirkei Avot cited above). In today's Hebrew, the "ten Egyptian plagues" are called *'eser makkôt Miṣrayîm*, "Ten Plagues of Egypt." Our word "plague" comes from the Latin *plaga* ("blow," "thrust," "stroke," Greek *plēgē*), entering English via Christianity and the translation of the Bible. It thus has a religious significance ultimately deriving from the plagues in Exodus.

10. Thus, according to Diodorus, Ataxerxes III lost part of his army at Lake Serbonis during his second campaign in 343 BCE (Diodorus, *Bibliotheca historica* 16.46.5). According to the same source, a similar fate befell Antigonos Monophthalmos in 305 BCE (Diodorus 20.73.4).

11. Christoph Berner assigns the second version (drying out of the sea) to the oldest textual stratum and the first version (parting of the sea) to a more recent layer (stage 3); see *Die Exoduserzählung*, 404–405.

12. Poème §123–4 = Chaliand, ed., *The Art of War*, 52. The poem and report of the Battle of Kadesh are traditionally cited using the division undertaken in his edition by Charles Kuentz. For a more recent edition of the hieroglyphic text, see Kitchen, *Ramesside Inscriptions*. See von der Way, *Die Textüberlieferung Ramses' II*; Fecht, "Das Poème über die Qades-Schlacht"; J. Assmann, *Ägypten*, 285–304.

13. Chaliand, ed., *The Art of War*, 52–53; translation modified.

14. Chaliand, ed., *The Art of War*, 53–54.

15. Kitchen, *Ramesside Inscriptions*, 131–133.

16. On this religious significance, see the "proclamations of divine power" genre discussed in chapter 2.

17. Shalev, *Thera*, 129–130.

18. Through these layers of ash, it is possible not only to synchronize widely separated sites belonging to different cultures but also to anchor them in an absolute chronology with the help of scientific dating methods. The dates provided by the natural sciences and by archaeology diverge by a century, however. That has made the Thera eruption one of the most widely discussed problems of archaeology. The Thera catastrophe had earlier been linked to the fall of Minoan culture on Crete around 1450 BCE. Crete lies around 100 kilometers south of the island and must have been badly affected by the catastrophe. That has since been called into question for chronological reasons. The dating of the eruption to 1620 BCE (+ / – 20 years) appears to have been methodologically secured, whereas the archaeological evidence does not permit the end of Minoan culture to be pushed back 150 years. The discrepancy with Egyptian chronology is even more serious. The pumice lumps in Avaris were found in a layer already belonging in the early eighteenth dynasty, a period following the expulsion of the Hyksos that has been dated to around 1530–1500 BCE. 1630–1600 or 1530–1500 BCE: that is the question. To an outside observer, a hundred years here or there may seem too trivial a matter to provoke heated debate. For Egyptian chronology, however, these hundred years present a still insoluble dilemma.

19. Velikovsky, *Ages in Chaos*.

20. Walton, *Diodorus of Sicily*, 281; Redford, *Pharaonic King-Lists*, 281–282.

21. See Stern, *Greek and Latin Authors*, 1:20–44. Tacitus, too, characterizes the Jewish idea of God as monotheistic and aniconic; see p. 198 with note 32.

22. This historically attested personage in the reign of Amenophis III must lie hidden behind the affix "Paapis" in Manetho. See Wildung, *Imhotep und Amenhotep*, 274–275.

Wildung points out that prophesying impending disaster is considered a typical sign of wisdom in Egyptian literature.

23. The name is commonly explained as "Osiris-Sepa." Chaeremon uses the form "Pete-seph," which can only be explained as *P3-dj-Sepa*, "Given by Sepa." Sepa is a minor deity and lord of a small town south of Cairo that the Greeks called Babylon. To Thomas Mann we owe the attractive interpretation of the name as "Osiris Joseph," i. e., "Joseph in the netherworld." The interpretation of the first element as "Osiris" had already occurred in Josephus, *Contra Apionem* §250 (*apò tou en Elioupólei theou Osireos*).

24. Funkenstein, *Perceptions of Jewish History*, 32–49; see Schäfer, *Judenhass und Judenfurcht*, 31–56, who likewise speaks of a "counterhistory."

25. Lysimachos, *Aegyptiaca*; excerpt in Josephus, *Contra Apionem* 1.304–311 = Stern, *Greek and Latin Authors*, 1:383–386.

26. Chaeremon, *Aegyptiaca Historia*, apud Josephus, *Contra Apionem* 1.288–292; Stern, *Greek and Latin Authors*, 1:419–421; Schäfer, *Judenhass und Judenfurcht*, 51–53; Redford, *Pharaonic King-Lists*, 287–288. On Chaeremon, see van der Horst, *Chaeremon*, esp. 8–9 and 49–50.

27. Cited in Gager, *Moses in Greco-Roman Paganism*, 49.

28. Stern, *Greek and Latin Authors*, 2:17–63; Schäfer, *Judenhass und Judenfurcht*, 53–56; Hospers-Jansen, *Tacitus over de Joden*; Redford, *Pharaonic King-Lists*, 289; Heine, "Ägyptische Grundlagen des antiken Antijudaismus." See also Bloch, *Antike Vorstellungen vom Judentum* (with an extensive chapter on the ancient and modern reception of the Tacitus chapter), and Bar-Kochva, *The Image of the Jews*.

29. Tacitus, *Historiae* 5.5.4 = Stern, *Greek and Latin Authors*, 2:19–20.

30. J. Assmann, *Moses the Egyptian*, 43.

31. Meyer, *Aegyptische Chronologie*, 92–95.

32. *Diodorus Siculus*, ed. Oldfather, 222–223.

33. Ryholt, "Egyptian Historical Literature," esp. 236–237.

34. Cairo National Museum CG 34183; Helck, *Urkunden der 18. Dynastie*, 2025–2032.

35. See Gnirs, "Die 18. Dynastie," 42–43; and Fischer-Elfert, *Abseits von Maat*, 39–40 with further references.

36. See Goedicke, "The 'Canaanite Illness'"; Goedicke, "The End of the Hyksos."

37. Singer, *Hittite Prayers*, 58.

38. See Levenson, *Death and Resurrection*; Finsterbusch, "Vom Opfer zur Auslösung."

39. See Bauks, *Jephtas Tochter*.

40. That is justly emphasized by Sarna, *Exploring Exodus*, 81–85.

41. According to the analysis of Christoph Berner, (1) belongs to P and (2) and (3) to Deuteronomist-influenced redactions (see Deut 16:1–7). See Berner, *Die Exoduserzählung*, 267–342.

42. Psalm 111:4 alludes to this: "He hath made his wonderful works to be remembered: God is gracious and full of compassion."

43. Keel, "Zeichen der Verbundenheit."

44. Cited in Otto, *Das Deuteronomium*, 82, in Stefan Maul's translation. I thank both Eckart Otto and Stefan Maul for their valuable support.

45. I use the Hebrew-German Pesach Haggadah edited by Rabbi Michael Shire et al. On the structure and meaning of the Haggadah, see Krochmalnik, "'Du sollst erzählen!'"

46. Shire et al., eds., *Pessach Haggadah*, 36.

47. Advertisement for the journal *Tikkun* in the *New York Times*, March 22, 2002.

48. Middleton, "Conversational Remembering."

49. Goffman, *Frame Analysis*.

50. Shire et al., eds., *Pessach Haggadah*, 14.

51. Shire et al., eds., *Pessach Haggadah*, 12.

52. Pessach is called *zĕman ḥĕrûtēnû*, "the feast of our freedom" (Shire et al., eds., *Pessach Haggadah*, 11). *ḥĕrût*, freedom, is not a biblical word, however. The Bible uses the word *'ăbōdâ*, "service," for Egyptian bondage as well as service unto God. It juxtaposes liberation in serving God with enslavement in serving Pharaoh.

53. Shire et al., eds., *Pessach Haggadah*, 18.

54. A. Assmann, "Vorbei ist nicht vorüber."

55. See J. Assmann, *Das Oratorium* Israel in Egypt.

56. Marx, *Händels Oratorien*, 100. On Charles Jennens, see R. Smith, "Jennens, Charles." See also Koldau, "Israel in Egypt." The premiere took place in the King's Theatre on April 4, 1739.

57. Ruth Smith refers to the war with Spain that lay in the air at the time; but it did not break out until a year later. There was therefore no victory to be celebrated. R. Smith, "Handel's Israelite Librettos."

58. Handel, *The Ways of Zion Do Mourn*, ed. Chrysander. The author of this scripture collection is the clergyman Edward Willes.

59. The chorus, "He spake the word," is based on the Serenata a tre con strumenti by Alessandro Stradella, No. 10, Sinfonia concertata con il concertino della dama . . . , Chrysander, *Händels Werke Supplement III*, 33–35. In Handel's version, two choruses appear in place of the two instrumental groups (Concertino and Concerto). Handel added the demisemiquaver runs to his prototype.

60. Drawing on the Sinfonia No. 1 of the Serenata by Stradella; Chrysander, *Händels Werke Supplement III*, 2–5.

61. See J. Assmann, *Die Zauberflöte*, 336–337.

62. Compare the Chorus, "Help! Help the king" in *Belshazzar*, which expresses the Babylonians' reaction to the writing on the wall and the king's horror.

63. Drawing on the organ fugue HWV 605.

64. See Hirschmann, "Sublime Strokes."

65. See R. Smith, "Handel's Israelite Librettos."

66. Goltz, "Die biblische Gestalt," esp. 20–24.

67. *Evening Post*, April 5, 1739, cited in Goltz, "Die biblische Gestalt," 16.

PART THREE: THE COVENANT

1. Schoenberg, *Moses und Aron*, act 3, scene 1.

2. Schieder, ed., *Die Gewalt des Einen Gottes*, 27.

3. Otto, *Das Deuteronomium*, 378.

CHAPTER SEVEN: THE CALLING OF THE PEOPLE

1. Philo of Alexandria, *De legibus specialibus* 2.2.29.

2. Actually vultures' wings, but known to posterity as eagles' wings. See the chapter "The Eagle Speech" in Buber, *Moses*, 101–108. Vultures have female, maternal connotations, emphasizing protection and care.

3. Following Markl, *Der Dekalog*, 63 (with note 132). The customary translation, "property," says nothing, since the whole earth belongs to YHWH anyway. The word *sĕgullâ* derives from the Akkadian *sikiltum*, the origin of the Latin *sigillum*. It denotes something like a treasured belonging, a jewel.

4. On the meaning of "seeing" and "hearing" in Old Testament anthropology, see Janowski, *Konfliktgespräche mit Gott*, 85–97.

5. Sloterdijk, *In the Shadow of Mount Sinai*, 44.

6. *terra nostra mundi totius est templum*, Asclepius 24; see Cancik, "Tempel der ganzen Welt," 47–48.

7. In the almost 300-page entry on "People, Nation" in Brunner, ed., *Geschichtliche Grundbegriffe* 7:141–431, the biblical concept of a people goes unmentioned. The Bible is similarly neglected in the article "Constitution," 6:831–899. On the political dimension of the covenant, see Walzer, *In God's Shadow*, even if Walzer posits a concept of the political that makes the biblical covenant idea appear as "antipolitics."

8. The book of Job protests against this—in many respects disastrous—construction of the connection between deeds and their consequences.

9. Heine, *A Biographical Anthology*, 435 (Geständnisse): "Now I chiefly honor Protestantism for its services in the discovery and propagation of the Bible. I say 'discovery,' for the Jews, who had preserved the Bible from the great conflagration of the second temple, and all through the Middle Ages carried it about with them like a portable fatherland, kept their treasure carefully concealed in their ghettos. Here came by stealth German scholars, the predecessors and originators of the Reformation, to study the Hebrew language and thus acquire the key to the casket wherein the precious treasure was enclosed."

10. Freud, letter to Lou Andreas-Salomé, January 6, 1935 *Briefwechsel*, 222.

11. Freud, *Moses and Monotheism*, 123.

12. Freud, *Moses and Monotheism*, 105.

13. Quoted in Bein, *The Jewish Question*, 655.

14. Quoted in Bein, *The Jewish Question*, 655–656.

15. The God of Shechem is called *Ba'al běrît*, "Lord of the Covenant": that is a god responsible for ensuring that contracts and pledges are honored.

16. See Schwienhorst-Schönberger, *Das Hohelied der Liebe*.

17. Nietzsche, *On the Genealogy of Morals*, 42–43; translation modified.

18. With his concept of "phobocracy," Peter Sloterdijk also credits the Jews with a pessimistic anthropology (*In the Shadow of Mount Sinai*, chapter 4). That this cannot be the whole truth of the "Sinai Schema" is demonstrated by the continued existence of the Jewish people to the present day. His concept of "total membership" similarly brings to mind the Nietzschean straitjacket.

19. See J. Assmann, *Das kulturelle Gedächtnis*, chapter 5.

20. See the impressive work by Carr, *Writing on the Tablet of the Heart*.

21. 2 Kings 22:3–20; 23:1–3; see 2 Chronicles 34:8–33. See also Diebner and Nauerth, "Die Inventio des spr h-twrh in 2 Kön 22"; Römer, *The So-Called Deuteronomistic History*, 49–56.

22. See, above all, A. Assmann, *Ist die Zeit aus den Fugen?*; A. Assmann, *Das neue Unbehagen an der Erinnerungskultur*.

23. Augustinus, *Enarrationes in Psalmos* (64.2), cited in Voegelin, *Anamnesis*, 279–280. The citation reads in full: "Incipit exire qui incipit amare. Exeunt enim multi latenter, et exeuntium pedes sunt cordis affectus: exeunt autem de Babylonia." In Voegelin's free translation: "They begin to depart who begin to love. Many there are who depart and not know it. For their walk of departure is a movement of the heart. And yet they depart from Babylon."

Augustine follows a tradition that interprets the psalm as a song composed by the prophets Jeremiah and Ezekiel when they set out from Babylon on their return to Jerusalem ("In cuius titulo positi sunt etiam duo prophetae, qui illo tempore in captivitate fuerunt, Ieremias et Ezechiel, et cantabant quaedam, *cum inciperent exire*"). Augustine interprets Babylon and Jerusalem in the light of his distinction between *civitas terrena* and *civitas Dei*. Whether a person belongs to one or other of the two *civitates* is determined by love: love of worldly goods (*amor saeculi*) characterizes the inhabitants of Babylon, while love of God defines the citizens of Jerusalem. Whoever loves God begins to depart from the world. Even if what Augustine had in mind here was the departure from Babylon as the epitome of the *civitas terrena* and the entry into the *civitas Dei*, with the keyword *exire* he is moving in the parameters of the symbolically condensed Exodus story.

In his commentary to Psalm 114 (113), Augustine likewise interprets Egypt as a cipher for the secular world that we must leave behind us in order to become citizens of the heavenly Jerusalem, "just as the Israelites could not have been led into the Promised Land had they not previously departed from Egypt" (Heither, *Schriftauslegung*, 35).

24. Assuming that these references to covenant and exodus are not later additions but original prophetic speeches. Becker, "Die Wiederentdeckung des Prophetenbuches," has contested this, as did Nissinen before him, *Prophetie, Redaktion und Fortschreibung*. On bridal and marital metaphors in Hosea, see Zimmermann, *Geschlechtermetaphorik*, 104–112.
25. An allusion to the episode told in Numbers 25; see below, chapter 8.
26. Day, "Yahweh's Broken Marriages"; see also Zimmermann, *Geschlechtermetaphorik*, 104–112 (Hosea), 112–117 (Jeremiah), 117–137 (Ezekiel, Deutero-Isaiah, Trito-Isaiah).
27. Adoption as a son, engagement, and marriage are all images for the covenant as a relationship established through love and free choice, not predetermined by biological, historical, or any other factors.
28. Joshua 9 tells how the Gibeonites acceded to the covenant by pretending to be immigrants (like the Israelites). When it was discovered that they were Canaanites after all, they were demoted to performing menial duties rather than being kicked out of the covenant.
29. Herodotus, *Histories* 8.144. We should bear in mind, though, that "Greekness" as conceived by Herodotus was not a national unit in the political sense but existed scattered throughout the (then) known world in the form of city-states and colonies.
30. Lapinkivi, "The Sumerian Sacred Marriage"; Pongratz-Leisten, "Sacred Marriage and the Transfer of Divine Knowledge."
31. See Schwienhorst-Schönberger, *Das Hohelied der Liebe*; Gerhards, *Das Hohelied*.
32. See Zimmermann, *Geschlechtermetaphorik*.
33. Rikala, "Sacred Marriage in the New Kingdom."
34. In their commentary on the Psalms, Friedhelm Hartenstein and Bernd Janowski place Psalm 2 in the "late Persian or early Hellenistic period," seeing verses 7–9 as an older relic integrated into this late psalm (*Psalmen*, 76–77).
35. In Jeremiah 31:9, too, God looks ahead to the new covenant by calling Israel/Ephraim his firstborn: "For I am a father to Israel, and Ephraim is my firstborn."

CHAPTER EIGHT: TREATY AND LAW

1. Perlitt, *Bundestheologie*, 157. There is broad consensus that the "anterior Sinai pericope" (19–24) belongs among the non-Priestly elements of the Book of Exodus. At issue is only whether the Priestly Source, understood as a source text, dispensed with the pericope entirely or whether, understood as a compositional stratum, it drew on and incorporated the pericope. I follow the second option here.
2. Perlitt, *Bundestheologie*, 158.

3. See von Rad, "Das formgeschichtliche Problem des Hexateuch."
4. In Hosea, *běrît* has no political significance but refers instead to interpersonal relations; see C. Koch, *Vertrag*, 250–251.
5. Steymans, "Die literarische und historische Bedeutung"; Otto, *Das Gesetz des Mose*, 119.
6. On this concept, see my book *Herrschaft und Heil*, 63–71.
7. See C. Koch, *Vertrag*, 252–265.
8. See Janowski, "Jahwe der Richter." On Egypt, see Spiegel, "Der Sonnengott in der Barke."
9. So far as Egypt is concerned, see my book *Ma'at*.
10. Cited in Y. Blumenberg, *"Der Auszug aus Ägypten,"* 175.
11. From Goethe's sonnet "Natur und Kunst."
12. Compare: "And YHWH declared unto you his covenant, which he commanded you to perform, even ten commandments; and he wrote them upon two tables of stone" (Deut 4:13). "These words YHWH spake unto all your assembly in the mount out of the midst of the fire, of the cloud, and of the thick darkness, with a great voice: and he added no more. And he wrote them in two tables of stone, and delivered them unto me." See Köckert, *Die Zehn Gebote*; Peter-Spörndli, *Die Zehn Worte vom Sinai*; Markl, *Der Dekalog*.
13. If we keep to syndetic and asyndetic constructions, then Deuteronomy 5 is a pentalog with the Sabbath commandment in the middle (Konrad Schmid with reference to Köckert, *Die Zehn Gebote*).
14. According to Köckert, *Die Zehn Gebote*, 35.
15. Diesel, *"Ich bin Jahwe,"* 224–238, reads the formula in this way and translates: "I alone am YHWH." According to this reading, the formula is not a self-introduction on God's part but a claim to exclusiveness.
16. Köckert, *Die Zehn Gebote*, 50, translates with reference to a clause in Esarhaddon's loyalty oath (in Manfred Krebernik's interpretation): "You should listen to everything that he [the king] says and do all that he commands and seek out no other king and no other lord besides him." See also C. Koch, *Vertrag*, 143 with note 192.
17. Jacob, *Das Buch Exodus*, 555.
18. Jacob, *Das Buch Exodus*, 561, disputes the translation of *qannā'* as "jealous." In his view, jealousy is "the reprehensible affect of a selfish passion that wants a woman all to itself." Here, it is a case of "aggrieved love" (see Song 8:6–7) and "zeal for the woman's honor." These things should not be seen as mutually exclusive, however. In any event, jealousy pertains to love and not to punitive vindictiveness, an attribute frequently ascribed to the "God of the Old Testament" from the Christian point of view.
19. See Grund, *Die Entstehung des Sabbats*. There is already a discrepancy between the two versions in how the commandment begins. In Exodus we read: "Remember the Sabbath day" (*zākôr 'et-yôm haššabbāt*), whereas Deuteronomy enjoins: "Observe the Sabbath day" (*šāmôr 'et-yôm haššabbāt*). *Šāmar* is the customary word for "observing" (keeping, following, holding, upholding) commandments; a *šômēr miṣwôt* is a Jew who upholds the commandments. In the Sabbath song, *Lěkâ Dôdî* ("Come, my beloved"), reference is made to both versions in the verse, "remember and observe in a single commandment" (*zākôr wěšāmôr bědibbûr 'ehād*). Both verbs are also connected with *běrît*, "covenant." In this connection, the difference emerges clearly: it is God who "remembers" (*zākar*) the covenant and Israel that "observes" (*šāmar*) it. See Grund, *Die Entstehung des Sabbats*, 163, note 86.
20. Furthermore, the justification provided by liberation theology moves the Sabbath commandment too close to the social commandments of human compassion, where it has no place (according to standard Jewish and Christian readings).

21. At most we could think of taboos on working on unlucky days, as encountered in Meso-potamian and Egyptian techniques for identifying propitious (or unpropitious) days. Hemerology, as the practice is called, is prohibited in Israel along with all other forms of divination. It may well be the case that the Sabbath commandment, with its distinc-tion of the seventh day, aims to put a stop to all other ways of distinguishing between days.

22. Jacob, *Das Buch Exodus*, 577. See also Zerubavel, *The Seven Days Circle*. Moshe Idel has drawn attention to the link between Sabbath and Saturn, the planet of the seventh weekday in ancient cosmology; Idel, *Saturn's Jews*. Saturn is associated with the Golden Age, the world turned upside down and melancholy.

23. Grund, *Die Entstehung des Sabbats*, 185.

24. With regard to the ban on coveting, Bernhard Lang writes: "My interpretation is as follows: it is a matter of protecting the entire estate (wife included) of a man who is away from home for long stretches of time, for example on extended trading trips, at war or in captivity. The wife he leaves behind is not allowed to remarry until a given period has elapsed (not specified in the text of the commandment); she is also forbidden from giving away the property of her husband." See Lang, " 'Du sollst nicht nach der Frau eines anderen verlangen.' " In the *Odyssey*, Penelope observes the commandment by awaiting the hero's return for twenty years (a decade of war + a decade's voyaging).

25. This is how Thomas Aquinas, *Summa Theol.* 1–2, qu. 100 "De Decalogo art. 6 re-spondeo," categorized the commands of the second table: "et nulli nocumentum in-feeratur neque opera neque ore neque corde." See Schenker, *Recht und Kult im Alten Testament*, 63, note 93.

26. According to Oswald, "Bundesbuch."

27. The announcement that the people will be led by an angel blatantly contradicts 33:2, where God makes exactly the same proposal only for it to be rejected by Moses: God himself should lead the people (33:12–16). God then agrees to this.

28. See Welker, "The Power of Mercy."

29. On this concept, see Assmann, Krippendorff, and Schmidt-Glintzer, *Ma'at Konfuzius Goethe*.

30. Othmar Keel has drawn particular attention to this aspect; see Keel, "Leben aus dem Wort Gottes?"; *Kanaan —Israel—Christentum*, 10; "Der zu hohe Preis der Identität," 97.

31. Reinhard, *Globalisierung des Christentums?*, 18.

32. See Ilany, "From Divine Commandment to Political Act."

33. In the terminology of the Priestly Source, however, a covenant is not "cut" but "estab-lished" (*hēqîm*), e.g., Exodus 6:4; Genesis 6:18.

34. This is made clear in Jeremiah 34:18–19. Schwartz, *The Curse of Cain*, 21–32, discusses the violence of this rite. On pp. 22–23 she refers to other passages that establish the nature of the rite as self-imprecation.

35. Albertz, ed., *Geschichte und Theologie*, 509.

36. In the terms of speech act theory, a distinction needs to be made between illocutionary and performative acts. In its illocutionary dimension (i.e., the level of intended mean-ing), the Codex Hammurabi can be understood as a codification of established law. In its performative dimension, however, what matters is its success in achieving its in-tended effect, and the Codex did nothing of the sort. While the Codex Hammurabi functioned as a classical work of legal literature, and as such was often copied onto clay tablets as part of scribal education, it never acquired the status of established law.

37. See Vernus, "Les 'decrets' royaux."

38. Mellinkoff, "The Round-Topped Tablets."

39. A. Assmann, "Exkarnation."
40. Pap. Leiden I 344 vso IX.9–X.1 ed. Zandee, *Der Amunhymnus* 3: Tf. pl. 9–10 = ÄHG, appendix 1, strophe 18.
41. Stele of Kuban, ÄHG No. 237, 36–39.
42. On the doctrine of the "living law," see Ehrhardt, *Politische Metaphysik*, 1:168ff.; Goodenough, "Die politische Philosophie des hellenistischen Königtums."
43. In his dialogue on the Statesman, Plato articulates his doctrine of the inappropriateness of laws fixed in writing to a world of human things that is in a constant state of flux. Dead writing can never adequately correspond to this world, only the justice incorporated in the "wise ruler." On this distinction between (written, "excarnated") law and (ideal, "incarnated") justice, see Derrida, "Force of Law."
44. Altenmüller, "Hu"; Zandee, "Das Schöpferwort im Alten Ägypten."
45. Thus we read in Deuteronomy (17:14–20):
    "When thou art come into the land which YHWH, thy God, giveth thee, and shalt possess it, and shalt dwell therein, and shalt say, I will set a king over thee, like as all the nations that are about me; Thou shalt in any wise set him king over thee, whom YHWH, thy God, shall choose: one from among the brethren shalt thou set king over thee: thou mayst not set a stranger over thee, which is not thy brother. [...]
    And it shall be, when he sitteth upon the throne of his kingdom, that he shall write him a copy of this law in a book out of that which is before the priests the Levites; And it shall be with him, and he shall read therein all the days of his life: that he may learn to fear YHWH, his God, to keep all the words of this law and these statutes, to do them: That his heart not be lifted up above his brethren, and that he turn not aside from the commandment, to the right hand, or to the left: to the end that he may prolong his days in his kingdom, he, and his children, in the midst of Israel."
46. Otto, "Vom Rechtsbruch zur Sünde," 48, regards the "measures to protect the weak" in the Covenant Code as the "gateway to an explicitly theological grounding of the law." He further distinguishes between a profane legal code (Ex 21:12–22:1.6) and a "proto-Deuteronomic redaction" based on God's law. The latter forms a theological framework with altar laws and injunctions to show mercy (20:24–26; 21:2–11.13–17.20–27.30; 22:1–2, 9–10, 15–16).
47. Porphyrius, *De abstinentia* 4.10.3–5.
48. From the Abydos stele of Ramses IV, Cairo JE 48 831. Peden, *Egyptian Historical Inscriptions*, 159–174.
49. Varille, "La stèle du mystique Béki."
50. See Merkelbach, "Ein agyptischer Priestereid," "Ein griechich-ägyptischer Priestereid," and *Die Unschuldserklärungen und Beichten*; see also Grieshammer, "Zum 'Sitz im Leben.'"
51. So-called "temple entrance texts"; see Grieshammer, "Zum 'Sitz im Leben,'" 22 ff. (for a list of such inscriptions, see page 22, note 14). Grieshammer refers in this context to Psalms 15 and 24 as "temple entrance liturgies"; see K. Koch, "Tempeleinlaßliturgien."
52. From the inscription Edfou III 360–61 = Kom Ombo II 245.

CHAPTER NINE: RESISTANCE

1. Goethe, "Israel in der Wüste," 229–230.
2. On these scenes, see also Frankel, *The Murmuring Stories*.
3. Römer, "Exode et Anti-Exode," 162.

4. The keyword *lûn*, "murmuring," only appears in Exodus 15–17, Numbers 14–17, and then (in a similar context) in Joshua 9:18.

5. In the original pre-Priestly version of the Exodus narrative, before the interpolation of the Sinai pericope (Ex 19–Num 10:10), these scenes seamlessly followed the scenes of murmuring on the way to Sinai.

6. R. Schmitt, *Der "Heilige Krieg" im Pentateuch*.

7. See Pirkei Avot, an early Jewish collection of sayings that found its way into the Mishnah as a tractate, 5:1–9, where there is a collection of "tens" in the Bible. Following the ten plagues and ten miracles in Egypt, there is a list of the ten "temptations" with which "our fathers tempted God in the wilderness." See also Lang, "Die Zahl Zehn und der Frevel der Väter."

8. See Römer, "Exode et Anti-Exode."

9. See Janowski, "Psalm 106, 28–31."

10. Goethe, "Israel in der Wüste"; see also Hartwich, *Die Sendung Moses*, 95–108. Goethe had already prepared this essay in 1797 for Schiller's *Horen*, although it was not published until 1819, when it appeared in the *Notes and Essays for a Better Understanding of the West-Eastern Divan*. The essay was based on even older sketches.

11. Goethe, "Israel in der Wüste," 230.

12. Strangely enough, this is discussed in our own historically oblivious age as the controversial argument of a Heidelberg Egyptologist.

13. Freud, *Moses and Monotheism*, 80.

14. Freud, *Moses and Monotheism*, 85.

15. Freud's essay "Constructions in Analysis" was composed in 1937, while he was working on the Moses book. In that essay, he compares the techniques by which the psychoanalyst forms a picture of the past from the fragments at his disposal to the reconstructive work carried out by the archaeologist.

16. I maintain this despite the objections of M. S. Smith, *God in Translation*. See also Pongratz-Leisten, ed., *Reconsidering the Concept of Revolutionary Monotheism*.

17. Freud, *Moses and Monotheism*, 128. In a letter to Arnold Zweig dated September 30, 1934, he writes more exactly: "Faced with the recent wave of persecution, one asks oneself again how the Jews have come to be what they are and why they have attracted this undying hatred. I soon discovered the formula: Moses created the Jews. So I gave my work the title: *The Man Moses, a Historical Novel*." Freud and Zweig, *Briefwechsel*.

18. Sellin, *Mose*; see also Schoeps, "Die jüdischen Prophetenmorde." Ernest Jones, *The Life and Work of Sigmund Freud*, 400–401, writes that Freud had been informed by A. S. Yahuda that Sellin had retracted his thesis of Moses's murder. Freud did not place much importance on this and responded: "It might be true all the same." Yahuda's claim is also completely unfounded. On the contrary, Sellin strengthened his thesis with new arguments six years later (in an essay from 1928) and he stuck to it in later publications as well. The only argument he would later retract was his identification of the "suffering servant" in Deutero-Isaiah with Moses, proposing that it instead be applied to Deutero-Isaiah himself; see Sellin, "Die Lösung des deuterojesajanischen Gottesknechtsrätsels" (from 1937). Sellin's richly documented, densely argued text must have left a deep impression on Freud. It still makes for fascinating reading today, not only due to its strong thesis of Moses's murder, which it supports with a wealth of (unfortunately inconclusive) passages, but also because of the immense significance it ascribes to the theme of guilt-ridden historical remembrance—a topic that preoccupied Freud as well. Baltzer, *Deutero-Jesaja*, has revived Sellin's theory that the "suffering servant" and Moses are one

and the same, endeavoring to support it with a plethora of new observations and arguments.

19. Sellin, *Mose*, 49–50.

20. So far as I am aware, the only scholar following Freud to have taken Sellin's thesis seriously, even if he ultimately rejects it, is Lust, "Freud, Hosea, and the Murder of Moses." However, Lust limits himself to a passage in Hosea (12:15–13:1), without considering the many other passages in Hosea adduced by Sellin in support of his thesis, let alone engaging with the great line of tradition that Sellin draws via Jeremiah, Deutero-Isaiah, Nehemiah, and Zechariah all the way to Jesus.

21. See Steck, *Israel und das gewaltsame Geschick der Propheten*, 265 ff., and Schiffner, *Lukas liest Exodus*, 385. Both authors emphasize that Luke situates Stephen in the tradition of Deuteronomistic prophecy.

22. Sellin, *Mose*, 52–53.

23. So far as this group is concerned, Albert de Pury proposed the prophetic circles of the ninth and eighth centuries as well as (drawing on H. W. Wolff and R. R. Wilson) the oppositional landed Levites of the Northern Kingdom. The "Yahweh-alone movement" (Morton Smith) subsequently arose from these circles. See de Pury, "Erwägungen."

24. Sellin, *Mose*, 114.

25. For example, it goes unmentioned in Odil Hannes Steck's 380-page, richly annotated monograph on Israel and the violent fate of the prophets (*Israel und das gewaltsame Geschick der Propheten*), even though both books largely cover the same ground. See, however, Hartwich, *Die Sendung Moses*, 199–202, who discusses Sellin in some detail.

26. M. Bauks (in a letter) refers in this context to van Ruiten and Vandermeersch, "Psychoanalyse en historisch-kritische exegese."

27. The fact that the tradition of the "violent fate of the prophets" is an ideological construct only makes the situation more interesting. As Othmar Keel reminds me, no prophet is recorded as having suffered a violent death.

28. See chapter 9 §2 and Janowski, "'Er trug unsere Sünden.'" Janowski does not mention the link to Moses postulated by Sellin, however.

29. Aurelius, *Der Fürbitter Israels*, esp. chapter 5, 127–202.

30. Freud, *Moses and Monotheism*, 134.

31. Freud, *Moses and Monotheism*, 86.

32. Baltzer, *Deutero-Jesaja*. Baltzer postulates a tradition that commemorated Moses as a man of sorrows who suffered for the sins of his people, a tradition that established a framework for later interpreting and commemorating the death of Christ. See also Aitken, *Jesus' Death in Early Christian Memory*.

33. Baltzer's interpretation has not met with widespread acceptance in the scholarly community, however. For more recent discussion, see Janowski and Stuhlmacher, eds., *Der leidende Gottesknecht*. Konrad Schmid also objects that, "precisely in the Servant Songs, it is clear that [. . .] they refer to different figures, such as Israel (explicitly in 49:3), the prophets themselves, Cyrus, but also Moses. His decision for Moses alone rests on his thesis of the literary uniformity of Isa 40–55." R. G. Kratz has published a forceful—perhaps overly forceful—critique of Baltzer on www.bookreviews.org.

34. The expression "syncretism" or "syncretistic," which has become commonplace in discussions of the preexilic form of the YHWH religion, is not entirely correct. We are not dealing with a mixture of Canaanite religion and YHWH religion, but the YHWH religion customary at the time, which worshipped YHWH as official deity and head of a small pantheon.

35. See Römer, "Exode et Anti-Exode."

36. Steck, *Israel und das gewaltsame Geschick der Propheten*, 125.
37. Steck, *Israel und das gewaltsame Geschick der Propheten*, 133.
38. Steck, *Israel und das gewaltsame Geschick der Propheten*, 110 ff. refers to texts like Psalm 79; Ezra 9:6–15; Nehemiah 1:5–11; Psalm 106; Nehemiah 9:5–37; Tobit 3:1–6; 4QDib-Ham I, 8-VII:2; Daniel 9:4b–19; Baruch I, 15–3:8.
39. On the continuity of Moses, the period in the wilderness, and later prophets and Levites, see Wolff, "Hoseas geistige Heimat."
40. Von Rad, *Theologie des Alten Testaments*, 293.
41. "It is striking that no historical connection can be demonstrated between the sorrowful features of the Deuteronomistic image of Moses and the Deuteronomistic idea of the violent fate of the prophets" (Steck, *Israel und das gewaltsame Geschick der Propheten*, 201, note 4). He refers to the Servant Songs in only two footnotes (16, note 4, and 201–202, note 4).

CHAPTER TEN: THE INSTITUTIONALIZATION OF DIVINE PRESENCE

1. The catalog of ships in the *Iliad*, spanning 275 verses, is comparable in length (2.484–759).
2. This question also preoccupied the rabbinical commentators; see Leibowitz, *Studies in Shemot*, 2:644–653. The great medieval scholar R. Moshe ben Nahman (Ramban, Nahmanides), even counted five catalogs, three summary and two extensive:
    1. The detailed instructions given to Moses (chapters 25–27)
    2. The summary instructions Moses is told to pass on to Bezalel (31:6–11)
    3. The summary demands for contributions from the Israelites (35:5–19)
    4. The detailed reports of the Tabernacle's construction (31:5–37)
    5. The summary approval of the construction by Moses (39:33–43)
    Ramban explains the repetitions with recourse to God's love: the Tabernacle was dear to him as the instrument by which he comes to dwell with his people.
3. See Keel, *Geschichte Jerusalems*, 2:916–944 (with many illustrations).
4. On the expiatory function of the golden panel on the ark, see Janowski, *Sühne als Heilsgeschehen*, 277–341.
5. See Janowski, *Ecce Homo*, 75 ff.; Janowski, *Ein Gott, der straft und tötet?*, 312–315.
6. *Kěrûb* is a Semitic word that also forms the basis of the Greek *gryphos*, "griffin." Keel nonetheless argues for an anthropomorphic being; see the following note.
7. See Janowski, "Keruben und Zion." See also Keel, *Geschichte Jerusalems*, 2:918–923, with copious illustrations from the Mesopotamian and especially Egyptian tradition of anthropomorphic beings standing face to face, with wings outstretched, protecting a deity in their midst.
8. See Keel, *Geschichte Jerusalems*, 2:929–943.
9. On the precedence of time (Sabbath) over space (Temple), see the important commentary provided by Krochmalnik, *Schriftauslegung*, 131–137.
10. Propp, *Exodus*, 2:376–377. See also the many passages—including in the context of Zion theology—where there is talk of God "dwelling" (*šākan*) in the temple. See Janowski, "Die Einwohnung Gottes."
11. Janowski, "Keruben und Zion," 262.
12. Janowski, "Ich will in eurer Mitte wohnen"; Janowski, "Die Einwohnung Gottes."
13. Moses erects an altar in Rephidim following the victory the Amalekites, but it is never mentioned again (Ex 17:15).
14. See also Moberly, *The Old Testament of the Old Testament*, who places great emphasis

on the difference between the world of the patriarchal narratives and "Mosaic Yahwism."

15. Janowski, "Die Einwohnung Gottes."

16. Leibowitz, *Studies in Shemot*, 2:471–486; see especially the list of parallels between the account of creation and the building of the *miškān*, pp. 479–481. See also Janowski, "Die Einwohnung Gottes," 22, and Janowski, "Tempel und Schöpfung."

17. Exodus 25:8; 29:45–46; Leviticus 26:11; Numbers 5:3; 35:34; Deuteronomy 32:51.

18. Janowski, "Ich will in eurer Mitte wohnen."

19. Heinrich, *Parmenides und Jona*, 114.

20. According to a press release from May 24, 2011; see www.elk-wue.de / aktuell / detailan sicht-pressemitteilung / ?tx_ttnews[tt_news]= 28556&cHash=8aa6ce6d26 (accessed November 5, 2014).

21. This turn of phrase interprets the Levites' massacre of their own brothers and sons as a sacrificial offering for YHWH.

22. Schieder, ed., *Die Gewalt des Einen Gottes*, 23.

23. Nietzsche, *On the Genealogy of Morals*, 38.

24. H.-C. Schmitt, "Die Erzählung vom Goldenen Kalb."

25. Mann, *Joseph und seine Brüder*. See Assmann, *Thomas Mann und Ägypten*, 76–83.

26. Uehlinger, "Exodus, Stierbild und biblisches Kultbildverbot," 47–48.

27. Pfeiffer, *Das Heiligtum von Bethel*, 62.

28. On the motif of substitutionary suffering, see Janowski, "Er trug unsere Sünden."

29. Sidur Sefat Emet, English translation in Weinberg, *Patterns in Time*, 168.

30. Philo, *De fuga et inventione*, in Wendland, *Philonis Alexandrini Opera*, 3:146; English translation in J. Assmann, *Moses the Egyptian*, 87. Philo deals with Exodus 33:23 in similar fashion in *De mutatione nominum* (Wendland, 3:157–158), and in *De posteritate Caini* (Wendland, 2:168–169).

31. See my book *Moses the Egyptian*, 122–143.

32. Scoralik, *Gottes Güte und Gottes Zorn*; Franz, *Der barmherzige und gnädige Gott*.

33. The custom of cooking meat in milk or yogurt is already attested for the Canaanite church in the nineteenth century BCE through the Egyptian tale of Sinuhe, and it is still typical of Syrian cuisine today. See H. Fischer, "Milk in Everything Cooked," 97–99. In Lebanon there is even a lamb dish called "milk of its mother" (*laban 'ummu*).

34. Schoenberg, *Moses und Aron*, 291–449.

35. Schoenberg, *Moses und Aron*, 264–267.

36. Cited in Strecker, *Der Gott Arnold Schönbergs*, 134.

37. Schoenberg, *Moses und Aron*, 291.

38. Schoenberg, *Moses und Aron*, 293.

39. Letter to Eidlitz, March 1933; *Briefe*, 188.

40. Schoenberg, *Moses und Aron*, 312–328.

41. Schoenberg, *Moses und Aron*, 329–330.

42. Schoenberg, *Moses und Aron*, 330–332.

43. Schoenberg, *Moses und Aron*, 333–334.

44. Schoenberg, *Moses und Aron*, 349–360.

45. "Orgy of destruction and suicide," 391–436, followed by an "erotic orgy," 437–441.

46. Freud, *Moses and Monotheism*, 112–113; translation modified.

47. Schoenberg, *Moses und Aron*, 454–455.

48. Schoenberg, *Moses und Aron*, 456–457.

49. Schoenberg, *Moses und Aron*, 462.

50. Schoenberg, *Moses und Aron*, 463–478.

51. Quoted in Strecker, *Der Gott Arnold Schönbergs*, 109.
52. Schoenberg, *Moses und Aron*, 478–481.
53. Schoenberg, *Moses und Aron*, 501–502.
54. Regarding the functional equivalence and mutual exclusion of cult image and Torah, Michaela Bauks refers to the essay by van der Toorn, "The Iconic Book," 229–248.
55. For a convincing justification for this dating, see de Pury, "Pᵍ as the Absolute Beginning."
56. But see also Fritz, *Tempel und Zelt*.
57. Bark, *Ein Heiligtum im Kopf*, 21.
58. Lang, "Der redende Gott," 191–192.
59. Quack, "Das Buch vom Tempel."
60. Bark, *Ein Heiligtum im Kopf*, 133–162.
61. A later example of this genre referred to by Quack is the "temple scroll" of Qumran.
62. Bark, *Ein Heiligtum im Kopf*, 48.
63. According to Konrad Schmid, the tavnit passages are probably a later addition in Exodus 25–31; see Schmid, "Der Sinai und die Priesterschrift."

CONCLUSION

1. Freud, *Moses and Monotheism*, 3.
2. K. Koch, "Der Tod des Religionsstifters"; Smend, "Mose als geschichtliche Gestalt."
3. A. Smith, *Chosen Peoples*; Walzer, *Exodus and Revolution*.
4. A. Smith, *Chosen Peoples*.
5. Weber, *Economy and Society*, 391.
6. See Graus, *Lebendige Vergangenheit*, 81–89; here also material on the corresponding Bohemian (89–109), Bavarian (109–111), and Saxon (112–144) legends of origin and ancestry.
7. A. Smith, *Chosen Peoples*, 124–125.
8. See Heynoldt, "Die Bedeutung des Sarmatismus." Sarmatism was also expressed in an orientalizing costume that made the Poles practically indistinguishable from the Turks.
9. See Bauks, "Les notions de 'peuple.'"
10. Pečar, ed., *Die Bibel als politisches Argument*; Pečar, *Macht der Schrift*.

BIBLIOGRAPHY

ABBREVIATIONS

ÄHG   Jan Assmann, *Ägyptische Hymnen und Gebete*, 2nd ed., Fribourg, 1999
BETL   Bibliotheca Ephemeridum Theologicarum Lovaniensium
BN   Biblische Notizen
BZAW   Beihefte zur Zeitschrift für Alttestamentliche Wissenschaft
FAT   Forschungen zum Alten Testament
FzB   Forschung zur Bibel
IBAES   Internet-Beiträge zur Ägyptologie und Sudanarchäologie
JBL   Journal of Biblical Literature
JBTh   Jahrbuch für Biblische Theologie
JES   Journal of Ecumenical Studies
JSOTS   Journal for the Study of the Old Testament Supplement
KuD   Kerygma und Dogma
MDAIK   Mitteilungen des Deutschen Archäologischen Instituts Abteilung Kairo
MIO   Mitteilungen des Instituts für Orientforschung
NGWG   Nachrichten von der Gesellschaft der Wissenschaften zu Göttingen
SE   Ernest Jones, *Standard Edition of the Complete Psychological Works of Sigmund Freud*, 24 vols., London, 1943–1974
SyBU   Symbolae Biblicae Upsalienses
VT   Vetus Testamentum
WUNT   Wissenschaftliche Untersuchungen zum Neuen Testament
ZAW   Zeitschrift für Alttestamentliche Wissenschaft
ZPE   Zeitschrift für Papyrologie und Epigrafik
ZThK   Zeitschrift für Theologie und Kirche

COMMENTARIES

Albertz, Rainer. *Exodus 1–18*. Zürcher Bibelkommentare. Zurich, 2012.
Childs, Brevard S. *The Book of Exodus*. Kentucky, 1974, 2004.
Fischer, Georg. *Das Buch Exodus*. Neuer Stuttgarter Kommentar Altes Testament. Stuttgart, 2009.
Heither, Theresia. *Schriftauslegung: Das Buch Exodus bei den Kirchenvätern*. Neuer Stuttgarter Kommentar Altes Testament. Stuttgart, 2002.
Jacob, Benno. *Das Buch Exodus*. Stuttgart, 1997.
Krochmalnik, Daniel. *Schriftauslegung: Das Buch Exodus im Judentum*. Neuer Stuttgarter Kommentar Altes Testament. Stuttgart, 2000.

Leibowitz, Nehama. *Studies in Shemot Exodus*. 2 vols. Jerusalem, 1981.
Propp, William H. C. *Exodus*. The Anchor Bible. 2 vols. New York, 1999, 2006.
Stuart, Douglas K. *Exodus*. The New American Commentary. Vol. 2. Nashville, 2006.

OTHER LITERATURE

Abush, Tzvi. "Ishtar's Proposal and Gilgamesch's Refusal: An Interpretation of the Gilgamesch Tablet 6, lines 1–179." *History of Religions* 26 (1986): 143–187.
Aitken, Ellen B. *Jesus' Death in Early Christian Memory: The Poetics of Passion*. Göttingen, 2004.
Albertz, Rainer, ed. *Geschichte und Theologie: Studien zur Exegese des Alten Testaments und zur Religionsgeschichte Israels*. BZAW 326. Berlin, 2003.
Altenmüller, Herwig. "Hu." In *Lexikon der Ägyptologie*, vol. 3. Wiesbaden, 1977. 65–68.
Altmann, Peter. *Festive Meals in Ancient Israel: Deuteronomy's Identity Politics in Their Ancient Near Eastern Context*. BZAW 424. Berlin, 2011.
Assmann, Aleida. "Exkarnation: Gedanken zur Grenze zwischen Körper und Schrift." In Jörg Huber, ed., *Raum und Verfahren: Interventionen*, vol. 2. Basel, 1993. 133–155.
———. "Im Dickicht der Zeichen: Hodegetik—Hermeneutik—Dekonstruktion." *Deutsche Vierteljahresschrift* 70 (1996): 535–551.
———. *Erinnerungsräume: Formen und Funktionen des kulturellen Gedächtnisses*. Munich, 1999. English: *Cultural Memory and Western Civilization*, trans. D.H. Wilson. New York, 2011.
———. "Impact and Resonance: The Role of Emotions in Cultural Memory." Lecture held at Södertörn University, May 18, 2011.
———. "Vorbei ist nicht vorüber." *Kulturaustausch* 4 (2013). http://cms.ifa.de/pub/kultur austausch/archiv/ausgaben-2013/zukunft/vorbei-ist-nicht-vorueber/.
———. *Ist die Zeit aus den Fugen? Aufstieg und Fall des Zeitregimes der Moderne*. Munich, 2013.
———. *Das neue Unbehagen an der Erinnerungskultur*. Munich, 2013.
Assmann, Aleida, and Jan Assmann, eds. *Kanon und Zensur. Archäologie der literarischen Kommunikation 2*. Munich, 1987.
———. *Hieroglyphen: Stationen einer anderen abendländischen Grammatologie*. Archäologie der literarischen Kommunikation 8. Munich, 2003.
Assmann, Jan. *Ma'at: Gerechtigkeit und Unsterblichkeit im Alten Ägypten*. Munich, 1990.
———. "Akhanyati's Theology of Light and Time." In *Proceedings of the Israel Academy of Sciences and Humanities*, vol. 7, no. 4. Jerusalem, 1992. 143–176.
———. *Das kulturelle Gedächtnis: Schrift, Erinnerung und politische Identität in frühen Hochkulturen*. Munich, 1992.
———, ed. *Text und Kommentar*. Munich, 1995.
———. *Ägypten: Eine Sinngeschichte*. Munich, 1996.
———. *Moses the Egyptian: The Memory of Egypt in Western Monotheism*. Cambridge, Mass., 1997.
———, ed. *Gerechtigkeit*. Munich, 1998.
———. *Das verschleierte Bild zu Sais: Schillers Ballade und ihre griechischen und ägyptischen Hintergründe*. Stuttgart, 1999.
———. "Fünf Stufen zum Kanon: Tradition und Schriftkultur im frühen Judentum und in seiner Umwelt." In *Münstersche Theologische Vorträge*, vol. 1. Münster, 1999. 11–35.
———. *Herrschaft und Heil: Politische Theologie in Altägypten, Israel und Europa*. Munich, 2000.

———. "Das Geheimnis der Wahrheit: Das Konzept der 'doppelten Religion' und die Er-findung der Religionsgeschichte." *Archiv für Religionsgeschichte* 3 (2001): 108–134.

———. *Tod und Jenseits im Alten Ägypten.* 2nd ed. Munich, 2003.

———. *Die Zauberflöte: Oper und Mysterium.* Munich, 2005.

———. "Monotheismus und die Sprache der Gewalt." In Peter Walter, ed., *Das Gewaltpotential des Monotheismus und der dreieine Gott.* Freiburg, 2005. 18–38.

———. *Religion and Cultural Memory.* Stanford, 2005.

———. *Thomas Mann und Ägypten: Mythos und Monotheismus in den Josephsromanen.* Munich, 2006.

———. "Myth as 'historia divina' and 'historia sacra.'{~?~thin space}" In Deborah A. Green, ed., *Scriptural Exegesis: The Shapes of Culture and the Religious Imagination. Essays in Honor of Michael Fishbane.* Oxford, 2009. 13–24.

———. "Cultural Memory and the Myth of the Axial Age." In Robert Bellah, ed., *The Axial Age and Its Consequences.* Cambridge, Mass., 2012. 366–407.

———. *Religio Duplex: How the Enlightenment Reinvented Egyptian Religion.* Trans. R. Savage. Cambridge, 2014.

———. *Das Oratorium* Israel in Egypt *von Georg Friedrich Händel.* Stuttgart, 2015.

Assmann, Jan, Ekkehard Krippendorff, and Herwig Schmidt-Glintzer. *Ma'at Konfuzius Goethe: Drei Lehren für das richtige Leben.* Frankfurt am Main, 2006.

Augustinus Hipponensis. *Enarrationes in Psalmos.* http://www.augustinus.it/latino/espo sizioni_salmi/index2.htm.

Aurelius, Erik. *Der Fürbitter Israels: Eine Studie zum Mosebild im Alten Testament.* Coniectanea Biblica 27. Stockholm, 1988.

Babbitt, Frank, ed. *Plutarch's Moralia V.* Cambridge, Mass., 1962.

Baltzer, Klaus. *Das Bundesformular.* 2nd ed. Neukirchen-Vluyn, 1964.

———. *Deutero-Jesaja.* Gütersloh, 1999.

Bark, Franziska. *Ein Heiligtum im Kopf der Leser: Literaturanalytische Betrachtungen zu Ex 25–40.* Stuttgart, 2010.

Bar-Kochva, Bezalel. *The Image of the Jews in Greek Literature: The Hellenistic Period.* Berkeley, 2010.

Bauks, Michaela. "Les notions de 'peuple' et de 'terre' dans l'oeuvre sacerdotale (P^g)." *Transeuphratène* 30 (2005): 19–36.

———. *Jephtas Tochter.* FAT 71. Tübingen, 2010.

Becker, Uwe. "Die Wiederentdeckung des Prophetenbuches: Tendenzen und Aufgaben der gegenwärtigen Prophetenforschung." *Berliner Theologische Zeitschrift* 21.1 (2004): 30–60.

———. "Das Exodus-Credo: Historischer Haftpunkt und Geschichte einer alttestamentlichen Glaubensformel." In Becker, ed., *Das Alte Testament—ein Geschichtsbuch?! Geschichtsschreibung und Geschichtsüberlieferung im antiken Israel.* Leipzig, 2005. 81–100.

———. "Von der Staatsreligion zum Monotheismus: Ein Kapitel israelitsch-jüdischer Religionsgeschichte." *ZThK* 102 (2005): 1–16.

———. "Julius Wellhausens Sicht des Judentums." In Martin Keßler and Martin Wallraff, eds., *Biblische Theologie und historisches Denken: Wissenschaftsgeschichtliche Studien aus Anlass der 50. Wiederkehr der Basler Promotion von Rudolf Smend.* Basel, 2008. 279–302.

Beckman, Gary. "Plague Prayers of Murshili II." In William W. Hallo, ed., *The Context of Scripture,* vol. 1. Leiden, 1997. 156–160.

Bein, Alex. *The Jewish Question: Biography of a World.* New York, 1990.

Bergson, Henri. *Materie und Gedächtnis: Eine Abhandlung über die Beziehung zwischen Körper und Geist*. French original, 1896. Berlin, 1982.

Berner, Christoph. *Die Exoduserzählung: Das literarische Werden einer Ursprungslegende Israels*. FAT 73. Göttingen, 2010.

Bickerman, Elias. "Ritualmord und Eselskult." In *Studies in Jewish and Christian History*. Leiden, 1980. 842–857.

Bietak, Manfred. *Avaris, the Capital of the Hyksos: Recent Excavations at Tell el-Dab'a*. London, 1996.

Bloch, René. *Antike Vorstellungen vom Judentum: Der Judenexkurs des Tacitus im Rahmen der griechisch-römischen Ethnographie*. Historia Einzelschriften 160. Stuttgart, 2002.

Blum, Erhard. *Studien zur Komposition des Pentateuch: Zeitschrift für die Alttestamentliche Wissenschaft*. Berlin, 1990.

Blumenberg, Hans. *Work on Myth*. Trans. Robert M. Wallace. Cambridge, Mass., 1988.

———. *Lebensthemen*. Stuttgart, 1998.

Blumenberg, Yigal. *"Der Auszug aus Ägypten bleibt unser Ausgangspunkt": Die verborgene Tradition in Sigmund Freuds Der Mann Moses und die monotheistische Religion*. Frankfurt am Main, 2012.

Bolter, David, ed. *Remediation: Understanding New Media*. Cambridge, Mass., 1999.

Bori, Pier Cesare. *The Golden Calf, and the Origins of the Anti-Jewish Controversy*. Atlanta, 1990.

Brinkschröder, Michael. *Sodom als Symptom: Gleichgeschlechtliche Sexualität im christlichen Imaginären—eine religionsgeschichtliche Anamnese*. Berlin, 2006.

Brunner, Otto, ed. *Geschichtliche Grundbegriffe*. 8 vols. Stuttgart, 2004.

Brunner-Traut, Emma. *Altägyptische Märchen*. 8th ed. Munich, 1989.

Buber, Martin. *Moses: The Revelation and the Covenant*. Oxford, 1946.

Bultmann, Christoph. *Der Fremde im antiken Juda*. Göttingen, 1992.

Cancik, Hildegard. "Tempel der ganzen Welt." In Sibylle Meyer, ed., *Egypt: Temple of the Whole World*. Cologne, 2003. 41–57.

Cancik, Hubert. "Erinnerung/Gedächtnis." In *Handbuch religionswissenschaftlicher Grundbegriffe*, vol. 2. Stuttgart, 1990. 299–323.

Carr, David. *Writing on the Tablet of the Heart: Origins of Scripture and Literature*. Oxford, 2005.

Chaliand, Gérard, ed. *The Art of War in World History*. Berkeley, 1994.

Chrysander, Friderich. *Händels Werke Supplement III*. Leipzig, 1902.

Crüsemann, Frank. *Die Tora: Theologie und Sozialgeschichte des alttestamentlichen Gesetzes*. Munich, 1992.

———. *Bewahrung der Freiheit: Das Thema des Dekalogs in sozialgeschichtlicher Perspektive*. Gütersloh, 1993.

Dahood, Mitchell. *Psalms III*. The Anchor Bible. New York, 1970.

Day, Peggy. "Yahweh's Broken Marriages as Metaphoric Vehicle in the Hebrew Bible Prophets." In Martti Nissinen and Risto Uro, eds., *Sacred Marriages*, 219–241.

Debus, Jörg. *Die Sünde Jerobeams: Studien zur Darstellung Jerobeams und der Geschichte des Nordreichs in der deuteronomistischen Geschichtsschreibung*. Göttingen, 1967.

Deist, Ferdinand. "The Dangers of Deuteronomy." In F. Garcia Martinez, ed., *Studies in Deuteronomy in Honour of C. J. Labuschagne*. Leiden, 1994. 13–29.

Delling, Gerhard. *Die Bewältigung der Diasporasituation durch das hellenistische Judentum*. Berlin, 1987.

Derrida, Jacques. "Force of Law: The 'Mystical Foundation' of Authority." In *Acts of Religion*. New York, 2002. 230–298.

Dever, William G. *Who Were the Early Israelites?* Grand Rapids, 2003.

Diebner, Bernd Jörg, and Claudia Nauerth. "Die Inventio des spr h-twrh in 2 Kön 22: Struktur, Intention und Funktion von Auffindungslegenden." *Dielheimer Blätter zum Alten Testament* 18 (1984): 95–118.

Diesel, Anja Angela. *"Ich bin Jahwe": Der Aufstieg der Ich-bin-Jahwe-Aussage zum Schlüsselwort des alttestamentlichen Monotheismus.* Neukirchen-Vluyn, 2006.

Dietrich, Walter, ed. *Ein Gott allein? JHWH-Verehrung und biblischer Monotheismus im Kontext der israelitischen und altorientalischen Religionsgeschichte.* Fribourg, 1994.

Diodorus Siculus: Bibliotheca Historica I–II.34. Ed. C. H. Oldfather. Cambridge, Mass., 1933.

Döhling, Jan-Dirk. *Der bewegliche Gott: Eine Untersuchung des Motivs der Reue Gottes in der Hebräischen Bibel.* Freiburg im Breisgau, 2009.

———. "Reue Gottes (AT)." In Michaela Bauks, Klaus Koenen, and Stefan Alkier, eds., *Das wissenschaftliche Bibellexikon im Internet* (WiBiLex). Stuttgart, 2006. Accessed December 3, 2015.

Donner, Herbert. *Geschichte des Volkes Israel und seiner Nachbarn in Grundzügen.* Vol. 1, *Von den Anfängen bis zur Staatenbildungszeit.* Göttingen, 1984.

Dörrie, Heinrich. *Leid und Erfahrung; die Wort- und Sinn-Verbindung pathein—mathein im griechischen Denken.* Wiesbaden, 1956.

Douglas, Mary. *In the Wilderness: The Doctrine of Defilement in the Book of Numbers.* Oxford, 1993.

———. *Thought Styles: Critical Essays on Good Taste.* London, 1996.

———. *Jacob's Tears: The Priestly Work of Reconciliation.* Oxford, 2004.

Ehrhardt, Arnold A. T. *Politische Metaphysik von Solon bis Augustin,* vol. 1. Tübingen, 1959.

Eisenstadt, Shmuel, ed. *The Origins and Diversity of Axial Age Civilizations.* Albany, 1986.

Fecht, Gerhard. "Die Israelstele des Merenptah." In Manfred Görg, ed., *Fontes atque pontes: Festschrift Hellmut Brunner.* Wiesbaden, 1983. 106–138.

———. "Das Poème über die Qades-Schlacht." *Studien zur Altägyptischen Kultur* 11 (1984): 282–333.

Finkelstein, Israel. *The Bible Unearthed: Archaeology's New Vision of Ancient Israel and the Origins of Its Sacred Texts.* New York, 2001.

———. *Das vergessene Königreich: Israel und die verborgenen Ursprünge der Bibel.* Munich, 2014. English: *The Forgotten Kingdom: The Archaeology and History of Northern Israel.* Atlanta, 2013.

Finsterbusch, Karin. "Vom Opfer zur Auslösung: Analyse ausgewählter Texte zum Thema Erstgeburt im Alten Testament." *VT* 56 (2006): 21–45.

———. *Deuteronomium: Eine Einführung.* Göttingen, 2012.

Fischer, Georg. *Jahwe unser Gott: Sprache, Aufbau und Erzähltechnik in der Berufung des Mose (Ex 3–4).* Fribourg, 1989.

Fischer, Henry. "Milk in Everything Cooked." In *Egyptian Studies I: Varia.* New York, 1976. 97–99.

Fischer-Elfert, H. W. *Abseits von Maat: Fallstudien zu Außenseitern im Alten Ägypten.* Würzburg, 2005.

Fishbane, Michael. *Biblical Interpretation in Ancient Israel.* Oxford, 1985.

Flavius Josephus. *Against Apion.* Trans. John M. G. Barclay. Leiden, 2007.

Frankel, David. *The Murmuring Stories of the Priestly School: A Retrieval of Ancient Sacerdotal Lore.* Leiden, 2002.

Franz, Matthias. *Der barmherzige und gnädige Gott: Die Gnadenrede vom Sinai (Exodus 34,6–7) und ihre Parallelen im Alten Testament und seiner Umwelt.* Stuttgart, 2003.

Freud, Sigmund. *New Introductory Lectures on Psychoanalysis.* London, 1974.

———. *Moses and Monotheism.* In SE 23. 3–137.

———. "Constructions in Analysis." In SE 23. 257–269.

Freud, Sigmund, and Lou Andreas-Salomé. *Briefwechsel*. Ed. Ernst Pfeiffer. Frankfurt, 1966.
Freud, Sigmund, and Anna Freud. *Briefwechsel 1904–1938*. Ed. Ingeborg Meyer-Palmedo. Frankfurt am Main, 2006.
Freud, Sigmund, and Arnold Zweig. *Briefwechsel*. Ed. Ernst L. Freud. Frankfurt am Main, 1984.
Fritz, Volkmar. *Tempel und Zelt: Studien zum Tempelbau in Israel und zu dem Zeltheiligtum der Priesterschrift*. Neukirchen-Vluyn, 1977.
Funkenstein, Amos. *Perceptions of Jewish History*. Berkeley, 1993.
Gager, John. *Moses in Greco-Roman Paganism*. Nashville, 1972.
Galvin, Garrett. *Egypt as a Place of Refuge*. Tübingen, 2011.
Gardiner, Alan. *Late-Egyptian Stories*. Brussels, 1932.
———. *Late-Egyptian Miscellanies*. Brussels, 1937.
Gerhards, Meik. *Die Aussetzungsgeschichte des Mose: Literar- und traditionsgeschichtliche Untersuchungen zu einem Schlüsseltext des nichtpriesterschriftlichen Tetrateuch*. Neukirchen-Vluyn, 2006.
———. *Das Hohelied: Studien zu seiner literarischen Gestalt und theologischen Bedeutung*. Leipzig, 2010.
Gertz, Jan Christian. *Tradition und Redaktion in der Exodus-Erzählung: Untersuchungen zur Endredaktion des Pentateuch*. Göttingen, 2000.
———. "Mose und die Anfänge der jüdischen Religion." ZThK 99 (2002): 3–20.
Gnirs, Andrea. "Die 18. Dynastie: Licht und Schatten eines internationalen Zeitalters." In André Wiese, ed., *Tutanchamun: Das Goldene Jenseits. Grabschätze aus dem Tal der Könige*. Basel, 2004. 27–44.
Goedicke, Hans. "The 'Canaanite Illness.'" *Studien zur Altägyptischen Kultur* 11 (1984): 91–105.
———. "The End of the Hyksos in Egypt." In Leonard H. Lesko, ed., *Egyptological Studies in Honor of Richard A. Parker*. Hanover, 1986. 37–47.
———. *The Quarrel of Apophis and Seqenenre*. San Antonio, 1986.
Goethe, Johann Wolfgang von. "Israel in der Wüste." In *West-östlicher Divan*. Ed. Hendrik Birus. Berlin, 2010. 229–248.
Goffman, Erving. *Frame Analysis: An Essay on the Organization of Experience*. New York, 1974.
Goldstein, Bluma. *Reinscribing Moses: Heine, Kafka, Freud, and Schoenberg in a European Wilderness*. Cambridge, Mass., 1992.
Goltz, Hermann. "Die biblische Gestalt des 'Volkes Israel': Ein christlich-orientalischer Typos in Händels Oratorium *Israel in Egypt*." *Händel-Jahrbuch* 52 (2006): 13–24.
Goodenough, E. R. "Die politische Philosophie des hellenistischen Königtums." In Hans Kloft, ed., *Ideologie und Herrschaft in der Antike*. Darmstadt, 1979. 27–89.
Görg, Manfred. "'Der starke Arm Pharaos': Beobachtungen zum Belegspektrum einer Metapher in Palästina und Ägypten." In *Hommages à François Daumas*, vol. 1. Montpellier, 1986. 323–330.
Graf, Friedrich Wilhelm. *Moses Vermächtnis: Über göttliche und menschliche Gesetze*. Munich, 2006.
Graus, Frantisek. *Lebendige Vergangenheit: Überlieferung im Mittelalter und in den Vorstellungen vom Mittelalter*. Cologne, 1975.
Greenberg, Moshe. "The Redaction of the Plague Narrative in Exodus." In Hans Goedicke, ed., *Near Eastern Studies in Honor of F. W. Albright*. Baltimore, 1971. 243–252.
Grieshammer, Reinhard. "Zum 'Sitz im Leben' des negativen Sündenbekenntnisses." *Zeitschrift der deutschen morgenländischen Gesellschaft* Supplement 2 (1974): 19–25.

Griffiths, John. *Plutarch's* De Iside et Osiride. Cardiff, 1970.
Grund, Alexandra. *Die Entstehung des Sabbats.* FAT 75. Tübingen, 2011.
Grusin, Richard. "Premediation." *Criticism* 46 (2004): 17–39.
Halfwassen, Jens. "Der Gott des Xenophanes: Überlegungen zu Unsprung und Struktur eines philosophischen Monotheismus." *Archiv für Religionsgeschichte* 10 (2008): 275–294.
Händel, Georg Friedrich. *The Ways of Zion Do Mourn.* Ed. Friedrich Chrysander. G. F. Händels Werke 11. Leipzig, 1861.
———. *Israel in Egypt.* Ed. Friedrich Chrysander. G. F. Händels Werke 16. Leipzig, 1863.
Hani, Jean. *La religion égyptienne dans la pensée de Plutarque.* Paris, 1976.
Hardmeier, Christof. "Die Erinnerung an die Knechtschaft in Ägypten." In Frank Crüsemann, ed., *Was ist der Mensch . . . ? Beiträge zur Anthropologie des Alten Testaments.* Munich, 1992. 133–152.
Harrauer, Christine. " 'Ich bin, was da ist . . .': Die Göttin von Sais und ihre Deutung von Plutarch bis in die Goethezeit." *Wiener Studien: Zeitschrift für Klassische Philologie, Patristik und lateinische Tradition* 107/108 (1994–95): 337–355.
Hartenstein, Friedhelm. *Psalmen.* Biblischer Kommentar 15/1. Neukirchen-Vluyn, 2012.
Hartwich, Wolf-Daniel. *Die Sendung Moses: Von der Aufklärung bis Thomas Mann.* Munich, 1997.
Heine, Heinrich. *A Biographical Anthology.* Philadelphia, 1956.
Heinen, Heinz. "Ägyptische Grundlagen des antiken Antijudaismus: Zum Judenexkurs des Tacitus, Historien V 2–13." *Trierer Theologische Zeitschrift* 101 (1992): 124–149.
Heinrich, Klaus. *Parmenides und Jona: Vier Studien über das Verhältnis von Philosophie und Mythologie.* Basel, 1982.
Helck, Wolfgang. *Die Beziehungen Ägyptens zu Vorderasien im 3. und 2. Jahrtausend v. Chr.* 2nd ed. Wiesbaden, 1971.
———. *Urkunden der 18. Dynastie: Urkunden des ägyptischen Altertums Heft 22.* Berlin, 1984.
Hendel, Ronald. "The Exodus in Biblical Memory." JBL 120 (2001): 601–622.
———. *Remembering Abraham: Culture, Memory, and History in the Hebrew Bible.* New York, 2005.
———. "Cultural Memory." In Hendel, ed., *Reading Genesis: Ten Methods.* New York, 2010. 28–46.
———. "The Exodus as Cultural Memory: Egyptian Bondage and the Song of the Sea." In Thomas E. Levy, ed., *Israel's Exodus in Transdisciplinary Perspective: Text, Archaeology, Culture, and Geoscience.* New York, 2014. 65–77.
Herrmann, Siegfried. *Israels Aufenthalt in Ägypten.* Stuttgart, 1970.
Heynoldt, Anke. "Die Bedeutung des Sarmatismus für das Nationalbewußtsein und die Kultur des polnischen Adels zwischen dem 16. und dem 18. Jahrhundert." *Kultursoziologie* 7 (1998): 6–57.
Hirschmann, Wolfgang. "Sublime Strokes: Händels Kompositionswissenschaft und die Ästhetik des Erhabenen." In Hirschmann, ed., *Händels "Messiah": Zum Verhältnis von Aufklärung, Religion und Wissen im 18. Jahrhundert.* Halle, 2011. 17–41.
Hoffmeier, James K. "The Arm of God versus the Arm of Pharaoh in the Exodus Narratives." *Biblica* 67 (1986): 378–387.
———. *Israel in Egypt: The Evidence for the Authenticity of the Exodus Tradition.* New York, 1997.
Hornung, Erik. "Die Israelstele des Merenptah." In Manfred Görg, ed., *Fontes atque pontes: Festschrift Hellmut Brunner.* Wiesbaden, 1983. 224–233.
Horst, P. W. van der. *Chaeremon: Egyptian Priest and Philosopher.* Leiden, 1984.

Hospers-Jansen, Anna. *Tacitus over de Joden.* Groningen, 1949.

Houten, C. van. *The Alien in Israelite Law.* JSOTS 107. Sheffield, 1991.

Idel, Moshe. *Saturn's Jews: On the Witches' Sabbat and Sabbateanism.* London, 2011.

Ilany, Ofri. "From Divine Commandment to Political Act: The Eighteenth-Century Polemic on the Extermination of the Canaanites." *Journal of the History of Ideas* 73 (2012): 437–461.

Janowski, Bernd. *Sühne als Heilsgeschehen: Studien zur Sühnetheologie der Priesterschrift und zur Wurzel KPR im Alten Orient und im Alten Testament.* Neukirchen-Vluyn, 1982.

———. "Psalm 106, 28–31 und die Interzession des Pinchas." *VT* 33 (1983): 237–248.

———. "'Ich will in eurer Mitte wohnen': Struktur und Genese der exilischen Schekina-Theologie." In *Der eine Gott der beiden Testamente.* JBTh 2. Neukirchen-Vluyn, 1987. 119–147.

———. *Gottes Gegenwart in Israel: Beiträge zur Theologie des Alten Testaments.* Neukirchen-Vluyn, 1993.

———. "Tempel und Schöpfung: Schöpfungstheologische Aspekte der priesterschriftlichen Heiligtumskonzeption." In *Gottes Gegenwart in Israel,* 214–246.

———. "Keruben und Zion." In *Gottes Gegenwart in Israel,* 247–280.

———. "'Er trug unsere Sünden': Jesaia 53 und die Dramatik der Stellvertretung." In *Gottes Gegenwart in Israel,* 303–326.

———. "Jahwe der Richter—ein rettender Gott. Psalm 7 und das Motiv des Gottesgerichts." In *Die rettende Gerechtigkeit,* 92–124.

———. *Die rettende Gerechtigkeit.* Neukirchen-Vluyn, 1999.

———. *Konfliktgespräche mit Gott: Eine Anthropologie der Psalmen.* 2nd ed. Neukirchen-Vluyn, 2006.

———. "Die kontrastive Einheit der Schrift: Zur Hermeneutik des biblischen Kanons." In *Kanonhermeneutik: Vom Lesen und Verstehen der christlichen Bibel.* Neukirchen-Vluyn, 2007. 27–46.

———. *Ecce Homo: Stellvertretung und Lebenshingabe als Themen Biblischer Theologie.* Neukirchen-Vluyn, 2007.

———. *Die Welt als Schöpfung.* Neukirchen-Vluyn, 2008.

———. *Ein Gott, der straft und tötet? Zwölf Fragen zum Gottesbild des Alten Testaments.* Neukirchen-Vluyn, 2013.

———. "Die Einwohnung Gottes in Israel." In *Das Geheimnis der Gegenwart Gottes: Zur Schechina-Vorstellung in Judentum und Christentum.* WUNT 318. Tübingen, 2014. 3–40.

Janowski, Bernd, and Peter Stuhlmacher, eds. *Der leidende Gottesknecht: Jesaja 53 und seine Wirkungsgeschichte.* FAT 14. Tübingen, 1996.

Jaspers, Karl. *The Origin and Goal of History.* New Haven, 1953.

Jericke, Detlev. "Hebräer / Hapiru." In Michaela Bauks, Klaus Koenen, and Stefan Alkier, eds., *Das wissenschaftliche Bibellexikon im Internet* (WiBiLex). Stuttgart, 2006–. Accessed December 3, 2015.

Jones, Ernest. *The Life and Work of Sigmund Freud.* Vol. 3, *The Last Phase, 1919–1939.* London, 1957.

Kaiser, Otto. "Die Ausländer und die Fremden im Alten Testament." In Peter Biehl, ed., *Heimat—Fremde.* Neukirchen-Vluyn, 1998. 65–83.

———. *Zwischen Athen und Jerusalem.* Berlin, 2003.

Kant, Immanuel. *Kritik der ästhetischen Urteilskraft.* In *Werke in 10 Bänden,* ed. Wilhelm Weischedel, vol. 8. Darmstadt, 1968.

Keel, Othmar. *Die Welt der altorientalischen Bildsymbolik und das Alte Testament: Am Beispiel der Psalmen.* 3rd ed. Zurich, 1980.

———. "Zeichen der Verbundenheit: Zur Vorgeschichte und Bedeutung der Forderungen von Dtn 6,8f und Parr." In Pierre Casetti, ed., *Mélanges Dominique Barhélemy: Etudes bibliques offertes à l'occasion de son 60e anniversaire.* Fribourg, 1981. 159–240.

———. *Göttinnen, Götter und Gottessymbole: Neue Erkenntnisse zur Religionsgeschichte Kanaans und Israels aufgrund bislang unerschlossener ikonographischer Quellen.* Freiburg im Breisgau, 1992.

———. "Der zu hohe Preis der Identität oder von den schmerzlichen Beziehungen zwischen Christentum, Judentum und kanaanäischer Religion." In Manfried Dietrich, ed., *Ugarit: Ein ostmediterranes Kulturzentrum im Alten Orient,* vol. 1. Münster, 1995. 95–114.

———. "Leben aus dem Wort Gottes? Vom Anspruch und vom Umgang mit den Schriften des Alten und Neuen Testaments." In Alois Schifferle, ed., *Pfarrei in der Postmoderne? Gemeindebildung in nachchristlicher Zeit.* Freiburg im Breisgau, 1997. 95–109.

———. *Kanaan—Israel—Christentum: Plädoyer für eine "vertikale" Ökumene.* Franz Delitzsch-Vorlesung 2001. Münster, 2002.

———. "Die Heilung des Bruchs zwischen israelitischer und 'kanaanischer' Kultur." In Vertikale Ökumene, Bibel + Orient Museum Freiburg (Switzerland), 2005. 11–26.

———. *Die Geschichte Jerusalems und die Entstehung des Monotheismus.* 2 vols. Fribourg, 2007.

———. "Seth-Baal und Seth-Baal-Jahwe—interkulturelle Ligaturen." In Gerd Theissen, ed., *Jerusalem und die Länder: Ikonographie—Topographie—Theologie.* Göttingen, 2009. 87–108.

Kerling, Marc. *"O Wort, du Wort, das mir fehlt": Die Gottesfrage in Arnold Schönbergs Oper Moses und Aron.* Mainz, 2004.

Kessler, Rainer. *Die Ägyptenbilder der Hebräischen Bibel: Ein Beitrag zur neueren Monotheismusdebatte.* Stuttgart, 2002.

Kitchen, Kenneth. *Ramesside Inscriptions.* Vol. 2. Oxford, 1971.

Klatt, Norbert. ". . . des Wissens heißer Durst." *Jahrbuch der deutschen Schillergesellschaft* 29 (1985): 98–112.

Knauf, Ernst Axel. *Midian: Untersuchungen zur Geschichte Palästinas und Nordarabiens am Ende des 2. Jahrtausends v. Chr.* Wiesbaden, 1988.

Koch, Christoph. *Vertrag, Treueid und Bund: Studien zur Rezeption des altorientalischen Vertragsrechts im Deuteronomium und zur Ausbildung der Bundestheologie im Alten Testament.* BZAW 383. Berlin, 2008.

Koch, Klaus. "Tempeleinlaßliturgien und Dekaloge." In *Studien zur Theologie der alttestamentlichen Überlieferungen.* Neukirchen-Vluyn, 1961. 45–60.

———. "Der Tod des Religionsstifters: Erwägungen über das Verhältnis Israels zur Geschichte der altorientalischen Religionen." KuD 8 (1962): 100–123.

Köckert, Matthias. *Die Zehn Gebote.* Munich, 2007.

Koldau, Linda Maria. "Israel in Egypt (HWV 54)." In Michael Zywietz, ed., *Händels Oratorien, Oden und Serenaden.* Laaber, 2010. 268–286.

Koschorke, Albrecht. "Exodus: Gesetzgebung und Landnahme im kulturellen Gedächtnis Europas." In Anna Heinze, ed., *Grenzen der Antike: Die Produktivität von Grenzen in Transformationsprozessen.* Berlin, 2014. 27–37.

Kratz, Reinhard G. *Die Komposition der erzählenden Bücher des Alten Testaments.* Göttingen, 2000.

———, ed. *Divine Wrath and Divine Mercy in the World of Antiquity.* Tübingen, 2008.

Krauss, Rolf. *Das Moses-Rätsel: Auf den Spuren einer biblischen Erfindung.* Munich, 2001.

Kristeva, Julia. *Revolution in Poetic Language.* New York, 1984.

Krochmalnik, Daniel. " 'Du sollst erzählen!' Die Haggada von Pessach." In Ingrid Schoberth, ed., *Urteilen lernen: Grundlegung und Kontexte ethischer Urteilsbildung.* Göttingen, 2012. 197–207.

Krüger, Annette. *Das Lob des Schöpfers: Studien zur Sprache, Motivik und Theologie von Psalm 104.* Neukirchen-Vluyn, 2010.

Laboury, Dimitri. *Akhénaton.* Paris, 2010.

Lactantius. *The Works of Lactantius.* Trans. W. Fletcher. Edinburgh, 1871.

Lang, Bernhard. *Jesus der Hund: Leben und Lehre eines jüdischen Kynikers.* Munich, 2010.

———."Le dieu de l'Ancien Testament est-il un dieu jaloux?" In Hedwige Bouillard-Bonraisin, ed., *Jalousie des dieux, jalousie des hommes.* Turnhout, 2011. 159–171.

———. *Buch der Kriege—Buch des Himmels: Kleine Schriften zur Exegese und Theologie.* Leuven, 2011.

———. "Von der kriegerischen zur nativistischen Kultur: Das alte Israel im Lichte der Kulturanthropologie." In *Buch der Kriege—Buch des Himmels,* 25–43.

———. "Die Leviten: Von der Gegnerschaft einer kriegerischen Priesterzunft gegen Ahnenverehrung und Bilderkult." In *Buch der Kriege—Buch des Himmels,* 45–82.

———. "Die Zahl Zehn und der Frevel der Väter." In *Buch der Kriege—Buch des Himmels,* 83–107.

———. " 'Du sollst nicht nach der Frau eines anderen verlangen': Das 9. und 10. Gebot im Licht altorientalischer Rechtsgeschichte." In *Buch der Kriege—Buch des Himmels,* 109–117.

———. "Der redende Gott: Erfahrene und erfundene Offenbarung im Alten Testament." In Jan Assmann, ed., *Orakel und Offenbarung: Formen göttlicher Willensbekundung.* Munich, 2013. 181–208.

———. "Der Mann Mose und die mosaische Religion: Eine kleine Bibelkunde." In Rolf Schieder, ed., *Die Gewalt des Einen Gottes,* 56–78.

Langston, Scott M. *Exodus through the Centuries.* Blackwell Bible Commentaries. Oxford, 2006.

Lapinkivi, Pirjo. "The Sumerian Sacred Marriage and Its Aftermath." In Martti Nissinen and Risto Uro, eds., *Sacred Marriages,* 7–41.

LeClerc, Jean. *Historia Universalis a Creatione Mundi ad Caroli Magni Tempus.* Amsterdam, 1696.

Lepper, Verena. *Untersuchungen zu pWestcar: Eine philologische und literaturwissenschaftliche (Neu-)Analyse.* Wiesbaden, 2008.

Leuenberger, Martin: "JHWHs Herkunft aus dem Süden: Archäologische Befunde—biblische Überlieferungen—historische Korrelationen." ZAW 122 (2010): 1–19.

Levenson, Jon D. "Is There a Counterpart in the Hebrew Bible to New Testament Antisemitism?" JES 22.2 (1985): 242–260.

———. *The Death and Resurrection of the Beloved Son.* New Haven, 1993.

Lewis, Brian. *The Sargon Legend.* Cambridge, Mass., 1980.

Lichtheim, Miriam. *Ancient Egyptian Literature.* Vol. 3. Berkeley, 1980.

Lohfink, Norbert. "Gewalt und Monotheismus: Beispiel Altes Testament." In H. Düringer, ed., *Monotheismus—Eine Quelle der Gewalt?* Frankfurt, 2004. 61–78.

Loretz, Oswald. *Ḫabiru-Hebräer: Eine sozio-linguistische Studie über die Herkunft des Gentiliziums cibrí vom Appellativum habiru.* Berlin, 1984.

Luiselli, Michela M. *Die Suche nach Gottesnähe: Untersuchungen zur Persönlichen Frömmigkeit in Ägypten von der Ersten Zwischenzeit bis zum Ende des Neuen Reiches.* Wiesbaden, 2011.

Lust, Johan. "Freud, Hosea, and the Murder of Moses." *Ephemerides Theologicae Lovanienses* 65 (1989): 81–93.

Lux, Rüdiger. "Der Zweite Tempel von Jerusalem—ein persisches oder prophetisches Projekt?" In Uwe Becker, ed., *Das Alte Testament — ein Geschichtsbuch?! Geschichtsschreibung und Geschichtsüberlieferung im antiken Israel.* Leipzig, 2005. 145–172.

MacDonald, Nathan. "Issues in the Dating of Deuteronomy: A Response to Juha Pakkala." *ZAW* 122 (2010): 431–435.

Manetho. *History of Egypt and Other Works.* Trans. and ed. W. G. Waddell. Loeb Classical Library. Cambridge, Mass., 1940.

Mann, Thomas. *Joseph und seine Brüder.* Ed. Jan Assmann, Dieterich Borchmeyer, and Stephan Stakorski. Frankfurt am Main, 2017.

Markl, Dominik. *Der Dekalog als Verfassung des Gottesvolkes. Die Brennpunkte einer Rechtshermeneutik des Pentateuch in Exodus 19–24 und Deuteronomium 5.* Freiburg im Breisgau, 2007.

Marx, Hans Joachim. *Händels Oratorien, Oden und Serenaden.* Göttingen, 1998.

Melammed, E. Z. " 'Observe' and 'Remember' Spoken in One Utterance." In Ben-Zion Segal, ed., *The Ten Commandments in History and Tradition.* Jerusalem, 1990. 191–217.

Mellinkoff, R. "The Round-Topped Tablets of the Law: Sacred Symbol and Emblem of Evil." *Journal of Jewish Art* 1 (1974): 28–44.

Merkelbach, Reinhold. "Ein griechisch-ägyptischer Priestereid und das Totenbuch." In *Religions en Égypte hellénistique et romaine.* Strasbourg, 1967. 69–73.

———. "Ein ägyptischer Priestereid." ZPE 2 (1968): 7–30.

———. *Die Unschuldserklärungen und Beichten im ägyptischen Totenbuch, in der römischen Elegie und im antiken Roman.* Giessen, 1987.

Metzler, Dieter. "A. H. Anquetil-Duperron (1731–1805) und das Konzept der Achsenzeit." *Achaemenid History* 7 (1991): 123–133.

———. *Kleine Schriften zur Religion und Geschichte der Antike und deren Nachleben.* Münster, 2005.

Meyer, Eduard. *Aegyptische Chronologie: Abhandlungen der Preussischen Akademie der Wissenschaften.* Leipzig, 1904.

Middleton, David. "Conversational Remembering and Uncertainty: Interdependencies of Experience as Individual and Collective Concerns in Team Work." *Journal of Language and Social Psychology* 16.4 (1997): 389–410.

Moberly, Walter. *The Old Testament of the Old Testament: Patriarchal Narratives and Mosaic Yahwism.* Minneapolis, 1992.

Molke, Christian. *Der Text der Mescha-Stele und die biblische Geschichtsschreibung. Beiträge zur Erforschung der antiken Moabitis (Arḍ el-Kerak 5).* Frankfurt am Main, 2006.

Moran, William L. "The Ancient Near Eastern Background of the Love of God in Deuteronomy." In Frederick E. Greenspahn, ed., *Essential Papers on Israel and the Ancient Near East.* New York, 1991. 103–115.

Mosès, Stéphane. "Ich werde sein, der ich sein werde." In *Eros und Gesetz: Zehn Lektüren der Bibel.* Munich, 2004. 65–79.

Na'aman, Nadav. "The Exodus Story: Between Historical Memory and Historiographical Composititon." *Journal of Ancient Near Eastern Religions* 11 (2011): 39–69.

Nicolaus Cusanus. *De docta ignorantia I* (1440). Ed. H. G. Senger. Hamburg, 1993.

Nietzsche, Friedrich. *On the Genealogy of Morals.* Trans. Carol Diethe. Oxford, 1996.

Nissinen, Martti. *Prophetie, Redaktion und Fortschreibung im Hoseabuch.* Neukirchen-Vluyn, 1991.

Nissinen, Martti, and Risto Uro, eds. *Sacred Marriages: The Divine-Human Sexual Metaphor from Sumer to Early Christianity.* Winona Lake, 2008.

Nock, Arthur Darby, and André-Jean Festugière, ed. and trans. *Corpus Hermeticum.* 2 vols. Paris, 1972.

Noegel, Scott B. "Moses and Magic: Notes on the Book of Exodus." *Journal of the Near Eastern Society* 24 (1996): 45–59.

Nordheim, Eckhard von. "Der große Hymnus des Echnaton und Psalm 104: Gott und Mensch im Ägypten der Amarnazeit und in Israel." *Studien zur Altägyptischen Kultur* 7 (1979): 227–251.

Osman, Ahmed. *Moses, Pharaoh of Egypt: The Mystery of Akhenaten Resolved.* London, 1990.

Oswald, Wolfgang. "Bundesbuch." In Michaela Bauks, Klaus Koenen, and Stefan Alkier, eds., *Das wissenschaftliche Bibellexikon im Internet* (WiBiLex). Stuttgart, 2006–. Accessed December 3, 2015.

———. "Auszug aus der Vasallität: Die Exodus-Erzählung (Ex 1–14) und das antike Völkerrecht." *Theologische Zeitschrift* 67 (2011): 263–288.

Otten, Heinrich. "Ein kanaanäischer Mythos aus Boghazköy." MIO 1 (1953): 125–127.

Otto, Eckart. "Vom Rechtsbruch zur Sünde." In *Sünde und Gericht.* JBTh 9. Neukirchen-Vluyn, 1994. 25–52.

———. *Das Deuteronomium.* Berlin, 1999.

———, ed. *Mose: Ägypten und das Alte Testament.* Stuttgart, 2000.

———. "Mose und das Gesetz: Die Mose-Figur als Gegenentwurf Politischer Theologie zur neuassyrischen Königsideologie im 7. Jh. v. Chr." In Otto, ed., *Mose: Ägypten und das Alte Testament,* 43–83.

———. *Gottes Recht als Menschenrecht: Rechts- und literaturhistorische Studien zum Deuteronomium.* Wiesbaden, 2002.

———. *Mose.* Munich, 2006.

———. *Das Gesetz des Mose.* Darmstadt, 2007.

Oz, Amos. *Jews and Words.* New Haven, 2012.

Pakkala, Juha. "Jeroboam without Bulls." ZAW 120 (2008): 501–525.

———. "The Date of the Oldest Edition of Deuteronomy." ZAW 121 (2009): 388–401.

———. "The Dating of Deuteronomy: A Response to Nathan MacDonald." ZAW 123 (2011): 431–436.

Pascal, Blaise. *Pensées and Other Writings.* Oxford, 2008.

Pečar, Andreas, ed. *Die Bibel als politisches Argument: Voraussetzungen und Folgen biblizistischer Herrschaftslegitimation in der Vormoderne.* Munich, 2007.

———. *Macht der Schrift: Politischer Biblizismus in Schottland und England zwischen Reformation und Bürgerkrieg (1534–1642).* Munich, 2011.

Peden, Alexander J. *Egyptian Historical Inscriptions of the Twentieth Dynasty.* Jonsered, 1994.

Perlitt, Lothar. *Bundestheologie im Alten Testament.* Neukrichen-Vluyn, 1969.

Peter-Spörndli, Ursula. *Die Zehn Worte vom Sinai: Die Rezeption des Dekalogs in der rabbinischen Literatur.* Berlin, 2012.

Pfeiffer, Henrik. *Das Heiligtum von Bethel im Spiegel des Hoseabuchs.* Göttingen, 1999.

———. *Jahwes Kommen von Süden: Jdc 5; Hab 3; Dtn 33 und Ps 68 in ihrem literatur- und theologiegeschichtlichen Umfeld.* Göttingen, 2005.

Plutarch. *De Iside et Osiride.* In *Religionsphilosophische Schriften,* trans. and ed. Herwig Görgemanns. Düsseldorf, 2003. 135–292.

Pongratz-Leisten, Beate. "Sacred Marriage and the Transfer of Divine Knowledge: Alliances

between the Gods and the King in Ancient Mesopotamia." In Martti Nissinen and Risto
Uro, eds., *Sacred Marriages*, 43–73.

———, ed. *Reconsidering the Concept of Revolutionary Monotheism*. Winona Lake, 2011.

Porphyrius. *On Abstinence from Killing Animals*. Trans. Gillian Clark. London, 2013.

Pury, Albert de. "Le cycle de Jacob comme legend autonome des origines d'Israël." In J. A.
Emerton, ed., *Congress Volume Leuven 1989*. Leiden, 1991. 78–96.

———. "Gottesname, Gottesbezeichnung und Gottesbegriff Elohim als Indiz zur Entste-
hungsgeschichte des Pentateuch." In J. C. Gertz, ed., *Abschied vom Jahwisten: Die Komposition des Hexateuch in der jüngsten Diskussion*. BZAW 315. Berlin, 2002. 25–47.

———, ed. *Le pentateuque en question: Les origins et la composition des cinc premières livres
de la Bible à la lumière des recherches récentes*. Le monde de la Bible 19. 3rd ed. Geneva,
2002.

———. "Erwägungen zu einem vorexilischen Stämmejahwismus: Hos 12 und die Ausein-
andersetzung um die Identität Israels und seines Gottes." In Walter Dietrich, ed., *Ein
Gott allein?*, 413–439.

———. "P^g as the Absolute Beginning." In T. Römer, ed., *Les dernières rédactions du Pentateuque, de l'Hexateuque et de l'Ennéateuque*. BETL 203. Leuven, 2007. 99–128.

Quack, Joachim F. "Der historische Abschnitt des Buches vom Tempel." In Elke Blumen-
thal, ed., *Literatur und Politik im pharaonischen und ptolemäischen Ägypten*. Cairo, 1999.
267–278.

———. "Das Buch vom Tempel und verwandte Texte: Ein Vorbericht." *Archiv für Religionsgeschichte* 2 (2000): 1–20.

Quaegebeur, Jan. "On the Egyptian Equivalent of Biblical Hartummim." In Sarah Israelit-
Groll, ed., *Pharaonic Egypt, the Bible and Christianity*. Jerusalem, 1985. 162–172.

———. "La designation (P3)Hry-tp: PHRITOB." In Jürgen Osing, ed., *Form und Maß*.
Wiesbaden, 1987. 368–394.

Rad, Gerhard von. *Theologie des Alten Testaments*. Vol. 1. Munich, 1957.

———. "Das formgeschichtliche Problem des Hexateuch." In *Gesammelte Studien zum
Alten Testament*. Munich, 1958. 9–86.

Ramirez-Kidd, J. E. *Alterity and Identity in Israel*. BZAW 283. Berlin, 1999.

Redford, Donald B. "The Literary Motif of the Exposed Child." *Numen* 14 (1967):
209–228.

———. "The Hyksos Invasion in History and Tradition." *Orientalia* 39 (1970): 1–51.

———. *Pharaonic King-Lists, Annals and Day-Books: A Contribution to the Study of the
Egyptian Sense of History*. Mississauga, 1986.

Reinhard, Wolfgang. *Globalisierung des Christentums?* Heidelberg, 2007.

Reinhold, Carl Leonhard. *Die hebräischen Mysterien oder die älteste religiöse Freymaurerey*.
Leipzig, 1788. Reprinted and ed. Jan Assmann. 2nd ed. Neckargemünd, 2006.

Renan, Ernest. "Qu'est-ce qu'une nation?" In *"Was ist eine Nation?" und andere politische
Schriften*. Vienna, 1995.

Riedweg, Christoph. "Initiation—Tod—Unterwelt: Beobachtungen zur Kommunikations-
situation und narrativen Technik der orphisch-bakchischen Goldplättchen." In Fritz
Graf, ed., *Ansichten griechischer Rituale*. Stuttgart, 1998. 359–398.

Rießler, Paul. *Altjüdisches Schrifttum außerhalb der Bibel*. Augsburg, 1928.

Rifkin, Jeremy. *The Empathic Civilization: The Race to Global Consciousness in a World in
Crisis*. New York, 2010.

Rikala, Mia. "Sacred Marriage in the New Kingdom of Ancient Egypt: Circumstantial Evidence for a Ritual Interpretation." In Martti Nissinen and Risto Uro, eds., *Sacred Marriages*, 115–144.

Rofé, Alexander. *Introduction to the Composition of the Pentateuch.* Sheffield, 1999.

Römer, Thomas. "Exode et Anti-Exode: La nostalgie de l'Egypte dans les traditions du désert." In Römer, ed., *Lectio difficilior probabilior? L'exégèse comme expérience de décloisonnement.* Heidelberg, 1991. 155–172.

———. "Competing Magicians in Exodus 7–9: Interpreting Magic in the Priestly Theology." In Todd E. Klutz, ed., *Magic in the Biblical World: From the Rod of Aaron to the Ring of Solomon.* London, 2003. 12–22.

———. *The So-Called Deuteronomistic History.* New York, 2005.

———. "The Exodus Narrative according to the Priestly Document." In Sarah Shectman, ed., *The Strata of the Priestly Writings: Contemporary Debate and Future.* Zurich, 2009. 157–174.

———, ed. *Einleitung in das Alte Testament.* Zurich, 2013.

Rousseau, Jean-Jacques. "Considerations on the Government of Poland." In *The Social Contract and Other Later Political Writings.*Cambridge, 1997. 177–259.

Ruiten, Jacques van, and Patrick Vandermeersch."psychoanalyse en historisch-kritische exegese: De actualiteit van Freud's boek over Mozes en het monotheïsme: op zoek naar het 'echte feit.' " *Tijdschrift voor Theologie* 34 (1994): 269–291.

Rüterswörden, Udo. "*Deuteronomium.*" In Michaela Bauks, Klaus Koenen, and Stefan Alkier, eds., *Das wissenschaftliche Bibellexikon im Internet* (WiBiLex). Stuttgart 2006–. Accessed December 3, 2015.

Ryholt, Kim. "Egyptian Historical Literature from the Greco-Roman Period." In Martin Fitzenreiter, ed., *Das Ereignis: Geschichtsschreibung zwischen Vorfall und Befund.* IBAES 10. London, 2009. 231–238.

Sa-Moon, Kang. *Divine War in the Old Testament and in the Ancient Near East.* New York, 1989.

Sanders, James A. *From Sacred Story to Sacred Text.* Philadelphia, 1987.

Särkiö, Pekka. *Exodus und Salomo: Erwägungen zur verdeckten Salomokritik anhand von Ex 1–2, 5, 14 und 32.* Göttingen, 1998.

———. "Concealed Criticism of King Solomon in Exodus 2." BN 102 (2000): 74–83.

Sarna, Nahum. *Exploring Exodus: The Origins of Biblical Israel.* 2nd ed. New York, 1996.

Schäfer, Peter. *Judenhass und Judenfurcht: Die Entstehung des Antisemitismus in der Antike.* Berlin, 2010.

Schenker, Adrian. *Recht und Kult im Alten Testament.* Fribourg, 2000.

Schieder, Rolf, ed. *Die Gewalt des Einen Gottes: Die Monotheismus-Debatte zwischen Jan Assmann, Micha Brumlik, Rolf Schieder, Peter Sloterdijk und anderen.* Berlin, 2014.

Schiffner, Kerstin. *Lukas liest Exodus: Eine Untersuchung zur Aufnahme ersttestamentlicher Befreiungsgeschichte im lukanischen Werk als Schrift-Lektüre.* Stuttgart, 2008.

Schiller, Friedrich von. "Die Sendung Moses." Ed. Helmut Koopmann. In *Sämtliche Werke IV: Historische Schriften.* Munich, 1968. 737–757. Reprinted in C. L. Reinhold, *Die hebräischen Mysterien,* ed. Jan Assmann, 129–156.

Schipper, Bernd Ulrich. *Israel und Ägypten in der Königszeit: Die kulturellen Kontakte von Salomo bis zum Ende der Königszeit.* Fribourg, 1999.

Schmid, Konrad. *Erzväter und Exodus: Untersuchungen zur doppelten Begründung der Herkunft Israels innerhalb der Geschichtsbücher des Alten Testaments.* Neukirchen-Vluyn, 1999.

———. "Der Sinai und die Priesterschrift." In Reinhard Achenbach, ed., *"Gerechtigkeit und Recht zu üben" (Gen 18, 19): Studien zur altorientalischen und biblischen Rechtsgeschichte, zur Religionsgeschichte Israels und zur Religionssoziologie.* Wiesbaden, 2009. 114–127.

Schmitt, Hans-Christoph. "Die Erzählung vom Goldenen Kalb Ex32* und das Deuteronomisische Geschichtswerk." In Ulrike Schorn and Matthias Büttner, eds., *Theologie in Prophetie und Pentateuch*. BZAW 310. Berlin, 2001. 311–325.

———. "Erzvätergeschichte und Exodusgeschichte als konkurrierende Ursprungslgenden Israels – ein Irrweg der Pentateuchforschung." In Anselm A. Hagedorn, ed., *Die Erzväter in der biblischen Tadition. Festschrift Matthias Köckert*. BZAW 400. Berlin, 2009. 241–266.

Schmitt, Rüdiger. *Der "Heilige Krieg" im Pentateuch und im deuteronomistischen Geschichtswerk: Studien zur Forschungs-, Rezeptions- und Religionsgeschichte von Krieg und Bann im Alten Testament*. Münster, 2011.

Schneider, Thomas. *Ausländer in Ägypten während des Mittleren Reiches und der Hyksoszeit I: Die ausländischen Könige*. Wiesbaden, 1998.

Schoenberg, Arnold. *Briefe*. Mainz, 1958.

———. *Moses und Aron: Opera*. Ed. Christian Martin Schmidt. London, 1984.

Schoeps, Hans-Joachim. "Die jüdischen Prophetenmorde." SyBU 2. Uppsala, 1943. Reprinted in *Aus frühchristlicher Zeit. Religionsgeschichtliche Untersuchungen*. Tübingen, 1950. 126–143.

Schramm, Gottfried. *Fünf Wegscheiden der Weltgeschichte*. Göttingen, 2004.

Schwartz, Regina. *The Curse of Cain: The Violent Legacy of Monotheism*. Chicago, 1997.

Schwienhorst-Schönberger, Ludger. *Das Hohelied der Liebe*. Freiburg, 2015.

Scoralick, Ruth. *Gottes Güte und Gottes Zorn: Die Gottesprädikationen in Exodus 34,6f und ihre intertextuellen Beziehungen zum Zwölfprophetenbuch*. Freiburg im Breisgau, 2002.

Sellin, Ernst. *Mose und seine Bedeutung für die israelitisch-jüdische Religionsgeschichte*. Erlangen, 1922.

———. "Hosea und das Martyrium des Mose." ZAW 46 (1928): 26–33.

———. "Die Lösung des deuterojesanianischen Gottesknechtsrätsels." ZAW 55 (1937): 177–217.

Seters, John van. "A Contest of Magicians? The Plague Stories in P." In David P. Wright, ed., *Pomegranates and Golden Bells: Studies in Biblical, Jewish, and Near Eastern Ritual, Law, and Literature in Honor of Jacob Milgrom*. Winona Lake, 1995. 569–580.

———. *Hyksos: A New Investigation*. New Haven, 1997.

Shalev, Zeruya. *Thera*. Trans. H. Sacks and M. Greenberg. New Milford, 2010.

Shire, Michael, et al., eds. *Die Pessach Haggadah*. Berlin, 1998.

Simpson, W. K., ed. *The Literature of Ancient Egypt*. New Haven, 2003.

Singer, Itamar. *Hittite Prayers*. Leiden, 2002.

Sloterdijk, Peter. *In the Shadow of Mount Sinai*. Cambridge, 2015.

Smend, Rudolf. "Mose als geschichtliche Gestalt." In *Bibel, Theologie, Universität: Sechzehn Beiträge*. Göttingen, 1997. 5–20.

Smit, Dirkie. "Justification and Divine Justice." In Michael Weinrich and John P. Burgess, eds., *What Is Justification About?* Grand Rapids, 2009. 88–112.

Smith, Anthony. *Chosen Peoples: Sacred Sources of National Identity*. Oxford, 2003.

Smith, Mark S. *God in Translation: Deities in Cross-Cultural Discourse in the Biblical World*. Grand Rapids, 2010.

———. "God in Translation: Cross-cultural Recognition of Divinity in Ancient Israel." In Beate Pongratz-Leisten, ed., *Reconsidering the Concept of Revolutionary Monotheism*, 240–270.

Smith, Morton. *Palestinian Parties and Politics That Shaped the Old Testament*. New York, 1971.

Smith, Ruth. "Handel's Israelite Librettos and English Politics 1732–52." In *Göttinger Händel-Beiträge*, vol. 5. Göttingen, 1993. 195–215.

———. "Jennens, Charles." In Anette Landgraf, ed., *The Cambridge Handel Encyclopedia*. Cambridge, 2009. 355–357.

Spencer, John. *De legibus Hebraeorum ritualibus et eadem rationibus libri tres*. London, 1685.

Spiegel, Joachim. "Der Sonnengott in der Barke als Richter." MDAIK 8 (1939): 201–206.

Stadelmann, Rainer. "Die 400-Jahr-Stele." *Chronique d'Égypte* 79 (1965): 46–60.

———. "Vierhundertjahrstele." In *Lexikon der Ägyptologie*, vol. 6. Wiesbaden, 1986. 1039–1043.

Staubli, Thomas. "{~?~thin space}'Eines Tages trieb er das Vieh über die Steppe hinaus...': Der exegetisch-homiletische Impuls. Bibel / Kirche / Welt: Verdichtung am Dornbusch." *Schweizerische Kirchenzeitung* 166 (1998): 10.

———. "Antikanaanismus. Ein biblisches Reinheitskonzept mit globalen Folgen." In Peter Burschel, ed., *Reinheit*. Vienna, 2011. 349–388.

Steck, Odil Hannes. *Israel und das gewaltsame Geschick der Propheten: Untersuchungen zur Überlieferung des deuteronomistischen Geschichtsbildes im Alten Testament, Spätjudentum und Urchristentum*. Neukirchen-Vluyn, 1967.

———. *Moses und Aron: Die Oper Arnold Schönbergs und ihr biblischer Stoff*. Munich, 1981.

Stern, Menachem. *Greek and Latin Authors on Jews and Judaism*. 3 vols. Jerusalem. 1974–1984.

Steymans, Hans Ulrich. *Deuteronomium 28 und die adê zur Theronfolgeregelung Asarhaddons: Segen und Fluch im Alten Orient und in Israel*. Fribourg, 1995.

———. "Die literarische und historische Bedeutung der Thronfolgeregelung Asarhaddons." In Jan Christian Gertz, ed., *Die deuteronomistischen Geschichtswerke*. Berlin, 2006. 331–349.

———. "DtrB und die adê zur Thronfolgeregelung Asarhaddons? Bundestheologie und Bundesformular im Blick auf Dtn 11." In Georg Fischer, Dominik Markl, and Simone Paganini, eds., *Deuteronomium—Tora für eine neue Generation*. Wiesbaden, 2011. 161–192.

Strecker, Stefan. *Der Gott Arnold Schönbergs: Blicke durch die Oper* Moses und Aron. Münster, 1999.

Stricker, B. H. "Asenarii I." *Oudheidkundige Mededelingen uit het Rijksmuseum van Oudheden te Leiden* 46 (1965): 52–75.

———. "Asenarii II." *Oudheidkundige Mededelingen uit het Rijksmuseum van Oudheden te Leiden* 48 (1967): 23–43.

———. "Asenarii III." *Oudheidkundige Mededelingen uit het Rijksmuseum van Oudheden te Leiden* 52 (1971): 22–53.

———. "Asenarii IV." *Oudheidkundige Mededelingen uit het Rijksmuseum van Oudheden te Leiden* 56 (1975): 65–74.

Stroumsa, Guy G. "John Spencer and the Roots of Idolatry." *History of Religions* 41 (2001): 1–23.

Theissen, Gerd. *Der Schatten des Galiläers: Jesus und seine Zeit in erzählender Form*. Gütersloh, 2008.

Tilly, Michael, and Wolfgang Zwickel. *Religionsgeschichte Israels*. Darmstadt, 2011.

Toorn, Karel van der. "The Iconic Book: Analogies between the Babylonian Cult of Images and the Veneration of the Torah." In Toorn, ed., *The Image and the Book: Iconic Cults, Aniconism, and the Rise of Book Religion in Israel and the Ancient Near East*. BETL 21. Leuven, 1997. 229–248.

———. *Scribal Culture and the Making of the Hebrew Bible*. Cambridge, Mass., 2007.

Trampedach, Kai. *Theokratie und theokratischer Diskurs: Die Rede von der Gottesherrschaft und ihre politisch-soziale Auswirkungen im interkulturellen Vergleich*. Tübingen, 2012.

Tück, Jan-Heiner. "Verborgene Menschheitsreligion? Jan Assmann oder der Preis des Kosmotheismus." http://www.perlentaucher.de/essay/verborgene-menschheitsreligion .html. Accessed June 9, 2017.

Türcke, Christoph. *Jesu Traum: Psychoanalyse des Neuen Testaments.* Springe, 2009.

Uehlinger, Christoph. "Exodus, Stierbild und biblisches Kultbildverbot." In Christof Hardmeier, ed., *Freiheit und Recht: Festschrift für Frank Crüsemann.* Gütersloh, 2003. 42–77.

Ussher James. *The Annals of the World.* Ed. Larry Pierce. Green Forest, 2003.

Utzschneider, Helmut, and Stefan Ark Nitsche. *Arbeitsbuch literaturwissenschaftliche Bibelauslegung: Eine Methodenlehre zur Exegese des Alten Testaments.* Gütersloh, 2001.

Varille, Alexandre. "La stèle du mystique Béki (No 156 du Musée de Turin)." *Bulletin de l'Institut Français d'Archéologie Orientale* 54 (1954): 129–135.

Velikovsky, Immanuel. *Ages in Chaos: From the Exodus to King Akhnaton.* Garden City, N.Y., 1952.

Veltri, Giuseppe. *Eine Tora für den König Talmai: Untersuchungen zum Übersetzungsverständnis in der jüdisch-hellenistischen und rabbinischen Literatur.* Tübingen, 1994.

Vernus, Pascal. "Les 'decrets' royaux (*wd nsw*): L'énoncé d'auctoritas comme genre." In Sylvia Schoske, ed., *Akten des vierten internationalen Ägyptologenkongresses Munich 1985.* Hamburg, 1991. 239–246.

Voegelin, Eric. *Anamnesis: On the Theory of History and Politics.* Vol. 6 of *Collected Works.* Columbia, Miss., 2002.

Voltaire. "Essai sur les moeurs et l'esprit des nations," §XXII: "Des rites égyptiens." In *Œuvres de Voltaire,* ed. M. Beuchot, vol. 15. Paris, 1829. 102–106.

Walton, Francis. *Diodorus of Sicily.* Cambridge, 1967.

Walzer, Michael. *Exodus and Revolution.* New York, 1985.

———. *In God's Shadow: Politics in the Hebrew Bible.* New Haven, 2012.

Way, Thomas von der. *Die Textüberlieferung Ramses' II. zur Kadesch-Schlacht: Analyse und Struktur.* Hildesheim, 1984.

———. *Göttergericht und "heiliger Krieg" im Alten Ägypten.* Heidelberg, 1992.

Weber, Max. *Economy and Society.* Berkeley, 1978.

Weimar, Peter. *Untersuchungen zur priesterschriftlichen Exodusgeschichte.* FzB 9. Würzburg, 1973.

———. "Priesterschrift." In Michaela Bauks, Klaus Koenen, and Stefan Alkier, eds., *Das wissenschaftliche Bibellexikon im Internet* (WiBiLex). Stuttgart, 2006–. Accessed December 3, 2015.

Weinberg, Mattias. *Patterns in Time: Rosh Hashanah.* Jerusalem, 1989.

Weippert, Manfred. "'Heiliger Krieg' in Israel und Assyrien: Kritische Anmerkungen zu Gerhard von Rads Konzept des Heiligen Krieges im Alten Israel." In *Jahwe und die anderen Götter: Studien zur Religionsgeschichte des antiken Israel in ihrem syrisch-palästinensischen Kontext.* Tübingen, 1997. 71–97.

———. *Historisches Textbuch zum Alten Testament.* Göttingen, 2010.

Welker, Michael. "The Power of Mercy in Biblical Law." *Journal of Law and Religion* 29.2 (2014): 225–235.

Wellhausen, Julius. *Prolegomena zur Geschichte Israels.* Berlin, 1883.

———. "Die Rückkehr der Juden aus dem babylonischen Exil." NGWG (1895): 166–186.

Wendland, Paul, ed. *Philonis Alexandrini Opera Quae Supersunt.* 6 vols. Berlin, 1896–1915.

Westermann, Claus. "Boten des Zorns: Der Begriff des Zornes Gottes in der Prophetie." In Jörg Jeremias, ed., *Die Boten und die Botschaft: Festschrift Hans Walther Wolff.* Neukirchen-Vluyn, 1981. 147–156.

Wettengel, Wolfgang. *Die Erzählung von den beiden Brüdern: Der Papyrus d'Orbiney und die Königsideologie der Ramessiden.* Fribourg, 2003.

Wildung, Dietrich. *Imhotep und Amenhotep: Gottwerdung im alten Ägypten.* Munich, 1977.

Willi-Plein, Ina. "Ort und literarische Funktion der Geburtsgeschichte des Mose." VT 41 (1991): 110–118.

Winkler, Heinrich. *Geschichte des Westens: Von den Anfängen in der Antike bis zum 20. Jahrhundert.* Munich, 2010.

Winter, Urs. *Frau und Göttin.* Fribourg, 1987.

Witte, Markus. "Von der Weisheit des Glaubens an den Einen Gott." https://www.perlentaucher.de/essay/von-der-weisheit-des-glaubens-an-den-einen-gott.html. Accessed June 9, 2017.

Wolff, Hans Walther. "Hoseas geistige Heimat." In *Gesammelte Studien zum Alten Testament.* Munich, 1964. 9–35.

Yavetz, Tzvi. *Judenfeindschaft in der Antike: Die Münchner Vorträge.* Munich, 1997.

Yerushalmi, Yosef Hayim. *Zakhor: Jewish History and Jewish Memory.* Seattle, 1982.

———. *Usages de l'oubli.* Paris, 1988.

Zandee, Jan. "Das Schöpferwort im Alten Ägypten." In *Verbum: Essays on Some Aspects of the Religious Function of Words Dedicated to Dr. H. W. Obbink.* Leiden, 1964. 33–66.

———. *Der Amunhymnus des Papyrus Leiden I 344.* 3 vols. Leiden, 1992.

Zenger, Erich. *Einleitung in das Alte Testament.* 8th ed. Stuttgart, 2008.

Zerubavel, Eviatar. *The Seven Days Circle: The History and Meaning of the Week.* Chicago, 1985.

Zimmermann, Ruben. *Geschlechtermetaphorik und Gottesverhältnis: Traditionsgeschichte und Theologie eines Bildfelds in Urchristentum und antiker Umwelt.* WUNT 2/122. Tübingen, 2001.

Zuntz, Günther. *Persephone: Three Essays on Religion and Thought in Magna Graecia.* Oxford, 1971.

ILLUSTRATION CREDITS

FIGURE 1   Egyptian Museum, Cairo. Photo from P. Montet, La stèle de l'an 4000 retrouvée. Kemi IV, 1931 (1933). Plate XI

FIGURE 2   *Die Bibel in Bildern*. Leipzig (Georg Wigand), 1860. Illus. 44. © akg-images

FIGURE 3   Ed. by the Noar Halutzi Meuhad, the Zionist Youth intending to emigrate to the newly formed state of Israel (Noar Halutzi Edition). From Y. H. Yerushalmi, *Haggadah and History*, 2nd ed. New York, 1976. Plate 179

FIGURE 4   © akg-images

FIGURE 5   Ashmolean Museum, Oxford. © akg-images

FIGURE 6   © akg-images / Erich Lessing

FIGURE 7   No. 4 from the series, "The Story of Exodus," 24 gouaches in preparation for 24 color lithographs. Centre Georges Pompidou, Paris. © akg-images

FIGURE 8   © akg images / Roland and Sabrina Michaud

FIGURE 9   © akg-images / Erich Lessing

FIGURE 10   Y. H. Yerushalmi. *Haggadah and History*, 2nd ed. New York, 1976. Plate 44

FIGURE 11   Photo: Wikimedia Commons (Licence CC-BY-SA 3.0) / Dnalor_01)

FIGURE 12   © akg-images

FIGURE 13   British Library, Ms. Oriental 2884, fol. 17. © akg-images / British Library

FIGURE 14   British Library, Ms. Sloane 3173, fol. 16 v. © akg-images / British Library

FIGURE 15   Paris, Bibliothèque Nationale de France, Douce 211, fol. 63. © akg-images

FIGURE 16   © akg-images / Erich Lessing

FIGURE 17   © akg-images

FIGURE 18   © akg-images / De Agostini Picture Lib. / G. Dagli Orti

FIGURE 19   © akg-images / Erich Lessing

FIGURE 20   London, British Museum EA 9901/3. From J. Assmann, *Tod und Jenseits im Alten Ägypten*. Munich, 2001. Illus. 6, pp. 104

FIGURE 21   London, British Museum EA 10471/13. From J. Assmann, *Tod und Jenseits im Alten Ägypten*. Munich, 2001. Illus. 7, pp. 106–7

FIGURE 22   The National Gallery, London. © The National Gallery, London / akg-images

FIGURE 23   *Biblia, Das ist, Die gantze Schrifft Alten und Newen Testaments*. Verteuscht: Durch Martin Luther. Strasbourg 1630

FIGURE 24   *Biblia, Das ist, Die gantze Schrifft Alten und Newen Testaments*. Verteuscht: Durch Martin Luther. Strasbourg, 1630

FIGURE 25   *Biblia, Das ist, Die gantze Schrifft Alten und Newen Testaments*. Verteuscht: Durch Martin Luther. Strasbourg, 1630

FIGURE 26   Painted on the ceiling of the Scuola Grande di S. Rocco, Sala Grande, Venice. © akg-images / Cameraphoto

FIGURE 27   British Library Add. Ms. 11639, fol. 743. © akg-images / British Library
FIGURE 28   *Biblia, Das ist, Die gantze Schrifft Alten und Newen Testaments.* Verteuscht:
            Durch Martin Luther. Strasbourg, 1630
FIGURE 29   B. Reicke and L. Rost, eds. *Biblisch-Historisches Handwörterbuch*, vol. 3.
            Göttingen, 1966, col. 1873–1874
FIGURE 30   B. Janowski. *Ein Gott, der straft und tötet?* Neukirchen, 2013. Illus. 2, p. 304
FIGURE 31   *Hermann Witsius: Miscellaneorum sacrorum libri IV, Lib. II, Dissertatio I:
            De Tabernaculi Levitici Mysteriis*, edition secunda. Amsterdam, 1695. P. 403
FIGURE 32   *Hermann Witsius* (see illus. 31). P. 405
FIGURE 33   © akg-images / Werner Forman
FIGURE 34   *Biblia, Das ist, Die gantze Schrifft Alten und Newen Testaments.* Verteuscht:
            Durch Martin Luther. Strasbourg, 1630
FIGURE 35   © akg-images / Erich Lessing
FIGURE 36   © akg-images
FIGURE 37   The National Gallery, London. © The National Gallery, London /
            akg-images
FIGURE 38   Gemäldegalerie Berlin. © akg-images
FIGURE 39   Doge's Palace, Venice. © akg-images / Cameraphoto
FIGURE 40   S. Pietro in Vincoli, Rome. © akg-images / Andrea Jemolo

INDEX

Names and concepts that recur throughout the book, or those discussed in chapters of their own, are not included in the index: covenant, Egypt, exodus, faith, god, liberation, law, memory, monotheism, Moses, pharaoh, prophets, redemption, religion, revelation, Sinai, temple, and Torah.

CPSIA information can be obtained
at www.ICGtesting.com
Printed in the USA
LVHW090230010920
664738LV00003B/460

9 780691 2031